CW01096233

The Long White Mountain, Or, a Journey in Manchuria: With Some Account of the History, People, Administration and Religion of That Country

Sir Henry Evan Murchison James

30127 07588661 9

Nabu Public Domain Reprints:

You are holding a reproduction of an original work published before 1923 that is in the public domain in the United States of America, and possibly other countries. You may freely copy and distribute this work as no entity (individual or corporate) has a copyright on the body of the work. This book may contain prior copyright references, and library stamps (as most of these works were scanned from library copies). These have been scanned and retained as part of the historical artifact.

This book may have occasional imperfections such as missing or blurred pages, poor pictures, errant marks, etc. that were either part of the original artifact, or were introduced by the scanning process. We believe this work is culturally important, and despite the imperfections, have elected to bring it back into print as part of our continuing commitment to the preservation of printed works worldwide. We appreciate your understanding of the imperfections in the preservation process, and hope you enjoy this valuable book.

DS
782.3
.J27

THE

LONG WHITE MOUNTAIN

THE

LONG WHITE MOUNTAIN

OR

A JOURNEY IN MANCHURIA

WITH SOME ACCOUNT OF THE HISTORY, PEOPLE, ADMINISTRATION

AND RELIGION OF THAT COUNTRY

BY

H. E. M. JAMES

OF HER MAJESTY'S BOMBAY CIVIL SERVICE

WITH ILLUSTRATIONS AND A MAP

LONDON

LONGMANS, GREEN, AND CO.

AND NEW YORK: 15 EAST 16th STREET

1888

Suffolk County Council

30127 07588661 9

Askews	Jan-2011
	£22.99

TO

HERBERT JAMES ALLEN, Esq., F.R.G.S.

H. B. M. CONSUL AT NEWCHWANG

THE REV. JOHN ROSS

OF MOUKDEN

AND

M. L'ABBÉ RAGUIT

OF PA-YEN-SHU-SHU

IN MY COMPANIONS' NAME AND MY OWN

I DEDICATE THIS BOOK

AS A TOKEN OF KIND REGARD

Christmas 1887

PREFACE.

THE journey which we made through Manchuria last
year would not warrant the production of a new book
of travels, solely on the ground of the variety of its
incidents or the value of its geographical results. But
Manchuria possesses many points of special interest.
From a valley on the outskirts of the Long White
Mountains there sprang a petty Tartar chieftain, nearly
three hundred years ago, who challenged the power
of China, and whose sons, after a determined struggle,
conquered the Celestial Empire and placed on the
throne the present dynasty. Russia, in the years 1858
and 1860, lopped off the Amur and part of the Primorsk,
or Maritime province, leaving only the present Manchuria between the Muscovite and the capital of China.
As the scene of a great conflict in the past, for supremacy over Eastern Asia, and perhaps of a still greater
in the future, Manchuria merits alike the attention of
historical students and contemporary statesmen. Moreover, the rapid rise of the little Manchu nation to a
pinnacle that enabled it to impose an outward and

visible badge of humiliation upon the innumerable
millions of its conquered enemies, followed by its
equally rapid transformation, until its institutions,
language, and even its national entity, became absorbed in those of the subject race, is one of the
most striking incidents in Asiatic history. To the
economist and administrator the province is full of
interest; its fertility, its resources in gold, iron, coal,
timber, and other products, and the vast numbers of
colonists which these have attracted, make it a conspicuously progressive country, although suffering from
an endemic pest of brigandage, from a corrupt staff of
officials, and hampered by many obstacles needlessly
put in the way of trade and of the accumulation of
wealth. For the ethnologist, Manchuria has attractions
arising from the variety of peoples found within her
limits—Russians and Chinese, Mongols and Manchus,
Tungusians and Coreans. To the military inquirer, she
reveals the spectacle of officers seizing with one hand
the latest scientific implements of war, and refusing to
drop from the other the oldest and most obsolete—the
gingall and the Tartar bow and arrow. The student of
comparative religion and the earnest Christian believer
may both learn much from Manchuria, partly because
her existing religion is a mixture of superstitions widely
separated in origin, and partly because two missionary
bodies, at opposite poles of the Christain faith, have
successfully begun the task of replacing heathenism
by the knowledge of Christ. Finally, the geography
of Manchuria is so little known to Europeans that,

in a map issued not so very long ago by the Royal
Geographical Society, a chain of snowy peaks, 10,000
to 12,000 feet high, was inserted, which has been
found to be purely imaginary. For these reasons I
have thought it worth while to put into a connected
form a sketch of Manchuria, its history, its people,
its administration, and its religion, followed by an account of our journey through the country, including
the ascent of the Long White Mountain. This mountain has given rise to many myths during the last three
thousand years, but to none more contrary to fact than
that which has created a whole range of peaks covered
with eternal snow. My work will, at any rate, serve
as a foundation on which others, better informed, may
build hereafter.

The records of an Oriental country scarcely ever
travel beyond the wars and achievements of its successive rulers. A great part of my historical sketch
is, therefore, necessarily confined to the deeds of the
early Manchus; but I have endeavoured to throw light
upon the causes which raised them from mere raiders,
like Mahrattas in quest of tribute, to administrators
and sovereigns far greater than Scindiah or Holkar.
In tracing the history of the existing dynasty down to
the reign of the present Emperor Kuang Hsü, I have
treated of the wars with England and their causes at
greater length than I originally intended; but, although
these wars are of recent date, so much misapprehension
prevails concerning them that a restatement of the facts
seems advisable. For a different reason, my readers

will be glad to hear again of General Gordon's campaigns, which probably saved the Manchu dynasty from extinction. They will also learn, both from the history and the wood-cut, that the doubts which the Abbé Larrieu has recently thrown upon an old friend, the Great Wall of China, are without foundation, at any rate as far as a portion extending three hundred miles inland from the sea is concerned; for that distance at least the Wall is really a substantial fortification, which has answered, and may answer again, the purpose for which it was built.

I have looked at the administration of Manchuria through Indian spectacles, so that the chapter upon that subject and upon religious beliefs may not, I fear, prove very interesting to the general reader. My views, too, upon opium will, I dare say, be unpopular, excepting amongst those who are really acquainted with the subject. I would recommend, therefore, any person who takes up the book solely from an interest in our travel or exploration to omit the first six chapters. And I would especially include in this advice the whole learned body of sinologues. In placing before the public a popular sketch of a Chinese province, it is necessary to describe various things which are familiar to foreigners in China, and to students of Chinese literature. Should, however, any Chinese scholar condescend to read this work, I hope he will be 'a little blind' to its errors; for, although I have spared no effort to ensure accuracy, an Anglo-

Indian writing upon China is sure to drop into some pitfall. Those who are interested in British trade with China may, perhaps, find some food for reflection in the statistics I give in Chapter V., which seem to indicate possibilities of an extended commerce with Manchuria.

I must acknowledge a great debt of gratitude to the Rev. John Ross, of Moukden, whose historical works are a mine of information for writers like myself. I have also to thank Mr. Ross for valuable MS. notes on different subjects, and for most of the illustrations. Much information has been obtained from the 'Chinese Repository,' an article in which contains a comparison between the Chinese and Manchu languages, from the 'China Review,' the 'Chinese Recorder,' 'Notes and Queries on China and Japan,' several excellent Consular Reports by Messrs. Meadows, Adkins, and Gardner, and from the 'Annales de la Propagation de la Foi.' M. Cordier's 'Bibliotheca Sinica' and Mr. Demetrius Boulger's 'History of China' have also proved most useful. The Jesuit narratives, and especially those of Bishop Palafox y Mendoza and Père Martini, throw a flood of light upon the conquest of China by the Manchus. A valuable paper by the Rev. J. MacIntyre is referred to in the body of the work. The value to students of Mr. Howorth's great 'History of the Mongols' is marred by want of an index.

A work called 'Journeys in North China,' by the Rev. Mr. Williamson, of Shanghai, includes an account of several expeditions to different parts of Manchuria; and a paper by Mr. E. Delmar Morgan, F.R.G.S., in the Royal Geographical Society's 'Proceedings' for 1872, describes a journey made in 1870, by the Archimandrite Palladius, chief of the Russian mission in China, from Peking by way of Moukden and Kirin to Blagovaschensk, on the Amur. Both works are illustrated by good maps, which we found very useful. I must also acknowledge the kind permission given me by Mr. Fleming, C.B., to use two of the illustrations from his work, 'A Ride on Horseback through Chinese Tartary,' and thank Mr. E. G. Ravenstein, author of 'The Russians on the Amoor,' for the translation of two letters from the 'Annales de la Propagation de la Foi.'

My special gratitude is due to Mr. W. C. Hillier, Chinese Secretary to Her Majesty's Legation at Peking, for his kindness in correcting the spelling of Chinese names and for other assistance. The spelling has indeed been a trial; but Indian experience taught me the necessity of following a proper scientific system, and, so far as one ignorant of Chinese could do so, from the first I endeavoured to follow that of Sir Thomas Wade. This system requires many diacritical marks, which are distasteful to the ordinary reader's eye; while, therefore, I have taken care to insert them on introducing a word for the first time, they will sometimes be found omitted in cases of repetition, especially if the name is a well-known one, as Kanghi or Kienlung. I must admit also a want of principle in transliterating

polysyllabic names, the component parts being sometimes separated by hyphens, and sometimes joined
together. But to Chinese scholars such names will present no difficulty, and to an ordinary reader a compact
is pleasanter than a straggling name.

The characters on the right-hand side of the cover
are Manchu, and those on the left Chinese. They represent Ch'ang-pai-shan, or the Long White Mountain;
Sung-hua Chiang, or the famous river Sungari; Moukden, or Shên-yang, the capital of Manchuria; and,
lastly, Kirin and Hei-lung Chiang, the central and
northern provinces of Manchuria.

The map, which I owe to the kindness of the
Royal Geographical Society, is founded on the latest
Russian maps in the Society's possession; but some
places, notably those in the newly settled tracts on the
Corean border and the Mongol frontier, have been
located by myself from a Chinese map. The situations
in such cases can be considered only approximately
correct. It is a matter for regret that the observations taken by Mr. Younghusband could not be worked
out in time for the final correction of the map. Mr.
Younghusband displayed untiring perseverance, and
it needed no ordinary resolution to stand outside at
nights, with a bitter wind blowing, and the thermometer below zero, waiting till a star rose to its
proper altitude. He also took compass observations
to fix the position of the hills and rivers as we passed
along. But his love of adventure induced him to extend his travels into Western China and Turkestan, and

his calculations had to stand over. It is his pencil, however, that has enabled my readers to see in the frontispiece the summit of the real 'Long White Mountain.'

H. E. M. J.

Christmas, 1887.

CONTENTS.

————·◦·————

CHAPTER I.

INTRODUCTORY.

CHAPTER II.

HISTORY.

CHAPTER V.

ADMINISTRATION.

CHAPTER VI.

RELIGION.

a

CHAPTER VII.

YINGTZŬ TO MOUKDEN AND MAO-ERH-SHAN.

CHAPTER VIII.

CH'ANG-PAI-SHAN MOUNTAINS.

CHAPTER IX.

T'ANG-HO-K'OU TO KIRIN.

CHAPTER X.

KIRIN TO TSITSIHAR.

CHAPTER XI.

TSITSIHAR TO SANSING.

APPENDICES.

LIST OF ILLUSTRATIONS.

FULL-PAGE ILLUSTRATIONS.

ILLUSTRATIONS IN TEXT.

OBSERVANDA.

a is pronounced as the *a* in father.

ai	„	„	aye.
ao	„	as in how.	
e	„	„ yet.	
ê	„	as the vowel sound in earth.	
ei	„	as in money with the n omitted.	
êrh	„	„ burr or purr.	
i	„	as the vowel sound in ease or tree.	
ih	„	„ „ „ chick.	
in	„	„ „ „ chin.	
i-g	„	„ „ „ thing.	
ia	„	as in the Italian piazza.	
iao		see *i* and *ao*.	
iu	„	eeyew or eeoo.	
o	„	as in holloa.	
ou	„	„ the ow in burrow.	
ü	„	„ the French eû, tu.	
u	„	„ the oo in too.	
uei	„	as the vowel sounds in the French jouer.	
ua	„	as in Juan, nearly ooar.	
ŭ	„	something between the i in bit and the u in shut.	
ch	„	as in chair.	
hs	„	„ hissing if the first i is dropped.	
j	„	nearly the French j as in jaune.	
k	„	as in king.	
sh	„	„ shall.	

The insertion of an apostrophe reversed after a consonant signifies that that consonant is aspirated.

Chuang	means	a village or hamlet.
Ch'êng	„	a walled town.
T'un	„	a village or settlement.
T'ai	„	a stage or military post.
Shan	„	a mountain.
Ling	„	a mountain pass.
Ho	„	a river.
Chiang	„	a large river.
K'ou	„	the junction of one or more rivers; sometimes also a mountain pass.
Tien	„	an inn.
Tzŭ	„	a dissyllabic particle, to which no meaning can be attached; also a son.
Pei	„	north.
Nan	„	south.
Tung	„	east.
Hsi	„	west.
Ch'ang	„	long.
Ta	„	great.
Hsiao	„	little, small.
Pai	„	white.
Hei	„	black.

'Cash' is a copper-alloy coin, valued at about six to one farthin

'Tael' is a Chinese ounce of silver, varying in weight and value according to locality and the price of silver; the present value may be taken at 4s. 10d.

'Li' is a Chinese mile, almost exactly one-third of an English mile.

'K'ang' is a brick platform, warmed by flues, in the interior of a house, used for eating, resting, and sleeping.

THE LONG WHITE MOUNTAIN.

CHAPTER I.

INTRODUCTORY.

In the winter of 1885 I was entitled to two years' furlough, and determined to spend part of it in China. By great good fortune I soon found a companion, Lieut. Younghusband, of the King's Dragoon Guards, and our plans were speedily formed for a journey in Manchuria, a country full of historical interest, which has been but little explored. Friends from China confirmed us in our choice, asserting that the climate in the north was better, and the people far pleasanter to deal with than in the south or west. The mountains were said to be full of tigers, deer, and other large game, so we were

B

sure to get plenty of sport. Last, but not least, the situation of Manchuria on the Russian and Corean frontiers marked it as a country to which public attention was likely one day to be attracted.

We left Calcutta on March 19, 1886, and proceeded to Hongkong by way of Penang and Singapore. We then carried out the tourist's usual programme—Canton, Shanghai, and Peking, including the Great Wall and the Ming tombs. As we neither saw nor did anything extraordinary at these places, I spare my readers any account of them, though I cannot refrain from saying that, to my judgment, Canton, with its crowded streets and beautiful shops, its temples and pagodas, and its mighty city of boats, is the city best worth seeing in the world except Pompeii, and Peking the dirtiest and most unpleasant. By the beginning of May we had sailed in a steamer from Tientsin to Yingtzŭ, the principal port in Manchuria (commonly but erroneously called Newchwang), and on May 19 we started for the interior.

Manchuria occupies the north-eastern corner of the Chinese Empire, being surrounded on the north and east by Russia, and on the south by Corea. The name signifies the country of the Manchus, a tribe of Tartars, of whom I shall have a good deal to say further on; but the word is unknown to the Chinese, having, as far as I can ascertain, been coined by French geographers. The ordinary Chinese name is Tung-san-shêng, or 'the three eastern provinces.' At the present day Manchuria includes roughly a tract which lies between lat. 52° and 40° N. and long. 122° and 131° E. Its existing boundaries are, on the north, the river Amur; on the east, the river Usuri, the river Sungacha, Lake Hinka, and part of the Russian province of the

Primorsk ; on the south, Corea, the Yellow Sea, and the Liao-tung Gulf ; and on the west, Mongolia. Its extreme length from Port Arthur, on the Gulf of Pechihli, to a point opposite Albazin, on the Amur, is about 900 miles ; and its breadth from Hulan-Pei'rh to Lake Hinka, about 600 miles as the crow flies. It lies north of the Great Wall, and therefore is not part of China Proper, which it joins only at its extreme south-western corner, but belongs to what ancient geographers called Tartary. It is divided into three provinces. The first is Feng-t'ien, i.e. ' heaven ordained ' (as it has been ordained as the source of the present ruling dynasty), in the south, with an area of about 50,000 square miles and a population of from 12,000,000 to 13,000,000. It is commonly called in histories Liao-tung, that is, the country east of the Liao river, and sometimes in maps Shing-king, the translation of the Manchu name for the capital, Moukden. Kirin is in the centre, containing about 90,000 square miles, with a population of about 6,000,000 to 8,000,000, and Hei-lung-chiang in the north, with 140,000 square miles (inclusive of a portion of Mongolia joined to it for military purposes), and a population of 2,000,000. These figures, which are founded upon a careful estimate by Mr. T. Taylor Meadows, a former British Consul at Newchwang, and my own observation, give a total of 280,000 square miles and a population of 20,000,000 to 23,000,000, and may be taken as approximately correct. The area of Manchuria is thus larger than the Austro-Hungarian Empire.

The three provinces of Manchuria would in India be called non-regulation provinces. Though the law administered is the same as in China, there is a military executive, the chiefs of which are all Manchus, and in the centre and north the same officers perform both military and civil duties. The most southerly, Fêng-t'ien, which is comparatively close to the capital—for it adjoins the province of Chihli, in which Peking is situated—has been for so many centuries subject to China that there is practically no outward difference between it and any other part of China Proper; but the other two provinces, though from time to time nominally subject to Chinese suzerainty, did not come under the direct government of Peking until 1644, when the Manchus took possession of the empire. With a very sparse population of nomad hunters, they were reserved as a nursery for Tartar soldiers, and also used as a place for the transportation of Chinese criminals. It is only since the year 1820 that colonisation by Chinese has been permitted in these regions, and for a long time after that life and property were so insecure that emigration languished. During the last twenty years, however, great strides have been made, millions of settlers have arrived, and the land is being re-claimed as rapidly as in Manitoba itself. But the two northern provinces are still very backward, swarming with brigands and bad characters. There is little un-occupied land in Fêng-t'ien, but vast areas lie unculti-vated elsewhere.

Manchuria is essentially a highland country, a land of mountains, rivers, and swamps; almost the entire south and east are occupied by ranges of hills which geographers have christened Ch'ang-pai-shan, from the name of the principal peak. The meaning is—'The Long White Mountains.'[1]   (Another name is Shan-alin,

---

[1] The word Ch'ang in Chinese, like the word 'long' in English, is used for distance as well as time. Hence some authorities call them the 'Ever-White Mountains.'

which is part of the corresponding Manchu term, Golding-shan-alin.) The inhabitants know the ranges by no specific name, though individual peaks and passes have separate titles—e.g. Lao-yeh-ling, or the Pass of Lao-yeh, the God of War, the favourite god in Manchuria. The mountains radiate in different directions without any apparent system, and the watersheds between rivers run in one part north and south, and elsewhere east and west. They form part of a series of volcanic hills, from 3,000 to 8,000 feet in height, which extend in the south far into Corea, and in the west into the Primorsk, as far as the Sea of Okhotsk. The plain country is limited to the fertile alluvial tract in the west of Fêng-t'ien, on the banks of the Liao Ho, and to the north and west of Kirin, in the region of Petuna, and where the Nonni drains a vast area of undulating steppes. North of the Sungari, the hills form part of a separate system, also volcanic, consisting of outlying spurs of the great Chingan Range. The principal rivers are the Yalu or Ai-chiang, the Tumen or Kaoli-chiang, the Sungari or Sung-hua-chiang, the Nonni, and the Hurka or Mu-tan-chiang. The three first rise within a short distance of one another, in the remote recess of the Ch'ang-pai-shan Mountains. The Yalu flows west into the Yellow Sea; the Tumen east into the Japan Sea, the two together forming the boundary between Manchuria and Corea. The Sungari, which is far the largest, is one of the most considerable tributaries of the Amur. It flows about 350 miles in a slightly north-westerly direction, and then, taking a sharp turn to the east, after a further course of 500 miles, falls into the Amur 150 miles above Khabarofka. The Nonni rises in the Chingan Mountains, north-west of Tsitsihar, not far from the Amur itself, and flows south, joining the

Sungari near Petuna. The Hurka rises about 120 miles
south-west of Ninguta, flows north-east and due north,
and joins the Sungari at Sansing, nearly 200 miles above
its junction with the Amur. Three other important
streams must also be numbered amongst Manchurian
rivers. The first is the Liao Ho, on which the port
of Yingtzŭ is situated. It rises far to the west in
Mongolia, and drains the low country west of the
Ch'ang-pai-shan Mountains. The second is the great
Amur, called by the Chinese Hei-lung-chiang or Black
Dragon River—in Manchu, Sakhalin—which divides
Manchuria from Siberia. The third is the Usuri, also
half Russian. It rises not far from Vladivostok, and
falls into the Amur near Khabarofka.

On the map will be seen marked two barriers of
palisades, one commencing at the Great Wall and passing by Yü-shih-ch'êng-tzŭ and K'uan-ch'êng-tzŭ to Fa-ta-
ha-mên, and the other starting from Fêng-huang-ch'êng,
on the Corean border, and meeting the first not far from
Kai-yuan. These barriers have no more existence at
the present day than the Roman Wall. They consisted
of long lines of wooden *chevaux-de-frise*, in the shape
of St. Andrew's crosses, and made it difficult for men,
and especially for cavalry, to pass. They were designed
by the Ming dynasty about four centuries ago, the first
to exclude Mongols from Liao-tung, and the second,
which is identified by some with a willow fence put
up by the Emperor Kanghi for a deer park, to keep
out Manchu and Tartar robbers. The wooden gate-
ways, or *mên*, are, however, still maintained as Customs
barriers, and all traffic passing through them must pay
'lekin' or transit dues. Only an occasional mound
or row of trees marks the line where the palisade
originally stood.

The capital of Fêng-t'ien, which is also the chief town in Manchuria, is Shên-yang, though on maps it will be found under its Manchu name, Moukden, or Shing-king, which means the 'capital of prosperity.' Almost all places and rivers in this favoured tract have two names, which differ completely. The first, which is the official name, and the one which will be found on most maps, is the Manchu word, the second the Chinese, and the latter is now in almost universal use with Chinese and Manchus alike. As vainly might the traveller in Manchuria ask for Moukden or Kirin, as the American for Eboracum or Byzantium. The only survey ever made, but that a remarkably good one considering the short time spent over it, was carried out by three Jesuit fathers in the years 1709 and 1710, under the orders of the Emperor Kanghi, and, as both Manchu influence and population were at that time predominant in Manchuria, the Manchu names were entered in the map and still have official precedence. Moukden is the headquarters of the Governor of Fêng-t'ien, who is also Governor-General of Manchuria. It is the finest of the 'fenced' or walled cities, of which Fêng-t'ien has at least thirty, enclosed by really magnificent fortifications laid out in regular parallelograms, a mile or even two miles each way. The walls in most cases are built of squared stone or brick, thick and massive at the base, and tapering gradually to the top, which is crowned by a crenellated parapet. Seen from outside, thick buttresses at regular intervals break the monotony of the long line of masonry. At each corner stands a flanking tower, and in the centre of each side there is a lofty fortified gateway, surmounted by a picturesque pavilion, or watch-tower, several stories high. Formerly the gates used to be closed every night at sundown, as is still done at Peking, but the custom is gradually falling into disuse, and at some towns the walls themselves are out of repair. Notwithstanding, there is a stately solidity about them lacking in the walls of Indian towns, even those at Delhi being small in comparison. In Manchuria, whenever a village or trading place develops in size or prosperity, its first aim is to build a wall, and in Central and Northern Manchuria we found many of quite recent construction, but for lack of funds or public spirit nowadays they are mere mud enclosures. Even Kirin, or Ch'uan-ch'ang, the capital of Central Manchuria, is only partly surrounded by a masonry wall, and that a miserable apology like the wall of a Clapham villa, the rest of it being made of mud, and so ruinous that we used to jump over it daily when we went out for a walk. Yet wretched mounds and ditches like this have even in the last two years sufficed to protect towns from regular armies of brigands. The capital of Hei-lung-chiang and Northern Manchuria is Tsi-tsi-har, or Pu-ku'ei, on the river Nonni. It also is surrounded by a mere mud wall.

The following are the chief military stations on the northern frontier: Hulan-Pe'rh and Aigun; on the east, San-sing, Ninguta, and Hun-ch'un; on the south, Fêng-huang-ch'êng, Chin-chou-ting, Port Arthur (Lu-shun-k'ou), Yingtzŭ, Chin-chou-fu, and Shan-hai-kuan. The principal port is Yingtzŭ. The chief commercial town in the interior is K'uan-ch'êng-tzŭ.

Towns in Manchuria are almost always laid out as in America, on a regular plan. The main street runs due north and south, and the second best crosses it at right angles, while parallel to these run a series of alleys of greater or less dimensions, according to the importance of the place. But so anxious are new comers to locate themselves in the high street, that it is not uncommon

A PAGODA.

to find a newly-formed settlement consisting of a single street a mile or two long with hardly the rudiments of any cross streets, though a more compact arrangement would be obviously better. The houses are all one-storied, the better class constructed of gray brick, faced and corniced with slabs and tiles of the same material, which admit of being carved into elaborate and delicate designs. These tiles last extremely well, and suffer nothing from exposure. Most buildings are designed after one stiff common-place rectangular pattern, with a slight attempt at ornament in the high-pitched roofs, the topmost ridge of which tails off at the end into an upward curve, somewhat like the prow of a gondola. The general outline and peculiar roof suggest a canvas tent as the primary *motif*, though there is no further proof than this likeness of origin. The yamens, or public offices, and temples are all built on precisely the same design, the more pretentious edifices having verandahs, the pillars and spandrels of which are carved and gaily painted. And occasionally a handsome pavilion, with gorgeously coloured eaves—that is a part to which the Chinese builder always pays special attention—may be seen in a great man's court-yard. Still it must be confessed that the Chinese do not shine in architecture. Almost the only buildings which can be called picturesque are the lofty old-fashioned towers or pagodas such as one sees upon willow-pattern plates, with a quaint roof jutting out from each story, like a dozen umbrellas on one stick. They are generally seven or nine stories high, the number being always an odd one, and sometimes reach 150 feet in height. Originally supposed to guard a shé-lí or relic of Buddha, or else a set of Buddhist scriptures, many of them have been built as monuments of affection, or in honour of distinguished men. Sometimes an idol may be found in the lower story, but their chief merit is supposed to consist in their drawing down good influences from heaven. In Manchuria, towers of the kind are confined to the limits of Fêng-t'ien. The temples occasionally have pretty little bell-towers, with deeply curved roofs of the same design, and 'p'ai-lou,' or triple memorial arches, both in wood and stone, are often very elegant. Yet, Chinese understand the grouping of buildings harmoniously, and a street is very striking to the eye owing to the multiplicity of gorgeous sign-posts and advertisement boards. The finest sign is that of the pawnshops, which in Manchuria fulfil the functions of banks. It consists of a lofty pillar fastened at the base between two massive granite blocks, and from the upper part of it projects the carved effigy of a dragon's head gaily painted and gilded. Obelisks far finer than Cleopatra's Needle, with handsome Chinese hieroglyphics in gilding all the way down, tall lamp-posts carved to imitate pagodas, lofty Venetian masts from which depend glittering signboards of every shape, colour, and design, vie with one another in attracting attention. They are all fixed on the edge of the *trottoir*, so that, looking down the street, it appears one bright vista of masts, flags, and sign-posts. In some towns the streets are paved with wooden sleepers, which conceal hidden sewers; but as a rule there is no attempt at paving nor any thought of sanitation. In the high streets the ruts are several feet deep, and during the rainy season the roadway is churned into a slough of fetid black mud, in which carts often stick for hours, and occasionally get overturned. Then the filthy habits of a great part of the population, combined with the accumulation of market and house sweepings in any corner which is handy, and the free flow over the streets of house sullage, which in other parts of China is economically preserved for manure, combine to render a Manchurian town in some respects a pigsty which beggars description.

The land is exceedingly fertile, being generally a rich black loam. The principal crops are millet, wheat, maize hemp, barley, poppy, indigo, tobacco, rice, and beans The shortness of the season alone prevents two crops being raised, though turnips and vegetables may be grown on land cropped in the spring. Even in newly-reclaimed tracts the careful mode of tillage contrasts greatly with the loose, untidy fashion followed by the ryot in India. The ryot has certainly a more oppressive climate to contend with; still he is less stolid and methodical than the Chinaman, who gets up at two in the morning, works with hardly any intermission till dark, and then goes to bed at once, so as to rise again early the next day. The result is marvellous. Instead of scattering the seed broadcast, it is carefully planted in ridges at regular intervals apart, and the cultivator is for ever weeding, hoeing, or irrigating, so that each head of grain develops like a prize plant. There are three kinds of millet, each of which has several sub-varieties. First, there is the tall kaoliang, or *Holcus sorghum*. This is the jowar or cholam of India, where it forms one of the great food grains of the people, and the stalks are highly prized for cattle fodder. In Manchuria the grain is principally used for feeding mules and other animals, or else for distilling spirits, while the stems are converted into fuel (where no wood is to be got they are frequently the only fuel), or devoted to roofing houses and strewing the roadways of bridges, or the outer rind is stripped off and woven into matting. Secondly, there is the small millet, ku-tzŭ or hsiao-mi (*Setaria italica*), a plant about three feet high, something like the *Holcus spicatus* or bajri of India, only with a drooping head. This is the principal food grain. After the outer husk is removed it is boiled without any further preparation, and forms a most excellent substitute for porridge. The straw, which is particularly sweet, is chopped up fine with a sharp knife worked in a massive frame like the bread-chopper used in a workhouse in England, and, mixed with moistened kao-liang, makes the best fodder in the universe. It is singular that this staple, one of the finest imaginable for man or beast, has not spread to India. The third is the golden millet or huang-mi (*Panicum miliaceum*), a beautiful plant to look at, with a graceful drooping head, which is put to the same use as hsiao-mi. Wheat and barley are not of much account in Manchuria. Oats grow but sparingly. Maize is very common, and is eaten both green and dry. The hemp-plant grows to an enormous size and in vast quantities. The poppy, too, is found everywhere, and the plants are even finer than in India. Tobacco grows luxuriantly, of a mild quality, good enough for cigarettes. There is also a dry crop rice— that is to say, one that grows on dry land, and not in water, and which would possibly be very valuable in those parts of India where the rainfall is precarious. Last, but not least, come peas and beans. These form the great produce of Manchuria. From them oil is expressed of universal demand in Chinese cookery, and the residuum, pressed into great cakes, is either used as food for cattle or exported as manure for sugar-cane. Beans are also ground into a pulp with water and converted into a white jelly-like substance called bean-curd. It looks very good, and the Chinese consider it one of the greatest delicacies in Manchuria, though it has a disagreeable, rancid taste. Enormous quantities of both bean-oil and cake are exported annually to other parts of China.

Vegetables grow freely, both hardy and semi-hardy, such as melons, gourds, cucumbers, cabbage, lettuce, and turnips. The potatoes are as fine as I ever saw. Fruits are poor, except, perhaps, plums. There are a few peaches, and wild cob-nuts and filberts abound in the mountains. A good illustration of what cultivation will do for wild fruits may be seen in the haw or hawthorn berry. In Manchuria it grows to the size of a large gooseberry and makes excellent tarts and preserves.

Large quantities of tusser (in Chinese, t'u-ssŭ) or wild silk are produced in Liao-tung, as well as a little cotton. The hills are very rich in timber, minerals, and furs. The south slopes of the Ch'ang-pai-shan Mountains abound in magnificent trees, chiefly pines, which are floated to the mouth of the Yalu, and thence distributed to all parts of China. In the deep vales grows the famous ginseng plant, the most highly-prized medicine in the Chinese pharmacopœia. The wild root sells for 10*l.* or 12*l.* the ounce on an average, and large roots fetch fancy prices like large diamonds. When cultivated, it is worth only 4*s.* to 5*s.* a pound. A great article of export is deer-horns, which are also valued as medicine. A pair of them newly-sprouted and about a foot long, all velvet and blood, fetches from 50*l.* to 60*l.* The same when fully matured fetches only 7*s.* 6*d.*

As for minerals, we found in one place gold, silver, coal, and iron within a few miles of one another, and the gold and coal of Manchuria should have a great future before them. Meanwhile, I suppose, on the principle of

'Aurum irrepertum et sic melius situm,' the mandarins profess to prohibit gold-mining altogether. The miner, in fact, in the eye of the law, is on a level with the robber, and may be treated in the same fashion; and unfortunately the miner and the robber are in too many cases the same person. The death penalty is also inflicted on persons working coal without a licence. Theoretically it is sacrilege to dig into the bowels of mother-earth, and the sin of silver-mining was supposed to have contributed to the downfall of the Ming dynasty. But the Government at the present day has extensive coal-mines of its own near Peking, and there are licensed pits on a large scale both in Liao-tung and Kirin. Gold-mining, too, in Manchuria goes on merrily, either with the connivance of the local mandarin or in wild tracts beyond his cognizance. But not always. The day before we arrived at Sansing a miner lost his head; and a short while ago, when Russian subjects crossed the Amur to the gold-diggings at Yaksa, near Albazin, and quarrelled with the Chinese, the mandarins forcibly closed the works and exposed the mutilated bodies of their own subjects *pour encourager les autres.* Besides coal, there is first-class peat in many places.

The Ch'ang-pai-shan and Chingan Mountains also yield an abundant supply of sables, and Manchurian tiger-skins are far handsomer than Indian, with long silky hair. Squirrel, fox, lynx, and other furs are also plentiful. The rivers yield sturgeon, salmon, trout, and many varieties of fish, besides pearls of inferior quality.

Manufactures in Manchuria are not very advanced —in fact, just what might be expected in a country emerging from barbarism. There is but little weaving, as the cotton cloths which are in universal wear are imported from China, but dyeing establishments are numerous. Capital furniture, boxes, and coffins are made, elegantly painted and lacquered, as well as a kind of inlaid parquetry, and the carpenters are unrivalled in the manufacture of carts and cart-wheels. Tanning and the preparation of furs have reached a very high pitch of excellence, and the leather for shoes is good. There is also a little carving in marble.

The climate is temperate, at any rate in summer; the highest temperature we felt in the shade was 87° Fahr. on July 30. The rains commence in May, continuing almost without intermission till the end of August. The winter is severe; in the north the temperature goes down to 49° below zero Fahr., while even on the coast it reaches −10° Fahr. As long, however, as the north wind does not blow, it is an honest, dry, invigorating cold, far less disagreeable than the irritating chilliness of the Punjaub winter; but, when the north wind does blow, the less said about it the better.

The reader can now judge that, as countries go, Manchuria is well off; with a reasonably honest and intelligent administration, which encouraged rather than thwarted its development, its wealth would be unbounded, but it sadly lacks some of the most elementary requirements of either agricultural or commercial prosperity. First and foremost, roads are wanting; there are certainly tracks more or less defined from town to town, including the so-called imperial post-roads between garrison towns, but during the greater part of the year they are simply swamps impassable for carts. Traffic is confined to the winter months, when bog and stream are bound by rigorous frost. On the main lines of communication the worst pieces of quagmire and stream are bridged by the public-spirited efforts of local guilds, and in the north and east the same has been done by the soldiery for military reasons. But the difficulties are so great, and the distances so long, that commerce is positively choked. For instance, when there have been floods in the Liao basin, and grain becomes dear, it does not pay to import it from the mid-Sungari and northern districts, where it is almost a drug in the market. So, again, beans can only be sent south in the shape of oil, and grain in the form of liquor distilled from it. Even in Liao-tung it is computed that one-third of the grain is converted into whisky. Then there is no post. The imperial messengers only carry Government despatches, and, though merchants have established communications by couriers between some of the most important places, the convenience is by no means general. When we were staying at Pa-yen-su-su, a town of 25,000 inhabitants, we were unable to send a letter to Kirin, only a hundred and fifty miles off, and had to employ a special messenger. Telegraphs, it is true, are in the course of rapid construction, but they have been established solely for military reasons, and the offices are too far apart to be of much use to the public. Between Yingtzŭ and Hun-ch'un, a distance of six hundred miles, there are only three offices.

The absence of a silver currency also makes all money transactions inconceivably troublesome. The copper alloy 'cash,' about twenty-five or thirty of which go to the penny, is the only coin issued by the Government. It has a hole in the middle, by which numbers can be strung together, a practice that helps to preserve the coins; and an examination of a few strings taken at random enables one to realise better than almost anything else how ancient a people the Chinese are, and how conservative. A gentleman in my presence told his servant to bring a handful, and on running through them we found three coins of the Sung dynasty (of the eleventh and twelfth centuries), and one issued by Wu San-kuei, the Chinese general who helped the present dynasty to the throne two and a half centuries ago. Think of asking an English servant for change, and his bringing in, quite as a matter of course, some pence of William the Conqueror and a token of General Monk! Unfortunately, the Government issues the cash at a loss—that is, they receive less for it than it costs them to make. Naturally, therefore, they issue as little as they can, and there is a constant risk of the coin being melted up and converted into copper vessels. The 'Peking Gazette' occasionally fulminates threats against persons offending in this way, and anyone caught is executed. Even in Corea the melter of Chinese cash receives the same penalty. The Government might get out of the difficulty by issuing lighter or debased cash, and this has been sometimes done, though the Chinese do not like it. During the war with England the Emperor Tao-Kuang issued cash of half the usual weight, of which large numbers are still in circulation and count exactly the same as a cash of double weight on the same string. The result is that the cash, unwieldy, worthless, and inconvenient as they are—for two or three sovereigns' worth comes to a mule-load—are insufficient for the ordinary retail transactions of the country, and, as Government demands must be paid in cash, the poor are great sufferers. Nor may bankers send to other cities or provinces for a fresh supply, under a penalty of forfeiture of the cash and a few months' wearing of the cangue, or wooden collar. Matters are further complicated by the insertion of many bad or imitation coins in the strings. The

c

loss in this case falls on the last possessor, but the people use such strings freely. If, however, a cash was originally good, it is still a legal tender, even though it may have lost half of its weight.

The currency is supplemented by notes, which are issued by nearly every tradesman of a certain position, and even by well-to-do innkeepers. Occasionally a guild of traders regulates the issue of local notes, and in some places the licence of the magistrate is necessary, but as a general rule the trader issues them on his own responsibility. These notes, again, are only partially payable in cash, and are valueless a few miles away from the place of issue. Forgery is easy, and is an exceedingly frequent practice, so that Moukden and its neighbourhood swarm with counterfeits. In size and appearance, such notes much resemble our own, with an ornamental border, purposely made very elaborate in order to prevent imitation. The name of the issuing house, together with the unvarying portions of the date (with blank spaces left for the exact month and day of each), is printed in large characters. Instead, however, of receiving final validation from a manuscript signature, it is given, in accordance with Chinese official and trading custom, by means of elaborately carved stamps, with which red ink is used.

Then the tiao, or measure of value, varies in different parts of the province. It ought to represent a string of 1,000 cash, divided into sections of 100 each, and three tiao, in all 3,000 cash, are usually considered equivalent to the silver tael. As a matter of fact, the tiao at Yingtzŭ is only 160 cash, and eight to ten tiaos go to the tael; at Kirin the tiao is 500 cash, and three nominally go to the tael. But all these figures are subject to local and district variations. The tael itself is a 'liang,' or Chinese ounce of silver, worth formerly about 6s. 6d., but at the present time, when the value of silver is depreciated, only about 4s. 10d., and wholesale transactions are balanced in this metal. The silver is cast into ingots, which foreigners call shoes, shaped like a cocked hat, and which weigh about 53 taels each. But no two shoes are exactly alike, and the tael itself varies in different places. The Shanghai tael is less by about five per cent. than the Manchurian tael, and the Haikwan tael, which is used by the Imperial Customs department, differs from both. The exchange between copper and paper and copper and silver fluctuates from day to day, while on each transaction the money-changer exacts a small commission, called in Anglo-Chinese slang a 'squeeze.' For current expenditure travellers use what is called 'broken sycee,' i.e. ingots split up by a blacksmith into fragments varying from a quarter of an ounce to two ounces. Each of these must be weighed, when changed, and then not only are faults found with the fineness of the silver, but the different money-changers' scales vary. Finally, when any large remittance is made, as it must be, in silver, heavy blackmail must be paid to *messieurs les brigands*, or they would carry it off to a certainty. Still, in spite of these difficulties, which I suppose are found more or less over the whole of China, trade flourishes, thanks to the inextinguishable patience of the people.

Since I left China I see that the Government, or rather the Viceroy of Canton, is going to open a silver mint. If they can only make certain that no adulteration is practised, and prevent people clipping, under the pretence of testing, the silver coin when issued, the convenience will be enormous. But the success of the scheme is very doubtful. Just now at

c 2

Canton the money-changers clip and stamp every coined dollar which passes through their hands, thus unfitting it for currency afterwards.

Under Article IX. of the treaty of Tientsin, dated June 26, 1858, foreigners are entitled to travel in the interior of China under passports issued by their Consuls, and countersigned by the local authorities. The Consuls keep lithographed forms in stock, which need only the traveller's name to be filled in, so, as soon as our party arrived at Yingtzŭ we obtained the necessary documents, duly endorsed by the Taotai or Commissioner, without trouble or delay of any kind. Wherever we halted, the head magistrate or military commandant made a point of sending for our passports, but they were always returned without delay, and throughout our journey no impediment of any kind was met with from the officials. On the contrary, we could sometimes have spared the escorts which, thanks to Mr. Allen, the Consul's, kind intervention with the Governor-General of Moukden, were sent in one or two localities for our protection. After our travels were over, it turned out that our erratic wanderings in the mountains had been reported to Peking, and the Legations were requested to intimate to their Consuls that foreigners leaving the beaten track must not expect the local mandarins to be answerable for their safety. But, so long as we were in Manchuria, we could come and go as we liked.

•:

CHAPTER II.

HISTORY.

Aborigines of Manchuria—Discussion as to the name Tartar—Origin of the
word Manchu—Dynastic titles—Tribes now called Manchus—Personal
appearance of Manchus—Savages once inhabiting Manchuria—Ancient
dynasties ruling Liao-tung—Dynasties in the north—Bohai—Golden age
of Manchuria—Ketans—Nu-chêns—Mings—Effeteness of the Mings
—Nurhachu, the first Manchu—Legend of Li Fokolun and the birth
of Aisin-gioro—Discussion as to Odoli—Nikan—Nurhachu slays Nikan
—Nurhachu builds Lao-ch'êng—Builds Shing-king—His administration—Challenges the Ming—Defeats the Chinese—Takes Moukden
and Liao-yang—Chinese resistance—Ma Wên Lung—Chung Wan—
Repulse at Ningyuan—Tai Tsung passes the Great Wall—Shunchih—
Li-tzŭ-ch'êng—Ming Emperor commits suicide—Letters of San-kuei and
Prince Dorgun—Li-tzŭ-ch'êng defeated—Manchu dynasty established—
Ming princes—Prolonged war—Causes of Manchu success—Wretched
condition of China—Manchu army—Conciliatory measures—Popular
reforms—Conquest of India compared—End of Wu San-kuei and
Dorgun.

THE aboriginal inhabitants of Manchùria may, without
inaccuracy, be classed under the generic head of Tartars.
They have been known by that name at least for many
centuries past, and have as good a prescriptive right to
it as any other nationality. It is not clear who were
the rightful owners of the name originally; but the
general consensus seems to be that Ta-tar was an
appellation of a tribe of Mongols, adopted by or conferred on them about the time the victorious banners
of Jenghis Khan swept over Asia. The name was first
known to Christendom when the Mongols spread terror
in Eastern Europe about the time of their victory at

Wahlstadt[1] on April 9, 1241. And as the devout Christians of that age connected them with the legions of Tartarus, the letter 'r' crept into the first syllable. After that the term was applied to the Khanates of Kazan, Astrachan, and the Crimea, where Mongol kingdoms were established, though the conquerors soon forgot nationality and language alike, and were absorbed by the conquered.[2] A third region to which the term has been extended is Turkestan. A Chinese historian says that in 844 A.D. the Ketan dynasty expelled certain Tartars who took refuge beyond the bend in the Yellow River, and to this day the Persians call Turks Ta-tàrs. In this way the term Tartary has come to be used by Europeans vaguely for Manchuria, Mongolia, Turkestan, and other widely separated parts of Asia, and the inhabitants have been called Tartars.[3]

---

[1] Wahlstadt (literally 'town of corpses') is a village in Prussian Silesia, near Leignitz, where Henry II., Duke of Silesia, lost his life in a dreadful battle with the Mongols, after being defeated by Batu, the grandson of Jenghis Khan, on April 9, 1241. (On August 26, 1813, Field-Marshal Blücher obtained a victory over the French at the same place, in honour of which he received the title of Prince of Wahlstadt.) The Mongols overran Russia, Wallachia, Hungary, Poland—in fact, all Eastern Europe. They were never defeated, but on the death of Batu's uncle, Ogotai Khan, retired of their own free will, with their plunder, and eventually their power was split up into the Empire of China and different Khanates in Russia and Central and Western Asia.

[2] Hence the saying, 'Grattez le Russe et vous trouverez le Tartare.'

[3] A Chinese geography of 1461 mentions Mongols and Tha-tha-eul as two out of four nomad tribes who rose to great power in the times of the Sung and Kin dynasties (about the eleventh century). Other Chinese identify them with the early Moho, who, most authorities hold, did inhabit Manchuria. The Persian Abul Ghazi describes Tartars as living on Lake Buirnur, in the north-west corner of the Tsitsihar province. And in 1604 the Tha-ta people are spoken of as the descendants of the Yuen or Mongols, and inhabiting the Gobi or Shamo desert. Klaproth, from whom the above account is taken, adds that the Mongols themselves object to the name, as they connect it with the word Tatamai, 'to allure,' which would imply that they were robbers.

The Tartars of Manchuria all belong to the same great stock from which have sprung the Chinese, Mongols, Tungusians,[1] Japanese, and Coreans in the north, and the Thibetans, Siamese, and Burmese and kindred races in the south. They may be subdivided into three classes—the pure Mongols, inhabiting the extreme west and north-west; the Tungusians, in the north, a collection of very rude tribes confined to the banks of the Amur; and in the centre and south the Manchus proper, about whom I shall have most to say. Manchus, however, are not, and never were, a separate well-defined nation, as, for instance, the Coreans or even the Mongols themselves. They are rather the descendants of a congeries of petty nomad clans, half Mongol, half Tungusic, inhabiting the mountains between Corea and the Amur, who have been known at different periods of history by half a dozen different names, and who, in the seventeenth century, when their exploits first attracted the attention of Europeans, called themselves Nu-chêns. Why indeed they changed that title for the name Manchu is not quite evident. Klaproth asserts the word is Chinese, meaning, ' a well-peopled canton ;' but the early Manchus themselves said Manchu was the name of a place whence their dynasty sprang, or that it was the title of a mythical founder of the dynasty. Mr. Ross's explanation seems the most probable—that

[1] Tungusian is a term applied to the barbarous Turanian tribes inhabiting the region of the Amur. Mr. Ravenstein derives it from Dunkhu, or Tunghu, meaning, in Chinese, the Eastern Mongols. He adds that, according to Strahlenberg, the Arinians, a poor tribe on the Yenisei, called the Tungusians, Tonge-kze—i.e. ' people of three tribes '—which Bulichef (*Travels in East Siberia*, vol. i.) refers to the Reindeer Tungusians, or Oronchon ; the Tungusian fishermen of the sea-coast or Namki; and the Tagouris, or Daurians (called Solons by Du Halde), of North-east Mongolia, rearing cattle and tilling the soil. Klaproth derives it from Donke, a Tungusian word for ' men.' The word Ta-tzŭ, from which some derive Tartar, is applied by Chinese to Tungusians, Mongols, and, disrespectfully, to Manchus.

it is identical with the Chinese word 'ch'ing,' or clear, the title of the ruling dynasty of China, which the founder of that dynasty applied first to his own clan. In the East, when the inhabitants of a country are split up into small communes, each one under its own chief, a man of strong character will sometimes appear who conquers all the rest, and imposes upon them either the name of his own tribe or his own dynastic title.   And this is what happened to the people of Manchuria.

And just as the word English nowadays includes Gaelic- and Irish-speaking Celts, so the term Manchu now comprises, in addition to the mass of Manchus proper, who are the descendants of the Nû-chên tribes, Solon Manchus in the north of Hei-lung-chiang, who live by hunting, and Sibo Manchus farther south, who are akin to Mongols; the Goldis, or Yü-p'i Ta-tzǔ (literally, 'fish-skin' Tartars, from their wearing dresses made of salmon skin), who inhabit the lower reaches of the Sungari ; the Gilyaks or Ch'ang-mao-tzǔ, or 'long-haired Tartars,' who are found at the mouth of the Usuri, so called because they do not shave the forehead —these two are pure Tungusic—and others; all are now called Manchus.   They much resemble the Chinese in personal appearance ; indeed, a gentleman of great observation and experience, the late Mr. T. T. Meadows, went so far as to say that, putting aside language, manners, and dress—i.e. putting aside the results of training, and looking merely to the physical cha- racteristics of the naked silent man—he was unable to see any difference, whether as to features, sta- ture, or complexion, between Manchus, Mongols, and Northern Chinese.   I am inclined to think, however, that Mr. Meadows distrusted his powers of discrimi-

nation. On one occasion our party watched the
march past of a couple of thousand young Manchus
who had just been selected for employment in the
regular army, and they were easily to be distinguished
from the Chinese spectators around. The majority
were short and good-looking, brown as Italians or

A SOLON MANCHU YOUTH.

Sikhs, with high cheek-bones and dark ruddy com-
plexions. Their large hazel eyes were so little oblique
that, suitably dressed, they might have passed muster
as Caucasians, and their generally bright intelligent
look reminded us of Ghurkhas. Mr. Meadows was probably most familiar with the Manchus of Liao-tung,
who have mixed with Chinese for many generations

and adopted their manners. For Orientals are remarkably quick at picking up those slight *nuances* of de-
meanour and gait which mark different callings or even
races of men. A Bengalee lawyer at Calcutta, for
instance, has the undefinable but unmistakable profes-
sional air of his European *confrère*, and the artificers
in a Chinese arsenal can be recognised at once in the
street, walking home like English factory hands. But
in Manchuria, the farther from the coast one goes, the
greater the difference becomes, though it may never be
perfectly easy to detect. In the extreme north, where
the climate is rigorous and the means of livelihood
scanty, the indigenous tribes or clans are still wild barbarians, living by the chase, and ready, some of them,
to murder any intruder into their fastnesses ; in the
south, they have been civilised into Chinese.

The fact that China is at the present day ruled by
a Manchu dynasty is no doubt familiar to all ordinarily
well-informed persons, but the circumstances under
which the dynasty obtained possession of the throne
are not equally well known. I propose, therefore, giving
a brief sketch of the Manchus' rise and progress, describing in the first place their wars and the conquest
of China, and next, what I conceive will be of special
interest to Englishmen, the transactions which brought
them into conflict with Great Britain, in regard to which
considerable misapprehension has recently prevailed.
The first period of history has been investigated
lately by the Rev. John Ross, of Moukden,[1] and Mr.
Demetrius Boulger. But a comparison of these two
authorities with one another, not to mention the accounts of several Jesuit historians who were contemporaries of the first Manchu Emperor of China, brings

[1] *The Manchus.* By the Rev. J. Ross. Paisley: J. & R. Parlane, 1880.

to light considerable discrepancies, due very probably
to the inaccuracy, prejudice, or obsequiousness of the
Chinese authorities consulted in each case. I hope,
however, that my narration, though not agreeing with
any one historian throughout, will be found fairly accurate, and that it will be useful, not only in throwing
light upon the present condition of Manchuria and its
people, but in enabling my readers properly to appreciate the important part which this little corner of
China has played in the history of that ancient and
immense empire.

Ten or twelve centuries before Christ, the whole of
Manchuria is said to have been inhabited by savages,
who did not till the ground, and ate their meat raw.
In summer they lived on the hill-sides, and in winter
dug themselves pits in the ground. They wore only
a rag before and behind, and protected themselves
against the winter's cold by smearing themselves over
with lard. They were divided into clans. Those in
the north and east were always independent, but Fêng-
t'ien or Liao-tung was then, as it has always been, the
scene of perpetual triangular warfare between its indigenous inhabitants, the Coreans, and the Chinese, its
situation and fertility making it a kind of Chinese
Lombardy or Belgium. The catalogue of early conquerors is not very interesting, so I shall pass over
it briefly. In the south of Liao-tung, a kingdom
called Ch'aohsien was the earliest formed. According
to Chinese tradition, the first sovereign was Kitzŭ,
nominated B.C. 1122 by his elder brother, Wu Wang,
the founder of the Chow dynasty. Ch'aohsien was
conquered by the great Chinese dynasty of the Hans
in the second century B.C. When the power of the
Hans waned, Liao-tung first became a feudal kingdom,

and was ultimately appropriated by a dynasty called
the Northern Wei. The Wei were ejected by the Tsin[1]
in the third century. Meanwhile a Corean dynasty,
called Kaoli, had been rising into power in the north
of Corea, and in due course it overran and conquered
Liao-tung. Then another powerful Chinese dynasty, the
T'ang, came into being, which attacked and crushed
Corea, and in the seventh century Liao-tung was again
annexed to China. Meanwhile the tribes in the north,
the progenitors of the Manchus (originally spoken of
as Sishun and Suchen), were becoming sufficiently
civilised to form themselves into one or more organised
states, known successively as Fuyu and Yilow, then
Wuchi, and finally Mogo, which split up into two,
Heishui, or Black Water, in the north, and Sumo in
the south. The last-named developed into a powerful state called Bohai, which was recognised by the
Chinese Emperor early in the eighth century. Its
dominions embraced not only North and East Manchuria, but ultimately Liao-tung as well. This is said
to have been the golden age of Manchuria: every
glen was peopled, and every plain cultivated as far
north as the Amur. Learning flourished and literature
abounded.

In the tenth century a powerful tribe called Ketans
dispossessed the Bohai. They sprang originally, so it
is said, from the banks of the river Sira Muren, or else
from near Hu-lan, one of the northern tributaries of
the Sungari. As early as the seventh century they had
commenced a series of raids on China, which culminated
in their making good a lodgment in Peking itself. They

[1] This must not be confounded with the great Tsin dynasty which
flourished before the Hans, the last emperor of which built the Great Wall
of China.

ejected the dynasty called Sung, which had succeeded
the T'ang, and dubbed themselves the Liao, or 'iron'
dynasty. If tradition does not belie them, they were
a strange mixture of savagery and culture. They are
said to have delighted in drinking human blood. The
husband cut a small slit in his wife's back and drank—a
novel mode, says Mr. Ross, of showing the superiority
of the male sex. They were, however, hospitable and
lovers of strong drink; still better, they were artists,
and, when they entered China, had a literature[1] of
several thousand volumes. Some say that they conquered Liao-tung, taking their title from the river
Liao, and also subdued Corea; but others hold that
the Coreans occupied a great part of Liao-tung till the
time of Jenghis Khan. This question, however, need
not detain us.

The Nu-chêns, a tribe living between the Sungari
and the Hurka, overthrew the Liao, and established
themselves at Peking as the Chin, or 'golden dynasty.'
Thus Manchuria gave to North China a second dynasty.
The Chins, however, were swept away in the thirteenth
century by the resistless power of the Mongols, when
Kublai Khan, the grandson of Jenghis Khan, gathered
up the fragments of China and founded the Yuen
dynasty. Whether the Mongols actually ruled Manchuria or not is doubtful. In all probability the bulk
of the inhabitants followed them, as they had followed
the Ketans and Chins, to harry the rich cities and fertile
plains of China, while the cultivated fields of Manchuria
relapsed into bush, and the few inhabitants who were

---

[1] It is not clear whether the literature ascribed to the Bohai and Liao
dynasties was written or not. Mr. Ross is silent upon the point. If the
art of writing ever existed in Manchuria, it must have perished before the
end of the sixteenth century. (See pp. 34, 120.)

left supported themselves by hunting. In the fourteenth century, a fugitive priest turned robber, headed a successful rebellion against the Mongols, and for the first time for many centuries a really Chinese emperor took his seat upon the throne, and ruled the whole of China. The new dynasty was called the Ming. It lasted three hundred years, but, though it held Liao-tung and dictated terms to Corea, it never conquered the wild tribes of North Manchuria or Mongolia. The Ming dynasty perished in its turn. In Asia a David or a Baber may found a royal house, and the great men whom civil convulsions bring to the surface may play their part well in support of it; the first few princes may be men of iron will and keen sagacity; but inexorable destiny hangs over it. One day the sceptre falls into nerveless, luxurious hands, and then its doom is simply a matter of time. Such was the fate of the Ming. During the latter part of the sixteenth and the beginning of the seventeenth centuries the administration became utterly corrupt, the hand of the executive was paralysed by eunuchs and parasites of the court, and the people were crushed with intolerable oppression. So the time came for gallant little Manchuria, as a great English statesman would call her, to give yet another line of sovereigns to China, one that thirty years ago nearly perished like the Ming, but has gained a new lease of life, and now seems destined, in all probability, to be more powerful and enduring than any of its predecessors. For it enjoys the advantage, which they lacked, of an acquaintance with the resources of Western civilisation, resources which by degrees it is turning to good account.

In the year 1559, when the Ming Emperor Chia Ching was on the throne, in a secluded valley called Hotuala,

ninety miles east of Moukden and sixty from the frontier
of Liao-tung, there was born a Nu-chên named Novurh-
hochih, or Nurhachu.   At that period, Liao-tung, from
the Great Wall to a point about thirty miles east of
Moukden, belonged to the Emperor ; it was densely
populated and highly civilised, and formed as integral
a portion of the empire as any of the eighteen provinces
which constitute China Proper.   Outside Liao-tung the
country offered a great contrast.   The hills and vales
were divided amongst numerous little clans, constantly
fighting with each other, and so barbarous that the
Chinese treated them as outcasts and would hold no
dealings with them.   In one hundred miles square of
mountainous tract there were eleven, all independent
of one another.   Nurhachu was grandson of a petty
chief who owned half-a-dozen villages, one of a group
of five little holdings, which were the first to be consolidated into one state and called Manchu.   Years
afterwards, when his descendants had become great, a
miraculous ancestry was claimed for Nurhachu.[1]   But
poor and obscure kings, in the East especially, have

---

[1] The Chinese chronicle runs as follows: 'Immediately east of the pumice
peaks of the Ch'ang-pai-shan is a high mountain called Bukuli, at the foot
of which is the small lake or pool Burhuli. After bathing one day in this
pool, the maiden Li Fokolun found on the skirt of her raiment, placed there
by a magpie, a fruit, which she ate, and which caused her to give birth to a
boy of an appearance different from ordinary people, whence she called him
" You heaven-born to restore order to the disturbed nations." His surname
she called Aisin-gioro, his name Bukuli-yung-shun. She disappeared, and he,
embarking in a small boat, floated with the river stream. In the neighbourhood of a place where peoples of three surnames were at war he disembarked,
and was breaking off willow branches, when one of the warriors, coming to
draw water, saw him. Amazed at his strange appearance, the warrior
hastily retired to inform the people of the remarkable man he had seen.
The curious people went to the bank and asked his name and surname, to
whom he replied: " I am the son of the heavenly maiden Fokolun, ordained
by heaven to restore peace among you," and thereupon they nominated him
king, and he reigned there in Odoli city, in the desert of Omohi, east of

almost always had the vain ambition of being thought
descended from an illustrious ancestry.   Even Alexander the Great, not content with an heroic line,
claimed to be son of Jupiter Ammon, and rajahs in
India of humble pedigree have had their caste exalted by

Ch'ang-pai-shan.' Another version of the legend states that there were
three heavenly maidens, Angela, Changhela, and Fokolun. The first two
returned to heaven, while Fokolun remaiued on earth to nurse the miraculous
babe till he was grown up. Then she told him to wait till a man came to
fish. The fisherman came and adopted the boy, and Fokolun ascended to
heaven. Père Amyot, from whom this account is taken, identifies Fokolun
with a sixteen-armed goddess whom he calls Pussa, or the Chinese Cybele,
but described at the present day as a Boddhisatwa, a celestial candidate for
Buddhahood. The story continues that Aisin-gioro, in spite of his heavenly
birth, was put to death by his people, and only his youngest son, Fancha,
escaped by the aid of a magpie, which alighted on his head as he ran and
made his pursuers think him the stump of a tree. (The magpie is, therefore,
to this day the sacred bird of the Manchus.) Fancha fled from Odoli across
the Ch'ang-pai-shan (Long White Mountain) to Hotuala, and there, some
two centuries before Nurhachu's birth, he laid the foundations of the future
dynasty of China. Nurhachu himself is said to have given early indications
of his subsequent greatness. He was a thirteen months' child, had the dragon
face and phœnix eye, his chest was enormous, his ears large, and his voice
like the tone of the largest bell—so goes the tale.

The question whether Odoli has a real or only a mythical existence has
yet to be cleared up. Mr. Ross does not believe in it. The Chinese history
of Liao-tung places it 1,500 li, or 500 miles, east of Shing-king. The Jesuits
marked it on their map in 1709 about 200 miles north-east of Shing-king
and 100 miles south-east of Ninguta. Du Halde quotes Père Regis: ' Odoli
Hotun was very strong by its situation, being accessible only by a narrow
strip of land which rises like a causeway in the middle of the water. Here
are also to be seen great staircases of stone with other remains of a palace,
the like of which is observable nowhere else, not even at Ninguta.' But
Père Regis does not say he visited it, and he did not take any observations
of its situation. If it really exists, it may prove identical with Autun or
Tun-hua-hsion, which was wrongly placed by the Jesuits in the basin of
the Tumen, instead of the Hurka or Mu-tan-chiang. The name Odoli is
Manchu, and is now unknown to any of the inhabitants. I passed close to
Autun when travelling by myself from Hun-ch'un to Kirin, but could not
find an opportunity of visiting it. The learned Père Amyot (commenting on
a statement in the book of notes of the dynasty, to the effect that the
founder sat on the throne at Odoli for the first time, and called his kingdom
there by the name Manchu), says that Odoli was a simple hamlet, which the
Manchus surrounded by walls. It was therefore, in all probability, Lao-
ch'êng, Nurhachu's first capital. (See next page.)

complaisant Brahmans in the same fashion. So, leaving legend behind, let us revert to history.

When Nurhachu was twenty-four years old, his father and grandfather went to the assistance of another chief who had married Nurhachu's cousin, and who was being besieged by a countryman of their own named Nikan. Nikan, who had called a Chinese warden of the marches to his aid, by treachery obtained the surrender of the town, and Nurhachu's father and grandfather were slain. Nurhachu swore vengeance against the traitor and demanded his surrender from the Chinese, vowing at the same time that he would sacrifice 200,000 Chinese in honour of his father's funeral. But the Chinese, though they gave Nurhachu the bodies of his relatives and, to appease him, conferred on him a title with a gift of thirty horses, declared Nikan lord of the whole region. Nurhachu therefore collected a small force, but 130 men, and attacked the tribes with whom Nikan had taken refuge. In three years he had become so formidable, that the Chinese gave up the traitor, and Nurhachu executed him. The Chinese also agreed to have dealings with him, and they opened markets, where furs from the mountains could be bartered for Chinese produce.

In 1587 Nurhachu built himself a tiny capital in his hereditary estate, called Lao-ch'êng, or 'Old City.' A bank of earth two feet high, built along the foundations of a wall and enclosing a ploughed field, now marks this historic spot. Sixteen years later, when his power had developed, he chose a stronger position, two or three miles to the north, on the spur of a hill, which he called Shing-king (Hsing Ching), or the 'Capital of Prosperity.' After slaying Nikan, he beset himself to subdue the chiefs of the surrounding valleys, which he welded

D

into one compact state, and bestowed the name of
Manchu upon it. He then paid particular attention to
internal administration. His few laws were swift and
speedy in application and most strictly observed, while
no robber dared approach his land. His wise, impartial justice being known, people flocked to his standard
and acknowledged him king. Amongst other reforms,
he gave his countrymen for the first time a written
alphabet founded upon that of the Mongols. A
combined attack of Nu-chêns and Mongols failed to
break his power. Gradually he crept eastward to the
Yalu, and northward across the main range of the
Ch'ang-pai-shan Mountains to the Hua-pi Ho (Hwifa or
Khuifa of the maps) and other affluents of the Upper
Sungari, till, in 1613, just thirty years after his career
of conquest commenced, only one of the ancient Nu-chên
states in the neighbourhood, that of Yeho, close to the
Chinese fortress of Kai-yuan, was left.

Expeditions to the Hurka, the Swifun (Shui-fên),
and the Amur followed ultimately, and, by 1625, the
whole country to the Amur on the north and the Japan
Sea on the east had been annexed. But before that
he felt himself strong enough to challenge the mighty
power of the Ming. The reason was, that he was particularly ambitious of conquering and annexing Yeho,
but the Chinese officers on the frontier interfered and
spoiled his designs. Enraged at this, and knowing
probably that the Chinese power was both corrupt and
effete, he boldly determined on attacking both Yeho
and its supporter. So in 1617 he declared war against
China in the most formal manner, sending to the Emperor a statement of his seven 'hates,' or grievances
—a proceeding as ridiculous in the Emperor's eyes
as a summons to surrender from Sivaji would have

seemed to Aurangzebe. In 1618 he attacked and
captured Fu-shun, the nearest frontier town of Liao-
tung. Then, apparently repenting of his rashness, he
sent a letter full of respect to the Emperor, saying
he had only commenced the war to repel the violence
of the Chinese officials who had murdered his father,
and that he was ready to lay down his arms and give
up the town, if the Emperor would but grant him an
audience and do him justice. The Emperor at the
time was the well-known Wanli, at whose court the
famous Jesuit, Father Ricci, was received. Like Lord
John Russell, who forgot to answer King Theodore of
Abyssinia's letter, with the result that England was
dragged into a war with that potentate, so Wanli,
contemptuously or otherwise, neglected to reply to
Nurhachu. Worse than that, during the course of
the next year, a Chinese force, variously estimated
at 100,000 to 200,000 men (courtly historians are not
likely to have erred on the side of under-estimating
the force), was sent against him. The Viceroy of
Liao-tung, Yang Hao, divided it into four armies of
50,000 each, which advanced from different quarters
upon Shing-king. The Manchu chief had only 60,000
men all told, but he displayed consummate general-
ship. Just as Sivaji, of whom Nurhachu's career
continually reminds one, allowed Afzul Khan's army
to penetrate deep into the forest-clad glens of Per-
tab-garh before attacking them, so Nurhachu rested
patiently till the first Chinese division, under the general Tusung, had advanced forty miles into the hills.
When Tusung arrived at a low pass called Sarhu, he
made an entrenched camp, where he left part of his
force, pushing on himself with the remainder. Nurhachu
lay in ambush till he had passed, attacked the camp by

night and stormed it; then, pursuing the leading column, he utterly routed it, the general Tusung being killed. The victor then turned to meet the second division, which was advancing from the north. The general Ma Lin took up a strong position and fortified it with a triple fosse, two bodies of 10,000 each being posted on adjacent hills to cover his flanks. Nurhachu's fourth son, afterwards his successor, furiously attacked one of the outlying divisions, while his father advanced against the main body. The Chinese sallied out of their entrenchments to meet the foe, and, for a time, friend and enemy became involved in inextricable confusion. Had the second covering division then advanced, the fate of the Manchus would have been sealed. But the commander, a eunuch, fled without striking a blow; and in the end the Chinese, demoralised, no doubt, by the knowledge of the Sarhu disaster, were utterly routed. Ma Lin himself escaped to Kai-yuan, the most northern fortified city in Liao-tung, with but a handful of followers. The third and fourth corps were approaching from the south. They were ordered to remain on the defensive. But Nurhachu, it is said, dressing his men up in the armour and waving the banners of the defeated Chinese, rode into one of their camps, and, before his trick could be discovered, routed the enemy for the third time, killing Liu Ting, another of the generals. The main body of Liu Ting's infantry had been kept in reserve, together with a force, said to amount to 160,000, which the King of Corea had deputed to aid his suzerain. These were attacked in their entrenchments. The Corean commander went over to the enemy, and the Chinese forces were scattered. The fourth Chinese army had previously retreated, so Nurhachu's victory was complete. The Manchus were armed chiefly with bows and arrows, while the Chinese possessed cannon, gingalls, and matchlocks, vast quantities of which, together with other war material, fell into the hands of the Manchus. After resting a month Nurhachu marched against the remains of the Chinese army, which had garrisoned the strong city of Kai-yuan, and again routed them utterly; he then proceeded to attack Yeho, which was situated in the vicinity, and at last succeeded in annexing it. He hung the chiefs, and put to the sword all the Chinese soldiers he found in their cities. So at last the unity of the Nu-chên, or Manchu, state was accomplished.

In the year 1620 the Emperor Wanli died, after a long reign of sixty years. He was a weak prince, but before his death he took a prudent step, deputing an able general named Ting Pi to restore order in Liao-tung and punish the aggressive Manchus. So successful was Ting Pi in guarding the frontier, that for two years Liao-tung remained tranquil, and Manchu forays were unknown. Great bribes were offered by China to the Coreans, in order to secure their assistance in the enemy's rear, and a fleet was prepared at Tientsin for operations when necessary. But all these efforts were thrown away. In an evil hour the new Emperor, Tienchi, the grandson of Wanli, listened to court parasites, and recalled Ting Pi. A company of trained artillerymen from Macao, who might have rendered invaluable assistance, were, after a short trial, either from ignorance or jealousy, dismissed. Nurhachu then judged it time to make another attack. He had already removed his head-quarters nearer to the frontier, first to Jiefan and then to Sarhu, both places close to the scene of his great victory. In 1621 he recrossed the frontier, and attacked Moukden, then called Shên-yang. The town was well fortified and garrisoned, but the commandant, foolishly, was enticed into making a sortie, and by treachery his retreat to the city was cut off. Thus he and his men were destroyed, and the city, without a leader, soon capitulated.

Nurhachu then marched against Liao-yang, the capital of Liao-tung, which had witnessed a celebrated siege 1,000 years before, when the Han dynasty took it from the Coreans. It is still a large and important place. Ting Pi's successor, Yuen Ying Tai, made gigantic efforts to save it; but Nurhachu defeated the army sent to dispute his passage, camped before it, made a dry path of stones and earth across the moat, and took the town by fair escalade. Yuen Ying Tai and many of the chief officers committed suicide, and the capital of the province fell into the power of the invaders. On this occasion Nurhachu made all the inhabitants who were well disposed to him shave their foreheads and adopt the Manchu *queue*. This was to prevent disloyal Chinese who joined his standard from being mistaken by his own men for the enemy, and also to put a mark on them if they happened to return to their countrymen. That such a precaution should have been necessary is evidence of the strong family likeness which both Chinese and Manchus recognise in each other. All the country lying between Fu-shun and the Liao was annexed, together with the capital, which Nurhachu speedily converted into his own metropolis.

The Chinese took vigorous measures to reconquer their lost territory. Ting Pi was given command again, but a colleague was associated with him, who refused to take advice, and frittered away the troops at their disposal in small detachments; and he was hampered by obstacles which intriguers at Peking put in his way.

THE GREAT WALL OF CHINA.

The result was that he was unable to repel Nurhachu, who soon made a further advance, crossing the Liao, and ravaging all the country west of that river almost up to the Great Wall. Ting Pi and his colleague were recalled and executed. A valiant officer named Chung Wan, however, garrisoned Ning-yuan, a fortified town situated about seventy miles from the Great Wall. It formed the first line of defence to Shau-hai-kuan, itself a strategical place of the utmost importance, situated at the end of the Great Wall; being, in fact, the one practicable pass through the Wall, or, rather, through the mountains along the crest of which the Great Wall is built, and which separate Manchuria from the province- of Chihli, in which Peking is situated. Nurhachu not only failed to take Ning-yúan, but found it necessary to retire once more . behind the Liao, and he did not advance beyond it during the last five years of his life. History is silent as to the reason for this, but it was probably due to Chung Wan pressing him hard ; also because Nurhachu, with true sagacity, determined on reducing all the petty tribes along the Amur and bordering on the Japan Sea, so as to prevent the possibility of his being taken in the rear ; and lastly because a diversion was created on his flank by a great general named Ma Wên Lung, who for seven years maintained the cause of the Ming in the peninsula of Liaotishan (called in navy charts Kwantung, literally, ' East of the Wall '—a term properly applicable to the whole of Fêng-t'ien—or the ' Regent's Sword '), as well as on the borders of Corea. On one occasion Ma literally carried the war into the enemy's country, plundering Nurhachu's patrimony near Shing-king. And now the end of Nurhachu's career was approaching. In 1625 he moved his capital for the sixth and last time to Shênyang, the name of which he then changed to Moukden, or the 'Flourishing Capital.' In 1626 he took the field again, and made a desperate attack on Ning-yuan. He was, however, repulsed with great loss, the Chinese having mounted foreign guns on the walls, which Ma Wên Lung is said to have taken from a Dutch brig that was wrecked on the coast. Mortified at his defeat, he retired to a place called Ching-ho, where there are mineral springs. Here he fell ill and expired, in the sixty-eighth year of his age and the eleventh of his dynasty, which is now computed from 1615, a year or two anterior to the declaration of war with China. A year later the Ming Emperor died also.

Emperors in China have the privilege of nominating their successors. The Ming was succeeded by his brother Ts'ung Chêng, a weak personage and the last of his line, and Nurhachu by his fourth son Tai Tsung, a still more remarkable man than his father. In all the early fights with the Chinese, as at Sarhu and the taking of Liao-yang, the fourth Beira, or Prince, had been conspicuous for his Rupert-like courage and impetuosity, charging with his horse into the Chinese and dispersing them like sheep. The year after he assumed the reins of power he attacked the faithful Ma Wên Lung, whom bribes had failed to detach from his allegiance. The opportunity was favourable, as Ma Wên Lung's troops had quarrelled with and pillaged the Coreans, whose allies they were, and whose territory they were occupy-ing; and the Coreans appealed to the Manchu King for aid. Tai Tsung, according to some accounts, was un-successful, and, blaming the Coreans for his defeat, he turned upon them and ravaged their country. Ma Wên Lung then attacked in his turn, and there ensued

a general and bloody engagement, in which neither
side gained a decided advantage. Unfortunately for the
Chinese, this was the last blow that Ma Wên Lung was
able to strike for them, for in the course of the year he
died, as is universally believed, by poison administered
to him by Chung Wan out of jealousy.

After this, a kind of guerilla warfare went on for
five years; but Tai Tsung had no difficulty in ultimately
reducing the peninsula, and three of Ma Wên Lung's
officers, Kung, Gung, and Shang, went over to the Manchus and lived to play a leading part in the conquest of
China, under the name of the Three Princes. Tai Tsung
again attacked Ning-yuan, but failed, and, as long as it
stood, China south of the Wall seemed invulnerable.
Tai Tsung, therefore, determined to circumvent it; so
he formed an alliance with the Kortsin tribe of Mongols,
and in 1629, marching through their territory, passed
through the Great Wall north of Peking, and laid siege
to the mighty capital itself. Chung Wan, however,
heard of the manœuvre, and by forced marches arrived
at Peking in time to save it. Then, *more Sinico*, accusations of treason were made against him, and he was
put to death, some say by the Emperor's own hand.
The belief in his want of faith was very general at the
time, and to this perhaps may be ascribed the tale that
he murdered Ma Wên Lung. Chung Wan's successor
was by no means so able, but, in spite of that, Tai
Tsung found Peking too vast a city for him to capture,
so he returned to Manchuria by the way he went.

Tai Tsung's success, however, made him resolved to
secure a permanent road into China, and he soon gained
his object by assisting his friends the Kortsins against
Lindan, the chief of the Chahar Mongols, whom the
Ming Emperor had commissioned to attack the Manchus,

and who had, unluckily for himself, taken the opportunity of wreaking an ancient spite against the Kortsins as well.   Tai Tsung also judiciously cultivated the
Kortsin alliance by intermarriages and large subsidies,
and thus the Mongol road through the Great Wall continued always open to him.   Counting from the first
siege of Peking, for fourteen years the history continues
one melancholy record of raids by the Manchus upon
the northern provinces of China, where they plundered,
burnt, and murdered to their hearts' content, varied
by unsuccessful attempts to take Ning-yuan and the
cities adjoining, the possession of which by China prevented them from ever attempting to establish themselves permanently south of the Wall.   The misery and
loss of property and life from the Liao to Ning-yuan,
and throughout the provinces of Shansi, Chihli, and
Shantung, was enormous.   The Ming Emperor endeavoured to come to terms with his foe, but the
natural arrogance of the Chinaman on the one hand,
and the ambition of his successful rival on the other,
rendered the negotiations fruitless.   At last, in 1643,
just after a great marauding expedition had returned
from the province of Shantung, Tai Tsung [1] died.   He

---

[1] It is illustrative of the difficulty experienced in collating Chinese
histories, that Father Martini, a contemporary writer of the events which
follow, says that Tai Tsung died in 1636, and was succeeded by his son
Ts'ung Têh, who was the father of Shunche, the then reigning Emperor.
Du Halde's great work, published in 1735, gives the same account, and both
describe Ts'ung Têh as having been educated as a Chinaman, being very
popular with the Chinese, and dying just before the conquest of Peking.
Adrien Greslon (1671) confirms the last statement, and both Père de Rouge-
mont (1673) and Père Joseph d'Orléans (1688) say that Tai Tsung and
Ts'ung Têh were different persons. De Maillac (head of the Chinese survey
in 1708, and the author of a posthumous work which Mr. Boulger follows),
and Père Joveur, alias Vojeu de Brunem (1754), whose history is identical
with that of De Maillac, state correctly that about 1635 Tai Tsung changed
the title of his reign from T'ien Tsung to T'sung Têh, but add that he died
eight years before Peking was occupied, and that after his death a council

was an able son of an able father. The early Manchus were men who understood how to rule men.
No favouritism was allowed in the army. Tai Tsung
did not hesitate to cashier and disgrace his eldest
brother Amin, who misbehaved by retreating from the
city of Yung-ping, at the sight of a Chinese army,
while his brother was attacking Peking. The policy of
the Manchus towards their defeated foes was precisely
the Roman 'Parcere subjectis et debellare superbos.'
The Chinese officers were given the choice of adopting
the Manchu *queue* or losing their heads. Such as
took the former alternative, and joined the conquering
side, were treated with generosity and confidence.
When a great city south of the Wall called Yung-ping
was taken, and some deserter officers visited Tai Tsung,
he said to them : ' I am not like your Ming Emperor,
who has forgotten to treat his ministers with kindness.
All my ministers can sit by my side, speak out freely
what they think, and eat and drink in my company.'
When two massacres of Chinese had occurred, in order

of princes directed Manchu affairs. The fact is, Tai Tsung, T'ien Tsung, and
Ts'ung Têh were the same person. His Manchu, that is to say, his personal,
name may not be mentioned by the Chinese, and even Mr. Ross does not
give it. On succeeding Nurhachu, he adopted the title of T'ien Tsung, and
in 1636, the year in which he called his dynasty Ch'ing and proclaimed
himself an Emperor, he changed it to Ts'ung Têh. After his death the
dynastic title of Tai Tsung Wên, under which he now goes, was conferred on
him. Changing the title of a reign was once common in China, to comme-
morate some great event or for luck. One of the Han dynasty had eleven
different reign-titles in fifty-five years. An Emperor, therefore, must have
at least three names—the first his personal name; the second a title, one
or more, which he assumes on succeeding to the throne or during the
currency of his reign; and a third, which his successors confer, and by which
he should be known ever afterwards. Contemporary historians must use the
second, and foreigners generally adhere to that. Many of the Manchu
Emperors' reign-titles are very appropriate. Nurhachu called himself Tien
Ming, meaning ' By the Grace of God;' Shun-chih means ' Obedience and
Good Government;' and K'ang-Hsi, 'Tranquillising and Consolidating.' The
title Chia Ching has a flavour of irony about it, meaning ' Joy and Blessing.'

to restore confidence, not only houses and land, but wives and slaves were distributed amongst the next body who surrendered. The result was that the number of Chinese in the Manchu army exceeded the number of the Manchus themselves.

Tai Tsung was succeeded by his ninth [1] son, Shunchih, then a boy of five, who became the first Emperor of the present—i.e. Ch'ing—dynasty of China. His uncle, Prince Dorgun, better known as Ama-wang, or the 'Father Prince,' became Regent of the Manchus. Dorgun was preparing another raid into China, when the news arrived that anarchy in that country had at last reached its height, and the Ming dynasty and government had collapsed. The Emperor, who had begun well by executing the most mischievous of the eunuchs, a creature named Wei, found, like Louis XVI., that matters were past mending. For upwards of fifteen years South and Central China had been overrun by freebooters, who had gradually collected under two leaders. One of these was a Chinaman, the son of a peasant and a robber from boyhood, called Li-tzŭch'êng; to him the other, a Mahommedan, submitted. Li made himself *de facto* ruler of great part of China, assumed the imperial title, and, though plundering and murdering on a colossal scale, yet by treating kindly those who did not oppose him, and reducing their taxes, he had gained a vast number of adherents. At last he found himself in a position to march with a horde of followers against the capital, which he succeeded in taking in April 1644. The hapless Ming Emperor, deserted by his officers, cut his own daughter's throat, and then, following the example of the last Chin Emperor when conquered by the Mongols, hung himself to a tree. A

---

[1] One Jesuit historian calls him the second son, another a nephew.

short time before, he had nominated four officers with high-sounding titles to restore peace in different quarters of the empire, one of whom, Wu San-kuei by name, was defending the Manchu frontier. That officer, who had marched back on Peking in a vain attempt to save it, on hearing of his master's fate, addressed the following letter to Prince Dorgun:

San-kuei, weak as a mosquito, is holding Shan-hai-kuan. He had intended to act as a bulwark to the empire in the far East, and thus fortify the capital. He had not conceived the possibility of a robber entering the palace, nor did he imagine it possible that a host of ministers would turn traitors and then open the city gates. The preceding nine emperors are now in misery, for the temples to their memory are burnt to the ground. At the present Heaven is wroth and men indignant, while the minds of all are unsettled, not knowing whither to look. They wait for deliverance, for our kingdom has yet stores of brave men and virtuous. Hope is, therefore, not quite extinguished. Among the governors of provinces there are sure to be men like Chin Wên and Han Wu, and some man is certain to appear as deliverer. San-kuei has had exceeding great favours bestowed upon him by his Emperor. His mind is bent on revenging his master's death, but his means are narrow and his men few. With tears of blood he, therefore, entreats the Prince to aid us, and prays that the upright words of the only remaining faithful servant of the deceased Emperor may not be unheeded when he beseeches the Prince to send on his best soldiers. The Prince will march with his men, San-kuei with ours. We shall combine, reach the gate of the capital, and exterminate the robbers out of the palace. And if you, the kingdom of the North, aid my kingdom, can we offer you only money and goods? Yea, the very skin of our foreheads we shall be willing to cut off and throw at your feet. We dare not lie.

On receiving this delightful epistle the Regent instantly ordered troops and artillery to go forward, and replied as follows:

From the beginning it was my desire to be on good terms with the Ming, and despatches conveying my good intentions were constantly sent to the court at Peking. Had your court addressed us in the friendly terms of your letter just received, our soldiers would never have been called out to fight; and our one aim even at the present moment is to restore tranquillity to the empire, to ensure prosperity to the people, and to put an end to war. Since I heard that the robber took possession of the capital and caused the suicide of the Emperor, no hair is left on my head nor nails on my fingers, and the men I am now leading in the same spirit are determined to exterminate the robber and to rescue the people out of the 'water and the fire.' I rejoice exceedingly that the Count has sent me this letter, and in response I am now leading on my men. The Count is praised as a most faithful and upright minister, and if you, Count, desire to revenge the insult to your master, the Count must determine not to live under the same heaven as the robber. Though the Count was formerly mine enemy, there is no reason because of bygones to harbour suspicious thoughts. Kuaichung of old, fighting against him, fixed an arrow in the belt of Hwan, who, when he attained the kingdom, afterwards employed Kwai, treating him as a father. If the Count join me with his forces he shall be made Jinjiao Fan Wang [vassal king] of his native place. Thus, in the first place, he can avenge the wrongs of his master, in the second his own, and the rewards of wealth and honour will continue like the mountain and the river.

The Manchu and Chinese troops coalesced. Wu San-kuei and his men were induced by the Regent to shave their foreheads and don the *queue*, that there might be no mistake between the allied troops and the rebels. Li-tzŭ-ch'êng had secured the person of Wu San-kuei's father, and threatened to execute him if his son persisted in resistance, thus appealing to the Chinaman's keenest instinct, his sense of filial duty. Brutus-like, Wu San-kuei preferred the interests of his country, and, after an interview with his father, who piteously begged him to go back (though some say he encouraged

him to persevere), he steeled himself to the sacrifice
of his parent and ordered the advance. Li-tzŭ-ch'êng
thereupon executed the old man and disputed the
allies' passage through the Great Wall. He was, however, completely defeated, and the Regent, accompanied
by Wu San-kuei, entered Peking. Wu San-kuei now
thought the Manchus had done enough, so he came to
the Regent with rich gifts in his hands, thanked him
most heartily for coming, and intimated politely that
the Chinese would not detain him or his troops any
longer away from their country. The Regent replied
even more politely, that it was no trouble at all, but it
would show too much indifference to the tranquillity
of China if the Manchus went back so soon; that Li-
tzŭ-ch'êng would certainly return if they did, and, if
once they left, it would be too late for them then to
come back. He thought, therefore, that Wu San-kuei
had better go in pursuit of that robber, who had fled
with the plunder of Peking, while he, the Regent,
stayed at the capital and restored peace in the northern
provinces. Meanwhile, he begged Wu San-kuei would
keep for himself all the presents he had brought. Wu
San-kuei thought it desirable to acquiesce, and probably did not revert to the subject. Meanwhile, Tartar
reinforcements began to arrive. Where the carcass is,
there will the eagles be gathered together, and from the
north and west Fish-skin Tartars, Mongols, Calmucs—a
vast concourse of peoples and nations and languages—
assembled at Peking. According to Martini, dwellers
in Poland and on the banks of the Volga heard of the
crash of the Chinese Empire and came to share in the
plunder. In a very brief space the Regent determined
to remove the Manchu capital from Moukden, sent for
his nephew, the boy Emperor, and issued two pro-

clamations: one promising to all who submitted to the
new dynasty the same place and power which they had
held under the Ming, and the other announcing that
a relative of the last Ming Emperor, who had been
already proclaimed by certain officials, would not be
recognised.   He at once detached four armies in different
directions to occupy and pacify Northern China, and
with great judgment nominated Wu San-kuei, whose
whole family, to the number of thirty-six, had been
slain by Li-tzŭ-ch'êng (and whose memory is still exe-
crated by the Chinese as a traitor, loyal though they
may be to the *de facto* dynasty), as generalissimo in
the West, to clear the country from robbers and restore
tranquillity.   Li-tzŭ-ch'êng, who had fled with the
plunder of Peking, was pursued, and after eighteen
months' hard fighting his adherents were dispersed and
he himself slain.   But before that the Ta-Ming, or
'Great Bright,' had yielded the place to the Ta-Ch'ing,
or the 'Great Clear' dynasty; and the end of the year
1644 saw Nurhachu's grandson firmly seated on the
Dragon throne.

Space will not admit of my narrating in detail the
various steps by which the conquest of China was completed.   Though the fall of the capital gave the invaders an advantage that can hardly be overrated, still
it was only the beginning of the subjugation of the
empire.   The three northern provinces of Shansi,
Honan, and Shantung were securely occupied within
three months, and then the struggle began.   The adherents of the Mings proclaimed Prince Fu, a grandson of
the Emperor Wanli, with great pomp and rejoicing at
the southern capital, Nanking; and, had that prince
or any one of the whole family possessed the qualities
of a leader, the precedent of previous Tartar invasions

would probably have been repeated, and China would
have been divided, the Tartars establishing themselves
in Peking, and the indigenous dynasty maintaining
itself in the south. But Prince Fu, though supported
by Shu Kofa, an able minister of the late Emperor's,
was himself dissolute and worthless. His army would
not fight for him, and he came to a miserable end,
either drowning himself to escape capture or strangled
with a bowstring at Peking. Other princes, the best of
whom were Prince Tang and Prince Kuei, were proclaimed in different provinces, and many a gallant fight
was fought; but the Ming princes could not agree
amongst themselves, and the Manchus, after a prolonged conflict, killed or expelled them all.

There were also several serious rebellions to overcome in provinces which were amongst the first to be
annexed: one, headed by Kiang-tsai, the Governor,
in Shansi, which was very nearly successful, was due
to the brutality of a libertine follower of one of the
Manchu princes: another popular rising occurred in
Shensi: the Chinese general commanding in Kiangsi
turned against the new *régime*: and the Mahommedans
in the west, who never allow a century to pass without
a revolt, went also out on the war-path. Again, an
outlaw had to be crushed in the south-west who had
dubbed himself Si-Wang, or 'Prince of the West,' and
whose massacres, which are perfectly well authenti-
cated, for sheer brutality surpass almost anything on
record. For example, he killed in cold blood many thousands of women belonging to his soldiery, including his
own harem, to prevent their impeding him on the march,
and he seriously attempted to exterminate the population of the entire province of Szechuen. Meanwhile,
China was writhing in hideous and prolonged anarchy.

E

When Martini left the country in 1651—that is to say, seven years after the occupation of Peking—only twelve out of the eighteen provinces had been conquered by the Manchus, and the last of the Mings, Prince Kuei, who established a kingdom in the south-west of China, was not finally expelled for seven years more.

But although I have no time for even an abridged account of the conquest, a dreary catalogue of sieges and battles, expeditions and massacres, marked here and there with occasional bright spots of heroism on the part of the patriotic Chinese, it will not be out of place if I state briefly the main causes that enabled a small barbarous tribe, to be counted rather by hundreds than by thousands, to master a nation of 300,000,000 or more, every man of whom hated them. Mr. Boulger calls it one of the enigmas of history, but it seems to me susceptible of simple explanation. It was due to a concatenation of circumstances, almost all of which were in favour of the invader.

To begin with, the great bulk of any Oriental people consists of cultivators of the soil and petty traders, whose only desire is to be let alone by the authorities, and to be allowed to plough and sow, buy and sell, unmolested. If they have any choice, they favour the strong ruler, who will afford them protection for life and property. For at least one generation before the Manchu invasion, that protection had been unknown throughout the greater part of China. Where the imperial mandarins still ruled, the administration was corrupt and oppressive; and where rebellion had successfully reared its head, the people were at the mercy of common robbers and freebooters, who usually gave them the alternative of joining the rebel standard and swelling the devastating hordes, or else of sacrificing their lives.

Rebellion in China is not a mere tourney between rival chiefs, each with his barons and bands of retainers kept for the purpose, the soldiers fighting while the people look on ; not a rising *en masse* of the oppressed to overthrow a tyrant or a limited tyrannical class. It resembles more the devastating progress of the Huns or Mongols. The Chinaman, no less cruel and remorseless to his own brethren than he is to foreigners, marches through the land, plundering and murdering without pity or discrimination—before him is the garden of Eden and behind him a desolate wilderness. The bulk of the population, always timid and peacefully inclined, may not wish to join, but they have no help for it. Their houses are sacked and burned, and they themselves must either flee to the mountains and woods or follow the bandit leader. It is sickening to read the accounts of the destruction of populous cities, and the wholesale slaughter of the inhabitants by their own countrymen, with which the annals of the time are filled. Over and over again the population, not merely of beleaguered cities, but of provinces, were reduced to cannibalism, and a terrible famine in Western China was only an incident in the universal misery. In the most fertile districts scarcely one acre in ten remained under cultivation. At such a time the bulk of the population could not but welcome any rulers with power sufficient to restore internal peace.

Such a power the Manchus possessed in their active, lightly-equipped, and well-disciplined army. It is true that only a quarter of the soldiers were Manchus, with an equal number of Mongols, and fully one-half recreant Chinese, a proportion that was ever on the increase. But all were Manchus in their loyalty and obedience, and well enough drilled to be always ready to march at

half an hour's notice. A mounted trumpeter sounded
the advance, the brigadiers and commanding officers
knew, both from the call and from the place where
it sounded, which corps were to proceed, and in a very
short time the army would be under way, each regiment
following its banner, which was carried in front by a
mounted trooper, no man knowing why or wherefore,
or whither he was going, except the general officer
and his trumpeter. This system, says Martini, greatly
puzzled the Chinese, for when they imagined the army
was going one way they suddenly saw it change to
another. The cavalry led and the infantry followed, so
closely packed that all distinction between regiments
seemed obliterated. The knotty question of the transport of baggage was solved in a very simple way—there
was none; and there was scarcely any commissariat.
Officers and men foraged as they went on, content to take
the first food they could obtain, not caring whether their
meat was raw or cooked, horseflesh or camel's flesh,
for to them nothing came amiss. They lay on the bare
ground, with perhaps a horse-rug underneath them;
and their tents, when they had any, would be pitched
or struck so quickly that no delay was caused by using
them. So hardy were they, and fond of the open air,
that, if compelled to lodge in houses, they would pull
down the walls and only leave the roof standing above
them—an arrangement that prevented their being taken
by surprise indoors. And whenever they had the opportunity, they went out hunting. They had few firearms till they entered China, and employed only a few
Chinamen and Europeans for their artillery. Indeed,
their first cannon was not cast till 1631, and their great
weapons were the long-bow, short heavy swords, and
lances. They were capital riders—an accomplishment

acquired from the Mongols, their own native hills being unsuited for cavalry exercises—and they were trained in a fight to drop the reins and guide their steeds with their heels, so that both hands were free to use the bow and arrow. In battle their principle was to fall on, all at once, and carry everything before them with a rush. When attacking a town, instead of using trenches and batteries, they tied to their horses' tails a great number of ladders made of a rough piece of timber with pegs stuck through. The standard-bearer clapped spurs to his horse, and rode fiercely up to the foot of the wall, while the rest followed, shouting hideously to terrify the garrison, and, though great numbers fell, the survivors soon carried the position. When the enemy on the walls possessed firearms, the besiegers advanced on foot, the leaders carrying large planks, which they fastened together and held in front to receive the shot. Immediately behind followed a party carrying ladders, and the forlorn hope came last. They delivered the attack from four different quarters, and, after receiving the first volley of the enemy, planted the ladders and scaled the walls before the matchlocks could be reloaded. If the town had resisted obstinately and bravely, the garrison and inhabitants were put to the sword, without distinction of age or sex;[1] but if they surrendered quickly without much loss to the besiegers, they were given the choice of joining the foe and shaving their foreheads or of losing their heads. Those who turned traitor and submitted were treated with generosity and confidence, and the leaders were entrusted with commands, while recalcitrants had only

---

[1] The great city of Canton distinguished itself by an heroic and prolonged defence, and was in consequence given up for ten days to massacre and plunder.

torture and death to expect. Thus, mingled severity
and kindness made the subsequent revolt of a place
once conquered a matter of rare occurrence ; and when
a province was cleared of the enemy tranquillity was
soon restored, and the roads and highways became
perfectly safe for travellers.

As the conquest proceeded, the troops at the front
were constantly being recalled to Peking, and fresh
armies sent to replace them, all burning for plunder
and distinction. This prevented the garrisons from re-
laxing their vigilance, and the constant movement of
the troops kept the fact of the conquest fresh in the
minds of the Chinese.

But although the efficiency and bravery of their
army was the main secret of their success, the policy
of the Manchus in regard to the Chinese civil officials
was also very wise and far-seeing. Unlearned and illiterate themselves, they were aware that without the aid
of the mandarins they could not hope to administer the
country at all, while, as the most influential members
of society, it was obviously good policy to conciliate
them. Instead, therefore, of filling all high posts with
Manchus, they appointed Chinamen as before. In each
large town there was a Manchu garrison, and at the
head of each province there was a Manchu general ;
but the civil magistrates and the civil viceroy were
Chinamen, and possessed equal powers with the military officials. In case of any disturbance, both civil
and military were bound to act in concert. Thus, by
continuing to them their rank and pay, the mandarins
soon became reconciled to the loss of their hair, and
to the change of dress (in the time of the Mings the
Chinese wore wide sleeves nearly touching the ground,
which the Manchus made them change to tight ones),

as well as to the change of masters. The bent of the
Manchu and of the Chinese mind was much alike, so
they worked harmoniously together from the very commencement. Great importance was attached by the
Manchus to literary proficiency, which in China is
inseparably bound up with the civil organisation. Out
of imitation or rivalry, Tai Tsung himself commenced
examinations in the Manchu, Mongol, and Chinese
classics as early as 1636, and sixteen candidates were
in that year granted the degree corresponding to M.A.
Considering that the Manchus had no written language
before the year 1599, this is somewhat remarkable.

Another thoughtful act, well calculated to gratify
the adherents of the fallen dynasty, was the ordering
the sacrifices to be continued at the ancestral tombs of
Mings, a contrast to the action of the usurper, Li-tzŭ-
ch'êng, who had destroyed the temple in which the last
emperor worshipped his forefathers.

But although they adapted themselves easily to the
Chinese official system, and maintained the old officials,
the Manchus had certain rules, which were probably
distasteful to men of the old school, though the people
strongly appreciated them. (I am quoting from accounts over 200 years old, and it is probable that many
of the good points in the new administration were not
maintained very long.) They paid particular attention
to giving speedy and impartial justice to litigants:
Nurhachu had himself ordered in 1620 that anyone
with a grievance should post up a complaint on one of
the two trees outside his palace gate, where it would be
sure to catch his eye and receive his personal attention.
And after the conquest of China any mandarin caught
delaying or selling justice lost both office and head.
There was no possibility of prolonging trials, which,

says one worthy old historian, ' may seem somewhat
barbarous, and not very politic ; but the contrary excess
of prolonging trials by perplexing. causes with tricks
and fraudulent niceties; in going through all those
punctilios and orders of courts which seem only to
delay justice and make causes to be so long depending
that they can never be decided, this may perhaps not
seem less barbarous to these people.'   So also the leading Manchus scandalised the pompous Chinese mag-
nates by receiving petitions as they rode on horseback
through the streets, and answering them then and there.
And at all times of the day they were ready to give
audience—sitting with their four doors open, as one
would say in India.   And they let the parties go without making them prostrate themselves on the ground
or creep on their knees towards them, as the haughty
Chinese did.   All this made the Manchus exceedingly
popular with the vulgar.   Then they made the Chinese
mandarins all pay taxes, from which they had been free,
like the *noblesse* in France : remarking sarcastically that,
as the counsel and advice with which they had aided
their former sovereign had profited him so little, they
should assist the new Government with something more
substantial.   They also stopped the mandarins from
going in stately processions through the streets.   They
mocked them when they were carried in sedan chairs,
and told them to leave such things to their women, and,
though they did not positively prohibit such things, yet
the Chinese soon ceased using them, especially as the
Regent and others of the Emperor's uncles, and all the
great Manchu viceroys, were accustomed to ride about
on horseback, with only a small retinue of five or six
persons.

The Manchus, as was natural, treated their army

well. They raised the status of the soldiers and conferred great distinction on successful commanders, the Emperor himself sending magnificent gifts to them unsolicited; and as all descendants of the original Manchu army became pensioners of the State, the throne had always a reserve on whose fidelity absolute reliance could be placed.

As to the people, when they saw that a foreign yoke meant liberty to live without constant risk of having their throats cut, and that, except in the one essential matter of the hair, their manners and customs would not be interfered with, and that they would still as a matter of fact be governed by their own countrymen, they were pleased enough with the new order of things. The Manchus had next to no religion of their own, and did not interfere with the priests, or the temples, or the worship of the Chinese. They certainly gave a little trouble by opening recruiting depôts all over China, and compelling some of the people to learn the drill, giving prizes for good shots and flogging bad ones. But they made up for that by a measure which gave substantial relief to the masses. They remitted three years' arrears of taxes that had accumulated during the disorders following the death of the Ming Emperor. This was a concession to the pocket that went home to the feelings of the meanest. The new rulers, too, were a fine manly race, who inspired respect. They made war against vices which were then unknown to themselves, but common in China. Though women had, even with them, a position that in our eyes would seem degraded, yet on the whole they behaved to them with respect, and generally spared them in war. They also degraded the eunuchs, whose intrigues had been one great cause of the downfall of their predecessors, and

at one time contemplated dispensing with them altogether. For their only use was to guard zenanas, and
the Manchu women at that time were not immured
like so many prisoners, but walked about freely in the
cities and fields, and rode on horseback armed with
bow and arrow, and even hazarded their lives in battle,
thereby setting an excellent example to their Chinese
sisters.

To sum up, the conquest of China seems attributable to the natural willingness of the people to accept
a strong and stable dynasty for one that had left the
country in anarchy; to the military prowess of the Manchus; and to their wise and generous treatment of the
conquered race, especially of the official and lettered
classes, which made the change of masters as little
irksome to them as the circumstances admitted of.

Some people may feel tempted to draw a comparison
between the conquest of China by the Manchus and that
of India by the English. But the circumstances are
wholly different. In the first case, one barbarous nation
overcame another semi-barbarous one, and ended, as
anyone who has visited China is aware, by adopting all
the laws and customs, and descending to all the follies
and vices of the subdued race. In the other, Western
civilisation came into contact with the Eastern, and it
has steadily pursued the policy of raising the other to
its own high level. In the eyes of unthinking people
it would have been a better policy to imitate the Manchus, and to have continued working the administration with the native officials. But it would certainly
not have been so popular a policy with the masses
of the people, and the English people themselves
would not have consented to entrust a country, for
whose government they were responsible, to the tender

mercies of the native officials whom they found in possession.

Moreover, other things being equal, the Chinese are really able administrators, whereas the talent of natives of India lies in a different groove altogether. Now, however, that generations have passed, and a race of natives trained in European thought and casting away native ideas and habits is arising, everyone cordially wishes to see them employed in high and responsible posts. But for years to come the supply of capable men will be few, while the posts themselves are fewer. People who hear a clever native of India making a speech, think it strange so able a man should not be eligible for any lofty post in his own country, forgetting that very probably he has received but a poor education, that he is unfamiliar with the principles which guide the policy of the Government of India, that, in spite of association with Europeans, he retains customs out of harmony with the ideas of Englishmen, that his experience of public life has been small, and that his principal strength lies in intellectual alertness, combined with a very considerable power of public speaking. If they wish to injure the cause of the unrepresented millions of India, they cannot do better than support men of that class. At the same time, a steady pressure kept upon the Government of India towards enlarging the sphere for native officials' talents, and for the promotion of those who have shown proofs of their ability, will undoubtedly do good. The province of Mysore at this moment is an example of the capacity of English-trained natives, with a slight admixture of Europeans, to administer well and efficiently. She is a monument to the wisdom of those statesmen who—it is but a few years ago—steadfastly refused to annex her.

But I am wandering far away from the Manchus and their history. I will conclude this chapter by relating the fortunes of Wu San-kuei. He energetically upheld the new order of things, and pursued Ming pretenders even as far as Burmah. On his return he was created almost uncontrolled lord over three provinces. Strange to relate, in his old age he became intoxicated by power, and raised the standard of revolt. Once again were his sons and grandsons condemned to death, and they were allowed, as a great favour, to commit suicide with a white cord which the Emperor sent them, the youngest, a boy of ten, setting the example to his elder brothers. He died, still undefeated. His followers were then dispersed, and thirty-five years after he had raised the Manchus to the throne, by the order of the Emperor his bones were cut up and scattered over all the provinces as a warning to traitors. It is characteristic of China that even Prince Dorgun, the Great Regent, did not escape posthumous degradation. He died when his nephew was twelve years old, and shortly afterwards, on the apparently baseless charge that he had meditated usurping the throne, he was driven from the ancestral temple, and his sacrificial honours withdrawn. It is even said that his body was taken out of the grave and treated with every kind of ignominy, which, in a Chinaman's eyes, is the most terrible and abominable punishment that can be inflicted. But it may be hoped that his nephew's ingratitude did not take so brutal a form. On the other hand, in 1636 the posthumous title of T'ai Tsu Kao, or Great Ancestor, had been deservedly conferred on Nurhachu (the year in which the dynasty was named ' Clear '), and in 1648, four years after the entry into

Peking, the Emperor solemnly worshipped T'ai Tsu with the honours due to Shang-ti, the one Supreme Ruler of Heaven. He also canonised T'ai Tsu's imme-diate predecessors up to the fourth generation, giving them all Imperial titles—so honoured were the founders and ancestors of the dynasty.

CHAPTER III.

HISTORY—(continued).

Shunchih—Dutch embassy—Kotow—Human sacrifice—Emperor Kanghi—
Yungchêng—Kienlung—His cruelty—Defeats the Ghurkas—Receives
Lord Macartney—Chia Ching—Lord Amherst's Embassy—Effeminacy
of later Emperors—Taokuang—First war with England—Its causes—
Chinese outrages—Mandarins' support of the opium trade—Lin's oppres-
sive measures—Operations of war—Treaty—Macaulay's speech—Mr.
Gladstone's—Hsien-fêng—The Taeping rebellion—Successes of the insur-
gents—Ward's 'Ever-victorious Army'—General Gordon—Second war
with England—Yeh—Lord Elgin sent to China—Treachery of Chinese—
Summer Palace destroyed—Elgin's treaty—Tungchih—A *coup d'état*—
Prince Kung—The Empresses—Yunnan rebellion—Kuang-haü—The
Empress-Regent—Prince Chun—Li Hung Chang—Reconquest of Sun-
garia and Kashgar—The Kuldja question—Dispute with the French—
Chefoo convention—Recent English treaties with China—Present policy
of China—Bad results of Nurhachu's policy in Manchuria—Brigandage—
Gang robbery—Suppression of gambling—Corruption of mandarins—
Improvement in Manchuria—Poyarkoff explores the Amur—Russian
navigation prohibited on the Amur—Expeditions of the Russians—
Mouravieff—Ignatieff—Russian annexations—Hopes of China and Russia
in regard to Manchuria.

SHUNCHIH, the son of Tai Tsung, reigned for seventeen
years, and died in 1661, at the early age of twenty-
three. From the death of the Regent, which occurred
about ten years before, he had commenced administer-
ing the state himself, and, though he was very young,
his contemporaries extolled his kindness in private, and
his prudence and magnanimity in public affairs.[1]   The

[1] A very fine speech is put into his mouth by De Maillac, supposed to
have been addressed to the nobles on arriving at Peking, but it is certainly
not more authentic than those recorded by Thucydides. A better anecdote is related by Père d'Orléans. Shunchih was fond of visiting Father
Adam Schaal, the astronomer, who lived in the palace precincts. It was,

STAIRWAY AT THE PEI-LING, THE EMPEROR TAI TSUNG'S TOMB, MOUKDEN.

present penal code of China was published when he
had only been three years on the throne, and, though
the credit of that work must be given to his uncle, it
shows the spirit of reform which surrounded him. An
interesting narrative of his stately court is preserved
in the account of a Dutch embassy, which visited
Peking in July 1656, and stayed for three months.[1]
The Dutch found there arrived already embassies from
the Great Mogul of India, at that time the Emperor
Shah Jehan, from the Western Tartars (called Satatads),
and from the Dalai Lama of Thibet. They performed
the ceremony of *San kuei chiu ko'u*—that is to say,
kneeling before the Emperor three times, on each occasion striking the forehead on the ground three times,
or nine times in all.[2] But they were only permitted
to see the Emperor from a distance, and all they received in return for a lavish expenditure was a letter
allowing them to come to China once every eight years,
and to bring a hundred men, of whom twenty might
come to court to pay their respects. Russian ambassadors, who arrived about the same time, refused to

perhaps is, etiquette that a seat which the Emperor has once occupied shall
be covered with yellow silk and never profaned again by any less noble individual. But Shunchih was accustomed to sit down anywhere in the Father's
house, till the owner deferentially remonstrated, telling His Majesty there
would soon be no place left for him (the Father) to sit down upon. 'Oh,'
said the Emperor, 'you can sit anywhere. You and I do not stand upon
ceremony.'

[1] *Narrative of the Embassy from the East India Company of the United
Provinces to the Grand Tartar Chan Emperor of China, delivered by their
Excellencies Peter de Goyer and Jacob de Keyzer*. By Mr. John Nieuhoff,
steward to the Ambassadors. Translated by John Ogilvy, Esquire, Master of
His Majesty's Revels in the Kingdom of Ireland. London, MDCLXIX.

[2] Foreigners usually speak of this as the 'kotow,' but this is not strictly
accurate. There are eight grades of ceremonious salutations in China,
of which the kotow is only the fifth, consisting of one kneeling followed
by one knocking of the head on the ground. The form of obeisance described above is the eighth and last, and only the Supreme Being and the
Emperor are entitled to it.

kotow. Shunchih's death is said to have been caused
by grief at the death of his favourite consort, to whose
shade he is credited with having offered a human
sacrifice, consisting of thirty male and female attendants, though, according to other accounts, he only
desired them so to devote themselves, and they, being
Chinese, did not approve of doing so. It is quite
possible, however, that human sacrifices were known
to the early Manchus, and that the first story is true.
De Maillac says that they were accustomed to offer
slaves, women, horses, and arms at the funeral of their
princes; and Père d'Orléans relates that, after Shunchih's
death, his mother made a favourite young Tartar noble
follow him into the other world. The Chinese themselves once practised human sacrifice. The Emperor
Ying Tsung, in the fifteenth century, left special injunctions when he was dying that none of his concubines
were to be buried alive with him. Huc also mentions
only fifty years ago that in Mongolia slave children were
sacrificed in large numbers, and placed in the grave of
a chief, along with gold, silver, and other things, which
the deceased monarch might be supposed to need.

Shunchih was succeeded by K'ang-Hsi, better known
as the great Emperor Kanghi. He was Shunchih's third
son, and is said to have been born when his father was
only fifteen years of age. It is noteworthy that from
Shunchih downwards, for seven generations, the succession was handed without a break from father to
son, the present Emperor, Kuang-sü, being the first to
succeed as a cousin. Kanghi reigned sixty-one years.
He was the patron of the Jesuits, whom he employed
in making a survey of his empire, taking astronomical
observations, casting cannon, and in other ways. His
first task, one that occupied him seven years, was to

put down Wu San-kuei's rebellion, with that of the son
and grandson of the Princes Shang and Gung, mentioned
in the last chapter, who had been created princes in
the south like Wu San-kuei himself. By all accounts
he was an exceptionally able ruler, liberal-minded, but
of strong will and indefatigable application to business,
economical with state funds, and sincerely anxious to
promote the good of his subjects. He extended his empire as far as Khokand on the west, and to the confines
of Thibet on the south-west. He also expelled certain
Russian adventurers who had settled in the wild trans-
Amur country.

Kanghi's successor was his fourth son, Yungchêng,
who reigned thirteen years. He is said to have been
the fourteenth son, and by altering Kanghi's will to
have deprived of his inheritance the brother whom his
father had nominated. A famine occurred in his reign,
which he did his best to alleviate. But he was a narrow-
minded man, and took alarm at the spread of Christianity under the Jesuits, whom Kanghi had consistently
protected. He forbade their making any further conversions, and some members of his own family who
had accepted the truths of the Gospel were exiled to
Furdan, in Eastern Manchuria, now part of the Primorsk, and they eventually succumbed to the barbarity
with which they were treated.

Yungchêng's eldest son, Kienlung (Ch'ien-Lung),
reigned sixty years, nearly as long as Kanghi. This
Emperor received the first embassy from England,
under Lord Macartney, in 1793. Other Western powers
sent embassies to China in this reign; but their object
was misunderstood, the vain Chinese affecting to believe
that they were from feudatories sending tribute. Kienlung was another able man, and, like Kanghi, personally

F

administered the affairs of his vast empire. He subdued the tribes in the far west, in Ili, or Sungaria, and
Kashgaria ; but his wars with the aborigines of Formosa
and Kueichou brought him not much glory, and he was
disastrously defeated in Burmah. In 1785 there was
again a great famine, and, as a calamity of the kind
is attributed by the Chinese to the wickedness of their
ruler, to gain his people's favour he persecuted Christians for a time. He made strenuous endeavours to
regulate and check the inundations of the Yellow
River, which to this day are a source of perpetual loss
and misery to considerable tracts of country. He was
a munificent patron of arts and literature. Like the
rest of his people, he was a cruel man, and, after the
manner of the French nobles at the execution of
Damiens in 1757, attended by his whole court, he
witnessed the death by torture of the chiefs of a Mahommedan rising in Shensi ; at the same time he ordered
the extermination of the whole race of rebels. The
Lama form of Buddhism was much favoured by him.
He invited the Teshu Lama, who ranks in power and
sanctity next to the Dalai Lama of Lhassa, to pay him
a visit in Peking, and actually went as far as Sining, in
the remote province of Kansuh, to meet him. The
Lama died of small-pox at Peking the next year (1780),
and Kienlung erected a very beautiful marble monument to him in Peking, in the shape of a Thibetan
' chorten,' or ' dagoba '-shaped tomb,[1] and forwarded his
body in a golden coffin to the Dalai Lama at Lhassa.
The Ghurkalis, or Ghurkas, as they are now generally
called, a warlike caste which not long before had usurped
the kingdom of Nepal, invaded Thibet in 1791, took
Teshulumbo, the Teshu Lama's capital, and plundered it.

[1] Compare the illustration on the next page.

Kienlung resented this, and out of regard to his former friend he promptly sent a Chinese army, which defeated and drove back the Ghurkas. The Chinese commander, Sun Fo, evidently a general of great capacity, pursued them across the Himalayas with 40,000 men and menaced their capital, Khatmandu. The Ghurkas took fright, while the Chinese general himself was anxious to get back ; so the contest ended by the Ghurka Maharajah agreeing to acknowledge himself the vassal of

LAMA MONUMENT OUTSIDE MOUKDEN.

China, to restore the plunder he had taken from Teshulumbo, and ever afterwards to send a quinquennial embassy to China [1] It is to be said of Kienlung that he was less eaten up with senseless pride than his successors. Indeed, he was the last to preserve a lingering memory of his ancestors' contempt for pomp and show. When Lord Macartney arrived, the question arose

[1] Note A, ' India, China, and Nepal,' p. 413.

whether he should prostrate himself and knock his head on the floor. Lord Macartney, who had not taken exception to the inscription on the flags attached to his carriage, 'Ambassador bringing tribute from the country of England,' as he might not be supposed to read Chinese, said he was willing to prostrate himself if a Chinese noble, of equal rank with himself, would make a similar prostration before a picture of King George the Third. Failing this, he agreed to bend the knee on entering the Emperor's presence, as he would do before his own sovereign. This degree of homage Kienlung had the good sense to be content with (though his courtiers doubtless objected as strongly as they dared), and he gave Lord Macartney a right royal and courteous reception. The embassy, however, failed—a result that is partly attributable to Sun Fo, who thought the English had assisted Nepal in the war.

Kienlung abdicated, in the year 1795, in favour of his son Chia Ching, the first really bad emperor of the dynasty. He was idle and dissolute; he expelled the famous Père Amyot from China, and under his feeble administration piracy flourished in South China to such an extent that trade almost came to a standstill. So great was his unpopularity that his life was several times attempted—an unprecedented crime in the history of the dynasty. On one occasion the assassins forced their way into the heart of the palace, and, but for the bravery of his second son, Prince Meening, he would have been killed. He gave up the annual hunting excursions. When another British Embassy, under Lord Amherst, was sent to Peking, he insisted on the 'kotow'; the envoy refusing, was insulted; after which he sent a message to the Prince Regent, that, as England was far off, he need not take the trouble to send another

embassy. With his accession, the degradation of the
dynasty began. Indeed, the contrast is remarkable between Kanghi and Kienlung and the Emperor of to-day.
They enjoyed hunting and travelling about, they saw
their country and subjects, and ruled. The present
Emperor remains cooped up in his palace, is taught no
manly exercises, except archery and riding in a yard,
and without a chance of acquiring a love of field-sport,
though he may hunt in the park when old enough. If
he goes to a temple, foreigners are requested not to
look at him, and his subjects are all kept indoors. The
early Manchus disliked eunuchs. To-day the imperial
city is peopled with them, and instead of their being degraded as in Shunchih's time, in 1887 the head of the
Board of Admiralty, the present Emperor's own father,
could not go on inspection duty without a eunuch
being sent specially to look after him. The Manchus
no longer laugh at the Chinese for travelling in chairs,
for their greatest generals ride in them to battle ; and
their love of speedy justice, their hatred of corruption,
the freedom they allowed to their women, have long
been things of the past. The decadence began with
Chia Ching, and is due to the Chinaman's love of ceremony and luxury, corrupting and destroying all primitive Manchu simplicity.

Prince Meening succeeded as the Emperor Tao-
kuang, and reigned from 1821 to 1850. His intentions
were excellent, and he tried to repair many of his
father's cruel acts. An honest minister, named Sung,
was recalled from exile, prisoners unjustly confined
were released, and the palace was cleared of a horde
of evil characters. But he was very indolent, and
took no pains to purify the administration. He is
best known abroad as the Emperor who provoked the

first war with England. A popular modern historian, Mr. Justin McCarthy, forgetful of the condemnation passed on those who foul their own nests, has denounced England's part in that war, and a portion of the public, with that misplaced, if generous, sympathy which prompts some folk always to take an offender's side, no matter how worthy of punishment he may be, have been only too glad to chime in. It would seem to be a sufficient answer that statesmen like Viscount Melbourne, Lord John Russell, Viscount Palmerston, the great Duke of Wellington, and Lord Macaulay, were responsible for or approved of that war, and that Parliament and the country supported them. Still, as facts are apt to escape the memory, and a story, however groundless, comes to be believed if only repeated with sufficient frequency, the true facts of the case will bear restating.

The war was set afoot, in the words of Lord John Russell, 'to obtain reparation for insults and injuries offered to Her Majesty's Superintendent and subjects, to obtain indemnification for the losses the merchants had sustained under threats of violence, and, lastly, to get security that persons and property trading with China should be protected from insult and injury, and trade maintained on a proper footing.' It is the fashion to call it the Opium War, but, although the high-handed proceedings of the Chinese in reference to the opium trade constituted the ultimate *teterrima causa belli*, yet, if no opium had ever come to China, war would have been inevitable. For many years the trade with China, not in opium only, but in such harmless and useful articles as tea and silk, had been growing steadily. But British merchants and foreigners in general were treated by the Chinese like

dogs. As I have related, two attempts were made by
the British Government to induce the Emperor of
China to enter into diplomatic relations, which would
have enabled grievances on either side to be discussed
and removed in a civilised manner, but both came to
nothing. Dr. Williams, the learned author of 'The
Middle Kingdom,' and a strenuous opponent of the
opium trade, states that the failure of the second mission was really due to the utter misconception of their
true position on the part of the Emperor and his
officials; ignorance, pride, isolation, and mendacity, all
combining to keep up the delusion, which needed to
be overthrown by the exhibition of resistless force.

As a specimen of the manner in which the Chinese
behaved to English officials and subjects, their treatment of Lord Napier may be cited. On the expiry of
the East India Company's charter in 1834, Lord Napier
was appointed by the Crown to be Superintendent of
Trade at Canton. The Chinese refused to receive him.
They affected not to have approved the abolition of the
East India Company's monopoly, and wrote the following
letter :

The barbarian[1] Lord Napier has come to Canton without
having at all resided at Macao to wait for orders; nor has he
requested or received a permit from the Superintendent of Customs, but has hastily come to Canton—a great infringement of
the established law. The Custom-house waiters and others who
presumed to admit him, are sent with a communication requiring
their trial. But, in tender consideration for the said barbarian
being a new comer, and unacquainted with the statutes and laws

[1] The Chinese word is an offensive one, which the Chinese were so fond
of using, that a special clause (No. li.) was introduced into the treaty of 1860
prohibiting it for the future in Chinese official proclamations. Only a year
or two ago the Consul in Manchuria had to call attention to a notice containing the objectionable word, and the authorities withdrew it and apolo-
gised.

of the Celestial Empire, I will not strictly investigate. . . . If the said barbarian throws in private letters, I, the Governor, will not at all receive or look at them. . . . With regard to the foreign policy of the Company without the walls of the city, it is the place of the temporary residence for foreigners carrying on trade. They are permitted only to eat, sleep, buy, and sell in the factories. They are not allowed to go out or ramble about.

And Lord Napier was not received. For many years before that, outrages were committed by the Chinese, generally with impunity. In 1816, H.M.S. 'Alceste,' proceeding to Canton for the embarkation of Lord Amherst, was fired upon, but in that case the British captain promptly and effectually retaliated, as related · in Captain Basil Hall's delightful narrative. In 1821 a sailor, an American, was accused of causing the death of a Chinese woman, who tumbled out of a boat by accident. Abandoned by his Consul and those who should . have protected him, because the American trade had been temporarily stopped on account of the accident, he was cruelly strangled. On that occasion the American representatives expressed to the Chinese a sentiment which the British have never yet conceded, but which Mr. McCarthy probably approves: 'We are bound to submit to your laws while we are in your waters; were they ever so unjust, we will not resist them.' In the same year an unarmed party of men belonging to the English frigate 'Topaze' were set upon in a barbarous manner by the natives and severely wounded with spears when watering on shore, and two of them died of their wounds. But no redress could be obtained. And not only did the Chinese Government hold itself disdainfully aloof from the Government of England, but even its officers at

Canton would not condescend to communicate with the English merchants, or with the Superintendent of Trade, except through the medium of the Chinese merchants engaged in foreign business. Neither the executive nor the courts of justice could be approached direct. Trade was confined to a single port, Canton; and the merchants' residences were restricted to one row of houses on the banks of a crowded river. They were forbidden to take the exercise necessary to health, walking in the city of Canton or even into the country being forbidden, the hiring of the requisite number of servants was denied them, and, more than all, their wives and families were not allowed to come to Canton at all, but were compelled to reside at Macao, several days distant by water. The following extract from an Imperial Edict of March 8, 1835, will satisfy the reader of the literal truth of this description:

Barbarians residing in the factories will only be allowed to walk about on the 8th, 18th, and 28th, three days in the month. Each time there must not be more than ten individuals, and they must be limited to the hour of five in the evening to return to the factories. They must not be allowed to remain out to sleep or drink liquor. In case of any infraction of this law the hong merchants and interpreters will both receive punishment.

When barbarians petition on any subject, they should in all cases do so through the medium of the hong merchants, in order that the dignity of Government be rendered impressive.

And more than once the conduct of the officials became so outrageous that intercourse of all kinds was suspended, and only renewed again at the request of the Chinese themselves. In short, the position of the Superintendent and the merchants was for years intolerable.

It will perhaps be said that matters might not have

been so bad but for the opium trade, which the British carried on, contrary to the law of China. The exact contrary is the case. Had it not been for the profit the mandarins at Canton made out of opium, the likelihood is that all foreign intercourse, the tea trade and the rest of it, would have come to a standstill sooner than it actually did. It is admitted that the opium traffic was at one time nominally illegal, and that just before the war the Emperor was really determined to suppress it. But for half a century the law—for so an occasional imperial proclamation against opium may admittedly be styled—was a dead letter. From the Emperor in Peking to the meanest tide-waiter in Canton, all the officials revelled in the gains from opium. The post of 'Hoppo,' or Customs Commissioner, was generally given to a Manchu of the imperial household, generally a relation of some favourite sultana, sent to Canton to enrich himself with the golden harvest to be reaped there. On one occasion, when the Chinese merchants refused to carry on the traffic on account of the Viceroy's exactions, the Viceroy himself built four large boats and carried the opium on his own account. An eminent missionary, the Rev. W. H. Medhurst, D.D., states that the Government officers used to come regularly on board the receiving ships and demand so many dollars per chest, and Dr. Gutzlaff, another well-known clergyman, writes that the smugglers were regularly licensed by the Custom House officers, and the revenue cutters were sent to load the prohibited article. 'Daily,' he writes, 'are the Government boats passing with the "illicit pernicious drug" on board.' Besides that, so much opium was grown at that time in Yunnan and other provinces, where it found a ready sale, that the Governors themselves said that the inhabitants could meet their own demand in the event of not being able to obtain a supply from the outside barbarians. It is clear, therefore, that whatever grievances the Chinese may have had against the British, the importation of opium was not one of them.

What then happened? In 1839 matters came to a climax. The Emperor began to take fright at the balance of trade being against China, which he attributed to the large remittances of silver made to India in payment for opium imported from that country. Taokuang undoubtedly disliked the practice of opium-smoking, which had increased since the beginning of the century, mainly owing to the increase in wealth, prosperity, and population that followed the long and well-ordered reigns of Kanghi and Kienlung.[1] True it was that opium had not been introduced into China by the British, that, according to Sir Thomas Wade, the best living authority on the point, the English importation would not have supplied one per cent. of the population, and that within seven years after the war it was ascertained that the poppy was cultivated in ten of the eighteen provinces, that of Kansu being spoken of as rivalling foreign opium. True also it was, that to call the opium trade a smuggling trade was a confusion of terms. In 1839, however, as I have said, the Emperor took fright at the export of silver, and, without caring to inquire how the trade had grown up, or what dimensions it had assumed, he sent a special officer, named Lin, to Canton, with orders at once to put a stop to it.

[1] To a similar cause is due the increase in the consumption of spirituous liquors in India. Even though individual mistakes may have been made, the allegation that the Government or its officers have fostered it is untrue. The orders and practice are to keep it to a minimum, consistently with the repression of smuggling.

In anticipation of Lin's arrival proclamations were posted in the streets that all trade with foreigners was to be stopped, and when Lin came himself he showed at once his determination to carry out his orders without regard to considerations of courtesy. He peremptorily forbade any English merchant to quit Canton without his leave, and endeavoured to obtain possession of the person of Mr. Dent, the principal merchant. The British Superintendent, along with 200 British subjects, was kept in close confinement for a period of more than seven weeks; armed men paraded day and night before their houses, and threatened to deprive them of food and water, and even to take their lives. Lin menaced them by publicly executing a criminal outside their residences (asserting it was for opium-smoking), as a foretaste of what they might expect themselves. And, as evidence of their contempt for the British, the Chinese seized and broke up a ship called the ' Snipe,' though only carrying duty-paid tea and coffee. Eventually, Lin called on Captain Elliott, the Superintendent of Trade, to surrender all the opium the merchants had in stock; in order to save their lives Captain Elliott was obliged to comply; and he made over property to the value of two millions sterling, which Lin destroyed.

But this was not enough. Supplies were refused to British men-of-war, outrages on foreigners and ships were perpetrated, and Lin even wrote an insolent letter to the Queen of England, from which I give an extract:

The powerful instrumentality whereby the Celestial Court holds in subjection all nations is truly divine and awe-inspiring beyond the power of computation. Let it not be said early warning has not been given. When your Majesty receives this document, let us have a speedy communication in reply, advertising us of the measures you adopt for the entire cutting off of the opium in every seaport. Do not by any means by false embellishments evade or procrastinate. Earnestly reflect hereon. Earnestly observe these things.

Twenty-four junks menaced two British frigates, and, though the Chinese admiral was beaten off, the Emperor rewarded him for his victory and ordered his officers at Canton to put a stop once for all to the trade with foreigners. It was also announced that English merchants who had dealt in opium were going to be executed.

The end of it all was that Great Britain was forced to go to war. Hongkong was forthwith occupied and annexed, and the forts on the Canton River taken and destroyed. The Emperor sent peremptory orders to have the leaders of the barbarians sent in cages to Peking, and Sir Hugh Gough replied by taking Canton, and forty war-junks were destroyed. Amoy fell, Chinhai, and Ningpo. It was then determined to carry the war up the river Yang-tse-kiang, and Woosung, Shanghai, and Chinkiang were taken.[1] At last, when the British force was on the eve of taking Nanking, the Emperor gave in and sued for peace. And he was then obliged, besides paying for British property destroyed, to open five of his ports to trade on a fair and regular tariff, and to cede Hongkong. Dr. Williams remarks: 'War seemed to be the only way to break down the intolerable oppression of the Court of Peking.[2]

---

[1] The Manchu garrison at the latter place resolved on killing their wives and children and committing suicide afterwards, and many were caught in the act and rescued.

[2] To illustrate the treatment meted out during the war to foreigners, the cases of three shipwrecked crews may be mentioned. In 1840 a lady named Noble and the sailors rescued from the 'Kite' were confined in small cages, like wild beasts, and treated so cruelly that some of them succumbed to their sufferings. (Captain Anstruther, of the Madras Army, who was taken prisoner at Ningpo, was subjected to similar barbarity.) In September 1841

That a war would do it was quite plain to everyone acquainted with the character of that Court and the genius of the people, and the result has shown that the expectation was well founded.' And no one believes that, if the Emperor or his officers had behaved in a civilised or, at least, a reasonable fashion, and entered, if not into friendly relations, even into civil communication with the Queen and her representatives, any grievance they had in connection with opium would not have been considered. But they never gave the English the chance.

It may be urged that it was, after all, optional with the Emperor to allow the contraband traffic up till 1839, and then peremptorily to put a stop to it, and to seize the contraband drug if so he pleased. This is scarcely accurate. The Emperor, refusing communication with foreigners, allowed them to know no other law than the will of the mandarins at Canton, and the drug imported with the permission of the mandarins could not be called contraband. Undoubtedly the British would have admitted the Emperor's right to legislate as he pleased for the future, but he could not go behind what had been admitted in the past. As Macaulay put it :—

The British Government might doubt whether it were wise for the Government of China to exclude from that country a drug which, if judiciously administered, was powerful in assuaging pain and in promoting health, because occasionally it was

and March 1842 the ships 'Nerbudda' and 'Ann' were lost off the coast of Formosa. Upwards of a hundred passengers in the first-named, wretched Indian camp-followers, deserted by the officers of the ship, after being imprisoned for eleven months, were executed in cold blood under the direct orders of the Emperor, passed upon a lying report of a Manchu official called Talungah. Of the 'Ann,' out of fifty-seven persons, most of whom were also natives of India, all but eleven were executed, Mr. Gully, a merchant, being amongst the victims.

used to excess by intemperate men; they might doubt if it was
wise policy on the part of that Government to attempt to stop
the efflux of the precious metals from the country in the due
course of trade; they learned from history, and almost every
country afforded proof, which was strengthened by the existing
circumstances in England, that no machinery however powerful
had been sufficient to keep out of any country those luxuries
which the people enjoyed, or to prevent the efflux of the precious
metals when it was demanded by the course of trade; what
Great Britain could not effect with the finest marine and the
most trustworthy preventive service in the world, was not likely
to be effected by the feeble efforts of the mandarins of China.
But whatever their opinion on these points might be, the
Government of China alone, it must be remembered, was
competent to decide. That Government had a right to keep
out opium, to keep in silver, to enforce their prohibitory laws,
by whatever means they might possess, *consistently with the
principles of public morality and international law*; and if, after
having given prior notice of their intention to seize all contraband goods introduced into their dominions, they seized on
opium, we had no right to complain. But when the Government, finding that by just and lawful means they could not
carry out their prohibition, resorted to measures unjust and un-
lawful, confined our innocent fellow-countrymen, and insulted
the Sovereign in the person of her representative, then he
thought the time had arrived when it was fit we should interfere. The Imperial Commissioner began by confiscating property, and his next demand was for innocent blood. Now the
English in China felt that, although far from their native
country, and then in danger in a part of the world remote from
that which they must look to for protection, yet that they belonged to a State which would not suffer the hair of a head of
one of its members to be harmed with impunity. He felt
bound to declare his earnest desire that this most rightful
quarrel might be prosecuted to a triumphant close.

The debate from which this speech is taken was on
a motion of Sir James Graham that the Government
had contributed to bring on the war by failing to give

the Superintendent of Trade at Canton full and timely instructions, although he had asked for them more than once. Mr. Gladstone, who then sat on the Tory benches, took part in it, and it is remarkable that, even at that early period of his career, he showed that recklessness of language in support of the cause which he supported for the time being, for which at a later time he became so conspicuous. He justified the alleged poisoning by the Chinese of the wells on the line of the coast, a measure taken, as one Member of Parliament put it, to deprive of fresh water English women and children, who at least were not implicated in the opium trade, but who were expelled by the Imperial Commissioner at three hours' notice from Macao; and Lord Palmerston severely rebuked him in the debate, giving him credit at the same time for being the last man in the House deliberately and on reflection to stand up and defend doctrines so monstrous.

Taokuang was the last[1] Emperor who visited his ancestral home in Manchuria. He died in 1850, and was succeeded by his son, Hsien-fêng, or Hien-fung, then a lad of nineteen, a weak and brutal ruler, in whose time the Manchu dynasty nearly followed that of the Mings. In 1850 began the great Taeping[2] rebellion. Though not immediately connected with Manchuria, I must give a slight sketch of it, as it nearly ousted the dynasty, and, as long as Gordon's name lives, so long will Englishmen take an interest in the story. Few people outside China know, or recollect, that the

---

[1] So Mr. Ross informs me. Mr. Delmar Morgan states that Chia Ching was the last.

[2] Taeping is properly T'ai-Ping, literally ' Great Peace ' dynasty, the title which the leader of the revolt assumed, in imitation of the Manchus, who called their dynasty the Ta-Ching, or ' Great Clear ' dynasty, following their predecessors, who were the Ta-Ming or ' Great Bright ' dynasty.

Christian religion in some measure contributed to this frightful revolt.

The leader was a man named Hung-Siu-tsuen, son of a small farmer who lived about thirty miles from Canton. At the age of twenty-four he fell into a trance, and saw (so he believed) a venerable personage who showed him all the depravity of the world, and gave him a sword to overcome the evil spirits. He also saw a man who was to guide him in his conflict. In 1843 he read a Christian pamphlet, consisting of sixty-eight selected chapters of the Bible, and he conceived that the persons of his vision were the first two persons in the Trinity. He believed himself called to be Supreme Ruler of the Earth. In 1846 he studied two months with a missionary named Roberts, but left him and began making converts amongst his relations and friends. As a rule, the Chinese Government summarily executes the members of a new sect, assuming it to be a conspiracy. But in this instance no notice was taken, and the converts by degrees became strong enough to attack their neighbours who refused to be converted. In 1851 the Emperor sent three Manchu officials to quell the rising, but the army was corrupt and inefficient to a degree, and the insurgents easily defeated them; and then, as there is no *locus pœnitentiæ* for one who once opposes the Emperor's authority, Hung-Siu-tsuen, after suffering a siege at Yung-ngan for five months, burst through the cordon of troops that surrounded him and commenced a triumphant march across China. To emphasise his claims as a rival emperor, he followed the Manchu precedent of 200 years before and compelled his followers to abandon the Manchu *queue*, to allow the hair to grow on their foreheads, and to wear the loose garments left off since the

days of the Mings. Hence, amongst the Chinese, the
Taepings were known as the 'Long-haired rebels.' An
insurgent force in China grows like a snowball, and
3,000 followers soon grew to 80,000. They made for
Nanking (literally, the southern capital, and the city
next in importance to Peking, which is the northern),
and took it on March 18, 1853, putting the garrison,
including the Governor-General of the province, to the
sword. Shortly afterwards another body marched for
Peking itself, and reached Tientsin, only eighty miles
from the capital, in four months, defeating all the imperial troops sent against them. Their progress from
the south to the north of China was like that of the
locusts in Joel: they made a solitude, but did not call it
peace. Nevertheless, their leader was not equal to Li-
tzŭ-ch'êng, and, when all China seemed at his feet, he
failed to make a bold stroke for Peking. In 1855 his
armies began to retire; in 1856 it was evident the first
force of the movement was spent, and in October of
that year his principal lieutenant, Yung, was cut off with
20,000 men. By 1857 the Taepings were confined to
Nanking, Nganking, and the intervening rivers, and
Nanking was so closely invested that there, as well as
in other places, human flesh was openly sold in the
shambles. In 1860 they burst out once more, and
carried fire and sword over Kiangnan and Che-kiang,
the fairest and richest districts of China. To assist the
imperial troops, an American named Ward then organised a body of men, amongst whom were a number of
foreigners, and the Chinese gave it the name of the
'Ever-victorious Army.' The Taepings strenuously resisted, and even captured important places like Ningpo
and Hangchow. In 1862 they also attacked Shanghai,
which was protected by English and French sailors and

marines, assisted by Ward's force. But gradually the
' Ever-victorious Army' began to cope successfully with
them. Ward was wounded, and died in September,
1862. A colleague named Burgevine succeeded him, but
he was found incapable, and in April 1863 the late
General C. E. Gordon, R.E., then Major Gordon, assumed the command. His army never exceeded 5,000
rank and file, nearly all of whom were armed with
smooth-bores, supported by a weak force of artillery.[1]
He found the rebels in possession of an immense alluvial
flat, having a superficial area of nearly 50,000 square
miles. In fourteen months, leading on his men in
person, he fought twenty-four successful engagements,
received the surrender of two cities, and captured
ten other cities and fortified places. By November
28, Soochow, the Taepings' last great stronghold, protected, like Venice, by rivers and canals, capitulated.
It was on this occasion that the Chinese General,
the present well-known Viceroy of Chihli, Li Hung-
chang, executed the insurgent leaders, whom Gordon
meant to spare. It is customary to condemn Li in
consequence, but there is something to be said on his
side, and his action may have been not less justifiable
by the necessities of the case, than by the Chinese
laws of war. General Gordon resigned, but afterwards,
from motives of pure humanity, took up his command
again, and marched against the rebels at I-hang, where
he found the people reduced to such extremities that
they were feeding on dead bodies. Here he met with
a reverse, and was wounded while leading his men to

---

[1] There were two 8-inch howitzers, four 32-pounder guns, three 24-
pounder howitzers, twelve 12-pounder howitzers, ten American 12-pounder
howitzers, eight 4½-inch howitzers, fourteen mortars, and six rocket-tubes.

the attack.   But soon he took the field again.   Hang-
chou, capital of Chehkiang, surrendered in March 1864,
and Changchou Fu on May 11, and then, as Nanking
alone remained and the Imperialists were quite able to
deal with it, the 'Ever-victorious Army' was dissolved.
Nanking fell on July 19, and the rebellion was soon
after at an end—a rebellion which devastated the most
fertile provinces of China and cost, it is estimated, fully
25,000,000 lives.   The leader's fate is involved in obscurity, but it is believed he poisoned himself just
before the capture of Nanking.   For many years afterwards the rich lands which the Taepings wasted up the
Yang-tsze-kiang, once the garden of China, remained a
mere jungle, the haunt of the pheasant and deer, the
inhabitants having ceased to exist ; and to this day the
country has not recovered.   Amongst other things,
the great porcelain factories were annihilated, and it is
feared that the highest secrets of their beautiful art
have perished for ever with the artificers.   A little
incident brought the reality of the rebellion forcibly
home to myself.   While staying at Shanghai I proposed visiting Nanking to see the famous porcelain
tower, which I had learnt as a child to consider one
of the wonders of the world.   Great was my disappointment to learn that the Taepings had destroyed it
just thirty years before.

The other great event of Hienfung's reign was the
second war with England, as well as with France.   Mr.
McCarthy apparently finds pleasure in condemning this
war also, so the facts may be briefly recapitulated.
After a long series of insults, such as the refusal to allow
the English to enter the city of Canton, though a distinct
agreement to admit them had been made, and the
unwillingness of the Imperial Commissioner at Canton

to discuss questions with British officials except on terms degrading to them, an outrage was committed on a British lorcha (a fast-sailing river boat) called the 'Arrow,' sailing under British colours. The flag was torn down and the crew imprisoned, contrary to treaty and civilised usages alike. The Commissioner refused to apologise, and justified the act, which a fair and unbiassed historian like Mr. Boulger does not hesitate to characterise as the 'last of a long succession of acts showing the resolve of the ruling authorities at Canton to thwart and humiliate the English, just as it was the precursor of many outrages unknown in the practice of fair warfare and repugnant to human sentiment.' There being no telegraph to hamper the representatives of British power on the spot, and it being usual then to permit no insult to the British flag, the British Admiral took a junk by way of reprisal, and, as that failed to bring redress, he attacked and took some of the forts on the Canton River. The Imperial Commissioner, Yeh by name, a clever, but treacherous and most brutal Chinaman, who is said to have executed 100,000 persons for complicity in the Taeping rebellion, replied by offering a reward for foreigners' heads, and some foreigners were murdered in consequence, and their heads brought in for the reward. Yeh might have easily yielded had he pleased, and the Governments of the two countries would not have been embroiled; but he was stubborn. The Earl of Elgin was then sent out from home as Ambassador Plenipotentiary, to bring matters to a conclusion. Before he arrived, the Chinese fleet had been gallantly attacked and destroyed by Admiral Sir Michael Seymour, but military operations were delayed by the outbreak of the Indian Mutiny. In January

1858 Canton was taken, when evidence was obtained,
amongst other things, that two English and four French
sailors had been treated with fiendish cruelty in the prison
there till death had ended their sufferings. Yeh himself
was captured and sent to Calcutta, where he afterwards
died. Lord Elgin then wrote to the Principal Secretary
of State at Peking, saying he had occupied Canton and
would proceed to Shanghai with the French Commissioner, who had been instructed by his Government to
demand reparation for cruel murders of French subjects,
and open negotiations with the Chinese Government
there. On their arrival at Shanghai, the Commissioners
found a letter from the Secretary, refusing to meet
them, and telling them to go back to Canton and
discuss matters with the new Commissioner who had
been sent in Yeh's place. Lord Elgin saw it was no
use trying to deal any longer with subordinates, so he
determined to proceed to the capital, and sailed for
Peking. A passage was soon forced through the Taku
forts at the mouth of the Peiho (a navigable river
flowing past Peking, which lies about twelve miles from
its right bank), and then the Emperor yielded. In June
1858 a treaty was made, under which five more ports,
including Yingtzŭ, in Manchuria (called, by the treaty,
Newchwang), were opened to trade, and a British representative was to reside permanently at Peking, who,
it was expressly stipulated, should not be called upon
to perform any ceremony derogatory to him as representing the sovereign of an independent nation on a
footing of equality with China. The Treaty of Nanking,
which had been made at the end of the first war, was
silent on the subject of opium, but the drug had been
admitted without question ever since. So Lord Elgin
agreed that for the future it should pay thirty taels a

chest, or about eight per cent. on its value. Thus that long-standing cause of difficulty was removed.

The treaty was to be ratified at Peking, and in 1859 the Hon. F. Bruce, who was appointed the first envoy, started for the purpose. But on arriving at Taku the river was found blocked, the envoy was fired upon, and an attempt to force a way through failed. Warlike operations were therefore resumed, and in 1860 the forts at Taku and Peit'ang, not far from Taku, were taken, and the British and French armies landed. A meeting was then arranged between Lord Elgin and a Commissioner nominated by the Emperor. The late Sir Harry Parkes and the present Sir Henry Loch were sent forward to make suitable preparations at the place fixed, but, together with some other English officers and their Sikh escort, they were treacherously made prisoners. Our troops then advanced and defeated the Chinese General, who lost eighty guns. His name was Sankolinsin, a chief of the same Kortsin Mongols whose good offices to the early Manchus I mentioned in the last chapter. The Emperor fled to Jehol, beyond the Great Wall, the country seat where his great-grandfather had received Lord Macartney. The return of the captives was then demanded, when it was found that most of them had been treated with such frightful barbarity that they had succumbed to their tortures. Lord Elgin, therefore, decided to destroy the Yuen-ming-yuen, or Summer Palace, as it was Hienfung's favourite residence, and it was there that our hapless countrymen were tortured by the Emperor's own orders. This was done, and the palace lies in ruins to this day. The Chinese still demurred to Lord Elgin's terms, and not till within ten minutes of the time when they had been warned the gates of Peking would be blown open did they yield. Then the An-ting-mên, or north-west gate of the capital, was opened, the envoys entered in state, and a fresh treaty was made. It commenced with a humble apology from the Emperor, who agreed to pay an indemnity for the war, and compensation to the families of the murdered English and Sikhs; till this was paid the English were to occupy Tientsin, the north coast of Shantung, and Canton. It also re-enacted the provisions of the first treaty. Such is a brief account of the second English conflict with the Chinese. It resulted in the final abatement of China's intolerable pretensions to lord it over the rest of the world, and history will give it a prominent place amongst those wars which have directly contributed to the civilisation and welfare of mankind.

Hien-fung died on August 22, 1861, five months after the British envoy was installed at Peking. He left one son, a boy of five, named T'ung-chih. His father's will nominated a Board of Regency, headed by Prince Tsai, his nephew, the man who was chiefly responsible for the arrest of the English officers and men, and who, with some others, represented the reactionary party. Fortunately, Prince Kung, the late Emperor's brother, who had negotiated Lord Elgin's treaty, and who appreciated the importance of remaining on friendly terms with foreigners, prevailed on Hien-fung's principal widow, the Empress T'zŭ An, to proclaim herself Regent, and the persons of Prince Tsai and two leading members of his party were adroitly seized. Their arrest was followed by speedy execution, two of the conspirators being allowed to commit suicide, but the third and most dangerous, Su-Shun (who had been captured, while escorting the Emperor's coffin, by Prince Ch'un, another of the brothers), was put to death in public. The widowed Empress T'zŭ An, associated with T'ung-chih's mother T'zŭ Hsi, who, originally an inferior wife, was raised to the rank of Empress, then jointly assumed the reins of power, and Prince Kung was made their chief counsellor. His official post was head of the Tsungli Yamen, or Board of Foreign Affairs, an institution which hard experience had at last taught the Chinese the necessity of establishing.

At that time the Taeping rebellion and the foreign war had reduced China to the last stage of exhaustion. But as Mr. Lecky observes: 'In the social system, as in the physical body, the prostration of extreme illness is often followed, with a strange rapidity, by a sudden reflux of exuberant health. When nature has been brought to the uttermost extremities of anguish, when the population has been suddenly enormously reduced, when great masses of property have quickly changed hands, and when few except the most vigorous natures remain, it may reasonably be expected that the cessation of the calamity will be followed by a great outburst of prosperity.' So China began to revive, and soon her recuperative powers were marvellously shown. Prince Kung realised that China could no longer pursue her policy of isolation, and determined that, since foreigners must be endured, their arts and sciences should be made available for the benefit of his country. And, as freedom from external aggression is a nation's first and most important object, a commencement was made (even after a quarter of a century I fear the Chinese have not got much beyond that) by teaching some of the troops the mysteries of foreign drill and buying foreign muskets and cannon and men-of-war. The country quieted down, brigandage was suppressed, waste lands were cultivated, and trade revived in all

parts of the empire.   More than that, a Mahommedan
rebellion in Yunnan, the most southern province, which
had broken out in 1856 under cover of the Taeping
disturbances, was, in the year 1873, effectually stamped
out.   In other words, tens of thousands of the rebels
were massacred.   According to Mr. Boulger, twenty-
four large baskets full of human ears, as well as the
heads of seventeen chiefs, who are said to have been
put to death with excruciating tortures, were sent to
the Viceroy at Yunnan Fu.

Tung-chih died on January 12, 1875, at the early
age of eighteen.   The cause assigned was small-pox,
but he had already shown signs of impatience at the
restraint in which he was kept by the Empresses and
Prince Kung.   Suspicions, therefore, of foul play were
not wanting, the more so as his widow, the Empress
Ah-lu-tê, who was pregnant at the time, and who would
have been entitled to claim part in the regency, died
shortly afterwards, before the child was born.   She was
a lady of unusually attractive qualities, and her un-
timely fate will furnish material for Chinese poets in
after-generations.   Now for the first time since the
death of Nurhachu was the succession between father
and son broken.   The late Emperor's cousin, Kuang-su,
son of the seventh son of Taokuang, Prince Ch'un, the
same who had arrested Su-shun, born on August 15,
1871, was chosen to succeed.   One of the Empress-
Regents, T'zŭ An, called the Eastern Empress, as she
lived in the east part of the palace, died in 1881.   Her
demise also excited surprise, for rumour had it that
T'zŭ Hsi was the invalid, and remarks as to the difficulty
of two suns shining in one firmament were again commonly heard.   The surviving Empress, T'zŭ Hsi, is,
therefore, now sole Regent.   She is fifty-three years of

A MANCHU PRINCE—HIS HIGHNESS PRINCE CH'UN, FATHER OF
HIS MAJESTY THE EMPEROR OF CHINA.

age, and clearly a princess of great will and capacity.
A recent writer[1] states that Her Majesty has sufficient
force of character to disregard the trammels of etiquette when she pleases, holding *al fresco* court in her
garden, and taking lessons in archery and boxing.   In
1884, she summarily dismissed Prince Kung for neglect
of duty, in terms which would do credit to any ruler in
these days of modern mealy-mouthedness.   Failure in
the French war was the real cause.   Five days later a
few lines in the 'Gazette,' ordering the Grand Council[2]
always to consult Prince Ch'un on matters of great
importance, announced Prince Kung's successor.   Prince
Ch'un, who married the sister of the Empress, is even
more powerful than his brother.   He is head of the
Admiralty Board, another new department.   A sharp
administrator he is, as the officials found when he visited
Port Arthur in the spring of 1887, to inspect the forts
and the Northern Fleet.   Next to him in influence, but
not rank, is Li Hung-chang, Viceroy of Chihli, senior
member of the Grand Secretariat, and, outside the imperial family, the first civilian in the empire.   He is
directly entrusted with foreign military reforms, but he
does not sit on the Board of Foreign Affairs.

Little is known of what really passes within the
penetralia of the 'Purple Forbidden City,' as the precincts of the palace are called.   But it seems probable
that the Empress Regent will continue to exercise
power, if not to reign, as long as she lives.   The Emperor was considered old enough to govern not long
ago, when she might have retired.   But memorials

<hr/>

[1] Balfour's *Leaves from my Chinese Scrap-book*. Trübner and Co., 1887.
[2] The Grand Council corresponds somewhat to a Cabinet Council in
England, consisting of the members of the Grand Secretariat and the Chiefs
of Boards, or Departments.

appeared in the 'Gazette,' urgently requesting her to
continue to guide public affairs, with her reply, that,
much as she disliked it, she could not resist such en-
treaties, and she would therefore assist the young Emperor with her advice for some time longer. Prince
Ch'un has shown no signs, so far as is known, of
trying to free his son from tutelage. His own position
is, however, very delicate. He must kotow to his son
as Emperor, and the Emperor must kotow to him as
father, so they can only meet informally. Prince Ch'un,
indeed, endeavoured to retire altogether when Kuang-
Hsü was nominated Emperor, and, were the son now
to take the government into his own hands, the father
must undoubtedly retire, for they could not meet in
public. Possibly, therefore, Prince Ch'un[1] is like the
Empress, and thinks it best to defer the evil day.

It is a remarkable proof of the neglect into which
the traditions of the dynasty have fallen, that the Empress T'zŭ Hsi is entirely unacquainted with Manchu,
and all public business has to be transacted with her in
Chinese. The Empress T'zŭ An was equally ignorant.

The principal event in Kuang Hsü's reign has been
the reconquest of Western Kansuh, Sungaria, Kuldja,
and Kashgaria. In 1862, shortly after Tungchih's accession, a rebellion broke out amongst the Tunganis, a
Mahommedan people settled in the province of Kansuh, the same who had revolted against the last of the
Mings, and again in the reigns of Kanghi and Kienlung.
Large numbers of the Chinese were slain, and the garrisons of imperial troops were put to the sword. The
flame rapidly extended across the desert of Gobi, past
Hami and Barkul to Ili, and lastly to Kashgar. The

---

[1] As this was passing through the press, a report arrived of Prince
Ch'un's death, but it was afterwards contradicted.

Russians, fearing disturbances in their own borders, crossed over and occupied Kuldja in 1871 ; and in 1867 a soldier of fortune from Khokand, called Yakub Beg, made himself master of Kashgar, holding his own for twelve years, and on one occasion receiving a mission from the Government of India, who seem to have been misinformed as to the probable permanency of his rule. It took the Chinese some years of preparation before they could reassert their power. Eventually, in 1874, Tso-Tsung-t'ang, Viceroy of Kansuh, commenced sending forward detachments of troops to occupy the oases on the road, with colonists to till the ground and grow corn, and two years later his main body went forward. (This circumstance gave rise to the fable that Chinese armies plough the land as they march and raise their own supplies.) In 1876 the two chief strongholds of the Tunganis, Urumtsi and Manas, were taken, and in the year following Kashgaria also was reoccupied. Tso-Tsung-t'ang had the advantage of foreign rifles and cannon, but Manas held out for two months, so when it fell he determined to exterminate the inhabitants. Neither age nor sex was spared, and it has been estimated that 90,000 souls perished in one day. But that is the Chinese style of war. Severity has its natural effect, and it takes very few troops and costs very little to keep the conquered country afterwards. Should, however, any of the Western nations ever contemplate having China for an ally, they must be prepared for incidents of the kind.

After these events the Chinese Government called upon Russia to evacuate the territory which she had occupied in Ili. Russia demurred at first, but China was persistent. An ambassador named Ch'ung Hou negotiated at Livadia a treaty far too favourable to

Russia. On his return he was thrown into prison and
sentenced to be beheaded. The two countries were on
the brink of war, but, partly owing to the good offices
of the late General Gordon in 1880, China was re-
strained from committing herself, and in 1881, by the
treaty of St. Petersburg, the territory she longed for
was restored to her on payment of one million and a
half sterling.

A year or two later the Chinese had a dispute with
the French, whose advances in Tonquin and Annam
gave them cause for dissatisfaction. The Chinese kept
threatening war, never really meaning it, and when the
French took Bacninh, a provisional treaty was signed
between Li Hung-chang, the Grand Secretary, and
Captain Fournier. The French commander then proceeded to occupy the frontier posts mentioned in the
treaty. The Chinese resisted the march at a place
called Langson, and fired on the French ; the latter
then demanded an indemnity, failing which they attacked Foochow. They first obtained admittance to
the harbour, and destroyed the arsenal and some ships
at that place ; they also occupied Keelung and other
positions in Formosa as a material guarantee. In 1885
the Chinese defeated the French commander, Negrier,
and captured Langson. In the end, by the mediation
of Sir Robert Hart, the Inspector-General of Imperial
Customs, a peace was arranged. China recognised the
French protectorate over Annam and the possession
of Tonquin, and she paid no indemnity.

The chief transactions between England and China
during the reign of Kuang-Hsü are those arising out
of the murder of a British officer named Margary, who
was despatched to Yunnan to meet an exploring party
sent by the Indian Government from Burmah. Satis-

factory reparation not having been obtained, the British
fleet was strengthened in the China Seas. In 1876 an
agreement was signed at Chefoo, a watering-place in
Shantung, by the Minister and Li Hung-chang, by
which the Chinese agreed to pay an indemnity to Mr.
Margary's family, and to publish a proclamation en-
forcing upon local officials the duty of safe-guarding
travellers provided with proper passports. China also
promised to facilitate the despatch of a British mission
to Lhassa. England, on her part, agreed to consider
an amalgamation of the import duty on opium, which
had been fixed in 1858 at thirty taels a chest, with
the 'likin' or inland transit dues, which were previously
levied at varying rates in different provinces, and which
were ultimately fixed at eighty taels a chest. The first
two conditions were carried out at once, but it was not
till 1886 that the convention was ratified. In 1886
a second treaty was made, providing for the delimita-
tion of the English and Chinese territories, which the
conquest of Upper Burmah by England in 1885 had
made conterminous. This treaty contains one curious
provision, which proves the great change that has
taken place since 1860 in the foreign relations of China
and European Powers. The Chinese claimed to be
suzerains of Ava, and, with a view to satisfy Court
or popular prejudices, demanded that their suzerainty
should be recognised. England, on the other hand,
being desirous of keeping on good terms with China,
was ready to yield in matters of form, so long as she
gained the substance. She, therefore, agreed that the
authorities in Burmah should send to China every ten
years a present of local produce in charge of a native
official, on condition that her own administration of the
new province was to be left absolutely free and un-

fettered. The propriety of this has been questioned, on the ground that even trivial points of etiquette have an abnormal importance in the East, and, although the word 'tribute' has been carefully kept out of the treaty, still, unless the sending of presents implied something of the kind, there would be no object in making them; and it is thought, therefore, that the clause may be detrimental to our prestige with other Asiatic states. The concession ought, however, rather to be looked upon as another indication of the contempt of the practical British mind for form and tinsel, and of our readiness frankly to allow China to have her own way in matters of no real importance, when she behaves like a civilised power, and asks for what she wants in a civilised manner. England also agreed not to press the Thibet-mission clause of the Chefoo Convention. In the following year, 1887, she gave another proof of her goodwill, by entrusting the Chinese Government with Port Hamilton, an island at the entrance of the Japan Sea, which she had occupied as a naval station, but which she saw no need for retaining.

The present policy of the Manchu Government is to keep peace with foreign governments, but to make compromising alliances with none, and to devote all its energies towards strengthening the defences of the empire against foreign intrusion. Envoys are now sent to European Courts, and, under the influence of Li Hungchang, the Grand Secretary, all that Western mechanical appliances and skilled training can do is being gradually used to improve the army and navy. Internal tranquillity, though marred in 1877 by a terrible famine, which is supposed to have swept off seven million souls, is producing its natural results in the happiness and wealth of the people. Whether peaceful appliances, institutions, so varied but so necessary, as railways, good roads, the post office, an alphabet, the abolition of judicial torture, and the reform of the civil service, are to be added or not, the course of years will show. Young Chinese are beginning to learn foreign languages, and articles that appear in Western magazines and newspapers, as well as new works on military or naval matters, are regularly translated for the information of those in power; so, now that the revolution from the habits of two thousand years has begun, though it may be slow, we may depend upon its being sure.

It is time, however, to return to the history of Manchuria Proper. The first results of the victories of Nurhachu and his sons were disastrous to that country. It was not merely that the land suffered for many years under the awful scourge of war, but in one respect Nurhachu treated the inhabitants of Liao-tung as the Kings of Assyria and Babylon treated the Jews. No sooner had he occupied the Chinese territory than he commenced, in order to prevent plots, changing the people from one place to another; residents by the sea he moved inland, and the citizens of one city he sent to another. Thus, as Mr. Ross remarks, in their own land they were strangers amongst a strange people, and combination was rendered difficult. The horrors of transportation probably equalled the horrors of war, and the misery that followed was dreadful. Père Verbiest, who accompanied the Emperor Kanghi on a tour through Manchuria in 1682, wrote that 'only a few houses had been lately built within the inclosures of the old cities, few of brick and mostly thatched and in no order,' and that 'there remained not the least mark of a multitude of towns and villages that stood before the wars'; and in 1709,

H

nearly a century after Nurhachu's invasion of Liao-tung,
the Jesuit surveyors reported that 'the towns are of
little note and thinly peopled, and without any defence
except a wall half-ruined or made of earth, though some
of them, as Ichou and Chinchou, are very well situate for
trade.'   During the eighteenth and the first half of the
nineteenth century, Liao-tung slowly recovered, though
the policy of excluding settlers from Kirin and Hei-
lung-chiang, which was pursued up to 1820, prevented
any progress in the north.   And the constant presence
in those quarters of a mass of bad characters, transported or fled from justice, made crime, and especially
brigandage, endemic.   Towards the close of Hien-fung's
reign, when all efforts were being directed to the suppression of the Taepings and other rebels, the state of Manchuria became very bad.   Bands of brigands coalesced,
and highway robbery took the form of armed resistance
to the Government.   Nowhere, says the report of the
English Consul, were violence and lawlessness more rife.
Murders were of daily occurrence; no man went out of
his house unarmed; field labourers had their matchlocks
and spears strapped across their backs while working.[1]
Gangs of robbers seized and held to ransom the persons of high officials and even the principal towns.   One
set of ruffians levied a tax on goods leaving the British
settlement, which had been opened at Yingtzŭ in May
1861; and in the only case of resistance, the recusant, a
Canton merchant, was cut to pieces and his flesh distributed attached to pieces of paper on which was
written the word 'warning.'   The British Consul at
Yingtzŭ had to put that place in a state of defence, and
an attack seemed probable.   Ultimately some regiments

[1] This spectacle may still be seen in the Hulan district, north of the
Sungari.

arrived from Peking, and the chief rebels were attacked
in 1867. But it was not till 1872 that the Consul could
report that anarchy was at an end. One measure
which greatly contributed to the restoration of order
was the resumption by the Chinese of a sort of ' no
man's land ' or neutral territory, which had been left
between Corea and Liao-tung, and had become the resort
of bands of robbers. Colonisation being permitted,
the forests which sheltered the brigands disappeared,
and the tract is now under cultivation. Still, as our
Consul reported on another occasion, gang robbery by
bands of mounted men varying in strength from ten and
twenty to eighty or a hundred has always existed in
Manchuria ; and it exists—nay, abounds—to the present
day, the Chinese officials looking upon it as an inevitable
evil, like small-pox or fever. One year a gang actually
plundered Shing-king, the sacred capital of the dynasty,
and murdered the magistrate in charge; and the 'Peking
Gazette ' teems with reports from officials in Manchuria
describing skirmishes with robbers and promising to
use every measure to extirpate them. Thus in 1884
the Governor-General in Fêng-t'ien acknowledged that
gatherings for predatory purposes were by no means
rare. ' But,' said he, ' the forcible establishment of order
on the frontier in 1875, and the wholesale punishment
of brigandage and gambling, which go hand in hand,
together with the execution of all notorious gamblers,
has of late years done much to bring about a better
state of things, and brigandage is now limited to small
gangs. During the past few years more than two
hundred robbers have been executed by Ch'ung Ch'i, the
late Governor, and in and around the provincial capital
several hundred gamblers have been dealt with. I make
it a point of pursuing my predecessor's policy, which is

to let it be generally known that I will summarily
execute the promoter of any large gathering for gambling purposes and the head of any gang of armed men.'
So far so good; but the results are not even yet completely satisfactory. The highways are still unsafe.
We met a party of five brigands ourselves near Hulan,
and frequently heard of them as being in our neighbourhood. Our servant, who was sent to Yingtzŭ for
stores and money, was stopped on the imperial road between Moukden and Kirin, and a convoy following him
was plundered. Again, a missionary friend narrowly
escaped a band which plundered a caravan on the outskirts of Kirin just before we reached that place. At
the time we left Manchuria an insurgent named Ma was
out on the war-path with a hundred followers. They
had been tracked to a cave, which the troops were then
watching. Many other instances of this kind might be
cited. The plague is worst in the newly-settled colonies
in the north, where the banditti not only rob on the
highways but plunder villages and cities. They also
bind and hold prisoners to ransom, failing payment of
which the victim is ruthlessly killed, and his head
sent to his friends. The officials, no doubt, are active
in their way. The whole garrison of Tsitsihar was out
after the robbers when we were at that place; flying
columns were chasing them, and hundreds of heads had
been taken off in the year or two previous. Twice,
too, we met parties of brigands on the way to execution.
But a Chinaman is constitutionally slow to move, so the
light-footed robbers generally escape before the regulars
come up. Then the troops are often badly led and
behave shamefully, allowing the robbers to force their
way through them unharmed. Worst of all, the mandarins themselves are occasionally corrupt and in league

with the foe. It is not many years since a brigadier-
general gave the chief of a band an asylum in his own
house at Moukden, and more recently the officer in command at a large town in the north, a nephew of the
governor of the province, sold the place to the outlaws.
Fortunately he reckoned without his host, for the towns-
people turned out and gave the robbers a drubbing. Were
an Anglo-Indian superintendent of police in charge, I
would vouch for it that in twelve months gang robbery
would be rarely heard of.

With the exception of brigandage, however, Manchuria is now peaceful enough, and colonisation is
making enormous strides. For a backwoods country
and an unenlightened government, she is at this day
as prosperous and well-to-do as any territory in Asia.

Before concluding this chapter I must give an account of an event, or rather of a series of events, in
the modern history of Manchuria of vast importance
locally, and possibly big with consequences to the whole
world. I refer to the annexation by Russia of all the
Chinese territory north of the Amur, as well as of the
strip of coast lying between the Usuri and the Japan
Sea. The sketch which I shall now give my readers is
mainly founded on Mr. E. G. Ravenstein's excellent
work, 'The Russians on the Amur.'[1]

Up to nearly the middle of the seventeenth century,
the regions of the Amur were absolutely a *terra incognita* to the Russians, and the first expedition down the
river was undertaken in 1636, when an adventurer
named Poyarkoff succeeded in a journey from Yakutsk
to the mouth of the river. Other expeditions followed,
sometimes accompanied by as great barbarity to the
aborigines as the Spaniards showed to the Indians of

---

[1] *The Russians on the Amur.* Trübner & Co., 1861.

Jamaica; and by the end of 1682—that is to say, thirty-four years after the Manchu occupation of Peking—the Russians had settlements at Albazin on the Upper Amur, on several of its tributaries, and also on some rivulets falling into the Sea of Okhotsk. That territory was then, as now, sparsely populated by barbarous Tungusic tribes, Gilyaks and others, who lived by fishing and catching sables. The Russian advance was facilitated by the Manchu policy which forbade Chinese to settle or even trade in those regions. Every year mandarins went down the river in barges to collect tribute from the tribes in kind, but that was the extent to which the Emperor's paternal government interfered with the people. The Trans-Amur districts nominally formed part of the government of Hei-lung-chiang. The Chinese, then governed by the great Emperor Kanghi, resented the Russian encroachments. They attacked and took Albazin, and eventually, by the treaty of Nerchinsk, made in 1689 and done over again in 1728, the Russians were obliged to evacuate all the positions they had occupied. The map shows the frontier then agreed to. After that the Chinese, selfishly enough, it must be allowed, prevented the Russians from navigating the Amur, and a request made in 1805 for permission to use the river was refused. It must be remembered that the original disputes took place when Peter the Great was Emperor of Muscovy, and the comparative powers of Russia and China were very different from what they were two hundred years later. During the early part of this century, various officers pointed out that it would be an advantage to the Russian settlements in Kamschatka if their supplies were brought down the Amur. So in 1847 General Muravieff, afterwards Count Muravieff Amursky and Governor-General

of Eastern Siberia, sent an officer to explore the river.
Several surveys were made, and in 1851 the towns of
Nikolaiefsk and Mariinsk were founded on the Lower
Amur by the captain of a Russian man-of-war as ports
for the Russo-American Trading Company. In 1853
Alexandrovsk and Konstantinovsk were founded on
the sea coast. All these settlements, be it noted, were
in territory belonging to China by treaty. In 1854
General Muravieff applied to the local Chinese authorities for permission to send supplies for the Pacific
settlements down the Amur. The mandarins could
not give leave. But it was a case of ' necessity
knows no law,' for the Crimean war precluded the
possibility of any other way of victualling the settlements in question. General Muravieff therefore proceeded himself down the river with a large convoy of
barges, attended by 1,000 men and several guns.
In 1855 three more expeditions were sent, with 3,000
soldiers, 400 colonists, military stores and provisions.
Finally, General Muravieff again descended the river
with large supplies of men and money, and established
Russian stations along the whole of the left or northern
bank. The mandarins on the spot feebly protested, but
could do nothing, except count the steamers and barges
which went up and down; and the central government could do nothing, being in the throes of the Taeping rebellion. Eventually the Russians called upon the
Chinese to legalise what had been done, and, helpless as
they were, they agreed in 1858 to the treaty of Aigun,
by which the whole of the left bank of the Amur was
ceded to Russia. Extensive measures were taken immediately by Russia for colonising the new territory, which,
even before its legal cession, had, by a decree dated
October 31, 1857, been converted into the Primorsk,

or Maritime Province of Eastern Siberia, including Kamschatka and the eastern coast of the Sea of Okhotsk,
Nikolaiefsk being constituted the first capital. In 1860
the Chinese were in extremity. The Taepings were
masters of a great part of the empire, and the English
and French were at the gates of Peking. General
Ignatieff, the Russian Minister at the Chinese Court,
accordingly found it a favourable opportunity to demand more territory, and he induced the Emperor to
make a further cession of the whole of the east coast
of Manchuria, as far south as the Corean frontier,
without the semblance of a *quid pro quo*. It is in
the south of this strip that the port of Vladivostok has
been founded ; and it is because that port is closed by
ice for several months in the winter that newspapers
are continually crediting Russia with a desire to seize
part of Corea, where there are bays and creeks open all
the year round. Khabarofka, at the junction of the
river Usuri with the Amur, is now the head-quarters of
the sea-coast province, and Blagovaschensk of the province of the Amur, the Governors of both being subordinate to the Governor-General of Eastern Siberia,
whose head-quarters are at Irkutsk.

Whatever may be thought of Russia's behaviour in
obtaining possession of this territory when China could
not lift a hand to defend it, it must be allowed that
China had only herself to thank. It was intolerable
that a great continental highway like the Amur should
be closed for ever to commerce, and vast regions to
colonists, simply because of China's crass obstructive-
ness. Had the Chinese Government seemed likely to
give the regions of the Amur the semblance of a
civilised administration, our sympathies might have
been with her. But she pursued the insane policy of

keeping tens of thousands of square miles simply a
desert, and preventing the development of Russian civilisation in Eastern Asia. And Russia, to her credit, has
since the annexation spent large sums of money, and
made increasing efforts to develop prosperous agricultural communities and open out commerce in regions
of which China was, after all, only nominally mistress,
and by the cession of which she lost nothing.

For years after the annexation of the Primorsk, or
sea-coast province, it was generally believed that Russia
would shortly make a further advance and annex at
least the provinces of Hei-lung-chiang and Kirin. And
I believe it is not disputed that when the two countries
were preparing for war in 1880 over the Kuldja question, orders were given the Russian general to occupy
the frontier towns of Ninguta and Sansing. Since then
China has steadily followed the policy of arming her
troops with foreign weapons, teaching them foreign
drill, and fortifying the frontier; and rumour now has
it that when the opportunity offers, it is not the Russians that will advance into Manchuria, but the Manchus
who will attempt the recovery, if not of the Trans-
Amur regions, at least of the Tung-hai or sea-coast,
which was one of the first territories occupied by the
great Nurhachu before he commenced his descent upon
China Proper. Russia and China, however, are two
powerful, if unwieldy, nations, both thoroughly wide
awake, and both anxious rather to strengthen themselves by making the best of what they have, than to
weaken themselves by prematurely asking for more,
when that more means a certain and an expensive war.
So my own impression is, as it must be every one's
hope, that the *status quo* will not be altered for many a
long year to come.

The Rev. H. Lansdell, D.D., who travelled through Russian Manchuria in 1879, puts the number of Chinese and their congeners now settled in the Primorsk at no more than 3,000 to 7,000, though he says the number would be multiplied a hundred-fold were free emigration permitted. When the country was ceded, the Chinese Government, it is said, forbade its subjects any longer to colonise in the country with their wives. The rich, therefore, returned home, leaving the poor, who were joined by Manchu brigands and outlaws. The dislike to Chinese settling in the Primorsk is, I suspect, not confined to the Chinese Government. It is the Russians who do not encourage them—they find them so troublesome to manage. In fact, early in June 1887, when Russia was passing a decree aimed at German settlers, and forbidding foreigners to acquire or farm estates on the western frontier-zone from the Baltic to the Black Sea, a similar ukase was promulgated, on the representation of the Governor-General of Eastern Siberia, prohibiting Chinese emigrants and refugees who might cross into Russian territory from settling in the districts bordering on the Chinese and Corean frontiers. The prohibition was extended to Coreans, who are more docile, and have hitherto been welcomed on that account by the local Russian authorities. Indeed, a Corean colony is said recently to have been established by the Russians as far north as the banks of the Amur, opposite the mouth of the Sungari. The policy of excluding industrious settlers on either frontier seems scarcely wise, but I suppose the Russians know their own business best.

CHAPTER IV.

THE PEOPLE.

In Chapter II. I have explained that the Manchus who conquered China were a small branch of Tartars, allied to the Mongols and Tungusians, whose numerous roving clans were welded into one people by Nurhachu, and I have related how Nurhachu's descendants, with the aid of the Mongols and the Chinese themselves, occupied the Dragon Throne, left vacant by the suicide of the Ming emperor. I must now give an account of the twenty millions or so of people who inhabit Manchuria at the present day, and say something about their manners and customs.

Of the twenty millions, I should be exaggerating if I put down more than one million as Manchus, all tribes included; and of that million I doubt if more than ten per cent. can speak the Manchu language.

It is the old story over again, 'Græcia capta ferum victorem cepit.' The Manchus took China, and the Chinese have taken captive the Manchus. To put the matter plainly, Manchus are now a rarity in their own country, and most of the few that exist dress and speak like Chinese. They are to be found—first, at all garrison towns, where there are sure to be Manchu troops; next, in the neighbourhood of Manchu magistrates' offices, employed as police or messengers; and, thirdly, in the remote recesses of the mountains, where they live by fishing or the chase, as well as by the cultivation of the ground. The last class still talk Manchu, and, as far as their own native land is concerned, are to-day the historic representatives of the great Tartar clans who have thrice conquered China.

The explanation of the rarity of the Manchus is that, just as after the Ketan and Chin conquests all Northern Manchuria was deserted by its people, who followed their leaders into China, so when the Manchus conquered China they depleted the country to furnish garrisons for keeping the populace in check. And from that day onwards, whenever there was need for troops in China—to subdue the Taepings, for instance —Manchuria has been used as the great recruiting ground, for the Court knows it can depend on its own countrymen. Thus the native population has been drawn away, while Chinese immigrants have poured in by thousands and tens of thousands to occupy the fertile towns and villages which the soldiery have left. The Chinese possess a refined culture and literature of their own, and their overpowering numbers and influence have completely taken captive the rude, unlettered aborigines. The spoken Manchu language is fast going the way of Gaelic or Erse, and the written one is so far forgotten that not long ago two teachers had to be imported from Peking to Kirin to instruct the soldiers' children, on the express ground that the few Manchus who could write it were all wanted as office clerks, which is just as if the promoter of an Eisteddfod at Carmarthen were to send to London for a pair of bards. Notices may be seen posted up in Manchu, and in remote places knots of country-folk may still be heard talking it, but even that is rare. On the other hand, in the Purple Forbidden City it still flourishes, just as, I believe, Norman-French was fashionable at the English Court long after the English language was generally spoken. Still, even there it is becoming a little antiquated, for, as I have already said, the Empress-Regent herself does not know it.

Before the conquest of Liao-tung the Manchus had neither writings nor any form of religion above the rudest Shamanism or the invocation, by dancing and incantations, of certain good spirits in opposition to the devil, whom they dread.[1] Their intercourse with the Mongols taught them the Lama or Thibet form of Buddhism, also, curiously enough, called Shamanism, which has, therefore, always been favoured by the ruling dynasty.[2] But they have now adopted *en bloc*

[1] The word is derived from Shaman, a Tungusian sorcerer, a description of whose weird rites is given in M. de La Brunière's letter, Note D, pp. 433, 434. Evart Ysbrantes Ides, an envoy sent by Peter the Great to Peking in 1692, also gives a graphic description of Shaman devil-dancing.

[2] The term Shamanism in this case is derived from a Sanscrit word meaning tranquillity or indifference, significant of the mental attitude of Buddhist priests. The Abbé Huc has a story, that when the Manchus were marching upon Peking, the Emperor Shunchih consulted a Lama as to the success of the enterprise. The Lama bade him God-speed, on which the Emperor ordered him to come and ask for a reward when the Manchus got into Peking. He did so, and the Emperor gave him sufficient land to construct a Lamaserai, and revenues to support a thousand Lamas. But as early as 1642 the Dalai Lama of Lhassa sent an embassy to Moukden, and

the Chinese religious cultus, of which more will be said hereafter. Chinese customs they have assimilated, also their laws. The women have been conservative and have never cramped their feet—and very pretty little feet they have, only they hide them in hideous coffins of shoes. To their honour be it said, to this day no woman with crushed feet may enter the Imperial Court. It is a remarkable thing that when the Manchus entered Peking, a time when, one might think, they would have endeavoured to gain the good-will of the conquered subjects, with a marvellous audacity they insisted on dress reform throughout the vast Chinese Empire. I have already explained why Nurhachu made the Chinese soldiers who joined him cut off their long top-knots, shave their foreheads, and wear their back hair in pigtails. But now, I suppose for the same reasons, the whole Chinese nation was to follow suit. And, as if that were not enough, the men were to substitute narrow for full flowing sleeves to their coats. The women, too, were to cease torturing and maiming their little girls' feet. It is perhaps characteristic of the sexes that the men of China consented; but the women refused, and not even the fashion of the Court has induced them to reform their barbarous habit.[1] It must be said for the men, too,

in 1652 he came in person to Peking, where he was invested by the Emperor Shunchih with the title of 'Self-existent Buddha and Supreme Ruler of the Buddhist Faith.' Continued residence in China made the Manchus acquainted with Confucianism, and Kanghi personally favoured that system. But he and his successors have always ostentatiously patronised the Lamas, because of their unbounded influence over the Mongol chiefs, whom it is the policy of the Court to conciliate. Kienlung's attachment to the Thibetan Lamas has been already alluded to.

[1] Such is the force of fashion, that sometimes even Manchu women have commenced crushing their babies' feet. In 1838 and 1840 the Emperor Taokuang issued several edicts against the practice, and Manchu women may at the present day be seen wearing boots with enormously high heels,

that some of them preferred losing their heads to their hair. To the Manchus also it is that the Chinese officials owe the so-called buttons on their uniform hats or caps, the colours of which distinguish the various ranks. Tai Tsung was the inventor. The button is an ornament the size of a large marble, elevated an inch over the centre of the hat, and very conspicuous. The highest is transparent red; then come coral or opaque red, sapphire or transparent blue, opaque blue, crystal, opaque white, gold, worked gold, and lastly silver. The civil buttons count the highest, for in China, at every point, *cedunt arma togæ,* and a military officer with a clear red button will not be so much feared or looked up to as a civil functionary with an opaque blue one.

The fact that the whole race of male Chinese could be made all at once to change their *chevelure*—the Japanese were made to do exactly the same thing a few years ago, and all clerks in that Government's employment must now wear European garments too—shows how overdone is the respect which we English have been wont to pay to custom in India. Not till long after the commencement of the present century was the self-immolation of widows prohibited, and the swinging of devotees from hooks was permitted for a generation longer. We forget that Orientals, conservative though they be, resign themselves more quickly than ourselves to the inevitable, and that habit soon heals the soreness caused by innovations. A shake of the finger would stop an evil custom which has grown up

placed almost in the centre of the sole, which communicate to the whole figure that elegant tottering gait so much admired in those possessing the real 'Golden Lilies,' as deformed feet are called. Several accounts are given as to the origin of the horrible custom. The most probable of them attributes it to the courtiers of an Empress who was afflicted with club-feet.

only lately, but is very widespread—I mean the viru-
lent writing of the vernacular press, which is eating
like a canker into the fair stem of British rule.   But
partly from contempt, real or affected, for such writing, and also from the fear that cant would be talked
at home about liberty of the press, and, as has actually
happened before, that demagogues would use it for
purposes of party warfare, the authorities refrain from
moving, though the reform would be popular with the
most influential classes of native society.

The headgear of Manchu women differs slightly
from the Chinese, as well as some parts of their garments ; but a stranger would scarcely know the difference.   Manchus are betrothed, as in China, without
reference to bride or bridegroom.   They marry early,
though a few girls are maintained by their parents
until fully twenty—a custom that is not unknown
among the Chinese. Polyandry is unknown. Polygamy
exists, but outside official life is not the rule.   Indeed,
it is illegal for any save a mandarin, when he cannot
avoid being absent from his wife, or for a literary
graduate, to possess a second wife, provided the first is
under forty or has a son.   The usual, though not the
only, reason for a plurality of wives is the desire to
have a son.   The position of women is now very inferior, just as it is in China, where even the great Confucius, the one being on earth endowed with wisdom
unalloyed, put his wife away without a cause.

The Manchus are as great gamblers as the Chinese
at cards, dice, or any other game of chance.   Gambling, however, is illegal except at the Chinese New
Year, and has to be carried on in private.   Mr. Ross
tells me he has known men sit at cards for thirty-six
hours on end.   They are said to be now as grossly im-

moral as the Chinese, though, as far as mere appearances go, we saw no evidence of it in either case. One domestic institution still kept up is slavery. It dates from the time of Nurhachu, when thousands of the defeated Chinese were enslaved by their conquerors. Strict laws against runaways still exist, and might be enforced. In practice, however, there are myriads of families known to be legal slaves who are practically free. Lapse of time or the absence of their owners in Peking or other parts renders it impossible to prove anything against them. Many of them now own the properties they were originally left to cultivate. Large numbers of other slaves are merely cottiers cultivating their landlords' farms for a small grain rent. Actors and courtesans are generally recruited from this class, but many are employed in the army, or as police or office messengers. In fact, almost the only thing that distinguishes slaves is that civil office is not open to them. Domestic slaves are few in number, though officials frequently purchase young men and women as body servants for 20*l.* or 30*l.* apiece. The offspring of these become the property of their owners. A runaway slave must be restored to his master. Very often, however, the owner is pleased if his man disappears, as he is then free from the obligation of feeding and clothing him, and hired labour is found much cheaper and better. Ordinary private persons sometimes buy slaves to look after the family tombs, and the slaves have the grounds adjacent to live upon. Although children are the property of their masters, owners may not sell single individuals of a family; they must part with the whole or none; and the slaveowner's rights are confined to his slave's labour; though he beat, he may not torture him. The law forbids the sale of free persons as slaves, and, though

I

common in China Proper, such a thing is seldom heard of in Manchuria.

The Manchu race possesses certain privileges which may for a long time prevent their otherwise inevitable absorption into the mass of Northern Chinese. Every Manchu between fourteen and forty who can draw a bow is entitled to one tael, in some parts to two taels, a month—i.e. 5s. to 10s. One-fifth of this sum is lost on the way to the ultimate recipient, who gets enough to keep him from starvation but not sufficient for the attainment of the comforts even of the poor. He also gets his land at a lighter rate of taxation; in very out-of-the-way places he obtains it free. The Manchu also pays a lower property tax than the China-man. The fact that he enjoys these privileges and the hope of rising to something better makes almost every Manchu a hanger-on at some Manchu yamen, like the relatives of Government clerks and messengers in India. He is thus prevented from pushing his own fortunes, and the difference between him and a China-man, either as a farmer or a merchant, is consequently very marked. Indeed, few Manchus take to merchan-dise, though many cultivate their own land. They are exempt from competition for the lowest literary degree, so as to qualify for the lowest step in the mandarinate, but only ten [1] per cent. of the mandarins are drawn from their ranks. The only element, says Mr. Ross, which prevents their degradation is that of pride as the conquerors of China, considering themselves the better men. At the same time, the Manchus unques-tionably produce officials and diplomatists as able in proportion to their numbers as the Chinese themselves.

---

[1] In reality the proportion is only seven per cent. Over one per cent. are Mongol, and under two per cent. Chinese banner-men.

A Manchu youth must practise firing at targets at full gallop, wielding a heavy sword, lifting heavy weights, and other manly exercises. When he passes his bow-and-arrow drill he is enrolled under one of the banners, the same to which his father belonged. He may have to join a regiment and adopt soldiering as his profession, in which case he gets the pay of a regular; if not, he stays at home and cultivates or idles, and is called out for training twice a year.

The original unit of Manchu military organisation was ten men and an officer, called a *niru*, or an arrow. As the army increased, so did the number composing a niru, and it is now said to comprise eighty or ninety men. The number was at one time 300 men, and there was one captain, or tso-ling, over that number. The colonel, or ts'an-ling, commanded five tso-ling, and the tu-t'ung, or lieutenant-general, the head of the banner, commanded five ts'an-ling. Thus the normal strength of a banner was 7,500 men. Up to 1613 there were four banners, yellow, blue, red, and white—according to Martini, the order of precedence was white, red, blue or black, and yellow—to which were afterwards added four more of the same colours each, with a broad edge of some different colour, and that is the number at the present day.[1] At first the eight banners comprised Manchus alone; but, as Chinese and Mongol allies flocked to the Manchu standard, room had to be made for them, and ultimately the Chinese and South Mongol banners were created. Their final organisation was completed only a year before the conquest of

[1] The colour of the banners has no ethnic signification. Their use is supposed to have originated in the chase, to which they were taken by the leader of the hunt for signalling to lines of beaters when hunting hill-sides for deer, and Nurhachu imitated that system in war. The yellow banner now takes precedence because it is the imperial colour.

Peking. The Chinese banners comprised the Chinese living outside the Great Wall, and their descendants have privileges to this day akin to those of the Manchus. They are called Han-chün, literally, 'Chinese Division,' a title of which they are very proud. As the name implies, the Mongol banners are composed entirely of Mongols, and there are besides separate levies of Solons and Sibos and other northern tribes.

The bordered yellow, the plain yellow, and the plain white[1] are called the three superior banners, the remaining five are inferior, and there is a complete series for each of the three nationalities. A portion of the banner-men are divided into an inner and outer division. The inner division is composed of men called Pao-i, or Janissaries, who render suit and service, those of the three superior banners to the imperial household, and the remainder to different princely houses. Some are employed as guards for the imperial mausolea and hunting parks, and a select few, taken from the Manchu and Mongol banners only, composed of two or four men out of every tso-ling's command, form the Imperial Life Guards. These are armed with bows and arrows and swords. Another picked body, selected in the same way as the guards, is called the Vanguard Division, half of whom carry matchlocks, and help to guard the entrances to the 'Forbidden City.' A third is the Flank Division, composed of thirty-four men taken from each tso-ling. They practise archery and musketry, both on foot and horseback. The fourth, or Light Division, is meant to correspond somewhat to the Bersaglieri in Italy. They attack and defend with the sword and iron flail, a kind of clumsy life-preserver;

---

[1] So Mayer's *Chinese Government*. According to Mr. Ross, the bordered white takes precedence.

they also wrestle and perform somersaults and feats of leaping, which, when accompanied by wild shouts, after the manner of Red Indians, cannot fail, so they consider, to strike terror into their enemies' hearts. The fifth division consists of artillery and musketeers. There are also gingall men and a corps named 'Oıbo,' to carry 'deer-horn' fences, a kind of clumsy and scarcely portable wooden *chevaux de frise*, with which to laager the camp at night. Government offices and imperial cemeteries are surrounded by fences of this description, an example of which may be seen in the foreground of the illustration at page 149.

Peking itself is simply peopled by these banner-men. A careful register of their number is kept, and there are supposed to be not less than 90,000 or 100,000 at the capital, costing 100,000*l.* a month in cash, besides rations of rice. About 20,000 more are distributed throughout the principal towns of China. At Canton, for instance, there is a small Manchu garrison, under a Tartar general, supposed to be capable of overawing the place in case of a rising against the dynasty. When visiting Canton I saw a number of them practising with the bow. But they are a survival of the past, and the Tartar general has as little real power over Canton as the Constable of the Tower over London.

The figures I have given do not include the banner-men still living at home in Manchuria and Mongolia, who form a reserve, to be called out in emergencies The official numbers of the Chinese and Manchu banner men in Manchuria are—in Fêng-t'ien, 56,000; in Kirin, 60,000; and in Hei-lung-chiang, 67,000; in all, 183,000. But these statistics are very untrustworthy. Only a small proportion of these are in active employment, the rest being militia, only called out for training at intervals.

The banner corps are to this day as distinct from the Chinese regular forces as the yeomanry cavalry is, or used to be, from the army in England. Their original weapons were swords, long spears, and bows. The last is the Manchu weapon *par excellence*, and the use of

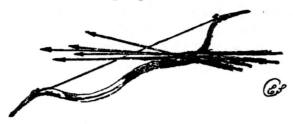

A MANCHU BOW AND ARROWS

it is still kept up.[1] Many of the archers are mounted, and it is a picturesque sight to see a squadron charge past wearing their round Tartar hats with strips of fur hanging behind, their bows at their backs and quivers at their sides.

The banner-men are looked upon as the flower of the Chinese army, but on the Government's own showing they are, or were till a few years ago, as a force inefficient, and as an institution corrupt to a degree. The 'Peking Gazette' of March 30, 1883, published the report of an officer charged to revise the organisation, which in the candid Chinese fashion discloses the following defects. First, Chinese are in

---

[1] The Manchu bow resembles the bow of Ulysses, which Homer calls παλίντονον τόξον—that is to say, when unstrung, it springs back till the inside assumes a convex shape, which proves it a powerful weapon. It is made of horn inlaid in wood, enveloped at the middle with cork from the Ch'ang-pai-shan forests. In size it is half-way between the powerful Turkish bow and the long and unwieldy Japanese. The arrows, which exceed three feet in length, are tipped with iron, and the feathers, taken from an eagle's wing, extend for ten inches up the shaft.

the habit of fraudulently enlisting, so much so that
half the banner-men are now supposed to be Chinese
and not Manchus at all. Secondly, large deductions
are made from the men's pay. Thirdly, substitutes are
constantly hired to pass the archery examination for
privates and the examination in reading for sergeants.
Fourthly, the grain issued to banner-men (outside
Manchuria the pay is made partly in tribute rice, which
is sent from the south to Peking for the purpose, and
forms one of the most fruitful sources of official pecula-
tion in all China) is so largely adulterated with sand
as to be unfit for food, and officers, granary clerks, and
rice merchants are in league with the banner-men to
sell rice due to them before it is issued. The Imperial
decree on this commanded the futu-t'ungs or lieutenant-
generals of the banners to lay down strict regulations
for the reform of these abuses, and there the matter
appears to have dropped.

But, in spite of ingrained corruption, the banner-
force has not stood wholly still of late years, and foreign
drill instructors are satisfied with the regiments, comparatively few though they be, which have passed
through their hands. Mr. Mayers, writing ten years
ago, said that the Shên-chi Ying, or 'Divine Mechan-
ism Army,' as the European-drilled field force is called,
even then numbered 18,000 or 20,000; and there are
authorities who assert that the total number at the present day does not fall short of 200,000. And though
foreign drill is not everything which an Oriental soldier wants — foreign discipline, foreign regularity of
pay, and foreign leadership being a-wanting—yet even
the drill by itself may count for something. To make
the army efficient has long been the darling aim of
Li Hung-chang. Immediately after the suppression of

the Taeping revolt he engaged a number of foreign drill instructors and founded an arsenal on an European model at Shanghai. In 1864 he established another at Nanking, and in 1866 the general Tso Tsung-t'ang followed with a third at Foochow. The instructors are mostly Germans. The Court allows Li Hung-chang undivided control over the foreign-drilled garrisons at Tientsin, Taku, and Port Arthur. If I am not misinformed, it was to battalions of his sending that the great destruction of brigands in Fêng-t'ien was due in 1867.

I may perhaps say in this place that the regular army of China, called Luh-ying, or the Army of the Green Standard, is computed by different authorities at anything from 500,000 to 1,000,000 men. This force is under the control of the viceroys of provinces, and its real and paper strength are probably very different. The men are used for all sorts of purposes besides military—as police, for the collection of revenue, and the like. The Luh-ying, which is composed entirely of Chinese, is generally considered more corrupt and effete than even the banner-corps.

The forces, foreign-drilled and others, in Manchuria are now very strong, and are supposed to number some 60,000 or 80,000, the main body being at Moukden, with detachments at various points on the frontier. Probably not less than 15,000 have learnt foreign drill. Many are armed with Remington repeating rifles, while the rest have muskets and Enfields of various dates and other miscellaneous weapons. There are also plenty of gingalls, large muzzle-loading blunderbusses which it takes two men to carry. There are a few batteries of foreign guns, but most of the field artillery consists of small-bore muzzle-loaders of no use in modern warfare. A review is a beautiful sight. There are almost as many banners as rifles, gigantic banners which take a whole man's strength to wield, and which in time of war would waste a good many useful fighting men. The Chinese Government, however, is now setting itself in earnest to drill the officers as well as the rank and file in European style; and in a few years, when the conservative old generals of the Taeping war have disappeared, there is no reason why the army should not become as efficient, if properly led and handled, as the Native army in India or the Russian in Central Asia. The worst of the present system is, that, although the regiments may do excellently on parade at Tientsin or Port Arthur, when they are sent to an out-station the men drift back, not unwillingly, to the old bow-and-arrow drill; and though, for form's sake, they may have to pass muster in both styles, yet they are not likely to be permanently improved so long as the 'Peking Gazette' continues to print old-fashioned inspection reports, such as that the spear drill was exceedingly good, the archery, turning warlike *culbutes*, and posturing, were very creditably performed, and that with the exception of the flail exercise, which was a little lacking in smartness, all the manœuvres of the regiment were worthy of the highest commendation. As the late Captain Gill, R.E., remarks: 'Prompt action, readiness of resource, ability to seize on the smallest advantage or to neutralise a misfortune, and the power to evolve fresh combinations, these are the qualities which make a soldier, and these are the very qualities that cannot co-exist with Chinese want of originality and reverence for antiquity.'

Great attention is, however, now being paid to the army of Manchuria. At the end of 1885, the Tartar

General of Foochow, called Mu-t'u-shan, was appointed special commander-in-chief for the frontier, and the supreme command hitherto exercised by the governors of provinces was taken away from them. (The new commander-in-chief has, of course, nothing to do with the civil organisation of the provinces.) When we were in Manchuria he was busy inspecting and selecting 15,000 of the cream of the militia banner-men for conversion into regulars. An arsenal has also been founded at Kirin. The pay of a regular foot soldier in Manchuria is three taels a month—say fifteen shillings. Mounted men receive seven taels, but they have to provide and feed their own horses. Uniforms and arms are provided by the Government. One of the worst points about the army, as with every other Chinese institution, is the waste and corruption that goes on. Thus, when escorts were sent with us to the eastern frontier, the men were for ever popping away with their repeating rifles at anything that took their fancy, and explained that they were allowed 600 cartridges a year merely to practise with. And many a nice weapon we saw almost ruined from rust and want of cleaning. The 'Peking Gazette' now and then contains a notification about some commanding officer who has been drawing pay for men who do not exist;[1] so that there

---

[1] On October 7, 1886, an Imperial Decree appeared in the *Peking Gazette* lamenting the death of Pao Ch'ao, formerly commander-in-chief of Hunan. His military services in the Taeping rebellion were referred to in the highest praise, and the Emperor's profound regret for his death was expressed. The posthumous title of Junior Guardian of the Heir-apparent was conferred upon him, he was to have a funeral at the public expense, the State historiographer was to prepare a record of his services, memorial temples were permitted to be erected to him, his eldest son was to succeed to the title of Earl, and two other sons and a grandson were to come to Court as soon as their term of mourning had expired. Alas! the lion being dead, the jackals began to howl, and it turned out that Pao Ch'ao had embezzled 100,000 taels, say 45,000*l.*, of public money. Down came the myrmidons of the law upon

is room for more military reform yet. The troops in Manchuria are paid by the Governor-General through their own commanders, who have paymasters subordinate to them. At present, money is required from Peking, as the provincial income cannot meet the demands.

The Chinese of Manchuria mostly come, as their ancestors did, from the two northern provinces of Chihli and Shantung. But if you ask a man what nationality he belongs to, he will not call himself a Chinaman. He will either say, ' I am a Min-jên '—i.e. a civilian—as distinct from the military, or, more frequently, he will call himself a Mân-tzu, or a Southerner. This, a term of reproach in South China,[1] where it is applied to the so-called barbarous aborigines of Hainan or Formosa, is used without opprobrium in Manchuria ; just as an Englishman might call himself a Southerner in Scotland, though the epithet 'Southron' in a Highlander's mouth would imply contempt. Dr. Lansdell says the word Manzu means 'Freemen;' but Palladius holds it originated in the reign of Kublai Khan, who sent large colonies of ' Mantszium '—i.e. Chinese soldiers —to the borders of Corea, to resist a Japanese invasion, which he feared after his own unsuccessful attack upon that country. In Manchuria, anyhow, the Chinese use it of themselves. Similarly, a Manchu will not call himself a Man-chou-jên, or Manchu, but a Ch'i-jén, or Bannerman, a term which would include Mongols and Chinese

the family of the deceased hero. His eldest son is, according to the latest accounts, in gaol, the second has absconded, and the servants have been tortured in vain to discover where the money is hidden. All that now remains of a once opulent and illustrious family are the two coffins containing Pao Ch'ao and his wife, lying unburied in an empty and confiscated house.

[1] Martini mentions that the Manchus, when first invading South China, mocked the Chinese with this epithet.

without the Wall. The Chinese of the north are a short, vigorous race, reminding one in features of the Newars of Nepal, who are Hindoos with a Thibetan strain. In stolidity of character they resemble the Mahratta Kunbi. They speak the Mandarin, or Court dialect of Chinese.

It is not difficult to pick up enough of this dialect to enable one to ask the road, talk about the weather, or get his wants supplied at a Chinese inn. But to do more, or carry on a conversation, is beyond an ordinary traveller's attainments. Newly-joined members of the British Consular Staff spend fully two years at Peking in studying the language before they are allowed to undertake official duties. For the benefit of Britons who have not been to China and who have only vague ideas on the subject, I may explain why it is that the language is so difficult. In conversation, the trouble lies, not in the pronunciation, nor in the accent, but in the tone in which each word has to be said. Consonants go for nothing, and *jên*, a man, the 'j' pronounced in the French way, may be, and is, pronounced 'rin'; *chi*, a fowl, may be, and is, called 'ki'—and no one cares. A speaker may accentuate his words like a grand secretary, or talk like a country farmer, and it won't matter. Never mind the accent, you must speak in the right tone of voice. For instance, the Chinese for 'Saddle the horse' is *Pei* (pronounced 'pay') *Ma*. But if you say 'Pay Ma' in your natural voice, as if you wanted a debt made over to your maternal parent, no one would understand you. You must say it surlily, 'Pay *Ma*,' with a complaining stress on the Ma, as if some one had been plaguing you to let him pay Pa, and you *insisted* on his paying Ma. Then only would your servant understand. There are four tones in Mandarin

Chinese; in the Cantonese dialect there are seven, and double that number in others; and the student has to practise for hours a day saying words and sentences over and over again, duly raising and depressing his voice for every single syllable; for if you use the cheerful tone when you ought to adopt the surly one, or *vice versâ*, the whole sense is altered, and without practice a good ear goes for nothing. I remember once wishing to see the inside of a *k'ang* or stove bed (my readers will hear a good deal about k'angs later on), which I was told was being repaired. I could say the two words for 'I want to see' intelligibly enough; but, though I knew the tone and did my best, I could not pronounce the word 'k'ang' in such a way as to convey to a sharp Chinese landlord any meaning whatever, and at last I had to get Fulford to interpret.

Then Chinese has no alphabet. Every separate word has a separate hieroglyph of its own, composed of from one to thirty-three lines and curves to represent it. These hieroglyphs have not, it is true, been created with entire disregard of system. There are 214 radical signs, and a character is formed by combining one of these with a so-called 'phonetic' or 'primitive' sign, of which there are 3,867. But it must not be supposed that by analysing the combination the meaning can be ascertained. In the vast multitude of cases it is impossible to trace or imagine any association between the meaning of the group and its component parts. Suppose, for example, you dissected a character, and found it made up of the symbols for a donkey and a bag of money. A superficial observer might guess it stood for a spendthrift, or, even taking it phonetically—ass-purse—might connect it in some way with slander. No such thing; it probably means the 'Flowery Constellation,' or the

' Ocean of Boundless Harmony.' The result is that a complete knowledge of the written language requires the memory to acquire and to hold, and the hand to be able to form at will a vast number of extraordinarily complicated characters, whose forms give no trace of their meaning. Let any of my readers look at a tea-chest, and imagine the labour of learning by heart every stroke in even four thousand of such characters as he will find there. That, however, is only the minimum number required for ordinary current work; 13,000 form the staple apparatus of the language, and fine scholarship involves the mastery of any number up to 30,000 or 40,000. One obvious but very serious disadvantage involved in this want of an alphabet is that there exists no possible means of expressing foreign proper names, or scientific or technical terms, in writing, but by using for that purpose (if the name be a polysyllable) a series of hieroglyphics, one of which is needed for every syllable, the Chinese language being monosyllabic; and, as each hieroglyph stands for a significant word, it follows that every such foreign word must be represented by several Chinese words, often with no sense connecting them, but, as often, forming a Chinese sentence the meaning of which is ridiculous. Moreover, the Chinese do not possess fit words to represent many of the sounds which occur in European languages, so that it becomes impossible to write them in Chinese without travestying them till they are scarcely recognisable. Thus, the word France is represented by three characters, which read Fa-lan ssǔ, and Scotland becomes Ssǔ-k'o-t'ê-lan. My own name, James, was turned into Chieh mai-ssǔ, three words signifying a fragrant plant, wheat, and to think.

Then, besides having no alphabet, Chinese has no

inflections, no genders or declensions, no tenses or conjugations. Inflections of number, time, and so forth, are designated by phrases. To denote the plural, it is necessary to subjoin some word of plurality. And so, whether a word is to be understood as a noun-substantive, a noun-adjective, as a verb, as an adverb, as a preposition, or as a conjunction, must in general be inferred or conjectured from the context or the order of the words, all of which is the occasion of extreme obscurity and uncertainty in both the spoken and written speech. The Chinese augment the obscurity by perverse rules of rhetoric and taste. It is bad taste to divide a composition into paragraphs according to the sense or argument, to employ conjunctions, particles, or even punctuation. A page is covered with words, each of which may represent any or all the parts of speech. There are no stops, and the words are arranged so as to place a particular word of dignity at the top of a paragraph or for some other puerile or fanciful purpose; and from this mass of words, made studiously obscure, the meaning must be extracted by conjecturally applying inflections, connections, particles, paragraphs, and all other means of precision or perspicuity. Certainly this very obscurity is the delight of sinologists, who love to trip each other up in the elucidation of difficult texts and proverbs, but it is unsuited to the ordinary wear and tear of the world's business.

But this is not all. The written and the spoken language are two different things, having little more connection than English and Arabic. It is bad enough that neither the sound nor meaning of a written word can be ascertained by looking at it or by analysing its component parts, but it is still worse when we come to the spoken tongue and find it a separate language altogether. But such it is, and it is as poor in the variety or the number of its words as the written one is rich. It is said that there are not more than 342 spoken words, all monosyllables, which, by the help of aspirates, tones, and accents, are augmented to 1,331. Yet by these the forty thousand odd written characters must be represented to the ear. It follows, therefore, that the same spoken word stands for innumerable written ones, and the hearer must guess by the context and the collocation of the words what the speaker wishes to convey. The word ' yen,' for instance, means tobacco, the eye, salt, smoke, opium, throat, why, how, a woman's smile, a eunuch, to soak, to delay, the margin of a stream, to pickle, good-tempered, colour, a word, a cliff, a wattle fence, to extend to, a banquet, hot, elegant, to triturate, eaves of a roof, to practise, to shut a book, scars, a wild goose, a swallow, &c., &c., &c. In fact, when in doubt, say ' yen,' were there not other words equally comprehensive in meaning.

The spoken sounds, too, being handed down by tradition only, vary in all parts of the empire. In consequence, the dialects, which are very numerous, while bearing no nearer relation to the written language than Portuguese and Italian do to Latin, differ *inter se* quite as widely as do those two languages, or even more so. A native of Peking might write a letter to a Cantonese which the latter would understand, but if he spoke to him he would have to employ pigeon-English [1] or else an interpreter. Even at Shanghai a servant from a place as near as Peking proved of no use when I went

[1] This is literally true. A ship-captain recently took on board some Chinese sailors at Hongkong, and at the next port, Swatow, only 200 miles away, the following kind of dialogue was overheard with the native bumboat men: 'How muchee?' 'Half-dollar.' 'You b'long big thief.' In Sumatra, the Chinese from different parts converse in Malay.

out shopping, for he could not understand a word that was said to him.

The general result of this is that an educated Chinaman is in this position. He can correspond with his fellow-countryman, but outside his immediate neighbourhood he cannot converse with him, unless he happens to have learnt the Peking dialect, which Government officials as a rule acquire. And the labour which would have made him a learned man in Europe has only just sufficed to convey to him the precise meaning of the sentences composing a few bulky but obscure tomes, whose contents, when mastered, are in many cases of as little value as the correct translation of a corrupt passage in a Greek play. Of the difficulties which foreigners experience in acquiring the language, or, when acquired, in coining words to express Western names—in short, in exchanging ideas upon any subject outside the ken of the ordinary Chinaman's experience, I have already spoken. I dare say my readers will feel inclined to agree with a writer in the Chinese Repository, that the language is the most imperfect, clumsy, and awkward of all the instruments ever devised by man for the communication of thought.

The Manchu language, on the other hand, possesses undeniable advantages compared with Chinese. It has an alphabet, the pedigree of which is curious. When Nurhachu first began his conquests, the Manchus had no written characters at all, and anything they wanted to indite had to be translated into Mongolian. So the conqueror determined on an alphabet of his own, and scholars invented one on a Mongol basis, with characters much resembling those of the Mongols. But the Mongol alphabet itself was of modern construction, having been compiled about the beginning of the

K

thirteenth century by, or under the orders of, another conqueror, the redoubtable Jenghis Khan, who also, it must be presumed, found the need of writing. His alphabet, again, was founded on that of an ancient race of Turks called Oigours, the progenitors of the Turks, who extend to this day from Kashgar to Belgrade. When these Oigours, or Turks, became Mahommedans, they adopted the Arabic character, but before that they had an alphabet of their own, consisting of fourteen, afterwards sixteen letters. That alphabet, in its turn, philologists trace back to the Nestorian Syrians, or else to the Zend. The Manchu characters have, therefore, a respectable ancestry of their own.

Manchu is, however, sometimes called a syllabic language, one in which the symbols represent syllables and not letters. The error arose in the following way. When the Chinese grammarians became acquainted with Manchu, being accustomed to their own written characters, each one of which stands for a syllable, they forthwith compiled a syllabary, closely resembling the Mongolian in the formation of the syllables, arranged in twelve classes, which, being augmented to meet particular requirements, was eventually made to include some 1,300 syllables. The Chinese student treats each of these as single letters, modifying its form according to its place at the beginning, the middle, or the end of a word of more than one syllable, and learning all of them by heart; but each syllable is resolvable into its original letters, of which there are six vowels and nineteen consonants. The writing, like that of the Oigours, commences at the left-hand corner and runs down the page, but it can be written and read with equal ease horizontally by turning the page round and reading from right to left. This circumstance led early travellers to say that Manchu could be read as well topsy-turvy as the right way up. The letters are easy to form, and can be written at speed. Just as the scribe, when writing a document in Mahratti, draws a line across the paper and hangs the remaining portions of the letters upon that, like a housemaid hanging clothes on a line, so the Manchu clerk draws a line down the page, and then adds right or left of it the strokes or points which are needed to complete the letters and form the words. The original pen was made of bamboo or reed, but a goose-quill or paint-brush, such as the Chinese use, is now most often seen.

Manchu has all the regular parts of speech, noun-substantive, noun-adjective, pronouns—personal, posses-sive, administrative—verbs, with conjugations four in number, declensions, participles, adverbs, prepositions or postpositions (as in Hindustani and Indian languages generally), conjunctions, and interjections; and one great advantage is that the adjectives, as in English, are indeclinable, and there is only one gender. Those who have tried to pick up a little German can realise what a comfort that means. The conjugations of the verbs, four in number, are for the most part regular, they having fewer irregularities of inflection than in most European languages. Auxiliaries are used, but not in greater number than in English and French. The rules of pronunciation, too, are few and simple, the sounds of the letters are guttural but easy to acquire, and in many other respects the facility of acquiring Manchu distinguishes it strikingly from the Chinese. The successive emperors of the Manchu dynasty have taken care to have every Chinese book of value trans-lated into Manchu, and valuable dictionaries and other elementary works have been compiled in Manchu and

Chinese. Yet, so wonderful are the ways of men, the Court and the people alike are now abandoning Manchu for the cumbrous and barbarous Chinese. If they had imposed their language rather than their pigtails on their conquered foes, how much better it would have been.

Chinamen, Mongols, and Manchus in Manchuria, all dress pretty much alike, mostly in cotton clothing dyed with indigo, loose trousers, and over the trousers a pair of breeches cut like a pair of fishing boots, long flowing smocks or coats with tight sleeves, and over the coats a large waistcoat, sometimes prolonged into an apron. The women wear long loose gowns, and their hair is dressed as wonderfully as that of English ladies at the

A 'RU-I,' OR SCEPTRE.

beginning of the century—in marvellous bows and frills, pierced by silver arrows and combs decorated with the blue feathers of the kingfisher. This is Chinese fashion; in former times, Manchu ladies used to wear their hair hanging down loose behind, not even plaited like their husbands'. On state occasions old ladies carry a 'ru-i,' a veritable sceptre, made of wood ornamented with jade, and they display it when receiving guests of ceremony. The 'ru-i' is a favourite present to make, as the two characters which compose the word mean 'Selon votre désir,'—'May your wish be accomplished,' so that people give it to their friends just as one would enclose a forget-me-not in a letter in England. (One of the presents made by the Emperor to Her Majesty the

Queen on the occasion of her jubilee was a 'ru-i' made of jade.) As winter comes on, garments padded with cotton wool are duplicated and reduplicated, till the thickness becomes something incredible, for the houses are not constructed with a view to being properly warmed. I am certain that, if an average comfortable Chinaman were peeled at Christmas time, about twelve coats and twenty waistcoats would appear in succession, all worn beneath a magnificent fur coat and cape. At that time even the commonest labourers are compelled to wear sheep-skins, with the wool inside, and caps made of foxskin. In towns, for going from house to house, people wear neat little ear gloves, called *erh-t'ao*, lined with fur and with silk outside, with a pretty little text or design in flowers upon them. It is a wonder that English ladies have not yet invented something of the kind ; but perhaps they would be thought 'unbecoming.' The Chinaman despises hand gloves, and wears instead long sleeves which come beyond the tips of his fingers, wherein he can hide them as in a muff. The ladies have a similar contrivance, which makes them, balancing themselves as they have to do on their mutilated feet, look exactly like dolls that have lost their hands, as the numberless plies of cloth of which the gowns are composed, or rather the number of actual gowns they wear, make the sleeves stick out of themselves, and one misses the hands at the end of them. The ordinary head-dress of the men is a black silk skull-cap, with a button at the top. Soldiers and civil officials wear in summer a mushroom-shaped straw hat [1] with a red tassel, so arranged that it streams all

---

[1] In Thevenot's *Collection of Voyages* (Paris, 1690) there is a picture of a mandarin with a two-storied mushroom hat, very like the pith hats used by the English in Bengal.

over the hat like a waterfall. In winter they change it
for the round Tartar cap, of the shape known twenty
years ago in England as the 'pork-pie.' Some soldiers
wear a neat black turban, like the men of certain Indian
regiments. As to the other extremity, shoes worn by
well-to-do people are very soft and comfortable, the
uppers of black velvet or silk, with thick felt soles.
But the common folk have a special shoe, called *ula*,
meant for rough work in fields and swampy ground.
This shoe, which Bishop Palafox calls a little buskin
without soles, is made of one single piece of leather,

MANCHU SHOES.

moulded into the shape of the foot, with a separate
tongue attached. It is drawn up tight by laces. The
space between the stocking and the shoe is filled up
with soft dried grass, a species which grows in the
valleys of the Ch'ang-pai-shan, and when pounded makes
a very comfortable lining. We saw many Cossacks
wearing shoes of the kind when we visited Novo-kievsk.
The grass is much valued as one of the peculiar products of Manchuria, the other two being sables and
gold, and it is so elastic that the sables sent to the
Emperor are always packed in it to prevent friction on
the rough roads.

Shall I weary my readers if I describe Manchurian dwelling-houses? It goes without saying that they vary in size, as well as material, with the features of the country and the wealth of the settler. In the forests they are log-huts; in moorland the walls are made of turf, or else sun-dried bricks; new settlers in the north run up very primitive wattle and daub huts, almost as frail as a house in a London suburb. A skeleton is made of poles, and between the uprights is suspended a series of strings, over which are hung roughly-made plaits of grass or rushes. These are first splashed with liquid mud, and then painted and repainted with the same till the whole becomes a solid mass, impervious to wind, rain, and cold. In the older districts and in towns, very substantial and well-built houses of brick or masonry are to be seen. The farm-houses stand in yards surrounded by lofty palings or walls, against which are built pig-styes and cow-byres and poultry-houses, exactly as you see them at home. The outer wall, however, is intended as much for keeping out robbers as for rural economy. On the great gate, which is always shut at night, are generally pasted two brightly-coloured prints, representing ferocious-looking warriors, to keep away evil spirits.[1] But, from the rich banker to the savage, all dwellings are alike in four respects, so far as circumstances admit. First, all face the south, because that is the quarter from which good influences come—(it has the incidental advantage of keeping the cruel north wind at the back). Secondly,

[1] The pictures are those of two soldiers, Ch'in Shu-pao and Hu Kung-teh, servants of the Emperor Tai Tsung, of the T'ang dynasty. The monarch being disturbed one night by spirits throwing bricks at his door, the two men came forward to keep watch, and the spirits gave no further annoyance. The Emperor, therefore, had their portraits painted on his door, and subsequent generations have continued the practice.

they are all one-storied. Thirdly, the front of the house
is filled with movable window-frames, with lattice-
panes of paper, not glass. As the summer advances
the paper can be torn away and the house ventilated,
or the windows can be removed bodily; and then, when
winter returns, the paper is very inexpensive to replace,
and, what is more important, it is far warmer than
glass,[1] which freezes and chills the room. Many a stifling
cottage in England would be better for windows of the
kind. Fourthly, built up against the wall, there is a
'k'ang' running down the whole length of the interior,
and communicating between room and room. Very
often there are two k'ahgs, one on each side. The k'ang
is a platform about two and a half feet high and five
feet broad, made of brick, the inside of which is filled
with a flue carried four or five times up and down the
whole length of the k'ang. At one end is a boiler, in
which the family dinner is cooked. Outside in the yard
is a chimney ten or twelve feet high, which creates a
draught through the flue. Thus all the smoke and
heat of the kitchen fire passes backwards and forwards
through the k'ang, warming it thoroughly like a stove,
and finally emerges through the chimney. The top of
the kang is covered with matting made of strips of
bamboo or the rind of the tall millet. The convenience
and economy of the k'ang are marvellous. Throughout
the day it serves as a place to sit and talk or gamble;
at meal times it is the dining-room, the food being
served on small tables a foot high, around which the
family squats. In the evening the beds are unrolled,
and it forms the general sleeping-place, the females'
apartment being partitioned off at one end. In the cold

---

[1] The use of glass is gradually extending. In well-to-do houses, the
centre pane of the window is often made of that material.

weather, with the thermometer below zero outside and below freezing point even within, a nice warm k'ang makes a most agreeable bed to sleep upon, besides serving as a stove to warm the room. In the better class of houses and in large inns each room has its own k'ang, and it is wonderful how little fuel is required to heat it. A boy lights a wisp of straw and stuffs it in a hole at the foot of the k'ang —so small a wisp very often that he has scarcely time to leave the room before it is burnt out—and it seems impossible so insignificant a fire can affect the great mass of brickwork. But in about half an hour a gentle glow pervades the top of the k'ang, and all the night long it remains delightfully warm. If in ignorance we ever ordered more fuel for the k'ang, we only made it insufferably hot. Occasionally in inns we found k'angs so scorching by reason of several series of dinners having been cooked, or because our beds were too near the boiler, that we were compelled to sleep on the floor or on tables, or else to lay a quantity of straw under our bedding to mitigate the heat.

Outside and in the courtyards of dwelling-houses, the Chinese love of flowers is displayed, but the varieties are few in number. Hollyhocks, balsams, blue larkspurs and roses are the favourites. The climate is too severe for any but the hardiest plants.

Talking of dinners, I ought to say that the people of Manchuria fare better as regards the inner man than people of the same rank of life in any part of the world I know. Provisions are very cheap certainly, but the people all seem natural-born cooks and make the most of their talents. All eat two heavy meals a day, and many of them three. The staple food is rice, or else *shyow* (*hsiao*), *mi* or small millet, boiled with

various condiments. One basin of grain makes three of
porridge. Appetising soups and stews are also made
of various vegetables. Fowls and ducks are consumed
in large quantities, and on great days a pig (itself an
economical animal to keep, as it uses up the refuse) is
killed. In a large inn one can get several courses, as
good as at an average country inn at home, for from eightpence to a shilling. They drink very moderately of a
liquor distilled from rice or millet, sometimes as strong
as whisky, generally as weak as beer. It tastes like
weak hot sherry, and is drunk warm. They are also
fond of boiling water, and always offer it to new arrivals,
that is to say, to drink. For they very seldom wash,
confining their ablutions to an occasional wipe with a
damp towel, steeped in boiling water and wrung out.

The furniture of a house or an inn is undeniably
scanty, as the k'ang fulfils so many functions. Shelves
exist, and chests, often gaily lacquered, take the place
of wardrobes. The little tables for the k'ang I have
already spoken of; there are also real tables and chairs,
the latter with solid wooden seats and stiff perpendicular
backs, most æsthetic and uncomfortable. The shops
have regular counters. The walls of the better houses
are hung with texts from the Chinese classics or poetical
couplets, written in an elegant running hand or archaic
letters, and sometimes with clever pen-and-ink sketches
freely done. At one house we saw some very good
paintings of pottery and relics of the Han dynasty
from the brush of no less a personage than the Commissioner for delimiting the Russo-Chinese frontier. A
reception room of any pretensions has always at one
end of it a couple of good porcelain vases on a table.
Wealthy Chinese are great *virtuosi*, and willing to pay
as high a price for good china as any *bric-à-brac* hunter

in Europe. A member of the British Legation at Peking told me a dealer had asked him as a favour to sell him back for a hundred and twenty dollars a pair of basins for which he had given only fifteen dollars a few years ago, as a Chinese collector wanted them to complete a set. ⁊The walls of inns, and the posts and cross-beams which support the roof, are generally decorated with rude coloured prints, or mottoes of welcome written in large characters on red paper, such as : 'Lift up your head and see joy,' or 'A good inn is a heaven on earth.' Then there are bits of good advice, such as 'Take care of your coat and hat,' 'A good master feeds his horse first,' 'Look after your mules yourself.' At the end of one room we saw posted up the laconic notice, 'Don't talk politics.'

Some of the Manchus used formerly to burn their dead, a custom they probably adopted from the Mongols, who, according to Abbé Huc, are like the people of Ladakh and Thibet, and practise cremation when fuel is obtainable. But it is probable that the majority always used coffins, as the Fish-skin Tartars do to this day. In modern times all classes imitate the Chinese, amongst whom cremation was once not entirely unknown, but who, as is well known, have a great respect for the bodies of the dead. Indeed, while living, they manifest as great an anxiety to be properly interred as old women in Cumberland, who would starve themselves rather than touch the hoard for 'putting them by, puir bodies ;' and when a man attains the age of sixty, a dutiful son can show no greater or more touching token of filial regard than to present him with a good substantial coffin. In our travels once or twice we saw the old man's 'casket' all ready for him in an out-house. The coffins are made of enormous size, and are closed in such a way as to make them air-tight. It is, therefore, quite possible to leave them above ground without creating an immediate nuisance, and, as underground graves cost money, the arrangement suits the Chinaman's love of economy. An emigrant, too, always cherishes the hope that his body will one day be taken away and buried in the family cemetery. The result is that in Manchuria, where half

ENTRANCE TO A FAMILY GRAVEYARD.

the people are strangers, the public burying-grounds and the environs of towns are covered with coffins, left there under the idea their relations will one day claim them; and though they may be seen now and then decaying, revolting spectacles are not so common as might be expected. Old settlers have their family burying-grounds, neatly walled in, with carved tombstones resting on the backs of tortoises, and often a handsome p'ailou at the entrance. (The tortoise is one of the nine offspring of the dragon, and is placed below the gravestone as an emblem of strength.) These family grounds are kept with great care, and are almost always planted with Scotch firs, which give them a solemn aspect. The imperial tombs at Moukden are very fine examples of Chinese respect for the dead; but they are not to be compared with the Ming tombs near Peking, which in their turn are tawdry and ephemeral when put by the side of the Mogul Emperors' tombs in India. Wood is so cheap in Manchuria that good coffins cost little, and every town of any pretensions does an enormous business in them. For a quarter of a mile on the river front at Kirin nothing is to be seen but huge piles of them; and there are great depôts also at K'uan-ch'êng-tzŭ and other places. In the winter twenty or thirty carts may be seen at a time on the roads laden with nothing but coffins, going to other provinces of China. Some coffins are very highly finished with paint and lacquer, and for these large sums are paid. A not uncommon spectacle is to see a woman weeping at her husband's tomb, and truly painful it is. And at certain seasons worship is paid to the dead by writing prayers on pieces of paper and burning them with incense at the tombs, and sometimes crackers are let off to scare away the evil spirits.

As to manners and customs in general, I have already said that the Chinese are extraordinarily industrious, and I have little to add to that. The upper classes, both Chinese and Manchu, are charmingly polite when interviewed—in fact, they rather overdo it—while in deeds they are very disobliging. The politeness, in fact, is superficial, as it must be where women do not mix in society. The old Manchu style

of salutation, bowing, stretching out the right hand,
and raising it to the mouth, which was not unlike the
Indian salaam, has been replaced by the Chinese habit
of closing the two fists, pressing them together against
the chest, and then bowing.   Amongst the lower classes
there are rude boors of course, and in towns and
large villages there is a blackguard residuum which
delights to mob 'kuei-tzŭ,' or 'foreign devils.'   Then
a white man is nearly everywhere such a novelty
that curiosity leads respectable persons, who ought to
know better, to pester him; and the extraordinary
national vanity of the Chinese makes them despise
strangers heartily and pay very scant regard to their
feelings.   The result is that, unless accompanied by
police, it is impossible to walk about the streets without being followed by a crowd, and very often a rude
crowd—in fact, no one who cares to travel comfortably should venture into the streets except on horseback or in a cart.   Hundreds of people surround the
stranger's lodgings; they wet their fingers and bore
holes in his paper window-panes, to which they apply
their eyes and watch him with untiring patience.   They
take especial interest in the wild beast if he happens to
be at his toilet or feeding, and occasionally they will
walk into his room unceremoniously and inspect him.
The sensation of being watched by fifty Argus eyes at a
time is curious at first, and now and again the wild
beast rushes out with a big stick or a cup of boiling
tea; but before long he accepts the situation philoso-
phically.   He answers meekly, even cheerfully, the everlasting repetition of ' What country do you belong to?'
' How old are you?' ' What are your clothes made of?'
' What did your gun cost?' He smiles while his garments
are felt by many dirty fingers and thumbs, concluding

by showing off the action of his gun and revolver. The nuisance was greatest in large towns; in rural places, where most of our time was spent, barring a little natural curiosity, the people were very civil and obliging, and in the mountains the hunters were capital fellows. The fact is, Northern Chinese are far better disposed to strangers than their countrymen in Central or Southern China. This may be attributed partly to their being accustomed to seeing people of other nations, such as Coreans and Mongols, and partly to natural temperament. Most of the Chinese settlers are great cowards, and brigands have an easy time with them. All, however otherwise refined, have certainly one horrible custom, to which one can never become reconciled. From the chief minister at his board to the captive in the dungeon, no matter how engaged or who may be present, a Chinaman—I scarcely know how to go on, but my description of the people would be incomplete if I stopped—is continually spitting upon the floor. The language of the lower orders is coarse, but not worse than Billingsgate. They all treat their women well, and are fond of children. The upper classes confine their wives and sisters to zenanas. In this, however, they are not worse than the educated Bengalee Baboo who knows 'Mill on Liberty' almost by heart.

I must not omit mention of the numerous communities of Chinese Mahommedans who are scattered over the large towns of Manchuria. In the streets they are indistinguishable from the rest of the people, as they shave their heads and faces, and wear the *queue* and Chinese dress. Their mosques, too, are built in true Chinese style, even (*proh pudor!*) to the images [1] of

---

[1] They are called Shou T'ou, and form another of the nine offspring of the dragon.

dogs, deer, and fabulous animals, with which the angles of the roofs are decorated—a fashion restricted to imperial buildings and temples. More than that, inside the entrance is placed a tablet, supported by dragons, in honour of the Emperor, such as the Chinese bow down before—a thing abhorrent to true believers. The walls are occasionally decorated with pictures—a thing forbidden by strict Mussulman law; while the minaret is represented by a regular umbrella-shaped pagoda, with a triple tier of balconies and roofs. The *kibla*, or niche pointing to Mecca, is generally ornamented with a complex and profuse array of texts. The pulpit, or reading-desk, is a movable wooden piece of furniture, in some cases standing almost in the entry of the mosque, or in a corner of that part of it which in a Christian church would be the nave. The Mussulmans practise circumcision, but seem generally ignorant of the history and tenets of their faith. But they insist on shoes being removed before entering the mosque, and they put on, when at prayers, a peaked cap like an Afghan's, with a turban round it. In one respect they contrast very favourably with their neighbours: the enclosures of their houses and mosques are kept scrupulously clean—oases in a wilderness of filth. Mr. Williamson, who stayed at some of their inns, speaks highly of them. They are always civil to strangers, and we found them invariably glad to see us.

On the southern borders of Manchuria, and especially in the Yalu Valley, a great many Corean settlers are met with, who are cultivating extensively, but principally as labourers or cottiers. It may be difficult to distinguish a Manchu from a Chinaman. Not so a Corean. He wears a mild and melancholy look, like a political martyr, and he has a development of yellowish-brown or black hair far greater than his Mongol and Tungusian neighbours, with whom beard and whiskers are generally conspicuous by their absence.   He is always dressed in dirty white garments, short coat, and very baggy trousers made of a kind of grass cloth.   An elaborate tall hat crowns his head, made of horsehair woven in large meshes, something like a bird-cage.   Those we saw were shaped like a Welshwoman's, often with long lappets hanging behind ; but in Corea hats vary in shape and size (*teste* Mr. Carles, who recently travelled there) almost as much as Englishwomen's bonnets.   Through the hat can be seen the hair twisted up in a knot on the top of the head after the ancient Chinese fashion which the Manchus abolished.   According to both Chinese and Corean law, neither country can be entered by a citizen of the other. The law is strictly enforced against Chinamen, and the penalty is death.   But Chinese colonists find Corean labour both cheap and plentiful, and the labourers themselves are willing and hard-working.   They are, therefore, encouraged to cross the Yalu, and till the waste lands.   The presence of the Coreans is supposed to be unknown to the Chinese mandarins, and on one occasion the Corean Government despatched an embassy with strict orders to have all their people sent back to their poverty-stricken homes.   While, therefore, Chinese are excluded from Corea, Corean emigrants are encouraged by Chinese settlers, and the local officials wisely connive at it.[1]

Corean women also dress in white.   They wear a long skirt, underneath which is a very tight bodice,

[1] On one occasion Corean settlers near Hun-ch'un formed the subject of a correspondence between the General there and the Corean Governor across the border, with the result that the Coreans were allowed to continue cultivating, on payment of rent in kind.—*Chinese Review*, xi. 262.

and pyjamas, and on their feet are shoes of straw or
string. They are ill-favoured, and go about with their
breasts exposed, which gives them a slatternly appearance. But those whom we met belonged to the lower
orders, which perhaps may account for their uncouth-
ness. The Chinese look with contempt on the Kaoli-
jên, though in days gone by they were masters of all
Fêng-t'ien, and fought bravely before they were driven
out. Coreans resemble Scotchmen in one respect—they
are capital fishermen.

The Coreans also possess an alphabet, which was
invented 400 years ago, and is, therefore, just twice
as old as the Manchu alphabet. In this respect they,
too, have advanced beyond the Chinese. Many people
do not know that the manufacture of alphabets is by
no means an uncommon thing even at the present day.
Missionaries have constantly to invent them, and officials
have been put to the same task in India. When we
conquered Sind, for instance, we found the work done
in Persian, a foreign tongue. Under the auspices of the
late Sir Bartle Frere, Sir Frederick Goldsmid invented a
written Sindhi character based on Persian, and Arabic.
It was first introduced into Government offices, and is
now generally used by respectable natives of Sind.
A few years later Sir William Merewether introduced
another, a character called Banya-Sindhi, for use by
Hindoo traders in Sind, who previously wrote a barbarous imitation of Marwadi, often unintelligible to
any one except the writer. So the art of Cadmus is
not yet wholly extinct, and it is to be wished that
the Chinese would cultivate it. The Corean alphabet
is phonetic and very simple; a long and a short stroke,
placed in varying positions, represent all the vowels.

Consonants are equally simple. But here I must stop. If any of my readers desire to know anything about the Corean language, they will find an interesting treatise on the subject in Chapter XIII. of Mr. Ross's 'Corea,' [1] on which I will not further trespass.

[1] *Corea.* By the Rev. John Ross. Paisley: T. and R. Parlane.

CHAPTER V.

ADMINISTRATION.

Tsung-tu, or Governor-General—Chiang-Chün, or military governors—Business of Governor-General—Boards—High Court—Chinese system replacing Manchu in Fêng-t'ien—Grades of officials—District magistrates—Their duties—Description of a Court—Civil justice—System in Kirin and Hei-lung-chiang—Inefficiency of Manchu military officers—Headmen of villages—Municipalities—Crime—Treatment of culprits—Cruelty and uncertainty of punishments—Torture—Civil and military police—Appeals—Extortion—Mandarins underpaid—Land tax—Poll tax—Salt monopoly—Tax on sales—Transit dues—Tax on distilleries—Tribute of furs—Maritime Customs—Imports in 1866 and 1885 compared—The opium trade—Moral aspects of opium—Large growth of opium—Decree against opium—Taxes on opium—Room for more English imports into Manchuria—'American' drills—Junk trade—Reforms needed in the administration.

ABOUT the year 1874, Ch'ung Shih, brother of Ch'ung Hou, who drew up the Livadia treaty with Russia (and who nearly lost his head in consequence), was nominated Chiang-Chün, or Military Governor of Moukden. He was the first to be styled, in addition, Tsung-tu, or Governor-General, the title of the highest provincial authority in China Proper, which is a civil one. Viceroys in China, like the Governors of some of the British Colonies, are also *ex-officio* Commanders-in-Chief within their jurisdictions, but the alteration was made to mark the introduction of a civil in lieu of a military, a 'regulation' in lieu of a 'non-regulation' *régime*. The change was effected on Ch'ung Shih's recommendation, and he was given a Lieutenant-Governor, with the rank of a Fu-yin, or Provincial Governor, for the civil

APPROACH TO THE GOVERNOR-GENERAL'S PALACE AT MOUKDEN—A DEER-HORN FENCE IN THE FOREGROUND.

administration of Fêng-t'ien, just as Lord Dalhousie was given a Lieutenant-Governor of Bengal. The military titles of Chiang-Chün, of the Governors of Kirin and Tsitsihar, were retained, and these two were made subordinate to the Governor-General of Moukden. The three Tartar generals are invariably Manchus, and are subject to the rule existing all over China, that their term of service may end at any time, but can rarely extend beyond three years, though in some cases it exceeds that period. At the same time that the Tartar General of Moukden became civil Governor-General, the Ch'êng Shou Yü, or Commandants of Garrisons, who formerly acted conjointly with district magistrates, were confined to their military duties alone. The Governor-General's pay is fixed at 18,000 taels, about 4,000*l.* a year, and the Lieutenant-Governor's at a third less. But they are ordered to draw only one-third of the sanctioned amount, as the finances of the empire are straitened. The Deputy-Governor, who comes next in order, is to receive only 2,000 taels.

The Governor-General seldom attends his yamen, or court, in person, but puts it in charge of a Manchu mandarin of the fifth or sixth grade, whose duties are confined to transmitting legal cases to the proper yamen for investigation. The Governor-General transacts all his business in his palace. He has as his servants a number of officials of various grades, who receive any documents for the Governor-General. These documents may refer to any kind of legal or administrative question, from the most trivial to the most serious, original cases or cases of appeal, whether handed in by official or private person, Manchu or Chinaman. The Governor-General appoints each case for trial either by one of his under-officials in the palace, or, and most frequently, by one of the tribunals outside the palace. In Peking there are six Boards or Great Departments, at Moukden there are five, that of Appointments being wanting. These Boards were established in 1631 by Tai Tsung, before the conquest of China, and they still survive, much after the fashion of the Governors and Councils of the minor presidencies in India, though not with so good a reason. To one of these Boards, according to the nature of the case, the Governor-General transmits the business presented to him for investigation. Besides the Boards, to which Manchus can present their case directly, there is a High Court for the trial of persons accused of capital crimes, and for the investigation of appeals from the provincial mandarins. This court takes cognizance only of such cases as are handed over to it by the Governor-General, who nominates the officials in charge of it. Except, however, for the fact that the Governor-General has dignified boards instead of secretaries to deal with, and that he has special charge of what I may call the Manchu military reserve in the native land of the dynasty, the duties of the Governor-General of Moukden scarcely differ at all from those of Governor-Generals in the provinces of China Proper.

The Chinese form of administration has now almost entirely superseded the Manchu in the province of Fêng-t'ien. There are still ten first-class commandants and five second-class exercising jurisdiction over Manchus, but these military courts no longer have jurisdiction over Chinese, whose business is transferred at once to the Hsien or Hien, the District Magistrate. There are fourteen of these, stationed at different towns of the lower province, the limits of which, in the north, extend even beyond the latitude of Kirin, as far as

Pa-chia-tzŭ, or Hwaitê, on the Mongolian frontier, in the south to the Corean boundary, and in the west nearly to the Great Wall. There are five inferior prefects (Chou-t'ung), five superior or Chou magistrates, three superior prefects (Chih-fu), and four Taotais. In the large towns there are also stipendiary police magistrates (Hsien-ch'êng). They exercise, each in his own grade, magisterial, judicial, and executive powers. The Taotai corresponds to a Commissioner in India, the Chih-chou or Chou-t'ung to a Deputy-Commissioner, who is district magistrate and judge, the Fu to the magistrate of the division of a district, and the Hsien to the magistrate of a Taluka, or subdivision of a district. The last is the unit of administration and the court of first instance. And there is one law which I cannot help commending, though the penalty for breaking it seems a little hard. Whether a complaint is made to a superior or inferior official, the case must be disposed of by the Hsien magistrate first of all, and if the complainant has gone to an officer of higher rank, his mistake is paid for by fifty blows with the bamboo. Few officers in India but are aware of the predilection of Orientals for going to the fountain-head for justice without applying to the inferior court first. In India once I remember a bundle of petitions, couched in rude and illegible vernacular, coming out from England, which had been addressed to Her Majesty the Queen direct; and to this day a very large proportion of the applications made to heads of departments in India are returned with the endorsement, ' This should be presented to such-and-such a subordinate official in the first instance.' The Chinese correct this tendency on the part of the public, which certainly gives unnecessary labour to officials and wastes their time. If, on the other hand, a subordinate officer decides a case himself instead of sending it to the district magistrate, he is degraded.

The district magistrate is compelled to inquire into serious cases like burglary or murder personally and on the spot, as used to be the case when I was a subordinate magistrate in India. I believe the High Courts at the present day discourage action of the kind, preferring that the magistrate should sit on the bench, and take the evidence in due form after it has been deftly moulded by the ingenious native police, instead of hurrying to the spot to see that no tales are concocted or innocent persons charged. The Hsien magistrate is also coroner, and the body must be left where it lies, absolutely untouched, till he has seen it. He has to report serious cases to his immediate chief, and, exactly as he would have to do in India, submit a monthly return of civil and criminal cases decided. He must settle them all within certain fixed periods. If he neglects his duty he involves not only himself but his superiors (who, though they may not have known anything about the matter, ought, it is considered, to have been looking after him better) in serious trouble. A rule, the policy of which our experience in India amply confirms, forbids an individual to hold a magistracy in his own province. Moreover, each public officer is changed periodically, and once every three years a report has to be made to the throne on the behaviour of every single official down to a very low rank. In short, if only the law were acted up to in China, there would not be so much to complain of. But there is all the difference in the world between the making of a rule and the carrying of it out, between the giving of an order and the seeing that it is obeyed ; and the main reason why Orientals fail so widely as administrators is that they neglect this cardinal distinction. They plume themselves on passing the most irreproachable orders, but what becomes of those orders afterwards they neither know nor care.

A magistrate's yamen in Manchuria is very like an Indian cutcherry. It stands in a courtyard surrounded by a lofty wall or a deer-horn fence. On the right and left of the entrance stand the gaol and quarters where the police and menials live. The main building contains a record room, a treasury, and the court room, in which official receptions take place. In the rear there are clerks' rooms, the magistrate's private residence, and miscellaneous offices. The magistrate lives surrounded by clerks and underlings, who are apt at soliciting or extorting bribes. Like the *amlah* in Bengal before the promulgation of the present Criminal Procedure Code, some clerks are deputed to take down evidence and prepare cases for subsequent trial and decision by the magistrate—an abominable system, which must always lead to a vast deal of corruption. And the pay of these clerks is so small that the Government and their superiors know they must live upon the people. I once visited a town magistrate's office in Canton while a case was being tried. The great man was sitting at a table in a high-backed chair, the only seated person in the room. Around and behind him were standing obsequious attendants, one of whom handed him his pipe occasionally for a puff. Before him lay a few law books, to which he referred occasionally, and before him knelt the complainant and witnesses, respectable merchants apparently, dressed in their best, who were arguing the case very respectfully, but with great pertinacity. It was easy to see that the magistrate was saying, ' Well, I would help you if I could. It is a hard case, but there is the law, and I can't do it.' In front of the magistrate, *vis-à-vis* to one another, were tied two miserable criminals who had refused to confess. They were suspended by strings attached to their thumbs and big toes, with their knees just touching the ground, while their *queues* were tied tightly to a post above them to keep their heads erect. Their eyes were half open, a slight foam oozed out of their mouths, but not a groan interrupted their heavy breathing.[1] Their thighs and buttocks were swollen, and the skin broken, the result of severe beatings. Outside in a basket sat another prisoner, whose ankles had already been beaten into a pulp, and who was unable to walk. Against the wall were placed the heavy bamboo, a flat segment of a bamboo about two inches in diameter, a lighter bamboo, a cane, and an iron chain, on which refractory persons who will not confess are made to kneel. Though illegal except in grave cases specified in the code, magistrates generally torture to make the accused confess. If an accused succumbs to unusually horrible tortures, the Emperor may degrade the magistrate, but it is often looked upon merely as an excess of zeal. Once a magistrate was reported for driving nails through prisoners' hands, using red-hot spikes, boiling water, and cutting the *tendo Achillis*. But the Viceroy gave him a good character, saying he hated bad men as he did his enemies, and that a little severity was suitable in that part of the country ; and the Emperor remarked that it was very difficult to find a magistrate who was not intimidated by the

[1] This is called the 'parrot's beam,' and is one of many illegal but frequently practised modes of torture; the only legal implements being, besides the light and heavy bamboo, an instrument for compressing the ankle-bones, five round sticks for compressing the fingers, the cangue, or heavy wooden collar, the iron chain, and iron handcuffs and fetters.

suspicions and resentments of others, and, since the culprits were wicked and abandoned wretches, there was
no cruelty inflicted, and the case might drop. Recently,
however, when a magistrate, who feared that a prisoner
was a sorcerer, to prevent his escape cut his *tendo
Achillis* and burnt his eyes out with quicklime, he
was suspended by the present Empress, and ordered to
be put on his trial.

Civil law in China takes up a very small part of
the code, civil disputes being treated as accusations of
criminal offences. Thus a suit· to obtain a horse is
brought in the form of an accusation that the horse has
been stolen, or for a field, that the defendant has committed mischief to the plaintiff's crops. And, however
the case may be decided, the losing suitor is almost
certain to be sentenced to a beating. In Manchuria, very
often both sides get it, and have to pay bribes besides.

In the province of Kirin, also, the Manchu form of
administration is being superseded by the Chinese civil
officials. In many of the large towns there are magistrates and prefects, as in Fêng-t'ien, and even in an
out-of-the-way place like Autun or T'un-hua there is a
regular Hien magistrate. But on the frontier, at Hun-
ch'un, Ninguta, and Sansing, for instance, the military
commandant is still supreme.

In the province of Hei-lung-chiang the Manchu
military officers still bear sway, and great are the
complaints against their inefficiency and corruption.
Judicial business is made the special charge of a
brigadier assisted by a legal secretary, and this brigadier, as the Governor of Tsitsihar reminded the
Government in a memorial not long ago, is chosen
for his military qualities, and not for his literary
or legal knowledge; so that the business is usually

left to the secretary. A Chinese prefect was appointed
to Hulan not long ago, and two magistrates have just
been given to Pei-tuan-lin-tzŭ and Pa-yen-su-su, though
the Manchu military mandarins still collect the taxes.
Bad as the regular Chinese magistracy is in many
ways, it is better than the Manchu military tribunals.

In the outlying patches of Mongolia, which, from
their position, would naturally be included in the
boundaries of Kirin or Hei-lung-chiang, the Chinese do
not interfere with the Mongol chiefs. When a town
of Chinese settlers springs up, the Chinese appoint a
magistrate, who levies taxation in the town from the
Chinese; but in rural places the Mongol is still lord.
He lets out the land, takes the rents, and administers
justice, except to Manchus. In the interior of the
Ch'ang-pai-shan Mountains, as well as in the hills between Pei-tuan-lin-tzŭ and the Amur, the arm of the
law has not yet made itself felt at all. We shall see
further on how public affairs are managed in tracts
like these.

Every large village has its one or more headmen,
called Hsiang-yao, who is elected by the people, but
installed in office by the magistrate of the district-city
under which the village is placed. If the village is
small, it joins with one or more similar villages in elect-
ing a headman. A policeman is also similarly elected.
Both these officials carry on their own avocations, and
have an allowance made them for their actual work.
This allowance, provided by a uniform tax per acre on
the land of those represented, is intended to indemnify
them for their expenses and loss of time.

Wherever there is a headman, there is a kind of
municipality with which he consults, and on whose
recommendations he acts when he has to engage in

litigation in behalf of the village or any portion of it. This municipality in the cities is composed of the principal merchants, who raise taxes on their shops, out of which they keep in repair the bridges, such as they are, within the neighbourhood of the city. Bridges in the country are kept up by subscriptions collected anywhere by a man or men interested in the locality. When town walls and yamens are in a dilapidated condition, the magistrate appeals for permission to rebuild. Sanction being obtained from Peking, a tax, as much as the 'guild' or municipality will permit without rebellion, is imposed on the town, and a subsidy is always needed besides from the exchequer. Such an opportunity is a mine of gold to the mandarin, as rare as it is desirable. It is the Hsiang-yao's duty to watch over the interests of the Government, to prevent Go · vernment land being illegally occupied, and give notice of crime and the like. He corresponds almost exactly to the Patil or Lumberdar or Gowda of India.

Except brigandage, crime is not rife in Manchuria. But when some unhappy wretch is accused and arrested, his plight is terrible. Torture by beating is all but universal, and the blows, administered on the mouth, palms of the hands, or buttocks, vary from five to two hundred, and are in proportion to what the magistrate is pleased to consider the amount of discrepancy between the statements of the accused and the actual facts. Then the treatment in gaol is frightful. Unless the criminal has means, he runs the risk of being starved, or in winter of being frozen to death. The medical missionary at Moukden gave me a heart-rending account of two poor peasants who came to · him, the one carrying the other on his back, nearly dead of rheumatism and frost-bite, as they had not been allowed any fire, with the thermometer below zero. Punishments are also, in some cases, inhuman. Emasculation still forms part of the penal code. For ordinary offences a fine or condemnation to wear the cangue, or huge wooden collar, for a certain time, or a beating, is the penalty, and perhaps there is not so much to be said against all this. But the slightest offence against the State is punished with death, sometimes in a terrible form. Last year, in a scuffle with brigands, a soldier was wounded, and all the brigands escaped but one. I scarcely like to describe his fate. His ankles were smashed, his legs forced outwards till his knee-joints were dislocated, and then he was cut into small pieces, alive. The last part of the punishment is what a hapless lunatic is subjected to, who, though admittedly mad, murders one of his parents, for madness is no excuse. The moral sense of modern Chinese seems to be no more affected by these judicial cruelties than was that of our ancestors in the days of the rack and thumb-screws; but custom hardens men to anything. An Englishman living in China, to whom I described the tortures related above, merely shrugged his shoulders and said, 'Well, it's the fellows' own fault; you have no idea how obstinate they are, and I dare say they were great brutes.' As for the 'ling ch'ih,' otherwise called the 'slow and painful,' or 'slicing process,' my friend said it was 'really not so bad as people thought; very often not more than eight or ten gashes were made.'

Even worse than the severity of the punishments is their uncertainty, influence by direct or indirect means counting far more than justice in the magisterial decisions. The fact that there are exceptions, whose praises are loudly sung by the people, does not affect

the general statement. About a dozen years ago such
an exception was the Governor-General at Moukden.
His principal subordinate officials combined to deceive
him; most of them were actually in secret league with
the powerful and numerous robber chiefs who then
flourished throughout the country, and provided these
chiefs with a secure shelter in their own houses if they
were hard pressed. This was generally known to all the
mandarins except the Governor-General. At present
matters are totally different at Moukden, and no
mandarin would dare be known as the accomplice
of a robber, though it is currently reported that the
two yamens set apart for the apprehension of thieves
are still in league with them. And, as I said a little
while ago, in the Hei-lung-chiang province the mis-
conduct of the military mandarins, from top to bottom,
was reported to us as terrible.

Police are both civil and military. The civil are
also subdivided. Some are set apart to clear the streets
before high officials, some keep the prisons, some wait
in the place of judgment to apply the bamboo, and
some serve writs upon those wanted at court. If the
accused have to be compelled to attend court, the military police are employed, and if these are inadequate
the regular soldiery is called in. Every magistrate has
both varieties of police in his yamen. Their pay is
composed of a small salary, and of what they can extort
by torture out of prisoners.

All capital cases must be sent to the head-quarters
of the province for trial, and witnesses as well. But in
very clear cases, when the magistrate can show incontro-
vertible proofs of guilt, the sentence can be passed by
the Governor-General, and carried out by the magistrate
on the spot. Except in cases of great emergency, no

sentence can be carried out if it requires confirmation. An appeal exists from any judgment to every provincial court in turn, and finally to the Court of Censors in Peking, even to the Emperor; but the process is long and costly, and is seldom resorted to except in extreme cases. There is practically no stay of execution of judgment on appeal, because the magistrate must obtain from the prisoner acceptance of the sentence before it can be carried out, and, as the consequences of refusal would be painful, the prisoner has no choice but to accept; so in most cases it is a relative of the aggrieved party who appeals. Sometimes even torture fails to elicit confession of guilt, and then the criminal is condemned under a statute providing that conviction may follow the clear and convincing testimony of a number of witnesses.[1]

Extortion by officials, in the form of excessive or illegal taxation, is uncommon. Only on the sale of oxen and horses is an illegal addition known to be made to the published tax, three per cent. being the legal tax, but five per cent. being the charged one. The buyer usually counteracts the addition by declaring the price less than the actual one, so that the deficiency falls upon the exchequer, which receives three per cent. on the declared value, the mandarin retaining two per cent. Bribery or extortion takes another form. As long as people keep outside the yamen they are practically beyond reach; but, once a lawsuit is originated, there is no finality to the extortion, except the exhaustion of one of the parties, and even then a decision may be evaded if there is hope of the other side continuing to make 'presents.' This, however, is true in its fulness only to cases of disputed property, where

[1] *Peking Gazette,* September 12, 1867.

the claims are sometimes difficult to resolve. In these cases the Chinese courts are veritable Courts of Chancery for procrastination and expense. The worst forms of extortion are those practised by the yamen underlings, who sometimes torture in order to extort perquisites.

The fact is that the mandarins and police are grossly under-paid, and they make hay while the sun shines, as officials in India did before the time of Lord Corn- wallis ; in other words, they make their money by selling justice and embezzling the taxes. We heard of one, far away from head-quarters, who, on a complaint being made to him, no matter whether of a civil or criminal nature, promptly clapped both accuser and accused into gaol, and then it was a race as to which could bribe the court most speedily and effectually. In India the native subordinate courts may occasionally indulge an itching palm and take money from both sides, but prudence, no less than honesty, compels them to return the bribe to the losing side. In Manchuria they are not so complaisant.

The great source of taxation is the land, and, pro- perly speaking, the only land exempt is the temple land ; but Manchu houses pay a lighter tax than Chi- nese, and in out-of-the-way places they pay nothing. Chinamen pay about a shilling an English acre. This is always the same, but the acre is a nominal one of movable extent. The acre of first-class soil is an acre by measurement, middling soil is double the size, and a taxed acre of inferior soil is three acres in extent. Any man can secure as much waste land as he chooses to pay stamp duty upon, which duty is very light. In Fêng-t'ien it is officially measured, and pays full assessment after three years. North of the Sungari, the immigrant has to pay down about half-a-crown

M

an acre English. He then gets the land free for five years, and afterwards pays fivepence to sixpence the acre. The annual tax must be paid by one instalment in the eighth month—i.e. after harvest—but it is open to the farmer to delay payment until the tenth month, when failure to pay is followed by a fine. If arrears accumulate for six years the land reverts to the State. The Hsiang-yao sees that no land is taken up unauthorisedly, and that transfers are duly registered. Occasionally runners are sent from the mandarins' offices to inspect boundaries and prevent frauds. The system closely resembles that prevalent in the Bombay Presidency, but the rates are a good deal lower; for in Bombay the assessment varies from tenpence to four shillings and sixpence an acre. But it must not be forgotten that the price of agricultural produce is very much lower in Manchuria, so the difference is not so great as it seems. All land must be measured by officials appointed therefor, and once in cultivation it is supposed to be, and taxed as if, always in cultivation. Forfeiture of title legally follows three years' fallowness from the fault or neglect of the owner, and possession may be taken of such land, with, of course, the concurrence of the local magistrate, by another who will cultivate it. The legal owner can evade this consequence by paying the legal tax for the uncultivated ground, thus leading the magistrate to believe that it is under cultivation. This is a check upon large appropriations of waste lands by Manchus or Chinamen. Private sale is absolutely free to Chinese, the buyer having to pay a tax of five per cent. to the magistrate, who registers the sale and stamps the deed of sale, without which not only is the deed invalid but the estate is subject to confiscation. However, in the country, many people run the risk to save the tax, and they are unmolested if they have no bitter enemy who will take the trouble and risk the chance of exposing the buyer. In the deed of sale and in the register the names and designations of buyer and seller are detailed, and the deed could not possibly be more simple. Manchu land is entailed, and so much of it only can be sold as is suitable for the site of a house or grave. It can be, and generally is, let to Chinese, who often get virtual possession of it by mortgage for a third of its value. Rent-free land is often given to Manchu officials, by way of a portion of their salary. Building and garden lands pay a tax in newly-laid-out cities, but not in the older towns. The land tax is payable to the district magistrate of every city, who hands it over to the Taotai, who accounts for it to the Governor-General. Lands which from providential causes have produced less than sufficient to support the owner are, upon petition, exempted from taxation for that year; but defaulters from personal reasons are first visited by yamen runners or the local headman, and, if persisting in defalcation, are prosecuted.

Next in importance to the land tax comes the poll tax, which, Mr. Ross calculates, comes to about sevenpence or eightpence for a Chinaman and a half or a third as much for a Manchu. The unit of tax is one tael per family or group of families, of whom a register is kept. In a country like Manchuria, where the population grows largely and registers are not kept up to date, it is easy to collect, without oppressing the people, a much larger amount of poll tax than the accounts show to be due, and the balance goes to the magistrate. I heard of one magistrate whose legal salary is only 20*l.*, with a grain allowance of 40*l.* or 50*l.*, but who makes 6,000*l.* or

8,000*l.* a year in this way. Such a district as his is known as a good one to the powers that be, and specially favoured magistrates are purposely sent there.

Like the Government in India, the Emperor has a monopoly of salt in Manchuria, as in the rest of China. This monopoly is worked by a limited number of merchants, to whom licences are granted by the Government and whose proceedings are subject to strict inspection and supervision. They receive licences to manufacture, and, before removing the salt, must also procure permits specifying the quantity they propose to convey away, the route, the district for which destined, and other particulars. For this privilege they pay a lump sum, according to contract. Any infringement of the rules, or smuggling, is very severely punished. The incidence of the duty varies, as the provincial government need only transmit to the central treasury the sum fixed by the Emperor, and keeps the rest for local purposes. It averages $\frac{1}{4}d.$ or a little more per pound. The retail price at the works is $1\frac{1}{4}f.$ to $\frac{1}{3}d.$ per pound, according to the quality of the salt, but in the interior, the cost of carriage and transit dues raise the price enormously. The 'likin' in many parts of China is equal to $\frac{3}{4}d.$ per pound. There are extensive salt-works close to Yingtzŭ.[1]

The heaviest tax imposed away from treaty ports is on property (houses or land) sold, which, if belonging to a Manchu, pays three per cent. ; if to a Chinaman, five per cent. There is also a tax on sales of goods and animals, which is frequently evaded. But the tax-gatherers have

---

[1] In some parts of China the Government allow a limited number of poor persons to sell not more than 14 lbs. of salt by retail, free of duty at the works. The extremely poor are thus enabled to get their salt at a cheap rate. I do not know if this is permitted in Manchuria.

power to inspect and check the merchants' books. Every cart unlading grain or other produce must pay one or two shillings. No octroi exists for municipal purposes, but liberty is accorded by custom for the underlings at the gate of any Customs station in the city to pull out a handful of millet-stalk or take a spadeful of coal from every fresh cart.

All goods-carts and animals passing through a Customs barrier have to pay transit dues, even if there happen to be half-a-dozen barriers. Such barriers are situated on the borders of every province and harass trade greatly. In Manchuria they are in the line of the old palisades and at the Great Wall.

Distilling, only known in Europe for seven or eight centuries, has been practised by the Chinese since the days of Confucius. Distilleries pay a tax of from 300 to 500 taels (say from 75*l.* to 125*l.*) per still in actual use, and irrespective of the strength of the liquor produced. There is no tax on the retail sale of spirits, so some future Chinese Chancellor of the Exchequer has a fine field before him. Spirits on leaving the distillery are of formidable strength, but when presented to guests at the inns or elsewhere they are watered to a considerable extent. There is a strong beer brewed from the small yellow millet about as strong and quite as expensive as the common whisky. The price of this latter is from 2*d.* to 3*d.* per English imperial pint. It is very intoxicating, and impregnated to a large extent with fusel oil. A chemist in Edinburgh extracted half an ounce of fusel oil from about 15 ozs. of spirit. An enormous quantity of spirits is drunk in Manchuria, and drunkenness is not uncommon at the Chinese New Year or any other feast. In the towns, drunken men are to be met with at all seasons, but not very often.

A special tribute of furs and fish is sent to the Emperor every year. An annual gathering is held of the nomad hunters at Tsitsihar, accompanied by their Tâ Shêng, or Superintendent, at which the tribute of 5,500 sable skins is levied, the Governor afterwards presenting them with money, corn, and clothing. A certain number of deer must also be killed for the Emperor's use. The fixed proportion is 1,200 from Fêng-t'ien, and half that number from each of the other two provinces; but the number actually sent is far less, and the 'Peking Gazette' contains an apology from the Tartar General of Kirin, explaining that he could not secure the requisite number. It is said that only the fat tail of the animal, which is considered a delicacy, is sent to Peking. Of ginseng also a certain portion must be sent. No tax is levied on persons cutting trees in the forest, but the purchaser of the timber pays three per cent. upon it when it comes to market.

As is generally known, one of the most fruitful sources of imperial revenue in China is the maritime customs, which, so far as foreigners at treaty ports are concerned, are under the control of the Customs service, mostly manned by Englishmen under the direction of Sir Robert Hart. The rates were arranged originally on a five per cent. *ad valorem* principle, but they only approximate to that at present. The receipts at Yingtzŭ in 1886 came to between 300,000 and 350,000 taels, say 55,000*l.* to 65,000*l.*

I cannot refrain from calling the attention of my readers to some items in the Customs statistics. In 1866 the value of imports at Yingtzŭ, excluding opium, was 212,000*l.*, and the value of opium imported was 572,000*l.* In 1885 the figures were 990,000*l.* and

29,600*l.* respectively, while the population has without doubt enormously increased in the twenty years. This means that foreign trade has indeed quadrupled, but opium has fallen off by more than half a million sterling. In other words, worthy gentlemen of the anti-opium league, your ~~dusky~~ fellow-subjects in India have lost revenue to that extent, and the poor, downtrodden Chinese, against whom unjust opium wars have been waged, have grown an equivalent quantity, and a good deal more, for local consumption and export in one corner of China alone. Is it possible now to talk of the iniquity of forcing Indian opium into China at the point of the bayonet?

However, the league may take comfort. The Chinese have cast covetous eyes upon the Indian opium revenue, and think (it is not very unnatural) that, as they are the people who consume the opium, it would be a nice thing if they could obtain the lion's share of the profits, and they are no longer afraid of the export of silver. They have been, since 1858, raising a duty on imported opium of some eight per cent., which brings them in nearly a million sterling, and they find it very useful. Five or six years ago they proposed that the Indian Government should extinguish its opium revenue in fifty years, and now they have induced the Government of Great Britain to consent that the duty on Indian opium, formerly thirty taels a chest, shall in future be 110 taels, the extra eighty taels to frank the opium through the likin (transit-due) barriers to the end of China. But, even if the Peking Government is itself honest, it cannot control the provincial administrators, who profit by the likin; nor can it prevent them from levying the dues over again under a pretext that the opium has been unpacked, mixed with other opium, or the like. So the new tariff means the enhancement of the old duty by nearly 300 per cent. Indian opium cannot stand this, for it comes at a time when the taste for it is dying out in China. People like the home-grown drug, because it goes farther and is better prepared than it used to be; just as in India coarse Trichinopoly cheroots have superseded the fine imported Manilla tobacco. What is more, the Chinese want money for ironclads and breech-loaders, and are determined to get it. The Indian opium revenue, therefore, will dwindle. The process will be gradual, as the Chinese are far too astute to kill at once the goose that lays the golden eggs, but the end is inevitable. The unrepresented Indian taxpayer will suffer a loss of some six millions sterling annually, which he will have to make up by increased taxation; but he is dumb, and the pious British distiller, whose fire-water never injured a soul, will congratulate himself that Great Britain has done the right and moral thing at India's expense.

Quæ quum ita sint, I hope I may be excused for saying something more about opium in its moral aspects. To my mind, it is one of God's good gifts, like wine that strengthens man's heart, or tobacco that soothes his nerves. In many cases I believe it does a man good, and finer specimens of humanity than some of the races of India who are accustomed to use it could not be seen anywhere. In China I can only remember meeting two, or perhaps three, of those frightful victims of excess which some graphic writers would have us believe all Chinamen are gradually becoming. Opium, as a luxury, is in general use in Manchuria, and a healthier, stouter set of people can nowhere be found. The pipe and lamp are to be seen in the parlour of every respectable banker or merchant,

and he takes a whiff after meals and offers it to his
friends with as little embarrassment or fear of its doing
any harm as if it were a good cigar. The fact is that,
taken in moderation and upon a full stomach, opium
is no worse than a cigar, and most sensible foreigners
in China will tell you so. On the other hand, the
drug undoubtedly has many disadvantages. The first,
and not the least, is that smoking it leads to a terrible
waste of time. (In India it is generally eaten or taken
in some liquid form, which is not open to this objection.)
The next is that the risk of moderate turning to immoderate smoking is certainly great. Mr. Ross thinks
the chances as many as ten to one in favour of excess
following moderation; but that seems to me exaggerated.
I have seen many elderly men who smoked and were
none the worse. Still, the consequences of excess in
opium (though it does not, like excess in ardent spirits,
lead to murdering your wife with a poker or hob-nailed
boot) are undoubtedly grievous and degrading to a
degree. The passion for it seems to exceed even the
craving for drink. In the case of the rich, who can
afford to buy it, it is only the individual who suffers;
but, when a poor man is the victim, he will sell house,
home, lands, and cattle, even wife and children, to
gratify his appetite, and every winter unhappy wretches
are found frozen to death who have parted with their
very garments to satisfy their craving. One bad point
about it is that those who cannot afford better, smoke
the opium ash out of pipes again and again. Mr.
Edgar, Commissioner of Customs at Newchwang, reports that in 1886 the price of Indian opium at that
port was 15 taels for 50 ounces, yielding 45 ounces
of prepared opium—a price actually lower than that
of the native drug, which cost 15·50 taels for 50 ounces

and only yielded 30 ounces of prepared opium. The reason why the native product maintained its ground so well, says Mr. Edgar, is that, in Manchuria, smoking the ash is much indulged in, and the home product may be resmoked some ten times, while the foreign drug will only bear smoking three times. Native prepared opium is, therefore, frequently mixed with the foreign for the sake of the ash. This is a deleterious habit, and here, according to many good authorities, lies most of the mischief for which opium is responsible in China. That opium-smoking has a disreputable smack about it, and that it is dangerous to commence, no proof is wanted. No one would willingly allow a young man, in whom he took an interest, to begin it if he had sufficient influence to prevent him. I myself interfered when a lad in our service was being taught it by a cartman, just as I would if I had caught him drinking brandy; and when the native Presbyterian community at Moukden were recently framing rules for their Church, of their own accord they resolved that no opium smoker should be a member, and it was the missionary himself who got them to make an exception in favour of elderly converts. Yet, admitting all this, and more too, such as that opium and gambling often go together just as do horse-racing and betting, I maintain that the possibly well-meaning, but to my mind Pecksniffian, outcry against opium is, for the most part, moonshine. Look at home. Half-a-dozen streets in London contain far more blear-eyed sodden cumberers of the earth, men made originally in God's image, than the streets of all the towns in Manchuria. Yet would any one say that the English race is being destroyed by drink? I fearlessly assert that the Chinese natives are not being ruined by the drug any more than the

Rajputs or the Thakurs of Marwar. I cannot doubt that a way will yet be found for the Chinaman to enjoy his valuable and pleasant luxury with as little risk or sense of doing wrong as an Englishman who smokes an Havana. Temperance is making its way at home, and so it will in China. Even if it were not so, it is now too late to complain. Take Manchuria, for example: she not only makes opium for her own consumption, but exports it largely. Most of it goes out by land, carried in light swift carts, which evade the Customs barriers in the palisades, and convey it to various ports of Northern and Central China. Some of it goes to Canton by sea, packed up like Indian opium to deceive the Southerners. And, as is well known, the provinces of Yunnan, Sechuen (Sze-chuen) and Honan grow it even more largely than Manchuria. The Government still persists in empty declarations against opium, and occasionally does something to show it is in earnest. As late as 1875 some officials in Manchuria actually tore up some poppy crops; two or three years ago the Empress caused a eunuch to be executed who had opened an opium divan in the Imperial Palace; and the 'Peking Gazette' for January 29, 1883, contains a decree—I am using the Throne's own words—earnestly requesting that all high officials, civil and military, Manchu and Chinese, and all members of the Hanlin College, the Supervisorate of Instruction, and the Censorate, who are addicted to opium-smoking, should purify themselves of the vice, and warning those guilty of outward assent and secret disobedience that they will be severely punished. But the mere circumstance of such a decree being necessary shows how the practice has developed in high places. Moreover, thunder the Emperor never so loudly, a people like the

Chinese cannot be treated like babies and deprived of a luxury which, for several generations, they have been accustomed to and still insist on enjoying. Experiments of the kind have been tried before. In the fourteenth century the Ming Emperor made tobacco-smoking a capital crime, and the great Tai Tsung strictly prohibited the same thing in the seventeenth century. To-day every infant smokes. If every poppy plant were destroyed to-morrow, fresh supplies would be smuggled in by sea or land. The Japanese, I believe, successfully prohibit the importation of opium into their kingdom, because it has the advantage of an insular position, and because the people have not yet become addicted to the drug. Let us hope they never will. But, now that the Japanese travel widely, if they should learn to like opium as much as many other foreign articles, their Government, however much they may desire to exclude it, will be unable to do so, and then, like wise men, they will regulate the traffic instead of pretending to suppress it. The philanthropists, who have already done much mischief by weakening the hands of the British Government in its negotiations with China, may rest assured that, though they may succeed in irreparably injuring Indian finance, they will not reduce the consumption of opium by the Chinese.[1]

Everything connected with opium being still illegal in theory, the mandarins in Manchuria find in it a most delightful way of replenishing their private coffers; for each one can impose on it any tax he likes, either on the farmers who grow the poppies, or on the wholesale dealers, or on the shopkeepers who retail it. Accordingly, we found taxation on opium varying in

[1] Note B, 'Opium,' p. 418.

every place we went to. At Kuan-ch'êng-tzŭ the tax on sales was said to be twenty per cent., and, as the great bulk of exported opium changes hands at this mart, the powers that be must make a good thing out of it. But the figure is probably exaggerated.

There is another point in the foreign trade of Manchuria which has an unpleasant interest for Englishmen, and that is the apparent failure of English enterprise to develop that trade as one would think it ought to be developed. In spite of the great growth of the population, the imports are not more than they were ten years ago (in 1876 they were 976,000*l.* odd, and in 1886 they were 989,000*l.*), and British goods are said to be losing ground. In the Customs returns in 1885 we read that there were 102,000 pieces of American drill imported to 9,000 English, and 187,000 pieces of American sheeting to 20,000 English. The report for 1886 tells the same tale: ' T. cloths,' it says, ' have decreased by 28,215 pieces. This diminution is traceable to their inferior quality. Formerly they were much in vogue among the well-to-do classes, and sold for one tael a piece, but the price has fallen to six or seven mace (i.e. ·6 or ·7 of a tael), and they are only fit, after dyeing, to be used for lining garments. Lustres and Orleans continue to decline on account of their flimsy texture. Turkey reds have fallen off some 14,402 pieces ; they are being replaced by American sheetings, which, when dyed locally, are equal to them in appearance and much more durable in quality. The following articles have advanced: English drills, 12,055 pieces ; American drills, 72,285 pieces ; American sheetings, 27,480 pieces. These goods, which are largely consumed throughout the province—i.e. in the districts of Kirin and the Amur—must continue to

advance, provided they do not disimprove in quality.'
On the other hand, Manchester merchants and their
representatives in Shanghai must be supposed to know
their own business best. And some of them tell me
that the Customs figures are misleading. Vast quantities of drill, really English, are, in their opinion, entered as American, because they arrive in small bales,
tied round with rope like American bales, a mode of
packing in favour with the Chinese. My informants
add that during 1886 and 1887 America has had, in
consequence of her home demand, no surplus cotton
goods to send to China. It is also clear from the Board
of Trade returns that exports of cotton manufactures
to China are increasing with regularity. Still, when all
is said and done, the trade with Manchuria seems to me
capable of much greater extension. It should at least
grow with the population. The entire population in
Manchuria wear stout calico, plain in summer and
wadded in winter, generally dyed with indigo. It ought
to be in the power of Lancashire to turn out a cheap
and popular article.

The principal items of imports now are (so-called)
American drills (174,000 pieces to 21,000 English),
American sheetings (214,000 to 24,000 English), grey
shirtings, (7,100 pieces), T cloths (61,000 pieces), cotton
handkerchiefs (27,000 dozen), cotton yarn (1,400 tons,
mostly, I believe, from Bombay), old metals (6,700 tons),
lastings (17,933 pieces), dyes (chiefly German aniline),
and matches (also foreign). Nothing is exported direct
in foreign vessels to foreign countries, with the exception of an occasional cargo to Japan. But the coasting
steamers, which bring foreign imports to the extent of
88,000 tons annually, go away laden with bean-cake,
from which the oil has been expressed, for manuring

sugar-cane in South China, and with beans themselves (109,000 tons).

There is also an extensive trade carried on by native junks. The imports are estimated only at 13,000 tons, valued at 1,090,000*l*., the main item being native cloth to the amount of 945,000*l*.; and the exports are 113,000 tons, valued at 900,000*l*., the principal article being bean-oil, worth about 650,000*l*. Here again are openings for British trade. Manchester should be able to provide something as good as the native cloth, and the British ship owners to carry some of the bean-oil. At present it is not given to steamers because, so it is said, the light wicker-work baskets in which it is carried are handled too roughly by the crews of steamers.

The figures above are for Yingtzŭ alone. There are also many little subsidiary ports—one in the Gulf of Pechihli, eleven on the coasts of the Kuan-tung peninsula, and two at the mouth of the Yalu. None are of much note, except the two last, for which timber is grown in the Ch'ang-pai-shan Mountains and floated down the river, and exported largely to all parts of China.

The Governor-General has to report to Peking the income and expenditure under every head except foreign import duties; but it must be taken for granted that an accountant would probably find some discrepancy between the accounts as received and those reported. This is equally true of the minor officials; so that, as I said before, the amount of the official salary is augmented at the cost of the imperial exchequer, even more than at the expense of the people. All taxes are for imperial purposes, a certain proportion being legally appointed for the expenditure of each yamen.

I append *in extenso* an Imperial Decree, dated

August 5, 1885, conveying the opinion of the powers that be on the corruption that pervades all classes of officials throughout China.[1] Unquestionably officialdom is rotten, and the country's finances will never be in order, nor will the people get justice till a reformer arises who will, in the first place, pay proper salaries to all classes of mandarins, and, secondly, organise an Imperial Accounts Department, as independent of the local Governors as the Imperial Customs Department. As Oriental countries go, however, a Chinese native of Manchuria has little to complain of, excepting indeed insecurity to life and property from brigandage. He is very lightly taxed. He can build or plant, sow or reap, without any sanitary, educational, police, statistical or other inspector interfering to make his life a burden to him. All he has to do is to avoid quarrelling with his neighbours and to keep out of the law courts, and he will live a peaceable, uneventful life, far less worried, either privately or officially, than a ryot of the Indore State or the tenant of a Hindoo Zemindar in Behar. He is a happy man.

[1] Note C, Decree on the subject of official corruption, p. 421.

CHAPTER VI.

RELIGION.

Extract from Kingsley's 'Heroes'—Applicable to the people of Manchuria—
Three religious cults—Buddhism—Confucianism—Taoism—Collection of
gods in a temple of Buddha—Ancestor worship—Neglected temples—
Local and tutelary deities—Roadside shrines—Sample of a countryman's
prayer—Worship of animals and animal characteristics—A medium—
An exorcist—Worship of disease—Other objects of worship—Fêng-shui
— Rural superstitions—Progress of Christian faith — Roman Catholic
missionaries—Verrolles—Venault—De la Brunière—Boyer—Mortality
amongst missionaries—Dubail—Roman Catholic churches—Absence of
images—Attitude of priests towards mandarins—Orphanages—Training—Statistics of conversion—English Presbyterian Mission—Irish
Presbyterian Mission—Scotch Presbyterian Mission — Medical Mission
—Medical statistics—Refuge for opium-smokers—Valuable work—Meeting-houses—Difficulties in mission work—Success—General remarks on
missionaries.

I TOOK up recently a copy of ' The Heroes,' by Charles
Kingsley, and I cannot help quoting a piece of the pre-
face, although written for children, for what Kingsley
says of the Greeks very well applies to the Chinese:

' For you must not fancy, children, that because the
old Greeks were heathens, therefore God did not care
for them and taught them nothing. The Bible tells us
it was not so; but that God's mercy is over all His
works, and that He understands the hearts of all people
and fashions all their works. And St. Paul told these
old Greeks in after times that they were God's offspring
as their own poets had said. And Clement of Alex-
andria, a great father of the Church, as wise as he was
good, said that God had sent down philosophy to the

N

Greeks from heaven as He sent down the Gospel to the
Jews.   But these Greeks, as St. Paul told them, forgot
what God had taught them, and, though they were
God's offspring, worshipped idols of wood and stone, and
fell, at last, into sin and shame.   For, like all nations
who have left anything behind them besides mere mounds
of earth, they believed at first in the one true God,
who made all heaven and earth ; but after a while, like
all other nations, they began to worship other gods, or
rather angels and spirits, who (so they fancied) lived
about the land : Zeus, the father of gods and men (with
some remembrance of the blessed true God) and Here
his wife ; and Phœbus Apollo, the sun god ; and Pallas
Athene, who taught them wisdom and useful arts; and
Aphrodite, the queen of beauty ; and Poseidon, the ruler
of the sea; and Hephaistos, the king of the fire, who
taught men to work in metals.   And they honoured the
gods of the rivers, and the nymph maids, who, they
fancied, lived in the caves, and the fountains, and the
glens of the forest, and all beautiful wild places.   And
they honoured the Erinnyes, the dreadful sisters, who,
they thought, haunted guilty men until their sins were
purged away ; and many other dreams they had, which
parted the one God into many ; and they said, too, that
these gods did things which would be a shame and sin
for any man to do.   And when their philosophers arose
and told them that God was one, they would not listen,
but loved their idols and their wicked idol feasts till
they all came to ruin.   But, at first, they worshipped
no idols, as far as I can find, and they still believed in
the last six of the Ten Commandments, and knew well
what was right and what was wrong ; and they believed
(and that was what gave them courage) that the gods
loved men and taught them, and that without the gods

men were sure to come to ruin. And in that they were
right enough, as we know, more right even than they
thought; for without God we can do nothing, and all
wisdom comes from Him.'

This description applies very fairly to the present-
day religion of the people of Manchuria, which, however, is much less poetical than the Greek mythology.
With the ordinary Manchu and Chinaman, religion is
a thing full of contrasts, a mixture of fetichism and
spirit-worship, superstition and philosophy. There are
three divisions of religious belief: Buddhism, not here
the carrying out of Buddha's teaching and the attainment of Nirvana, nor even, as we shall see later, the
corrupt version of the faith current in Mongolia, but
mere idolatry—in other words, the actual worship of
Buddha, or Fo as the Chinese call him, and the saints
and demigods with whom mythology has surrounded
him; Confucianism, which is mere agnosticism, empha-
tically declaring that the sole duty of man is with man,
and substituting blind and unintelligent obedience to
earthly parents for reverence to God; and Taoism,
originally also a kind of metaphysical cult, founded
by a philosopher called Lao Tzŭ, and enjoining retirement and contemplation as the effectual means of
purifying the spiritual part of our nature and returning to the bosom of Tao. (Tao itself is as difficult to
define as Nirvana, and has been variously described as
'a superior intelligence pervading the earth, refining
the nature of man, and removing the dross of his
mortality,' as 'a reaching after the unknown,' and as
'impalpable reason.') Taoism, which dates from about
600 B.C., or a hundred years before Confucius, soon
became corrupted, its priests pretending to be wizards,
and introducing the worship of spirits, and now the

N 2

term includes all that is not pure Buddhism or Confucianism. Taoists and Buddhists alike worship a variety
of each other's gods. A Chinese theologian (probably a
Buddhist himself) writes that Buddhism has borrowed
all that is best from Taoism, and Taoism all that is worst
from Buddhism, and Dr. Edkins, in his great work on
Chinese Buddhism, says it is the same to the people
whether it be a Buddhist or a Taoist temple; they
present offerings with equal willingness to either, and
whatever story is told of any idol they are willing to
believe it. There is, besides, the worship of ancestors
and endless local and tutelary deities, peculiar to different families and tribes, castes and professions, houses
and villages. Religion in Manchuria is a mixture, more
or less, of all the cults I have mentioned, fused together.

Chinamen are naturally very materialistic, but there
is a pretty large minority who are religiously inclined.
In neither respect, says Mr. Ross, do they differ largely
from the practical English character. Like the Greeks
of old, they retain a dim conception of the Supreme
Being, whom they call Shang-ti or Lao-tien-yeh, the Lord
of Heaven. This great God of all resides in heaven,
and has no immediate concern with man. In dire distress, however, they appeal to Him. They believe Him
all-powerful and all-seeing, but any other attribute
they do not consciously apply to Him, and they know
of no duty to Him. For, when the thought of duty
comes in, they turn to Confucianism, and confine duty
to their brother-men. Next in order to Shang-ti comes
the Hwang-ti, or Emperor himself. He is T'ien-tzŭ,
Son of Heaven, co-ordinate with Heaven and Earth, and
amenable to both. Pestilence and famine are due to
his maladministration, and evidence of Heaven's wrath
against him, and such calamities justify the people

(theoretically, that is) in rebelling. The Emperor's tablet is in every temple, and he can make and unmake gods or saints, besides conferring additional rank and dignity on those already in existence. Behind His Majesty follows a great assemblage of minor deities and deified heroes, before whose idols the worshipper bows, in the hope either of getting something he wants or averting some disaster. These idols are mixed up in the temples in a singularly indiscriminate fashion, indicating that the gods themselves are the least exclusive of divinities. Go into a temple of Buddha. You will find in the centre of the chancel Buddha himself, sitting cross-legged and majestic as in a Jain temple in Guzerat or a Lama-serai in Thibet. At his feet you will probably see an image of the Maitreya, or Coming Buddha, a jolly-looking god with an enormous paunch, and on each side a row of nine Arhan, or apostles (who, according to the tradition, first brought the knowledge of Buddhism to China), or else three Boddhisatwas, or successors of Buddha, who have nearly, but not quite, attained to Buddha-hood. So far, so good. But in the shrine or niche adjoining stands the figure of the 'Queen of Heaven,' the babe-embracing Niang-niang, or goddess of mercy, bearing a striking likeness to a Madonna, and, on each side, a series of copies of herself on a smaller scale, one holding two babies in her arms, another a single baby, a third displaying a human eye between her thumb and forefinger, a fourth a human ear, a fifth is represented as rubbing her stomach, and so on; so that whoever wants an heir, or suffers from ophthalmia, stomach-ache, or what not, can worship the appropriate figure. (Niang-niang, be it noted, is said herself to be only a female incarnation of a celebrated Boddhisatwa, named Avalokiteshvar.)

The niche on the other side of Buddha is devoted most probably to a statue of Kuan-fu-tzŭ, better known as Lao-yeh, the war god, a grim figure with long mustachios and beard, one of the most favourite gods in Manchuria, and the patron saint of the dynasty. He is a real historical personage, a general of note, who was canonised by imperial edict within our own times. Next door—nay, even in the next compartment of the same temple—may be found, seated comfortably side by side, Lung-wang,[1] the dragon prince (the Nâg-Raja, or Serpent King of India), who is the god of rain; Tsai-chin, the god of wealth, another canonised saint, who, however, had no connection with riches— he was a virtuous minister who died for righteousness' sake at the hands of a cruel tyrant; and perhaps Yen-wang, the god of the nether regions. And the gods of literature, agriculture, fire, are all to be found in their turn, some ideal, some historical personages. It seems strange that the founder of the dynasty never became a popular god; although his descendants paid him the honours due only to Shang-ti, and tales of his personal prowess still linger in the Ch'ang-pai-shan valleys, still his divinity has not impressed the vulgar mind. Perhaps it is because mandarins and all faithful Chinese must adore the tablet, not only of the Emperor's ancestors, but that of the Emperor himself, and a living dog is better than a dead lion. The personage inside a temple, however, is not always meant to be worshipped, for sometimes a temple is erected to a living man.

The Chinaman's worship apparently consists of a series of formal prostrations and the lighting some sticks

---

[1] According to Dr. Edkins, Lao-yeh and Lung-wang have been formally adopted into the Buddhist religion, along with the god of fire, Hua-kuang, the divine protector of monasteries.

of incense, which are stuck erect in a bowl before the idol, and allowed to burn themselves out. He also pays a priest for reciting formulæ, which are supposed to be efficacious. Prayer, therefore, in our sense there is none. To parody a line of Tennyson's, if the worshipper were questioned he would say, 'I thought I'd

TEMPLE TO THE GOD OF LITERATURE, ON THE CITY WALL, MOUKDEN.

done what I ought to ha' done and I comed awa'.' For in many cases even the priest is ignorant of the name of the divinity he has been adoring. Many thoughtful Chinamen who bow before the gods are, says Mr. Ross, entire unbelievers. Some of these who are mandarins must go to the temple as part of their official duty, like Naaman to the house of Rimmon — a circumstance which occasionally prevents believing men from becoming baptized and acknowledging themselves Christians. Others continue their ceremonies from habit or from a lingering fear lest there be something true in them after all. Thinking men of this class will often be found keen disputers on points of moral philosophy. They are, however, in a minority. The bulk of the people carry out their religious exercises in a very perfunctory way. Usually a temple is erected by some rich man or syndicate of wealthy merchants as a token of respect to the established church. The walls are adorned with pretty fresco paintings, illustrating the miracles of the Goddess of Mercy, saving people from a shipwreck, causing an executioner's knife to snap off when striking an innocent man's neck, and the like, or else portraying the tortures of the damned in the Buddhist hell. Then, after the gods, modelled in clay and of gigantic size, gaily dressed and gorgeously painted, have once been placed inside and the temple consecrated, they are left to dust and neglect. Time after time I have gone inside and found the idols utterly uncared for. A temple is not the sacred place to a Chinaman that a church is to a Christian, or even a stone daubed with red to a Hindoo. The Chinaman enters without removing either hat or shoes, talks and expectorates freely, and will eat, drink, and sleep in the very god's chamber as if it were a room in an inn. Whether it be the putting up of a little wooden tablet or the erection of a pretentious decorated temple, the service seems complete when once the building is ready, and the god needs, at any rate he gets, little further attention.[1]

[1] One peculiarity of some temples is that, like imperial buildings, they

Except in the large towns, there are few priests in
Manchuria, and they are nowhere very numerous. We
went one day to see service performed in a small chapel

A BUDDHIST PRIEST.

near Kirin, and, though on a much smaller scale, the
ceremony reminded one of Buddhist worship in Ladakh.

are allowed to have yellow tiles on the roof, and they all have the mysterious
Shou T'ou animals on the angles of the roof. The walls are coloured red,
like palace walls, concerning which a curious story is told. Once on a time
an Empress, finding her rooms much infested with vermin, was told that if
she painted them with the expressed juice of a pepper, which is red, the insects would disappear. The recipe was successful, so, in order that no one
but royalty and the gods should in future enjoy the comfort which she had
attained, she promptly decreed that no ordinary mortal should in future
use that particular colour.

Three or four priests stood in a row, headed by the senior in a black gown. They chanted the prayers while an acolyte rang a bell at intervals, and they all occasionally genuflected, bowing their heads to the ground. They were dirty, stupid-looking fellows, with close-shaven bullet heads. These priests are vowed to celibacy, but, if public report does not malign them, they live immoral lives.

In rural districts and far away from towns the Chinaman is very superstitious and a great worshipper of local demons and spirits. Nothing strikes a person travelling in Manchuria for the first time (perhaps the same is noticeable in other provinces) more than the number of little shrines to the *genii loci* which stand at the corners of the roads. The Rev. John MacIntyre, of Yingtzǔ, from whose interesting paper[1] on this subject I shall quote largely, describes them admirably. ' They are of all sizes, from one to eight or ten feet high. They are perched everywhere—in gardens, in the fields, at village corners, on lovely shady knolls just above the village or homestead, on beetling crags dominating the lofty mountain passes, and everywhere, even in the solitudes and on distant mountain peaks, wherever the fuel-cutter and the cattle-herd have had an errand. They are of all sorts. You have them of mud, or sun-dried brick, with a roof of reeds plastered over with mud. You have them of burnt brick, with a tile roof and some attempt at architectural taste. I have seen one such to the fox with a gable-light of ornamental tile work which was a remarkably good representation of a fox's head. You have them taste-fully constructed of a few slabs of limestone or granite,

[1] *J. R. A. S.*, China Branch, vol. xxi., new series, Nos. 1 and 2. Shanghai, 1886.

TEMPLE OF THE FOX, MOUKDEN.

where such are the natural products of the country. In the forest clearing an old trunk is made to do duty, scooped out or only burnt out according to the tools of the settler; and sometimes again you have handsome wooden cabinets divided into so many niches, each niche with its moveable door. In pottery districts they are as certainly of earthenware, a damaged water vessel being set bottom up, the size of a beehive, and with ·a hole punched in it just sufficient to admit the hand. And perhaps by far the most numerous are those roughly set together with a few rough stones picked up at random, with a flattish stone for roof, as mean-looking as any clumsily extemporised sparrow-trap. The cost is from nothing (not even five minutes' labour) up to a few pounds sterling. Therefore each homestead may have several, and you have whole batches of them at village corners. I have seen five or six in a row—a large one of burnt brick, a smaller one of the same material, and the rest of loose stones. It seems the rule rather to rebuild them than to repair the smaller ones, as new dedications frequently extend the row; while above them may be one or more in a state of ruin, and that while they are all to the same objects of worship. Wealth as a rule shows itself in burnt brick, and even No Man's Land,[1] with its abundance of stone and timber, displays numbers of neat brick structures in the most approved style of the plains, with little Venetian masts in front. The furniture of the shrines never varies. It is either a simple wooden tablet with the name of the object of worship inscribed on it in Chinese characters, or a rough daub of a picture, or a few uncouth

---

[1] Neutral territory on the Chinese and Corean frontier, recently annexed by China and colonised, on account of its having become a shelter for brigands. (See Chap. III. p. 90.)

clay figures, and of course, on a shelf in front, a dirty broken bowl for incense. The arched opening to the shrine is very small, often no larger than will admit a man's hand.'

A trio of 'Holy Ones,' consisting of the 'Spirit of the Hills,' 'Wu Tao,' and the 'God of the Ground,' are the most favourite objects of worship in these rustic shrines. The first is portrayed as a black fellow with an axe over his shoulder, and, maybe, a tiger or bear by

A ROADSIDE SHRINE.

his side. He is Lord of the Forests, and at the tops of the wildest passes in the Ch'ang-pai-shan Mountains we came upon his shrine. He is master of ginseng and gold and the other concealed treasures of the hills, and he protects the searchers for them from wild beasts. Wu Tao (literally 'five roads') is an exorcist of evil demons, and his aid is invoked in cases of spasms, epilepsy, and the like. His emblem is a sword. The duties of the God of the Ground are with the dead,

and all deaths must be reported to him. He carries a
crook like Mercury's *virga horrida*. Then there are
combinations of five, seven, or nine Holy Ones, taken
pretty much at random from the rural Pantheon.
There is the popular Lao-yeh, God of War, with his
sword ; the God of Wealth, with a bowl of cash or an
ingot of silver ; the Fire King, a demon with a dreadful
red face and three bulging eyes ; the King of Cows,
with the model of a cow ; the King of Horses, with the
model of a horse ; the King of Germinating Crops, with
a handful of rich millet in ear ; the King of Insects,
with a bottle gourd ; the Medicine King (a canonised
physician), with his bottle and pill-box ; and the Dragon
or Rain King, with white dragon whiskers. 'In other
words,' remarks Mr. MacIntyre, 'there is a genius or
presiding spirit in every department of human interest,
depicted generally under the guise of a human being,
each with his appropriate symbol. But the human
exterior counts for nothing. In the ancient services
of the ancestral temple a child was dressed in the robes
of his deceased grandfather and received the homage
due to him. So it is here : the men are mere dum-
mies, pegs upon which to hang a robe of ceremony.
And what is behind ? The robe in this case is nature,
the spirits, the essences of things ; so that this is the
voice of the rustic's prayer : " Grant me to dwell safely
in mine own land, free from plague of fire or water
or cankerworm ; give health of body and wealth of
goods, luxuriant crops and prosperous herds ; may
the hills yield me treasure and no scaith ; may no evil
demons cross my path ; and in death may my lot be
prosperous as in life." Such is the voice of the roadside tablets, and such is religion all over China, where
religion is native to the soil—a method of attaining

the good things of life and of warding off the evil. There does not seem to be much soul in it, travel as far as we will. Religion is a " recipe," and is only valued as such.' ' It is not that we do not appreciate your doctrine,' a talkative fellow remarked to Mr. MacIntyre once, with the hearty approval of a large audience ; ' it is that we don't want doctrine. But give us England's recipe whereby she has secured her enormous wealth, and there is not a man of us who will not become your follower.'

Besides tutelary genii, and in close competition with them for public favour, comes the worship of animals, or rather the worship of traits peculiar to certain animals as exhibited in mankind. And here we find undoubted traces of the Shamanism of the ancient Manchus. The sable-hunter in the forests worships the tiger as conscientiously as any Bhil in the Satpura Hills. If, like the Bhil, he confines himself to hunting deer or harmless animals, he makes a merit of sparing the noble beast ; while the man in the next glen, who has gone to the expense of a tiger-trap, catches his god if he can, and flays him with joy. In the plain country the fox and the stoat receive the greatest veneration. The fox is represented as a hoary old man with a foxy eye. He is the essence of cunning, and is fond of changing himself into a beautiful woman to deceive the unwary. He can bewitch you or cure you, and so revered is he that no place in a Manchurian temple is too high for him. Mr. MacIntyre mentions the singular fact that the highest words of the Christian faith, ' Ask and you shall receive,' form the invariable motto over the door of a fox temple. The fox (the animal) will leave medicine for you if you put offerings at the mouth of his hole. He will also (in his human or spiritual capacity) attend on people as a familiar spirit. Mr. MacIntyre relates that he baptized the wife of an old dealer in medicines, who was a noted fox medium. The account is interesting:—

From her tenth year she has had visitations from one of the Fox family, who gave herself out as Miss Fox So-and-so, from the Province of Yunnan. When the vision appeared, the medium either sat or reclined, and with closed eyes held converse as with an actual visitor. As a rule the medium was inactive, but she might put any queries she chose, and was sure of a frank answer. To hear her speak, this was precisely to her what the Daimonion was to Socrates—with this difference, that when she had urgent business and hasty errands (as in the collecting of her husband's accounts, which is altogether done by her), she felt as if helped along the road, got to a long journey's end 'without knowing it' and absolutely without fatigue. It sounds odd to hear that the last great manifestation was on the eve of her husband's baptism, and that the spirit, on being questioned, answered freely that she need not be anxious on account of her husband, as the doctrine was a true one. And as to her own duty, it was to follow her husband, as he without her could not be complete, and the doctrine for him would only be 'a half doctrine.' She is, judged by our own standards, a clever woman, is the 'business man' of the family, has seen a great deal of life in the way of trial and affliction, and is not at all the type one associates with spiritualism. It speaks well for her that all her four married daughters can read, that the two unmarried ones, young girls, are being taught also at her own expense, and have this year received baptism. She is confident her whole house will yet follow her.

Associated with the fox, but never to be confounded with him, comes the stoat, a mischievous elf but of great power in healing. A Roman Catholic missionary told me he was once invited to see an exorcist call in the aid of the stoat to cure a sick person. A hen was tied up by the sick man's head, and the sorcerer kept calling incessantly in an unearthly voice for the stoat to come. My informant got tired and went away ; but a Chinaman, who stayed and whom the priest thoroughly credited, reported that a short time afterwards a large stoat came out of a hole in the k'ang and made off with the hen, to the gratification of the relatives. The patient was, however, suffering from dropsy, so the stoat's powers of healing failed in that particular case. The serpent also is greatly feared and worshipped ; so is the hare, and so is the rat that feeds on beans, the staple crop, much like the locust in India in tracts which are affected by that devastating insect.

After animals the rustics worship disease. Naturally, small-pox has many votaries, as in India, though in China she is not a mere manifestation of a well-known dread goddess, but a separate deity by herself. A miserable broken-down-looking figure is known to everybody as 'His Excellency the Asthma,' and hard by you will see ' Mr. Muscle-and-bone-pain '; and there is one very repulsive divinity frequently seen in roadside shrines and large city temples alike, which aptly illustrates the ingenuity of the Chinese in spiritual matters. It would be too much to have a separate god for every single disease that flesh is heir to, so a deity has been devised, ' Mr. Imperfect-in-every-part-of-his-body.' The idol is most unpleasant in appearance, having sore eyes and a hare-lip, an ulcer here, a diseased bone there. To him a sufferer from any disease unprovided with a god of its own offers a symbol of the part affected, cut out in gilt paper or silk, and he goes away with the assurance that he will be cured. Occasionally a box full of prescriptions is placed before this loathsome-looking deity. Then, when incense has been burnt, the priest, after duly pocketing his fee, throws a pair of dice and takes out the prescription marked with the number that turns up. The patient carries it off to the drug shop, gets it made up, and, let us hope, profits much by swallowing it.

Lastly come miscellaneous objects of worship not easily classified, of which no images are found, but adoration is paid to the name inscribed on an oblong tablet of wood. The founders of the three religions, Lao-tzŭ, Confucius, and Buddha (in these days of unbelief Sinologues have arisen, who question the historic existence of the two former), local wizards or exorcists, the founder of a colony, the first settler in a valley, a spiteful man who died and was expected by his neighbours to haunt them, Spiritual Intelligences generally, Heaven and Earth, the Four Winds, the Four Points of the Compass, Thunder and Lightning, the Male and Female Principles—in fact, everything a man can conceive as influencing him spiritually gets a tablet. Sometimes, though rarely, one finds an offering before a roadside shrine, usually plates of rice, sugar, and the like. But the man who needs anything generally thinks it enough to write on a tablet the name of the spirit who can supply his needs, and the devotion expressed by that act suffices. It is remarkable that Confucius has never been deified. He has many fine temples, but they contain never more than tablets to himself and his chief disciples. 'He is venerated,' says a great authority, 'as the perfection of humanity and not the incarnation of divinity.'

In addition to what I may call their personal gods and spirits, though that expression is at best rough and inaccurate, the people of Manchuria are also profoundly impressed with a belief, common to the whole of China, in 'Fêng-shui.' The literal meaning of this word is ' wind and water,' and it implies the existence

o

of influences, belonging to the natural rather than to the spiritual world, pervading the earth and air around them, which must needs be propitiated by the individual who would live a prosperous life.

The main principle of these geomantic influences, as they are called, is this : All genial life-giving influences come from the south, and all those of an evil, deadening character from the north. They think that these influences proceed in as straight a line as possible, and that, if any high building be raised, it will divert the current from the places due north of it, and so injure the inhabitants in the direct line immediately beyond. For this reason they think that high church-towers, and even telegraph poles and railway signals, will compel the good spirits to turn aside in all directions, and so throw everything into confusion.[1] But it is important to note that this difficulty, which would appear to obstruct the introduction of many civilised appliances into China, is by no means insurmountable. The Emperor's will is law, even to the supernatural world ; and when he decides upon constructing railways, for example, it is not Fêng-shui or the people's dislike to them that will stop him. Every building must be situated with due regard to Fêng-shui, and it is a regular profession to report upon the ' Fêng-shui ' of houses, or to design them so that it may be as favourable as possible. (There is something analogous to this in India, where a pious Hindu will refuse to build a house, unless the rooms can be all constructed in rectangular shape and in size duly proportioned one to another.) If a screen is constructed in front of the main entrance of a house in China, its object probably is to exclude evil influences rather than the gaze of the outside

---

[1] Williamson's *Journeys in North China*, i. 16.

public, and a residence with good 'Fêng-shui' is as much sought after as a gravel subsoil and a southern aspect in England. Even tombs must be built with due regard to 'Fêng-shui.' That of Nurhachu at Moukden is, I am informed, a perfect example of the kind, being built on a hill which represents and propitiates the wind, with a river of water below it, on the genial south. It is supposed that if the spirit of the deceased is comfortable, and free from disturbing elements, so that it has unrestricted ingress and egress, the ancestor's spirit will feel well-disposed to his descendants, and will be enabled constantly to surround them and willing to shower upon them all the blessings of the spiritual world. So the Chinaman does his best to find a propitious site for the tomb, and will go any lengths to maintain it free from interference. Señor Amaral, a Governor of Macao, was murdered because, when road-making, he desecrated some tombs; and the first thing the mandarins do when a rebellion breaks out is to defile and destroy the graves of the rebels' ancestors. And it is for reasons of this character that railway cuttings in hills and through graveyards are disliked, though, as I have said, the Emperor's will *ipso facto* averts any disastrous consequences. As an instance of the active influence 'Fêng-shui' has upon people's minds, a medical missionary told me he thought he might get a site for a hospital cheaply because an unfortunate youth had recently hung himself in a garden there and so ruined its 'Fêng-shui,' which was already much deteriorated by the proximity of foreigners' houses.

I owe to Mr. Ross some examples of rural superstition in Manchuria, which bear a strong family likeness to tales of the kind in the Deccan. Every year a fair

is held at a place called Yao-chao-shan, about twenty
miles east of Moukden, which originated as follows.
Four dynasties ago a carter was going there, when his
cart stuck in a bog. Suddenly three ladies appeared,
who said to him, 'Give us a drive and your load will be
lightened.' The driver agreed, the ladies mounted the
cart, and instantly the mules were able to proceed. On
arrival at Yao-chao-shan, the ladies got down and disappeared, but next day near the top of a hill were
found three female images made of brass. Temples in
their honour were immediately built, and the goddesses
now reappear annually on the 18th day of the fourth
moon. Another belief is that drought is caused by a
man having died on an unlucky day. His body cannot
decay, but hair grows out of it, which, like Gideon's
fleece, absorbs all the moisture in the neighbourhood.
A remedy is found by placing a light on different hills in
succession, and at last, when it shines on the hill next
the unlucky man's grave, a corresponding light is seen
at that spot. The grave is then found and opened, lavish
honours are paid to the corpse, and then the clouds
do their proper work. Corpses have other uncanny
ways in Manchuria. If a person has died on an unlucky day, or with a black cat on the roof, or a black
dog in the room, the body, when laid out, is apt to
revive and run straight ahead until it overtakes a man,
whom it embraces and squeezes to death. It then
returns contented. It goes, however, perfectly straight,
with its eyes staring, so it can easily be eluded, and a
log of wood put in its way. This it hugs, and then
returns equally satisfied.

A Christian traveller may be expected to say what
progress the belief in the one true God and Saviour
has already made in Manchuria. There are two sets

of missionaries at work. The earliest in the field
were the Roman Catholics. In the reign of Wanli, a
celebrated Emperor of the Ming dynasty, who died in
1620, the first Catholic priest is said to have come to
Manchuria. It is presumed that he was only a visitor
from Peking, but there were converts in the province
three centuries ago, and they have never been wholly
wanting. There is a man above middle age in Liao-
yang whose family have been Christians for nine generations. Up to 1838 Manchuria formed part of the
diocese of Peking, but in that year Pope Gregory XVI.
handed it over to the French Société des Missions
Etrangères, and created it a separate charge. Mgr.
Verrolles, a missionary in Sechuen and Superior of the
Christian College there, was nominated the first Bishop
(of Colombie) and Vicar-Apostolic. After suffering
unheard-of difficulties and privations on the journey
across China, he arrived in 1840 to find in Manchuria a
widely-dispersed community of between 3,000 and 4,000
Christian souls, mostly immigrants from adjoining provinces. There were no churches, schools, or priests'
houses, and the only assistant on the spot was a
Chinese priest called Hsü. The bishop lost no time.
Without even providing himself with a *pied à terre*,
he travelled through the length and breadth of his vast
diocese, ministering to the spiritual wants of his flock
as best he could. In 1841 and 1842 two very eminent
missionaries arrived from Paris, MM. Venault and de
la Brunière. The latter was a gentleman of great
abilities and enterprise. While Mgr. Verrolles was
absent in Europe raising funds for his mission, he
was appointed pro-vicaire. In this capacity he took a
memorable journey to the Lower Amur, then almost a
terra incognita to Russians and Chinese alike, where he

was murdered by the Longhairs or Gilyaks. The scene of the crime is still called by the Russians 'The Island of the Martyr.' No news of him being received, his comrade, M. Venault, determined to go in quest of him, and succeeded in completely clearing up the mystery which hung over his fate. M. de la Brunière's last letter, written from the Usuri, and M. Venault's account of his journey four years later in search of his lost friend, are printed in the 'Annales de la Propagation de la Foi.'[1] These interesting documents testify, if any testimony were wanting, to the true Christian courage and devotion of these men of God—a devotion that is shared by their successors at the present day. M. Venault was by birth a nobleman, born in 1806 in the diocese of Poictiers. As a young man he was a courtier of the Restoration, but he gave up the world for Christ, was ordained a priest, and embarked for Manchuria. For forty-two years he laboured there without intermission, devoting his whole private fortune to his work, building churches and orphanages, relieving the sick and needy, and ever refusing to live better or more comfortably than the poorest of his flock. He died on January 12, 1884, the most truly and worthily venerated apostle of the faith in Manchuria.

In 1854 the mission was joined by two other priests, one of whom, Mgr. Boyer,[2] Bishop of Myrina, is the present coadjutor-bishop of the diocese. While sailing across the Gulf of Liao-tung in a junk with two other priests, to reach his post, the vessel was boarded by pirates. One of the three, M. Biet, who was on deck at the time, was instantly seized and thrown overboard.

[1] Vol. xx. 1848. A translation of them will be found in Note D, p. 423.
[2] Since this was written I regret to have to record the death of this excellent bishop.

Mgr. Boyer and the third priest, now Mgr. Tagliabue (the present Vicar-Apostolic of Peking, who lived to consecrate his early comrade), were down below. They were seized and tied to the mast while the pirates plundered the ship. Then came MM. Négrerie and Berneux. The former died by an accident, the other was consecrated Bishop for Corea in 1856. He was next in succession to two martyred prelates, Mgrs. Joubert and Farréol; and in ten years more he himself won the martyr's crown. After them came MM. Pourquié, Ménard, Colin, Malais, and Simon, all of whom died doing their duty. To the exertions of the latter are mainly due an elegant church, orphanage, and other buildings at Yingtzŭ. Since 1875 reinforcements have arrived in greater numbers, but a large proportion have perished from typhoid fever, caused, no doubt, by the filth of the Chinese cities in which their work is carried on. Amongst them may be mentioned MM. Neunkirche, Lamandé, Delaborde, Leformal, and Delecourt, mostly young men; but only last year a missionary of thirty-one years' service, M. Métayer, the revered superintendent of a large orphanage on the boundary of Mongolia, died of the same disease. As orphanages increased in numbers many Sisters of Mercy came from France to manage them, most of whom have also fallen victims to the climate. Of the first set of ten, who arrived shortly after 1875, only two now survive; and of a second set of nine who came later, only three are living. Mgr. Verrolles, the first bishop, to whom the present flourishing state of the mission is greatly due, died in 1878. With his flock, he had suffered much persecution on various occasions, and had once to fly the province. The first Christian church on a European model was built by him at Sha-kou, in the promontory of Kuantung; and by degrees similar buildings with modest parsonages were constructed at various places— viz. Yang-kuan, Pa-kia-tzŭ, Newchwang, Sha-ling, San-tai-tzŭ, Yingtzŭ, Wang-hao-tzŭ, and several others.

Mgr. Verrolles was succeeded by Mgr. Dubail, Bishop of Evelina, another of the early missionaries of Manchuria. He himself nearly perished by sea on his way to China, for his ship, the 'Lord of the Isles,' took fire in the latitude of Hai-nan. Mgr. Dubail and five other missionaries, along with the crew, twenty souls in all, were forced to take to the boats, and after eight days, during which they suffered the torments of extreme hunger and thirst, besides being very nearly swamped, they drifted on to the coast of Macao. So commenced a career of continued sacrifice and devotion. He was consecrated in 1879 at Sha-kou by Mgr. Ridel, another brave Corean bishop, who was taking refuge there during the last great Corean persecution. Under the auspices of Mgr. Dubail churches have been built at Se-kia-tzŭ, a very pretty one at Moukden, and another is at present under construction at Lian-hei-shan. The architect has been M. Chevalier, a priest of the mission since 1857, and an architect of considerable taste, sense, and skill his work proves him to be. The edifices are all of plain but elegant design, and very substantially built. They have been mostly constructed out of mission funds (the Church possesses valuable property in other parts of China), assisted by the labour of the converts, who are, as a rule, very poor. In one case, however, at Sha-kou, the mother church of the province, a rich Chinese family contributed nearly all the cost. The churches are conspicuous for a great distance owing to their lofty towers, which one cannot help thinking are a mistake. They offend the Chinese, who believe that they interfere with Fêng-shui. Therefore, partly on that account, and partly because high towers have a defiant look, which Christianity ought not to assume, let alone the fact that the construction costs a good deal of money, such elevated steeples are to be deprecated. At the same time, I must say it is a pleasant thing to see the Cross of Christ towering aloft in the distance, and, no doubt, the mission looks forward to the time when a converted nation of Chinese will view these steeples with veneration instead of hostility.

Mgr. Dubail[1] is now unfortunately suffering from bad health, so his coadjutor, Mgr. Boyer, aided by the pro-vicaire, M. Hinard, and the able procureur, M. Emonet, have of late carried on the work. Besides these there are just now twenty-four Catholic missionaries in Manchuria, as well as four native priests and some Sisters of Mercy. No one professing or calling himself a Christian can fail to be interested in the progress made by these good missionaries, for I suppose even the most fervent Nonconformist would admit that it is better to be a Catholic than a pagan. The Catholics set about their work in a different way from Protestants. Their main endeavour is to keep the families of existing Catholics true to the faith, and to depend for its extension on the bringing up of orphan children, whom they adopt or buy in large numbers. These children are taught useful trades, and a few of the best boys are selected to study Latin and theology with a view to entering the priesthood. Occasionally adults, dissatisfied with idolatry, are attracted by some Catholic friend, and come for instruction,

[1] Mgr. Dubail also is now dead, I regret to say.

which is gladly given them. But here the direct evangelising work seems to stop. There is little or no preaching to the heathen, the churches being reserved for converts only. The general result is that in about forty years the number of Catholic Christians has been raised to nearly 13,000. The number of boys and girls in orphanages is now about 1,200, besides 300 infants. Conversions of adults are returned at 300 to 400 annually, and about 5,000 pagan infants are baptized *in articulo mortis*. The orphanages are capitally managed by the sisters, and farms are attached to some of them. The children look as rosy and chubby and cheery as a mother's heart could desire, and the training given is of the highest possible value, raising, as it does, communities of moral God-fearing men and women amidst a race eminently selfish, cruel, and prone to gross self-indulgence.

A great mistake often made is to think that Roman Catholics succeed because the images and decorations and the outward show of their churches are attractive to the pagan mind. Exactly the reverse is the case. Except a set of rude pictures of the stations of the cross, with perhaps a figure of the patron saint of the church, or a small image of the Madonna on the altar, the churches are as devoid of ornament as a Methodist chapel. Instead of being an assistance, the images are a hindrance, and not a single Chinaman would ever become a convert because of, or by the aid of, images. A little reflection will show that, if conversion to a Chinaman meant a mere change of idols— the substitution of one Queen of Heaven for another, for instance—he, being a thoughtful person, would fail to see the advantage of any change, and would prefer to stay as he was. So any books given to Chinese by

Catholics are virtually Protestant. Not only is nothing said in favour of images, but they are fiercely assailed. The worship of ancestors even, a subject on which the early Roman Catholic missionaries, in their zeal to attract converts, were a little unsound, is now strictly forbidden. Again, instead of the priest performing the service in dumb show to a congregation, listless or irreverent, as may be so often seen in France or Italy, all the worshippers join in the service most heartily, kneeling throughout, and singing the hymns and responses in Chinese. Only on very great occasions is the entire service done in Latin, just as, at Christmas or Easter, an English country choir produces, after much practising, an anthem, as little 'understanded of the vulgar' as a Latin hymn by a Chinaman. Moreover, the example set by the priests is very fine. They live lives of the greatest austerity and self-denial—their rooms cold and bare of comforts as the entrance-hall of a workhouse, and their food simple and plain. They never dream of taking leave and enjoying themselves for a year amongst their friends at home. They are exiles for the whole of their lives. They have indeed forsaken houses, and brethren, and sisters, and father and mother, and lands for Jesus' name's sake; but they rely on His promise that they shall receive an hundredfold, and shall inherit everlasting life.

The attitude of the Catholic missionaries towards the mandarins has always been rather different from that of their Protestant brethren. When the learned Jesuits were employed by the great Emperor Kanghi, they enjoyed the rank and privileges of mandarins, from which it has become a common custom (I do not know if it is universal) for priests to assume official dignity, and their servants occasionally wear the dress of Go-

vernment *employés*.   They correspond with the local
magistracy, and, when one of their converts is mixed
up in a case, they are said to interfere unwarrantably
with the courts in their *protégé's* favour.   In Manchuria
they have certainly succeeded in getting sixty per cent.
of the local rates remitted to their flock, on the plea
that part of the money is spent in idol worship and
ceremonies, to which the converts have conscientious
objections.   They seem popular enough with the
vulgar, and the mandarins leave them alone, though
secretly disliking them, as a Chinese official is always
most apprehensive of any political interference.   Had
the Pope's scheme to have a legate in Peking been
carried out, it would have removed the greater part
of the hostility now felt towards the priests, and they
might have gained widespread favour.   Many priests,
though not all, dress like Chinese and wear the *queue*, a
practice which has been imitated by missionaries at the
opposite pole of Christian belief, the members of the
China Inland Mission, a body of devoted Evangelical
free-lances led by Mr. Hudson Taylor, but owning obedience to no Church.   These have no representatives
in Manchuria as yet.

The Roman Catholic faith bears a stately name
amongst the Chinese—T'ien Chu Chiao, or the religion
of the Lord of Heaven.   That of the Protestant missionaries they call the Yehsu Chiao, or the religion of Jesus.
(Would that the two Churches could be combined!)   The
Protestant missions are much younger than those of the
Catholics.   Shortly after the treaty port was opened
at Yingtzŭ in 1861, the Scottish Bible Society sent a
colporteur to Manchuria.   Then came a missionary of
the English Presbyterian ministry, the Rev. Mr. Burns,

who stayed for half a year and died. The Irish United
Presbyterians were next in the field, occupying Yingtzŭ
for a few years, when the Scotch United Presbyterian
Mission also established itself there. There are now
three Irish Presbyterian and four Scotch Presbyterian
missionaries labouring in Yingtzŭ and in Moukden.
One fell a victim to famine fever recently, while engaged in carrying relief to the victims of the great
floods of the Liao. From the two centres just named
the missionaries move in all directions. There are two
medical missionaries, one at Moukden, and one is about
to establish himself at Liao-yang. The Scotch and
Irish missions are on the most amicable terms, and
divide the country betwixt them. They have opened
stations at various points as far north as K'uan-ch'êng-
tzŭ, that in the capital, Moukden, being the most important. The Scotch mission began work at Yingtzŭ at
the end of 1872, and have now in the province of
Fêng-t'ien more than seven hundred baptized persons.
The number of baptisms increases every succeeding
year, and is all but exclusively confined to adults. Including the Irish Presbyterian Mission, there are probably somewhere about eight hundred baptized converts,
while very many more profess to be believers. Most of
them are actively employed in spreading a knowledge
of Christian doctrines, which are now becoming familiar
in every city and market town in the province, as well
as in many country villages. The most important result
of mission work hitherto is not the number already enrolled, but the remarkable difference—nay, contrast—
observable in the attitude of the people. Open hostility,
says Mr. Ross, has given place to indifference when not
to kindness, and suspicion has been largely changed into

confidence and respect. Out of this soil will the great harvest of conversions be reaped by a judicious, patient, and earnest mission in the future.

A school for both boys and girls was established at Yingtzŭ in 1873. A girls' school was opened at Moukden a few years ago, and one for boys has recently been added. The members scattered over the country are eager to possess a central Christian school for their children; but this natural and proper desire cannot as yet be met. Many scientific books have been sold in the bookshops connected with the Moukden chapel.

The Medical Mission merits special notice. Its objects are two: healing the sick and preaching the Gospel. Services for religious instruction are held in the waiting-room of the dispensary, which are largely attended, and at which many copies of the Bible are sold. From a spiritual point of view, there is more satisfaction in dealing with in-door than out-door patients; during the year 1886 thirteen of them were received into the Church by baptism, and Dr. Christie has the names of several others who gave evidence of being sincere believers before they left. In one year, upwards of 10,000 out-patient visits were made to the dispensary; over a hundred in-patients were taken in; 250 operations of different kinds were performed, and many visits made to sick persons in the town. Dr. Christie also holds training classes for his assistants, and gives lectures in chemistry to respectable young men in the town; his institution is, therefore, very popular. Medicines are given free to everybody. But medicine, like advice, is not valued when given gratuitously, and if a rich Chinaman can afford to pay, experience teaches the policy of making him do so.

Dr. Christie has fitted up a refuge for opium-smokers who desire to be cured of the 'habit.' The patient first binds himself under two sureties to acquiesce in detention for twenty-one days. From that hour he is given no opium, for Dr. Christie's experience tallies with the best opinions in India, that it is a mistake to attempt breaking off the habit by degrees, or by giving so called anti-opium pills, which frequently contain morphia. The first day the deprivation is felt slightly, but from the second to the fifth the patient's sufferings are severe, accompanied by vomiting, diarrhœa, and other symptoms, which are treated as they arise. On the eighth day the appetite for food returns, and the patient improves rapidly, till discharged at the appointed time. Dr. Christie had treated 150 cases when I saw him, and he estimated fifty per cent. were permanently cured. His Chinese friends put the proportion still higher, as much as eighty per cent.

Unquestionably, the work that is being done by the Presbyterian missions is of the highest possible value. The converts they make are really robust Christians, men who believe and trust in Christ from thorough conviction. Not till they have discussed the truth of the Gospel-narrative a hundred times over, and argued out the theory of the Redemption from a dozen different points of view, will they acknowledge themselves conquered. The thoughtful even amongst unbelieving Chinese have an undoubted conscience, as is proved, if proof were necessary, by the numbers of men of lives free from vice who betake themselves to a religious life; and when they find in Christ not only a free pardon for sin in the past, but a real protection, if they choose, against the attacks of temptation in the future; when they realise the substantial reward to be gained during the present life which the endeavour to follow Christ never fails to confer, a thing wholly apart from the great, but intangible, promises held out of bliss hereafter; when, moreover, they are taught that priestly power, the intervention of man between God and men, is a fiction, and that there is one mediator, Christ Jesus our Lord, they grasp at Christianity readily. And the Presbyterians are very strict in permitting entrance to their Church. The Chinaman's heart may be touched by the infinite pathos of the story of Christ; he may exhibit all the signs of repentance from sin, and of real belief in our Saviour; but that is not enough. The kindly and devoted but withal hard-headed Scotch missionary knows full well that men are apt to confound emotion and genuine conviction. Therefore, not only must the neophyte go through a considerable period of strict probation, but he must pass an examination in the Gospel of St. Luke and the Epistle to the Romans. And in case of doubt as to the convert's full sincerity, or failure on his part to reach the required point of theological and dogmatic knowledge, baptism is refused him. It is impossible to over-value the debt Christianity will owe in future years to the exaction of this high standard at the beginning; and the greatest praise is due to the stern common-sense of the missionaries, who refuse to be tempted by the prospect of adding so many more converts to their flock, or of displaying a large yearly outturn of work, in order that the foundations of the Protestant Church in Manchuria may be from the first securely and deeply laid. In India great devotion is sometimes accompanied by great want of sense. In many cases educated missionaries' time is spent almost entirely in teaching secular learning to heathen children

and young men, who do not profess to come as inquirers
after Christianity, but simply to get a good education
cheaply, and who are willing in return to sit in a room
hung round with Christian texts, and to listen to an
hour's lecture on the Bible every day. So much a mere
form does Christian instruction come to in these schools,
that I have known a case where a pagan Hindoo lad
who had learnt Christian theology just as a boy at home
learns classical mythology, and was quite as well up in
it, was appointed to hear the Scripture lessons of a
class of native Christian boys who were studying to be
catechists. No doubt such missionaries piously hope
that of the good and true seed which they scatter so
profusely a grain or two may germinate; but they seem
not to consider the waste, and the small value people
put on what they obtain gratis. Again, in India I have
known of missionaries baptizing large numbers of low-
caste men to whom the barest rudiments of Christianity
were scarcely known, and who had every motive for
becoming Christians, not from conviction, but because
their position amongst their own people was so degraded
that the profession of Christianity conferred respectability on them. The result of the Presbyterian efforts
in Manchuria is that every convert becomes himself an
ardent missionary amongst his own people. Mr. Ross
states, in a recent report, that of six hundred people who
have been baptized since he came to Manchuria, not
more than a dozen owe their conversion primarily and
chiefly to the foreign missionaries; the others have become disciples of these converts, and this spiritual seed
has produced within a dozen years the sixth or seventh
generation. These converts, many of them far removed
from the direct influence of the missionary, must of
course be instructed, and the principal use of mission-

P

aries now is, or soon will be, to teach the natives, who will impart further knowledge to these scattered members. Experience gained in other fields than Manchuria shows that success in gathering a Church depends more upon the native than the foreign agents. The missions which have native agents at work are successful, but those who do not possess such agents make little progress. The day is not yet, but it will assuredly come, when the Churches in China will require no foreign assistance. Meanwhile, the instruction and employment of all capable native Christians who are obtainable is necessary.

The following extracts from recent reports will show pretty clearly the sort of difficulties met with in extending the faith in Manchuria, and illustrate the precautions taken before baptism is administered. Mr. Ross writes:

In Liao-yang, the ancient capital, there are many inquirers, several said to be convinced believers, but not one baptism occurred during the year. The disheartened preacher, Liu Shou Sien, grieves over the weakness of these believers, declaring that they are terrified to join us at present, as all members have been dismissed from whatsoever position they occupied; and till the believers are in secret a stronger body than at present, he does not expect to see many making a public profession of their faith. One young man who had an excellent business was boycotted; his business failed; and as the Church would lend him no aid in any way, his faith after a year cooled down, and he has ceased attendance on Sabbath meetings. His case is left over to ascertain whether another year may not produce nobler feelings. Yet old Chiao, Mr. Webster's preacher, who is there at present, is joyfully exultant over the hopeful state of many literary men to whom he has been for some time communicating the doctrine of salvation by Jesus through faith. And Jang of Wulitaidsu has a company of from twenty to thirty literary and monied men pledged to publicly join the cause when their number amounts to a hundred—a number which he believes, with God's blessing, to see collected within three years.

The Rev. James Webster gives the following account of progress made at Tieh-ling (a large town north of Moukden, out of which he and Mr. Ross were driven once on a time by a howling mob) :

The troubles from without, with which the early days of our work in this city were associated, have happily passed away. The Gospel has been preached in the chapel daily, a large number have had prominently brought before them the salvation of God in Christ, many have been led to inquire more or less earnestly, and a few, to the number of fourteen souls, have been received into the Church by baptism. Of these, one—the first convert— has removed from Tiehling to do business in a young and grow- ing city among the eastern hills, where, before a people to some extent set free from the trammels of national conservatism, he witnesses a good confession. Another has suffered so much persecution through his profession of Christianity that he has had to remove his family and business to Moukden. They have all suffered more or less in this respect; but it is well perhaps —for the good of their own souls, and the furtherance of the Word of Christ.

Street-preaching in towns is not customary in China. It would attract hostile or at least troublesome crowds. So the Presbyterians construct upon the main streets wooden meeting-houses, open to all, where scoffers or seekers after truth alike can come in and listen. They are just the same as the lecture-rooms one sees at Canton, where teachers sit expounding the doctrines of Confucius. Any wayfarer can come in, take his seat, listen quietly, smoking and spitting the while, and, when he is tired, go out. In these meeting-houses the mis- sionary or a native elder of the Church, or a leading member, sits for hours every day preaching and arguing with all comers. The Chinese like it, and it helps to make the purity and reasonableness of Christian doctrines known. I have never seen a place where evangelical work was carried on in so thoroughly sensible and solid a manner as it is by the Presbyterians in Manchuria. The future results are known to God, and will be seen by coming generations of men.

To illustrate the missionaries' success I print[1] a very interesting account by the Rev. Mr. Webster of the creation of a Christian community by a blind man who had been treated by the Moukden medical mission for eye-disease. He remained in the hospital a month, learned the Gospel truth and believed it. Then he went home, with darkened eyes it is true, but with an enlightened soul, and made known to all the wondrous vision, as he called it, which he had received from on High. Many believed his testimony, and when Mr. Webster visited him he found him surrounded by more than twenty who were eager to follow their blind guide into the fold of Christ. Nine applicants then received baptism—one the schoolmaster of the village, who jeopardised (in fact, I believe he lost) his situation, another the eldest scholar, and another a leading member of the Hwan-yuen, a thoughtful Taoist sect in the neighbourhood. Incidents like these are indeed a proof that the Gospel has not yet lost its power.

Yet one word more about missionaries. Many worthy persons will be heard saying, especially laymen who have been to India and China, that missionaries are lazy, that they live comfortable lives in pleasant homes at treaty ports or large up-country stations, and that the few so-called converts they make are generally out-and-out rascals. Mr. Laurence Oliphant gave vent to this view in 'Piccadilly.' I would like to say a word

[1] Note E, 'The Blind Man of T'ai-ping-k'ou,' p. 446.

about this. Drones there are in every hive, and doubtless, in the Catholic and Protestant communions alike,
well-meaning, excellent men are to be found who came
out burning with zeal, and, overpowered by constitu-
tional placidity of character, or—not to put too fine a
point on it—by laziness, or else, finding that the world
is not to be evangelised in five minutes' time, have lost
heart, grown cold, and subsided into the position of
poorly paid, easy-going pastors of humble little native
flocks. But these are the exceptions. Nineteen out of
twenty Englishmen who go abroad have their own
pressing avocations to attend to, and have no time to
inquire what missionaries are doing, and know absolutely nothing of what is going on. Yet when they
return home and are questioned, dreading to display
their ignorance, ' because they have been there, you
know,' they treat their friends to abuse of missionaries,
or, at best, damn them with faint praise. I myself was
many years in India before I took the trouble to inquire
how things were managed, and then I was amazed at
the progress that was being made. If a lazy missionary
is occasionally found who prefers lawn-tennis with
white men to preaching to black men in the afternoon,
the whole body of earnest workers should not be condemned on that account. And as for the comfort in
which missionaries are said to live, all honour must
indeed be given to him who, in order to influence the
poor and degraded, takes up his abode and lives an
ascetic life amongst them. But that *rôle* does not
suit everybody, and it is just as well; for the missionary's house and surroundings, his little neatly-furnished
rooms, with sacred prints and texts decorating the
walls, his trim little garden, his wife so gentle and
kind to the timid native women—all these are a means

for humanising and civilising the heathen, who live, even the richest and best of them, in the midst of squalor and dirt. Merely from an economist's point of view, or a patriotic Englishman's, the example set by the missionaries, and the elevating results which inevitably follow the adoption of Christianity, are highly valuable. Occasionally, no doubt, a good man will be deceived, and a hypocrite will, for the sake of what he can get, make a show of conversion. But this is to be expected, especially in a country like India, where it costs the missionary so little to support a native, and a hypocrite can evoke sympathy by pleading expulsion from caste. Besides, no one pretends that conversion ensures entire freedom from sin and victory over temptation for ever, so converts will occasionally commit offences like other men. But it is a delusion that there are many cases of the kind. A magistrate in India will be impressed by one instance of a native Christian's misdoing rather than by hundreds of similar cases amongst the heathen around. At least, that is my own experience.

CHAPTER VII.

YINGTZŬ TO MOUKDEN AND MAO-ERH-SHAN.

Arrival at Yingtzŭ—Newchwang—Foreign settlement on the Liao—Auda-
cious thieves—Joined by Fulford—Carts in Manchuria—'Rattler'—
Our servants—Baggage—Money—Rate of discount—Plan of route—
Reach Moukden—Chinese inns—Opium-smoking—Inn charges—Insects
—Moukden—Tomb of Nurhachu—Tomb of Tai Tsung—Chinese banking
transactions—Hiring mules—Start from Moukden—The valley of the
Hwun—Yung-ling—Shingking—Settlers—The scenery—Hsin-min-pu—
T'ung-hua-hsien—Chinese horse-dealings—Flooding of the Hun-chiang
—Three months' rain—Timber rafts—A roadside inn—Picture of the
God of Wealth—Botanising—Pheasant shooting—Accident to Fulford
—Primitive coal-pits and iron-foundry—Difficulties and accidents on the
route—Mao-erh-shan—Garrison—Corean cultivators—Converts—Midges
and gadflies—Chinese system of loading mules—'The lunatic' mule—
System of travel.

YOUNGHUSBAND and myself, as I said at the commencement, arrived at Yingtzŭ on May 13, 1886. This place
is known to English officials and merchants as Newchwang, which is really the name of a town thirty miles
further up the Liao river. Newchwang, in fact, was
the port once, but, owing to the rapid accretion of land
at the mouth of the Liao, the shipping has gradually
moved down the river. Still, as Lord Elgin's treaty
contains the name Newchwang, the town where the
British Consul resides has always borne that name
amongst foreigners. The real name is Yingtzŭ, or Ying-
k'ou, and the approach to it up the river is guarded by
forts. The country around is entirely of modern forma-

tion. The various rivers flowing south bring down with
them a vast amount of alluvial deposit, which turns
first into salt marshes and then into rich cultivable
ground. Eighty years ago the site of Yingtzŭ was in
the sea, now it is four or five miles inland ; and every
year large tracts are reclaimed. The same thing is
going on at the mouth of the river Yalu.

The foreign settlement is built along the left bank
of the river, to the north of the Chinese town. It is
not very attractive in appearance, while the native
quarter is filthy. The most pretentious building is the
Custom House, on the river bank. At a little distance
comes the British Consulate, which stands back in a
spacious walled enclosure. Then come the houses of
two English merchants, Mr. Bush and Mr. Bandinel,
the doctor's and missionaries' residences, besides one or
two shops kept by Europeans. The country around
is flat, muddy, and uninteresting; but when the sun is
setting, the river crowded with quaintly-rigged junks,
and a stretch of reedy marshes beyond, make a pretty
effect, reminding one of a bit of Flanders. And the
hospitality strangers meet with must always fill them
with pleasant memories of the place. The environs
swarm with audacious thieves, who break into foreigners' houses or stables and walk off with anything they
can lay hands upon, from a drawing-room clock to a
pair of ponies. A year or two ago three soldiers were
caught breaking into a Chinese house adjoining the
settlement. Two got outside safely, but the third
stuck in the hole, and the inmates caught him by his
legs. His companions had probably never heard of
Rhampsinitus, but they chopped off their comrade's
head, lest, being captured alive, he might reveal their
names. Unfortunately, the precaution proved useless.

The crime was traced home, and in a brief space all three heads were swinging in cages by the side of the road.

At Yingtzŭ, Younghusband and myself were fortunate enough to be joined by Mr. H. Fulford, a young officer in the Consular Service, who was given leave to come. He was a capital linguist and understood Chinamen's ways, so we often had reason to be thankful that

A LONG CART, WITH SMALL MIXED TEAM.

he came. We started with a procession of six small carts. I beg the reader to note the word *small*; for there are two sorts of carts in use in Manchuria—the long and the small. The first is a low, heavy vehicle, drawn usually by seven mules or ponies, one in the shafts and two sets of leaders, three abreast, or, in difficult country, three sets of leaders, four abreast. The body rests on the axle, which rotates with the wheels. All the goods traffic of the country is conveyed by long

carts, and probably 100,000 or 120,000 of them come to
Yingtzŭ in the winter, each carrying a ton or more of
up-country produce. When used for light farm work,
smaller teams are required. Our carts were small carts
—light, covered vehicles, with one mule in the shafts
and two leaders, used by passengers and for the conveyance of small articles of value, such as opium or treasure. A small cart has been likened to a large Saratoga
trunk, placed two-thirds of the way down between two
substantial beams. Where they project in front, these
beams form the shafts, and the prolongation behind
serves as a frame on which to put baggage. The wheels,
and in fact every part of the vehicle, are made of the
toughest wood, and are so strong that if, as not in-
frequently happened in our experience, one rolled down
the side of a mountain, we felt little anxiety about its
coming to harm. The wheel of the small cart turns
round the axle, which is gripped only by the outer and
inner edges of the nave, and every five or six miles
the driver gets down and oils it. The axle itself is
prolonged about nine inches beyond the wheel, and
looks as if intended to fasten scythes to, Boadicea-
fashion, or at least to upset foot-passengers who happen
to approach too close. But this prong, apparently
useless at first sight, is really invaluable for harnessing
ropes to when the wheel sticks in the mud, and it
helps to save the cart and its contents in case of an
upset. The cart has no springs and no seat inside.
Natives spread bedding on the floor and squat on that,
but the shaking is simply agonising. We therefore
used to put a cushion on the shaft, and sit alongside
the driver, who always takes the left-hand side himself,
giving the right to his passenger. The shaft makes a
pretty comfortable seat, and it has the advantage that

one can jump down readily when game is close by. The Chinese do not think the outside seat so dignified as the inside, but that we did not mind.

The first of our attendants was a faithful friend of mine called Rattler, a large fox-terrier. Unfortunately he knew no fear—a virtue that more than once nearly led to his death, as he would defy half-a-dozen big Tartar dogs at a time. He was devoted to sport, and if we shot a duck, no matter how rough the rapids or how swift the current, in he would plunge for the pleasure of retrieving it. He had a capital nose, and when we got into the pheasant country and one of us winged an old cock, he would run the bird over mountain and dale for a quarter of an hour, the pheasant dodging backwards and forwards like a hare. Many a time the chase seemed to be lost, but Rattler never gave up; and soon the pheasant would be seen leaping out of the brushwood, and then Rattler would have him. The ' Hsiao Kou,' or small dog, was always a source of great interest to the populace. Indeed, he formed a bond of sympathy between us and them, as the Chinese themselves are fond of pet dogs—that is to say, pugs and such-like useless creatures—and Rattler was a proof that, ' foreign devils' as we were, there was at least one human trait in our composition.

We took three servants with us—one an English-speaking valet of about forty, Chang San by name, slow and stately, but sensible and useful; another man of fifty called Chu-Hsiu, whose master kindly lent him to me to prepare bird-skins; and the third was our cook. On the journey we picked up a boy called Chiang, an active and willing lad. These completed our staff. Our servants rode on the carts, in and outside of which our luggage was piled. Not taking warning by others' experience, we took too many guns and rifles and a load of useless ammunition. We hoped for large-game shooting, and, though there was plenty to be had, we soon found that, if we were to get over the ground and return in a reasonable time, we could not stop to look for it; besides, the summer undergrowth in the forests of Manchuria is as dense as in thick Indian Terai, so that stalking was next door to impossible. We should have done better had we taken less ammunition and more tinned provisions; but, on the whole, our baggage was on a very economical scale. We had a small Cabul tent, which was very useful when camping in the hills. Almost the only luxury we allowed ourselves was a sufficiency of Whitehead's soups and some French desiccated vegetables, which we found invaluable, and they took up no room. We had also a little arrowroot, milk, and Liebig's extract in case of sickness. It may interest teetotallers to know that we used hardly any intoxicating liquor. One of us was a water drinker; the second said he did not care about liquor and would drink water too; so the third did not like to be out of the fashion. We took, however, some brandy and whisky, and they proved valuable for medicinal purposes and to give away as presents. Tea was our great stand-by; but I am not sure that a little more alcohol and a little less tea would not have been better for us. Too much tea makes one irritable—I, at least, can testify to that. We carried with us twenty-five shoes of sycee—that is to say, ingots of silver—each shoe being worth, at the depreciated price of silver, a little over 12l. We also took a bill for ten shoes on Moukden, and some loose sycee—i.e. fragments of silver, and some small bank-notes. As we went on we used to change the ingots for broken sycee. We kept a small pair of scales to weigh each bit of this separately, and then the servants changed it for notes and strings of cash. In out-of-the-way places this money-changing gave a great deal of trouble. The merchants would say the silver was bad, or our weights were wrong, or they would refuse it altogether except at a frightfully high rate of discount, and no notes had a currency for more than a few miles away. However, Fulford undertook the duties of treasurer, and well he managed them, though at times his ingenuity and patience were sorely tried.

Our programme was first to go to Moukden, and strike thence due west to the Yalu river, to ascend that to its source, if we could, cross the watershed, and go down the Tumen to Hun-ch'un, visiting *en route* some of the snowy peaks we found marked on a map of the Royal Geographical Society, and which some authorities put at 10,000 to 12,000 feet high. As no European had ever visited this region, so far as we were aware, unless it were the Jesuit missionaries at the commencement of the eighteenth century, we thought some interesting geographical information might be obtained, as well as some rare specimens of natural history. From Hun-ch'un we meant to go to Ninguta along the frontier, thence to Sansing, the fortress which guards the navigation of the Sungari; Tsitsihar, the capital of North Manchuria; Aigun, visiting the Russian station of Bla-govaschensk, on the further bank of the Amur; and then back *viâ* Kirin, the capital of Central Manchuria, to Yingtzŭ. As the reader will find, we made our way to the centre of the Ch'ang-pai-shan Mountains, and from there, finding the road to Hun-ch'un impracticable, owing to the swollen state of the rivers, we made our way to Kirin, and then carried out the tour we had

planned, taking the places in reverse order, omitting
Aigun only for lack of time.

We started on May 19 from Yingtzŭ.   The second
day we passed the real Newchwang, containing about
50,000 inhabitants, with good shops.   The day after,
we came to Liao-yang, a fine old walled town, twice as
large as Newchwang, with a splendid old pagoda erected
in memory of Kung Yudua, one of the three officers of
Ma Wên Lung's army, whom I mentioned in Chapter II.

PAGODA SOUTH OF MOUKDEN.

as having joined the Manchus after that general's death,
and who rose to be dictators of part of Southern China.
At last, after travelling 120 miles through flat and not
very interesting country, where we saw the poppy growing for the first time (it is significant that people do not
fear planting it by the most frequented highway in the
country), we reached Moukden, or Shênyang.   This bit
of road gave us our first experience of Chinese inns,
which are a great institution throughout Manchuria.

Only in the wildest and most uncivilised tracts are inns not to be found. For the Chinese resemble Americans in this respect—whenever they make a new settlement, the first thing is to establish an inn, which fulfils the joint purposes of a saloon, a grocery, and a dry-goods store; and, though I will not say the accommodation is luxurious, still travellers may be thankful for it. The sign-post of an inn is always a fish carved in wood, suspended from the top of a lofty pole. From the mouth of the fish dangles a series of five or more hoops, adorned with a fringe of Turkey red or fancy paper, the significance of which I never was able to ascertain.

The hostelries on the Moukden high road are of a better class than most. An ordinary inn has only one general room, where all the guests eat and sleep in common; but these have little private rooms as well, about ten or twelve feet square, which are reasonably comfortable. To the new-comer the public rooms are the most interesting. The inns are one-storied, as all buildings are in Manchuria, and the public rooms occupy the main part of the interior. Imagine a long low room, with a brick platform about two a half feet high and five feet broad running down each side, and a passage about six feet broad in the middle. On these platforms the guests spread their bedding and recline till dinner is ready; then they sit up, curl their legs under them like the Grand Turk in front of a little table on which the basins of food are placed, and fall to. The guests are of all classes—respectable merchants, petty mandarins, supercargoes, cart-men. Each one has his own place assigned him, where, till dinner is ready, he reclines placidly, smoking a snuff-like tobacco out of a pipe with a tiny brass bowl and a long black wooden stem, or else a handy brass hookah ornamented with shagreen.

Sometimes a guest, probably a soldier or well-to-do merchant, smokes opium. This process, with the lamp, the little bit of opium stuck on a hair-pin and roasted in the flame, and the flute-shaped pipe, has been often described. I can only say that, after watching opium-smoking very often, I cannot conceive any human being submitting to it, for it is tedious beyond description. Over and over again I have looked on, but have hardly ever had patience to wait till the man actually began to smoke. He lies down, roasting the opium, for ever twiddling it round and round for a quarter of an hour or more, and not one puff does he get all the time. Clearly, a great deal of pleasure lies in the preliminaries, and, as I have said before, although I have seen hundreds of Chinamen engaged with the pipe during the nine months I was in China, I have very seldom seen anyone the worse for it.

But to return to inns. The charge for dinner and bed is very little, whether you have a private room or not—at the best inns, only about sixpence a night, *plus* an infinitesimal gratuity to the servants. Dinner costs sixpence or a shilling. We generally provided our own food, and then the charge included the use of fire and hot water. In no respect is the superiority of the Chinese over the people of India more apparent than in the fact that inns are common everywhere. In India, caste prevents anything of the kind, and the public rest-houses, constructed by Government or by charitable persons, are only used by poor Mahommedans and the lowest classes of Hindus. I must also bear honourable testimony to one good point in Chinese inns. During our whole tour, I only remember seeing one specimen of *Cimex lectularius*. *Pulex irritans* was common; but, thanks to Keating's powder, we were hardly molested by it. In some quarters the small cockroach abounded in millions; but he was so harmless and inoffensive that we soon learnt to ignore him, except perhaps when hunting under the pillow for one's watch and handkerchief in the morning, as it was a trifle vexing to pull out a handful of cockroaches as well.

Moukden is a fine town, with splendid walls, about a mile long on each side. To these walls we owed our first disagreeable experience of Chinese amenities; for, walking round them one evening, we attracted a crowd which took to hooting and pelting us, though no harm was done. The suburbs extend for a mile or more beyond the walls, and are also surrounded with walls, in this case made of mud. In the heart of the town is an inner wall, within the *enceinte* of which is a small palace, the walls and roofs covered with tiles of imperial yellow; but entrance is absolutely denied to barbarians. The hunters in the hills afterwards told us that Nurhachu's boots and pack (for, great man as he was, he began life as a pedlar, said they) were preserved in this palace as sacred relics. Though Moukden is now only a provincial capital, it contains upwards of 250,000 inhabitants, and still bears interesting traces of past grandeur. One of the finest objects in Peking is the Temple of Heaven, a splendid marble structure raised on three circular marble terraces with a lofty triple roof, where the Emperor offers sacrifices in person to Shang-ti for rain and for blessings on the spring sowings. The Emperor alone takes part in this ceremony, which is the most solemn religious function known to the Chinese. In imitation of this, Nurhachu's son, Tai Tsung, after that he had dubbed himself Emperor and commenced writing to the Ming as an equal, constructed a small Temple of Heaven at Moukden. It is

Q

a small enclosure some distance from the town, surrounded by a circular wall with an altar in the centre, now in ruins. Standing at this altar, the wall gives back a marvellous echo. There is likewise a Temple of Earth, which is square, in imitation of the one at Peking, but also now in ruins.[1] Four or five miles east of the town, on a hill, deep in a sombre grove of pines, stands a great mound, in front of which is a funeral hall, with an ante-chamber in front, the whole surrounded by a high wall. This is the Fu-ling, or Happy Tomb, where lies the T'ai Tsu, or great ancestor as he is rightly named, Nurhachu, the founder of the dynasty. The temple and walls bear the yellow imperial tiles. The south or principal gate is a handsome structure, with three openings and a richly decorated roof; and let into the wall on each side is a bas-relief in green majolica, representing a huge imperial dragon—that is to say, the dragon with five claws. This is the finest piece of fictile ware I saw in China. The road up to the gate passes first between two lofty p'ailous[2] of massive carved stone, the bases of the columns being carved into the likeness of frogs. Beyond are two pillars, each with a lion on the top, and, finally, two noble couchant lions guard the sacred portal. To the centre of each door is affixed a huge quaint knocker of copper, once richly gilt, representing a bull's head, of the same size and character as the large knocker of Durham Cathedral. The shrubs have grown wild in

[1] According to the Emperor Kienlung, Tai Tsung built these Temples of Heaven and Earth, and also the existing palace and walls of Moukden, in the fifth year of his reign (1631).

[2] A p'ailou is an *arc de triomphe* divided into three compartments, the middle one being the highest. It is an elaborate form of monument erected by the Chinese in honour of deceased worthies. In Manchuria it is generally made of brick or wood and covered with florid ornament.

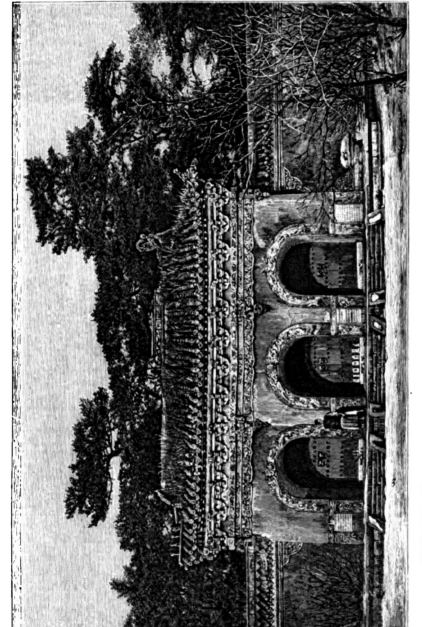

SOUTH ENTRANCE TO THE FU-LING, THE TOMB OF NURHACHU, FOUNDER OF THE MANCHU DYNASTY.

the park around, and roofs and paths are moss-grown. But on the whole the tomb is well kept up, and forms a fit resting-place for one who played a great part in his time, and made himself master of one of the most powerful and ancient of Oriental monarchies. No one but a Manchu may enter the enclosure—to a Chinaman the punishment would be death. North of Moukden is the Pei-ling, or northern tomb, also in a deep grove of ancient cedars, where lies Tai Tsung, Nurhachu's son. It is surrounded by delightful shrubberies full of hawthorn and other sweet-flowering trees, where pheasants were crowing in the balmy springtime. Outside the main entrance, at the top of a flight of steps, stands a splendid marble p'ailou,[1] a noble monument indeed, and at the beginning of the avenue leading up to it are two gigantic slabs resting on the backs of tortoises, which warn the traveller, in several different languages, 'Here every one must get off his horse.' A mile or two south of the town, near the crossing of the Hun river, one finds a trace of the old alliance between Tai Tsung and his friends the Mongols, in the shape of a huge dagoba-shaped monument,[2] exactly like the chortens one sees in Ladakh. It stands in a grove of ancient trees, not far from the south gate.

The Emperor Kienlung wrote a poem in praise of Moukden, which was translated by the learned Père Amyot, and attracted the attention of Voltaire, from whose pen it drew an epistolary poem asking certain questions of the imperial author as to the difficulties and requirements of versification in Chinese.[3] Kienlung's poem was printed in sixty-four different forms of Chinese writing. In this poem his Majesty narrates

---

[1] See illustration at p. 62.   [2] See illustration on p. 67.
[3] Boulger, *History of China*, vol. ii. p. 540.

that the site of Moukden was chosen by his ancestor, Nurhachu, in the tenth year of his reign,[1] which he had named the 'Providence of Heaven.' 'After considering all the dangers which might beset his good fortune, and the best way of avoiding them, "Let us seek," said he, "a place where the influences of bad fortune cannot molest me.[2] It is by going towards the centre that I shall prevent them from injuring me. The country of Shên-yang invites me. There I shall find the most benign influences; there will I fix my Court." His plan was no sooner resolved upon than carried into execution. Moukden was built, and became a sure defence against all the forces of the West.' One cannot help remarking that the allusions in this part of the poem can hardly have been palatable to patriotic Chinese.

We spent several pleasant days in Moukden, and made the acquaintance of the excellent Presbyterian missionaries. The cashing of a bill for 120*l.*, which we had brought from Yingtzŭ, gave us our first insight into Chinese banking transactions. Though drawn upon an inn, the inn-keeper said it was not for him, but for a guest who made his head-quarters there, and was away selling cloth at the time. Then, when the guest was found, he showed no anxiety at all to meet the bill. However, by the exercise of much patience, Fulford got it cashed at last, and another banker gave us a bill for a similar amount on Tsitsihar. No bills were to be got on Kirin or Hun-ch'un at all, so we had to carry the rest of our money in bullion.

It interests a new-comer to China to watch the work-

[1] 1625.
[2] In other words, a place with good Fêng-shui (see Chap. VI., page 193). Père Amyot gives an interesting account of the astrological calculations necessary to gauge the geomantic influences of a particular place, too long to quote here.

ing-out of all sums by the calculating machine. In a banker's shop or large inn the click, click of the balls is continually heard, often quite in a musical rhythm. Such indeed is the accuracy ensured by its use, and so quickly can it be worked, that the clerks in the Hong-kong and Shanghai Bank and foreign merchants' offices habitually call in a Chinese understrapper to verify their calculations with the 'suan-p'an.' The abacus, for such it is, is an oblong tray, about twelve inches by eight, divided longitudinally into two unequal com-partments, each containing a number of wires on which balls of black wood are strung in parallel columns. Those in the upper and larger compartment represent integral units, increasing decimally to the left as in our own system of numeration. In the smaller they repre-sent fives or tens. Almost the identical instrument can be seen in our own infant schools and toy shops. The Russians use it, and a Russian officer whom we met never added up a sum without it. The only objection to it is that the calculations are destroyed as the sum progresses, so in case of interruption or forgetfulness the sum must be begun over again.

Considerable difficulty was found in changing our carts for pack-mules, as no one was willing to venture into the unknown mountains. After first endeavouring to hire without success, our inn-keeper told us that once a week mules were brought to the market for sale, so we waited, resolving to buy ; but when the day came round, on our going to the place only one old animal was offered, perfectly worn-out and useless. We called on the Taotai, or Commissioner, to ask for assistance, but the great man was prudently not at home, and he afterwards sent a polite, but unsatisfactory message. At last, when almost in despair, a sergeant, who belonged to a regiment at Hun-ch'un and had relations who were mule-drivers, came forward and arranged terms with some men to accompany us. The rates were high, and the animals in bad condition, but there was no help for it ; so, at last, with the sergeant in attendance, we started. We had twenty animals—twelve for packs and three for our riding, as we thought ponies would not answer so well in the hills, three for our servants and two to carry the sergeant and muleteers by turns. The muleteers were three in number, but we found them insufficient, and we had to employ two more men on our own account.

A beautiful and exhilarating spectacle was our start from Moukden. Our wretched mules were much over-loaded and went very slowly; one was dead lame, and another so galled that he could hardly move. We ourselves were perched on native saddles covered with red blankets and heavy native stirrups ; for, rightly anticipating that we should not get much riding, we had left our own saddles behind. Fulford and I carried a revolver and a gun apiece to give us a *noli me tangere* air, and I carried also on my back a tin box for botanical specimens. Younghusband, as the scientific member of the party, was laden with more instruments than a subaltern in the Indian army going on field service. Over one shoulder was slung a telescope, over the other a pocket aneroid, round his neck dangled a prismatic compass, from his waist a thermometer ; a sketching-case was at his hip, and a notebook protruded from his breast-pocket. The sight was indeed calculated to impress the unsophisticated native. Unfortunately, that day all the troops had turned out and were lining the eastern road in expectation of a great warrior, the imperial military commissioner, whose arrival was looked for that morning. The populace had come in large numbers to see the procession, so our cavalcade had to run the gauntlet of both soldiers and crowd. They mocked us consumedly, occasionally tossing a playful bit of mud or dirt at us, and I am bound to say it was not comfortable. But eventually we got clear and out into the country, and then our spirits rose.

We left Moukden on May 29. Our road followed the valley of the Hwun, a large affluent of the Liao. The country was well wooded and very pretty. The second day we passed Fu-shan-ch'êng, formerly the frontier town of China, and the first which Nurhachu attacked. We then entered the hills, following the Sutzu Ho, a tributary of the Hwun, and passing Sarhu, the scene of the great and decisive battle between the Manchus and the Chinese, an account of which in Manchu and Chinese is inscribed on a fine marble slab erected on the spot in the forty-first year of Kienlung. On the fourth day we reached the village of Mu-chi, beyond which an avenue of ancient elms brought us to the foot of a small pass, the view from which was exquisite. Descending the hill, we entered the valley of Hotuala, whence the Manchu dynasty sprung. A few miles farther on we passed by an ancient palace consisting of nine little detached houses in a ruinous enclosure, and then came to Yungling, a village filled with soldiers, who guard a beautifully wooded hill on the top of which are situated the tombs of Nurhachu's ancestors. The base of the hill is surrounded by a decaying deer-horn fence, which takes in a circle of about twelve miles. Three or four miles beyond, on the top of a small detached hill, stands Yenden, or Shingking, 'the Capital of Prosperity,' now a petty village with decaying gates and walls, containing little more than an insignificant yamen or magistrate's office. Two miles south of it are the remains of Laochêng, his first capital, and I believe the original Odoli. Settlers are now taking up their abode in great numbers in this and adjoining valleys, and the forests are rapidly falling before the axe. The scenery in the neighbourhood is marvellously beautiful—woods and flowers and grassy glades—and to the lover of Nature it is simply a paradise. The first day I began to collect I found no less than five kinds of lilies of the valley, and it was common to see whole hill-sides covered with them, tempting one to stoop down, pluck a handful, take one long draught of the delicious smell, and then fling the flowers away. The maidenhair in this neighbourhood, *Adiantum pedatum*, is also very beautiful. Its delicate fronds radiate in a circle from the top of a slender stalk in the likeness of a shallow cup. Farther on, we came upon masses of sweet yellow day-lilies, which the Jesuit Fathers remarked upon nearly two hundred years ago, as of a beautiful colour and mightily esteemed. Besides, we found great crimson cyprepediums, wood anemones, sweet syringas, and familiar flowers like dog-violets and marsh-marigolds. Beautiful mandarin ducks haunted every pool and stream, and from the mountain tops the cock-pheasant's crow was heard on all sides.

At Yungling we bought a fresh mule and a pony, for from the first day we had given up our riding mules to relieve those which were overloaded. We then went on again between hills covered with wood, the country becoming more beautiful at every turn. Thirteen miles from Shingking, we passed Hsin-min-pu, a market town now rising into importance, which has been formed within the last twelve years. Before that the district had been the resort of brigands, and our sergeant, who had been employed in hunting them down, described how two hundred of them had been hemmed in, and shot in this very valley. We followed the Su-tzu Ho to its source in the hills, crossed the watershed about 2,000 feet above the sea, and on the ninth day after leaving Moukden we arrived at T'ung-hua-hsien, the seat of a resident magistrate, 160 or 170 miles from Moukden. It is but a small place, with one or two inns and a few shops, and scarcely contains more than 2,000 inhabitants. A lofty stone wall has been built round the town, which is charmingly situated on the Hun-chiang, a large tributary of the Yalu, flowing due south. But the site is a bad one, as only a year before the river overflowed, washed down great pieces of the wall, and filled the public offices with mud. Here we did our best to get more beasts of burden, and eventually we invested in three ponies and a mule, but our purchases were not on the whole satisfactory. The mule turned out to be blind and also vicious; at critical points on the edge of a precipice he would amuse himself by kicking off his load, and we all felt relieved when one day he suddenly refused to go on, and a few hours afterwards died. The ponies did well for a few days, but one after the other they developed the most frightful ulcers on the withers and became quite useless; from which it will be perceived that the Chinese horse-dealer got the better of us. We reduced our baggage, and sent back a cartload to Moukden (where it never arrived, by the way). We also substituted wicker-work panniers for various heavy boxes, and at last got the loads down to a reasonable weight. But we had started too late. At T'ung-hua-hsien the rains began, and continued for three months almost without cessation. To begin with, the Hun-chiang came down in flood, rising ten feet in a few hours, and we were detained by it more than a week. Whenever it cleared we went out to pick up a duck or a teal, and one day found a poor drowned Chinaman, whom it was nobody's business to take and bury. We called on the magistrate, a mandarin with a clear crystal button on his hat, a jade ring on his finger, and wearing a beautiful jade rosary, called ch'ao-chu, a thing said to have been worn by officials ever since the Dalai Lama brought one, made of golden beads, as a present to the Emperor Shunchih. He was civil spoken, but uncivilly did not return our call. Another day we went to see some gold-diggings, but they had been stopped in consequence of the diggers quarrelling. There was said to be a silver-mine in the neighbourhood, but we could not get so far. It was a sight to watch the great rafts of timber come floating down the Hun-chiang. The logs, after being cut, are pitched into the nearest ravine, and left there till the flood comes. Then they are caught at suitable points in the main channel, formed into rafts and steered down to the sea. The principal wood-yards are at Ta-tung-k'ou, at the mouth of the Yalu, where in summer upwards of 40,000 raftsmen are said to collect, and the timber covers a stretch of ground two and a half miles long by half a mile deep. We saw some enormous trees coming down, quite four feet in diameter, all cut into logs of one uniform length of fifteen feet. Almost the whole of China now sends to Ta-tung-k'ou for wood.

When the Hun-chiang fell sufficiently to allow a raft ferry to ply (for we had left bridges behind at Moukden), we crossed it and then followed a difficult path up a feeder of the Hun, amidst more glorious scenery, to avoid crossing the main river again. But we were once more brought up by an impassable stream, which kept us four days in a miserable roadside inn, in a valley called Lo-chuan-k'ou. As this was a fair specimen of the lodging we got in many places, I will try and describe it. Imagine a little thatched house about forty feet long, the roof open to the rafters and the windows only bare frames, the paper panes having disappeared. The door is in the centre, and a k'ang, as

INTERIOR OF AN INN.

usual, runs along the wall, covered with dirty matting, on which are piled rolls of foul old bedding, sheepskin coats, wadded cotton garments, pedlars' packs, and tra-vellers' gear of all kinds, while a dozen or two of the roughest labourers and farmers are squatting about, or eating or drinking or sleeping. On each side of the door as you enter is a cauldron, in which vast masses

of pork, soup, and vegetables are being cooked for travellers, and the pungent savour of these, mingled with
stale tobacco fumes, incessantly pervades the building;
for everyone smokes, from the old woman of seventy
to the boy or girl of ten. In the middle of the room
stands a primitive kitchen range, an oblong mass of
brick, about three feet high, hollow in the centre, with
an arched cover in which holes have been pierced for the
fire to heat the cooking-pots. In one corner stands the
large stone mill for grinding bean-curd, and in others
huge earthen jars, or watertight wooden boxes, in which
pickled cabbages and turnips are kept, and which emit
a horrible smell. The end of the building is boarded
off, so as to form a little room about eighteen feet by
ten, which is usually occupied by the landlord's family,
but on this occasion has been made over to us. One
side of it is occupied by a k'ang, which we use like the
Chinese, both for sitting, eating, and sleeping. (I can
assure my readers that one soon gets accustomed to tuck-
ing up one's legs like a tailor and eating one's meals so.
It is far more comfortable than reclining, as the ancient
Romans did—*crede experto.*) Various old chests, earthenware pots, rough boxes and shelves protect the household goods. Facing the door hangs a rude picture
of the God of Wealth, on one side of him a black
fiend and on the other a white angel, typical, it may be,
of the good and bad uses of money.[1] This picture is
flanked by two strips of red paper, bearing the legends,
'He who honours his father and mother is sure to grow

[1] The left hand in China is the seat of honour. The figure on the right
of the God of Wealth is the black-faced Hsi-yang Hui-tzŭ, the 'Western
Mahommedan'; in his hands he holds a vessel which magically converts
anything put into it into the precious metal—gold or silver—desired by the
person casting in. The left-hand pleasant personage is honorary only, as
far as I can ascertain. (Ross *in epist.*)

rich,' and ' He who cherishes his sons and grandsons is sure to grow rich.' The reader will notice that the growing rich is the main object of exertion to a China-man, as it is to the typical American, and no inn is ever found without a tablet to the God of Wealth. Below the picture is a table used as a sort of altar, on which stand a coarse iron incense burner, two pewter vases for flowers, and two pewter candlesticks. The most gorgeous temple has not a more complete paraphernalia for worship than this.

To return to our room. Ornamenting another wall are two coarse daubs. One represents two boys worship-ping a cash, as the symbol of wealth, and the other a confused battle-scene. The rafters and beams are black with the dirt of ages, and suspended from them dangle old bits of harness, sheepskins, baskets, and farming im-plements. The earthen floor is damp and full of holes. In the far corner stands the grindstone, on which a dirty youth periodically sharpens a knife to chop up millet stalks for the mules, and next to it is the flue of a disused cauldron, which has evidently done duty for some months as the receptacle for the sweepings of the floor. The landlord's family consists of an old grand-mother with a deep bass voice, who makes the beds and looks after the little ones. Every morning she comes in with her flock, carrying the family bedding, and we help her to stow it away on the top of the boxes. In the evening she comes for it again. The wife is the inn cook. We lie on the k'ang wearily reading,[1] listening to the rain and wishing it would cease. Occasionally a small child peeps in with an eye to a lollipop, or a

---

[1] Amongst other things, Fulford brought a quantity of old *Chambers's Journals*, which proved of incomparable value. Each number was a library in itself.

couple of ploughmen who have heard of the strangers' arrival come slouching in to look at us, for the meanest Chinaman needs no introduction to a 'foreign devil.' They gaze at us curiously and stolidly for a time; then one of them turns to his friend, bursts into a loud laugh as much as to say, 'Did you ever see such odd-looking brutes?' spits on the floor, and out they go again. Occasionally one of us would make an expedition through the slush and mud as far as the stream close by, to see if the water was falling; and so we spent our days, for the rain had caught us and we must wait for it to stop. It was just a little monotonous.

But when it cleared up we had delightful walks into forests and mountains, up charming wooded valleys and across grassy glades, dotted with oaks like an English park. I got half-a-dozen fresh kinds of ferns, and every day we came upon new flowers. The lilies especially were exquisite. On the cliffs grew a delicate crimson turncap, in the brakes a great cup-shaped tiger-lily, and the hill-sides were spangled with yellow day-lilies, and another kind, small and scarlet. There was a clematis, too, covered with masses of white star-shaped flowers exquisitely sweet. Fulford, who was the great shot of the party, got a beautiful and rare kingfisher and some hill partridges. Then the pheasants gave us sport. A cock-bird would crow on a hill-side, perhaps 600 feet above us, and then we would toil patiently up through the long wet grass, listening for the cry and putting Rattler on the scent. The moment the cock found we were after him he would make for the top of the hill like lightning. Rattler would follow almost as fast, while the guns came panting in the rear, generally just in time to see the bird dropping into the ravine below. But if ever we were in time to catch him, great was the rejoicing, for he made no mean addition to our larder. One day Fulford had a nasty accident. Threading his way along a deer-path in a forest, he stumbled on to a pitfall twelve feet deep, which had been set for deer, and instantly crashed down through it. Luckily it was so narrow that he could check his fall with his elbows, or he might have hurt himself seriously. The pit was so admirably concealed with leaves and twigs, no one could detect it. In this neighbourhood were some very primitive coal-mines. The entrance opened on to a very steep stair, the roof of which was supported by rotting stakes and brushwood, but all was so wet and grimy, we did not feel inclined to explore. A mining engineer who surveyed a coal-field near Moukden says the Liao-tung coal is equal to the best Cardiff. The pit-shaft is dug at an angle of forty-five degrees to a depth of about 500 feet, and the load, which is packed in two baskets, attached to the ends of a short carrying pole, weighs from seventy to ninety pounds. A strong man will do thirty trips a day. Close by the pit was an iron foundry, where they were making simple castings in moulds of sand. The furnace was a mere shell of clay, and was kept in blast by a gigantic pair of bellows, which four men kept going with a treadle.

When the rivers fell we started again and began with another accident. Our path led between the precipitous edge of a river on one side and an impassable bog on the other. Picking our way along, a mule tumbled into the river, knocking one of the men into the stream and hurting him somewhat badly. The pack was saved, but all Fulford's tobacco and some gunpowder was spoiled. Constantly deep streams had to be forded, causing us serious delay. The muleteers behaved well, stripping themselves naked, and taking the packs across on the strongest mules, one or two at a time. To avoid the rivers, we climbed a range called the Lao-yeh Ling, going up through forests to an elevation of 2,800 feet, to find that the road on the other side was only but the bed of a mountain torrent. It was really hard going; the mules tumbled occasionally, and one of them twice plunged all our guns into the river. But this was not surprising, considering the roughness of the stony bottom and the force of the water. We started at daylight, halted for two hours or so at mid-day to bait men and beasts, and then went on till night-fall, and thankful were we if we got out of the forest to a place of shelter before dark. At last we reached the Yalu, or Ai-chiang, a noble stream about 350 yards broad. The path along the bank was so narrow in many places that our packs could not pass and we had to hack away the rock and widen it. One very hot day the convoy had been waiting for some time while the road was being made practicable, till one of the mules which carried our silver got tired of waiting, plunged into the Yalu, and swam out into the stream. Luckily it swam back to the side and the pack fell off in about three feet of water. A little farther out, and 60*l*. worth of silver, and other baggage besides, would have been irre-trievably lost. Another day, descending a precipitous mountain side, we found the path broken away for some distance. What remained was only a foot broad and very crumbling, with a drop of some hundreds of feet below. However, the mules got safely across, though the blind one kindly tried to commit suicide by kicking up its heels in the middle. Once we had an alarm that Corean thieves were coming from beyond the Yalu to rob us, but it proved to be false, though

when we arose in the morning we found we had really
had unpleasant neighbours close to us, for two snakes
had left their skins, one of them quite five feet long,
in the k'ang chimney. Eventually we got to Mao-
erh-shan (literally, Hat Hill, from the conical top of a
mountain close by; it is a common name for a hill in
Manchuria). Mao-erh-shan is the last Chinese outpost
on the Yalu, about 280 miles from Moukden. There is
a small garrison of 200 men in a good walled enclosure,
besides a yamen and a few farmsteads. Here we expected to get supplies, but hardly any were procurable,
and we were reduced to Chinese pork and salted eggs,
neither of them attractive food.

The scenery around Mao-erh-shan is grand. Innumerable forest-clad hills rise one behind the other,
and in one direction the horizon is bounded by a dark
range so long and so level that one might fancy a
coach and four could be galloped along the tree-tops
for a week. The Yalu itself, a splendid stream, comes
sweeping round a bluff in a majestic curve, and on the
opposite side are the plains and hills of Corea, one
peak being crowned with a fort, resembling a Mahratta
' garh.' Numbers of Coreans have crossed the forbidden boundary, and cultivate the valleys with the
connivance of the mandarins. They are famous fishermen. A great many are Christians, and one of them
showed us a book which had been given him by a
missionary. In 1882 some of the Gospels translated
into Corean by Mr. Ross got into the hands of one of
them, who was baptized and returned to make known
the glad tidings to his fellow-colonists. The news he
brought kindled a flame which spread from house to
house and valley to valley. And when Messrs. Ross and
Webster visited them they saw their way to baptizing

R

eighty. Not the least hopeful feature in connection
with this movement is that it takes its stand on the
platform of self-support. The Coreans build their own
churches and support their own ordinances. Corean
houses are arranged after the fashion of Chinese, except
that they have no k'ang, or rather the whole floor is one
extensive k'ang, elevated about a foot above the ground,
and warmed by underground flues. It is an improvement on the Chinese arrangement.

In this region we became first acquainted with Corean oxen and horses. The first are gigantic animals.
Spanish bulls are huge, and so are buffaloes and Indian
bison, but for weight and strength and massiveness the
Corean beasts take the palm. Not even the celebrated
Amrut Mehal oxen in Mysore, the breed once renowned
for dragging artillery, can equal them. The horses,
on the other hand, are diminutive creatures, no bigger
than a large dog. They are much valued for their
strength and usefulness, and are very cheap to buy.
They are not in the least like the weakly miniature
ponies bred in India and England to carry children,
but are stout, well-made, spirited little beasts. The
worst point about them is that they are generally
vicious.

About this time we began to experience the greatest
plague of Manchuria, one to which former writers have
alluded—I mean the midges and gadflies. The misery
caused by insect pests is a stock theme with travellers,
too common perhaps to call for sympathy. And yet if
there be a time when life is not worth living, I should
say it was summer in the forests of Manchuria. The
midges are worst at night and in the early morning,
though they by no means object to the middle of the
day also. They come out in countless millions, and bite

like fiends. Mules and cattle are picketed at night to the leeward of fires, so that the smoke may protect them. At sundown all the doors and the windows of houses are shut tight, though the smoke and summer heat are stifling. Often a fire must be kindled on the floor, to fill the house with smoke, and, when it is filled full with Chinamen also, the atmosphere in the early morning can be better imagined than described. Men at the plough wear circlets of iron on their heads, on which are stuck bits of burning touchwood, and they carry pieces of it in their hands as well. Fortunately we had provided ourselves with green gauze veils, which were invaluable when we went to bed or when marching in the early morning, and at meals we enveloped ourselves with smoke. The gadflies were less annoying to ourselves than to our beasts, as they invariably selected any that were sick or tired. They did not appear till seven or eight in the morning, and retired at sundown; so, by marching before daylight, a little respite was obtained from their attacks. They were huge fat insects, and at this distance of time they seem to me to have been as big as stag-beetles. There are several kinds—one striped yellow and black, like a giant wasp—and the rapidity with which they can pierce a mule's tough hide is inconceivable. In a few moments, before one could go to its assistance, I have seen a wretched beast streaming with blood. Fortunately the gadflies are very stupid and slow, and easily killed. Once, when a mule had tumbled several times down hill, and was quite exhausted, Fulford and I had to stand over it, smashing the gadflies as they settled with slabs of wood, until night came on. I have no idea how many hundreds we killed, but we saved that mule's life. They did not often bite men, but occasionally a gadfly would try how a ' foreign devil's ' blood tasted, and then that ' foreign devil' jumped and made remarks.

I have mentioned once or twice that a mule's pack came off: the reason is that the pack is not tied to the animal, which is really a great advantage. In fact, I believe the Chinese system of loading mules is the best in the world. A frame is made of two pieces of tough wood, like a couple of boomerangs, which are bent into shape when green, then thoroughly seasoned and fastened together by cross-pieces. In appearance the frame is like the letter ' A,' with the apex rounded and the crossbar removed, the curved portion at the top fitting into the saddle and the legs hanging down on each side. It is, however, quite separate from the saddle, which is of wood also, with ridges along the edge both in front and behind. The load is first divided very accurately into two parts of exactly equal weight, and then tied on to either side of the frame very firmly, as a loosely-made pack galls the animal. Two men then catch hold of the frame by its feet, hoist it into the air, and drop it over the saddle, where, as it balances perfectly, it remains in position by its own weight. Then, when the convoy arrives at the half-way house and the beasts are to be fed, the whole lot of frames and packs can be lifted off the saddles in less than a minute, without untying one, and they can be replaced as quickly when the march is recommenced. Suppose a mule sticks in a bog; his burden falls off or is lifted off him in a trice, and it is put on again as soon as he has struggled to his feet. One disadvantage with packs certainly is that every evening the loads containing bedding, cooking-pots, and similar things must be untied, and done up again next morning, thus wasting time; but by utilising open panniers for small things we saved having to undo more than three or four packs at once.

Our mules looked a sorry lot when we started, but they improved on acquaintance. Younghusband's veterinary skill soon relieved their galls, and the cure of one enormous abscess was a real triumph of surgery. When not overloaded, the beasts worked right well. The leader was a splendid fellow, very big and strong, and as clever on his feet as a cat. He had a bell round his neck, and, when that stopped, we in the rear knew something was wrong ahead—a bad bit of bog, a steep crag, or an unfordable river. One of the best mules we surnamed the Lunatic, as he had a habit of turning sharply round and gazing wildly at his fellows in the rear, thus stopping the whole procession ; and if a halt was called and he got tired of waiting, he would commence charging about amongst the others, making the boxes of ammunition he carried resound again upon their flanks, and ending by knocking one or two of them down the hill. He liked doing this in specially tight places, when the others only wanted leave to hang on quietly by their eyelids. The beast that started on three legs became one of the best towards the end, while a good grey one gave in entirely and had to be led along empty. As long as we were in the hills, we kept down the packs as nearly as we could to 150 lbs., but along reasonably good tracks a mule will carry patiently 350 lbs. for twelve hours every day. Their masters fed them well with plenty of small millet-straw chopped fine, mixed with kaoliang (the large millet seed), and they flourished. After a hard day's work over marsh and moor they would be quite frisky, when, to all appearance, there was not a kick left in any one of them.

Our manner of life while the mule-men ruled us was regular and simple. We were up at dawn and had a cup of tea. Then the bedding packs were made up, which always took time, and by seven we were off and marched till eleven or twelve. Then after lunch we went on till nightfall. Fulford, being long of limb and fleet of foot, used generally to precede the cavalcade, and when he found any difficulty he called a council of war. A boy guided the old leader, alongside of whom walked a man with an axe to clear away trees and brush-wood. I followed half-way down the caravan, carrying my gun, but Fulford generally shot what there was, so my chief amusement was collecting plants. Younghusband brought up the rear, taking sights with his compass and heights with his aneroid, and seeing that no one lagged. When we came to really bad bits, we had all to bestir ourselves mending or clearing the track, lift-ing packs off and on, leading mules over delicate places, or catching them when they strayed off the path. In the evening we made a point of dining as soon as the cook allowed us. The meal was a frugal one—a plate-ful of preserved soup, some roast game and potatoes, and perhaps a pancake or plain rice pudding, made without milk or eggs, as such luxuries were not to be had; and when that was over, one of us read prayers and we went to bed *instanter*.

CHAPTER VIII

CH'ANG-PAI-SHAN MOUNTAINS.

Progress up the Yalu Valley impossible—Pack-road to Hun-ch'un—Gold-washers—Fording the T'ang Ho—Camping-out in the forest—A tiger-trap—An obstruction in the road—Difficult situation—Arrival at the head-quarters of a guild—Admission refused—The midges—An account of the guilds—Legislation—Gathering opium—The Old White Mountain—Fording a mountain torrent—A Manchu fisherman—Fulford meets a bear—Preparations for the sable season—A sable-trap—Deer-trap—Mushrooms—Source of the Sungari—Ascent of the White Mountain—The scenery—Flowers—The lake—The Erh-tao-chiang—The neighbourhood—Another route to Hun-ch'un—Du Halde's account of the White Mountain—The Jesuits' visit—Oumoune—Palladius' account—The Emperor Kienlung's—Père Amyot's—Botanical results—Birds—Butterflies.

THE affluents of the Upper Yalu, above the point where it makes its great bend to the south, are known by numbers—First, Second, Third, &c. Mao-erh-shan is situated between Number One and Number Two, and we were disappointed to find that progress up the main valley was impossible beyond this point. The river flows at the foot of precipitous hills, and, except for pedestrians, communication with the upper valleys is only practicable in winter, when the frozen river itself is the highway. We learnt, however, that a pack-road existed to Hun-ch'un, crossing the Lao-ling, as the ridge is called which divides the Yalu from the head waters of the Sungari, and striking the Tumen near its mouth,[1]

[1] For the benefit of future travellers I give the details as related to us by an old and possibly not very accurate man. Cross the Lao-ling, descend the T'ang River to T'ang-ho-k'ou, cross the Sungari, go down to the Sung-chiang, a tributary of the Sungari, thence to Ta-sha Ho, two days'

so we determined to try and reach Hun-ch'un by that
way. Accordingly we turned up the Erh-tao Ho, or
second river, crossing and re-crossing it till we got
tired, and in less than two days reached the top of the
range. The pass was 3,000 feet high. On the way
we met a number of people gold washing, or rather
we saw their works, for they heard our shots at
partridges and levanted, thinking we were soldiers
come to arrest them. On the highest point of the
Lao-ling is a small temple with a monument, and an
inscription praising the greatness and beauty of the
pass. We then descended through thick forests to a
farm-house beautifully situated in a clearing on the
banks of the T'ang Ho, a fine tributary of the Sungari.
Next day we forded this river several times till, the
water becoming too deep, we had to climb the hills
again. It was at this stage that the blind mule gave
in and had to be left behind, and next day it was found
dead. We also here enjoyed our first experience of
camping-out in a Chinese wood; and a thunderstorm
came on which made it moist and unpleasant, though
waterproof sheets between our bedding and the ground
protected us from the wet. We came across a party
of hunters in search of newly sprouted deer-horns,
which, as I have said before, are highly esteemed
amongst the Chinese for their supposed medicinal

journey, for which a guide will be needed. At Tasha Ho the road gets
better. Thence to Kusung Ho, then Si-nan-cha, over a range; then Hung-
chi Ho, where a cart-track begins; then to Erh-tao Ho, Yang-chi-kang,
Mata-kang, San-chia Ho, Mi-chiang, and Hun-ch'un. The distance is about
1,000 li, or 333 miles. We followed this route as far as the Sung-
chiang, but the rivers beyond were said to be impassable during the rains,
so we went on to Kirin instead. Later in the year I passed Mi-chiang and
Yang-chi-kang on the way to Omoso from Hun-ch'un. There are also
paths leading direct to T'ang-ho-k'ou from Hsin-min-pu and T'ung-hua-
hsien. (See also page 264.)

properties. They are only to be got at their best during a few weeks in the spring, so large parties are formed to hunt them. We also saw the fresh tracks of a tigress, and not far distant was a tiger-trap, a huge wooden cage baited with a pig. But the jungle was far too thick and extensive, and settlers too sparsely scattered and independent, for any idea of tiger shooting; we might have spent a month and not marked down one.

After two more days the path descended again to the T'ang Ho, which we crossed in a dug-out. The stream then became broader and more shallow, and we commenced fording it once more; and, though at one place the water was terribly swift and deep, and an accident seemed inevitable, we got safely over. We were pressing on for the point where it joins the Sungari, when it commenced raining heavily. Fearing lest the water should rise and cut us off, we pushed on after dusk, contrary to our usual rule, and just as the light failed we got over the last ford. We were then, as we found afterwards, barely a mile from our destination, but it took us a long time to get there. The path led into a narrow wooded gorge, skirting the very brink of the river, the water below us on one side, a precipitous hill on the other, and deep gloomy trees overhead. The sky was overcast, and we could not see a yard before us. We groped our way along in front of the mules till we were suddenly brought up by a rock three feet high in the middle of the path—in the dark it seemed double that height. To return or go forward seemed alike impossible, for the path was too narrow for the mules to turn, and it looked like staying there till morning, with the midges biting, thunder roaring and the rain falling,

and the tired mules ready to drop themselves and their
burdens into the river below.   We had also a suspicion
that our guide did not know the road.   However, one
of our men went on, and found the path did continue
along the river, so the mules were forced over the
obstacle (I never knew how they managed it in the
dark), and eventually, with only one pack missing, we
arrived at our destination—a large house in a yard,
surrounded by lofty palings.   It was then nearly midnight, and the great gate was shut.   We knocked
loudly, but to our dismay the inmates refused to open.
We spoke civilly and showed our passports, but all in
vain.   'Rules were rules,' and they would not open
their gates after dusk for the Emperor himself.   We
might possibly have forced our way in, but we thought
it better not.   So we pitched the tent, while the servants sheltered themselves under the high lichgate, if
I may apply that term to the shed which is built over
the entrance-gates of farms and inns.   There was a
noble mountain of firewood close by, so we soon had a
great blaze kindled and drove away the midges, which
were thick to suffocation, and about one in the morning
we got to bed.   The missing pack was found not very
far off, and thus all ended well.   But the midges that
night beggared all description, and we resolved never
to travel after dark in the hills again.

The place we found ourselves in was the head-
quarters of a guild, situated fairly within the precincts
of the Long White Mountains.   In theory these mountains are supposed to be sacred to the ancestors of the
reigning dynasty, and it is sacrilege to trespass in them.
Only a little while ago the official 'Peking Gazette' published a report from the Governor of Kirin, that in obedience to standing orders he had carefully searched all

the glens in the mountains to see if any wicked people were seeking for ginseng, and he had found the country quite quiet and free from intruders. And another imperial edict, in disposing of a Chinaman's petition to be allowed to cultivate certain land which the authorities reported to be within the limits of the Imperial Hunting Park, directed the presumptuous applicant to be severely punished.[1] As a matter of fact, the mandarins never dream of going into the mountains, and settlements are being founded rapidly. Some cultivate the land, or seek gold and ginseng in the ravines; others cut down timber, which is floated down the Sungari or the Yalu, or else live by the chase, hunting sables, squirrels, tigers, and deer.

The colonists form themselves into associations or guilds, with presidents, vice-presidents, and councils, who legislate for the community, and exercise powers of life and death. The existence of these guilds is known to the authorities of Kirin, who occasionally call on them, and not unsuccessfully, for assistance in hunting robbers. On such occasions the headman of the guild sends a circular round, and a hunter told us that, even if a man had got a deer in every pit, he must shoulder his matchlock and go; yet theoretically, as I have said, they have no existence before the law. Of course, as there are no mandarins, there is no taxation, except what the settlers impose upon themselves. Some items in their legislation are peculiar, but practical. We saw one proclamation warning people not to harbour certain bad characters, whose names were

---

[1] The Emperor Kanghi had a fence put up on the right-hand side of the road between Moukden and Kirin, not far from Ye-ho, to mark that all the mountainous country beyond was sacred, and reserved for imperial use. The tract immediately adjoining that fence is still called the Imperial Hunting Park, and it is so marked on the Chinese map.

given. A second forbade Coreans to fish. The Coreans,
be it noted, are employed in large numbers as agricultural labourers by the settlers, who want them, so they
said, to labour in the fields, and not waste their time in
sport. A third was for regulating the trade in ginseng,
and forbade any person buying or selling it before a
certain date. The penalty for transgression of that law
was, in the case of a rich person, a fine to the guild of

A COREAN FISHERMAN.

one pound of rice (a luxury in the hills), ten taels in
money, and two pigs weighing at least seventy-five
pounds each. If the offender were an outsider, and
therefore moneyless and unable to pay the fine, he was
to be beaten to death with sticks. This law was for the
protection of zealous ginseng seekers, who sought the
more remote valleys, and occasionally found the market
forestalled by less venturesome hunters returning before
the season was fairly over. The guilds are most efficient

institutions, and the only place within Manchuria where life and property may be said to be really secure is within their limits; although, from the configuration of the country, and the vast area of forests with which it is covered, robbers would, under ordinary circumstances, find there a safe refuge. In fact, it is a boast of the settlers that, even if a man drops a knife or a handkerchief, he is perfectly sure of getting it back again. The members collect at head-quarters in the winter, when their huts or homesteads are snowed up, to pass the time and discuss regulations for the public weal. The guild-house has, therefore, extensive accommodation, and it also serves as a store for supplies of grain and groceries, which are brought during winter along the frozen Sungari on sledges from Kirin. Till quite recently these little republics were looked on as dangerous, and the head of the guild next to T'ang-ho-k'ou was proclaimed at Kirin as an outlaw. A Governor, however, of more sense than usual sent an emissary in disguise to find out the real state of the case. His report was so favourable that the Governor invited the outlaw to Kirin; and he went there, leaving the spy as a hostage. He half expected his head would be taken off, but he was well treated, presents were made him, and he was told to go back and behave himself. No Peking official would dare penetrate to these remote valleys, or the Governor might get into serious trouble for his lenity; for, as I have said, the fiction of the region being sacred is still kept up at Court.

The T'ang-ho-k'ou guild-house is situated in a charming little sheltered nook in the hills, just at the junction of the Tang with the Sungari (or Sung-hua-chiang, i.e. 'Pine-flower River,' by which name it is locally known).

At this point the Sungari is a fine stream about two hundred yards broad. Behind the guild-house is a densely-clad hill, which keeps off the wind, and surrounding it is a fine farm which the president cultivates. The guild now numbers a thousand members, and all along the T'ang Valley a vast area of forest is in process of reclamation, chiefly by Corean labour. The beans that are grown, especially the French beans, were very fine; and a few acres were under poppies for home consumption. The juice is not extracted so scientifically as in India, the cuts in the poppy-head being made irregularly and the juice wiped off within five minutes of the incision instead of being allowed to exude and cake. The president of the guild was not at home, but the vice-president was—a lean, sour-faced old man, called Yen. He did not express the least regret at keeping us out in the rain, simply remarking that his rule was framed to exclude brigands. When the gate opened in the morning, he let us in and gave us a good apartment.

It was now time to search for the snowy peaks, which, as we understood from the map attached to the Rev. Alexander Williamson's book, 'Journeys in North China,' from Mr. Ravenstein and other sources, must be in the neighbourhood—snowy peaks from 10,000 to 12,000 feet high. Alas! Mr. Yen told us that there was not such a thing in Manchuria. There was, however, he said, one very celebrated mountain, the Lao-pai-shan, or Old White Mountain proper, about ten or twelve days' march off, from the top of which sprang the Yalu, the Tumen, and the Sungari. If we liked he could guide us there, but the road was very difficult to find, and he must come himself. We accepted his offer, loaded two mules very lightly and started, taking only one servant with us, and a boy to lead the mules over the bad bits. The path took us over mountain after mountain, through a dreary succession of gloomy swampy forests of giant oak, elm, pine, walnut, and plane, with dense thickets beneath, the home of the stag and the wild boar. In the evenings we would come to a small clearing with a hut, where ginseng was being· cultivated, and there we stayed for the night. Though we had brought the two strongest mules in our team, it was almost too much for them. They were constantly getting bogged, and it took us all we knew to extricate them. One of them was a timid brute that would make no attempt to help himself. Once he had to climb rather a nasty place, and, finding he could not manage it, gave up all for lost, tumbled over backwards, and rolled like a log to the bottom of the ravine ; and, even when his load was taken off and carried piecemeal, we had almost to carry him up. We had to wade the Sungari once, and painful it was with our bare feet; and then came a mountain torrent called the Shíh-t'ou Ho, or Stony River, which was worse. It was very rough and swift, like a nullah in Cashmere, while the stones had singularly sharp edges. In crossing it, Fulford stumbled and dropped his gun into the water, and Younghusband fell outright, cutting his hand severely. When we returned some days later, the stream was higher and more dangerous, and, but for Fulford's timely interposition, one of the mule-boys would have been swept away and drowned.

On the fifth day we reached a river called the Hei Ho, or Black River, and here we had to give up the mules altogether, as the bog beyond (the first place where we found larch-trees growing) was absolutely impassable for any beast of burden whatever. (We were told later on that a practicable pack-road did exist up another valley, but, as there were no huts along it, our guide did not take us that way.) We reduced our necessaries as much as possible, and the rest we made up into packs which we carried ourselves, with the aid of a hunter named Shih Tê-shêng, a very good fellow, who volunteered to come and help us. Old Yen himself did not feel equal to going any farther. As we had seen no chance of shooting large game, never doing more than catch a glimpse of a deer cross- ing the path, the one rifle we had brought so far was amongst the things now left behind; the natural result was that we missed getting a couple of bears. In the marshes a kind of dwarf bog-myrtle, with pretty white flowers, grew abundantly. Every year a quantity of it is gathered and taken down to a mandarin who is specially sent from Kirin for it, and it is forwarded to Peking to be made into incense for the use of the Emperor himself in sacrificing. But the mandarin, though supposed to gather it himself, durst not come within two hundred miles of the marshes where the plant is found. We stopped at nights in tiny little huts which the hunters have built on the banks of mountain streams. So tight a fit was it that we were obliged occasionally to lie head and tail on the k'ang, waking up to find a Chinaman's foot in one's eye. At the first hut there was a very jovial fellow, a Manchu, who gave us some fresh venison, and then, asking if we liked fish, volunteered to catch us some. He had a bamboo rod without a reel, a thick silk line, and a great coarse hook big enough to hold a salmon, to which he tied a tuft of deer's hair, converting it into a most ragged and primitive-looking fly. But in half-an-hour he was back with three first-rate trout, none of them less than a pound. We tried our hands with the rod, but the midges soon drove us in again. One day we came on a place where there were numerous droppings of bears, and a terrible smell withal. We halted for a rest, and Fulford and the guide were looking about when they ran right upon a bear, which was worrying away at the remains of a splendid stag. Fulford called out, and Younghusband and I ran up, putting swan-shot, the largest we had, into our guns; but by that time the bear had vanished. However, the guide got the antlers and feet and sinews of the stag, which he said would fetch a few taels. Fulford came upon another bear a few days later, so they are pretty common. The hunters complain they do a great deal of damage by pulling out deer from their pit-falls. We were shown a pair of soft horns that might have been worth 50*l.*, but which a bear had chewed till only about 3*l.* or 4*l.* worth was left. The hunters kill the bears when they can get them, but in this region the tiger is spared.

The everlasting tramping through the woods was a little tiresome, but we got new flowers and some very good birds. Here and there were large beds of wild strawberries, and a delicious purple barberry growing in vast quantities on bushes about four feet high. There were also wild gooseberries and currants, but they were good for nothing. A plant which I took for wild rhubarb afterwards proved, on examination at Kew, to be an entirely new species of saxifrage, with gigantic peltate leaves, which has been named *Saxifraga tabularis.* Many of the names of the places were Corean, and, in fact, the Chinese owned that, twenty years before, the ground was occupied by

s

Corean hunters, who drove them off till they were strong enough to reverse matters and chase the Coreans into their own territory, though not without the sacrifice of many lives. Mr. Carles, in his recent journey through North Corea,[1] found that the region was well known to Coreans, who call it the White Mountain, Paik-to-san.

The preparations for the sable season were just commencing. When the snow is on the ground, the sable, which is only the eastern variety of the British marten, likes travelling along the trunks of dead trees to keep its feet dry. So the hunters choose a fallen tree—they fell timber for the purpose—and drive two parallel rows of sharp pegs along the top, a few inches apart, forming a kind of little avenue for the sable to pass along. In the middle is placed an ordinary figure-of-four trap, above which a long sapling is suspended, which falls and crushes the animal. The hunters did not like to say much about their captures; but one of them told us that he and two friends had a thousand sable-traps and sixty deer-pits, and the take of one season came to only ninety sables and one deer with soft horns. One cruel but ingenious way of catching deer is to bury in their tracks a heavy circlet of iron, with spikes a couple of inches long pointing inwards, and forming an inner circle just large enough for a deer's foot to pass through. When once the wretched animal treads upon it and is caught, it can never get rid of its fetter. It drags it for a little distance through the wood, but soon sinks from terror and exhaustion, and the hunters run it down with their dogs. The sables are taken to Kirin, where the price varies from one to three taels (about 4s. 10d. to 14s. 6d.). The hunters

[1] *Proceedings R.G.S.*, May, 1880.

live comfortably on jerked venison and vegetables grown in their little gardens, and the spoils of the chase suffice to buy them flour and clothing. In one hut we were given a stew of jerked venison and cabbage, flavoured with mushrooms, and I could not wish for anything better. What I call mushrooms are a yellow fungus which grows in masses on decayed wood, and very good they are. At Hun-ch'un we found them a great article of export. This part of our journey was certainly the pleasantest. The hunters were kindly, good fellows, and unfeignedly glad to see us, very different from the ordinary Chinese or even the lonely ginseng cultivators.

At last, on the ninth day after leaving the guild, we began the ascent of the long-wished-for mountain. The lower slopes are covered with forests of birch and pine, but these gradually grew less dense, until we emerged on a delightful grassy plateau dotted with trees. It was like being transported into the Garden of Eden. The forests had certainly not been devoid of flowers, and some fine turn-cap lilies and orchids and blue-bells had lit up their gloom ; but now we came upon rich, open meadows, bright with flowers of every imaginable colour, where sheets of blue iris, great scarlet tiger-lilies, sweet-scented yellow day-lilies, huge orange buttercups, or purple monkshood delighted the eye. And beyond were bits of park-like country, with groups of spruce and fir beautifully dotted about, the soil covered with short mossy grass, and spangled with great masses of deep-blue gentian, columbines of every shade of mauve or buff, orchids white and red, and many other flowers. One gem of a meadow was sprinkled with azaleas bearing small yellow flowers, which looked at a distance like gorse.

Not that fair field
Of Enna, where Proserpine, gathering flowers,
Herself, a fairer flower, by gloomy Dis
Was gathered : which cost Ceres all that pain
To seek her through the world ; nor that sweet grove
Of Daphne by Orontes, and the inspired
Castalian spring, might with this Paradise
Of Eden strive.

Now for the first time, and up above us through the trees, we could see the ragged needle-like peaks of the Long, or Old White Mountain. As we marched along the plateau we heard the sound of streams rushing madly underground, and in one place we crossed a deep gully by a natural bridge, the banks of which approached so closely that we could almost jump across, while peering over we could see the mountain torrent roaring far below like the river Beas at its source. It would be easy for a careless walker to slip into one of these hidden water-courses and lose his life.

Finally, we arrived at a cottage called Tang-shan, at the base of a grassy hill which slopes down from the final heights of the Pai-shan. A short distance off, there are two splendid cascades, not very far apart, each about 150 feet high, one of which is called by the natives the real source of the Sungari proper. A mile or two away it forms a burn about ten yards across, on the edge of which is a fine hot-spring, 142° Fahr. The evening we arrived we climbed a hill seven hundred feet above the plateau, from which we had a grand view of the mountain. From that point there appeared in sight two sharp peaks, with a saddle between them, and the whole steep side below was shining white— not with snow, for there were only a few patches of it to be seen in clefts, but with wet disintegrated pumice-stone, large lumps of which we had noticed on the

banks of the Sungari on our road through the forests.
The westerly peak looks slightly the higher, but after
ascending the saddle we found it was lower than that
on the east, which is a splendid object—bold, sharp,
and jagged. Beyond it, farther to the east, on a rock-
broken sky line, stands another conspicuous pinnacle,
shaped like a serpent's tooth, and from this the shoulder
of the mountain slopes gradually down till it reaches
the plateau where the hut is situated.

The first day of our halt it rained, and we made the
ascent the next. We climbed the slope behind the
house, up to our waists in luxuriant wet grass, full of
tiger-lilies and other gorgeous flowers, and across a
stretch of moorland perhaps two or three miles broad,
covered with a dwarf white rhododendron, a lovely
little pink flower like an azalea, a pink heath, and other
flowers. Then we commenced the slope leading up to
the saddle. Even here, on the naked pumice, were
clumps of wild yellow poppies, dwarf saxifrage, a vetch,
and other botanical treasures. It was a steep climb,
reminding one somewhat of Vesuvius, except that the
rain had consolidated the loose pumice. At last we got
to the top and looked over the edge, and lo! at the
bottom of a crater on whose brink we were standing,
about three hundred and fifty feet below us, we saw
a beautiful lake, its colour of the deepest, most pellucid
blue, and, though the wind was howling above, its
surface as still as Lake Leman, reflecting the crown of
fantastic peaks with which the rugged top of the mountain was adorned. It was indeed a superb spectacle.
We judged the lake to be about a mile and a half
broad, and six or seven miles in circumference.

After enjoying the view for some time, Fulford
and I attempted to descend the crater. The hunter

guide refused to accompany us, partly because it was too steep, and also because no one who did get to the bottom would be allowed by the Spirit of the Lake to return. But he pointed out a place down which, he said, deer sometimes found their way to feed on the grass, of which we could see a narrow fringe in one place between the water and the base of the cliff. We succeeded in reaching about sixty feet from the bottom, through loose pumice and stones, but we were suddenly stopped by the cliff we were descending having crumbled away, leaving some fifteen or twenty feet of sheer perpendicular rock in front of us. With a rope we might have got down easily, but the descent was too risky without it, as the friable stone and the pumice it was embedded in gave no secure hold. Younghusband, in the meanwhile, had been boiling his thermometer in a cleft filled with snow, the only place where he could escape from the wind, and commenced the ascent of the eastern peak. It was very steep, and not unaccompanied with danger, as the foothold was treacherous, and, had he slipped, he might have rolled over the edge and dropped five or six hundred feet into the lake. However, he succeeded better than we did, and got up to the highest pinnacle, creeping out to the very edge of a peak of rock which projects over the lake like a bowsprit, and waving his hat to us. From below it looked as if nothing but an eagle could find a resting-place in such a position. He calculated the height to be 7,525 feet, but allowing for an error in the reading of the boiling-point thermometer, which he subsequently discovered, 500 feet must be added on to that. Even from the saddle the view of the surrounding country was very fine. Far away in Corea we could see forest-clad peaks which looked as if they might almost be as high as the Pai-shan, but all the hills in the immediate neighbourhood, including the Lao-ling— that is, the range we crossed after leaving the Yalu —seemed pigmies in comparison. So farewell to the idea of snowy peaks 10,000 or 12,000 feet high.

The lake itself is called by the hill-men Lung-Wang T'an, or the Dragon Prince's Pool, and it is sacred to the Dragon, who is the God of Rain. The Chinese account for its situation on the top of the mountain by calling it an ' eye of the sea,' an outlet through which the waters of the ocean force their way. From the north end of the lake there issues a small stream which is the source of the Erh-tao-chiang, or Second River,[1] the eastern branch of the Sungari, whose confluence with the main stream we visited a few weeks later. We would gladly have spent a week exploring this interesting neighbourhood; for the hunters said the sources of the Yalu were only ten miles from where they stood. They also told us a commissioner came not long ago from China to look for a boundary pillar erected in the fifty-first year of the Emperor Kanghi (A.D. 1712) to mark the Corean frontier, but that he could not find it for the snow. And only thirty miles beyond was the source of the Tumen, which they called the Ya-fêng. But we could not stay longer, as our

[1] The principal affluents of the Erh-tao-chiang are said by the hunters to be the Kutung (qy. Ku-sung) Ho, Ta-sha Ho, Fu-lu Ho, flowing into it from the north. On the south the first tributary is simply called T'ou Ta-pei Ho—i.e. First North River, and the rest are named in similar consecutive order. The upper affluents of the Sungari proper are, on the left bank, beginning from the south, Li-shu-k'ou-tzŭ, Erh-tao-hua-yuan, T'ou-tao-hua-yuan, Nar-hung, Mung-chiang, Sung-chiang, T'ang Ho, Shih-t'ou Ho, Hei Ho, Tu-i-pa Ho, Huapi Ho, Ti-tzŭ Ho, Wei-sha Ho. On the right bank, commencing from the confluence of the Erh-tao-chiang, the Yu-shih Ho, Wei-sha Ho, Sung-chiang. The hunters gave this catalogue of rivers to Fulford, but even they themselves did not seem quite clear as to the exact order in which each one came.

supplies were almost at an end, although some of the ginseng farmers and a hunter very kindly spared us some flour, and we had reserved a few tins of provisions for emergencies. Indeed, had it not been for Fulford's skill in shooting partridges, we should have had very little to eat. So hungry had we become, that, whenever we heard a shot fired, we used to ask if it was an old one or a young one, the old ones having more meat upon them. The birds used, when flushed, to fly up into the trees, and it required a very quick eye to distinguish them in the boughs. It seems a doubtful compliment, but Fulford certainly was a capital shot at sitting birds.

So we reluctantly determined to return to T'ang-ho-k'ou. Had we come earlier in the season, with plenty of supplies, we might, we now discovered, not only have visited the Long White Mountain and explored the frontier, but found a way out to Hung-chi Ho, which was said to be only seventy miles away, and from that point the road on to Hun-ch'un is easy. But, in addition to our other difficulties, the ice had broken up the previous winter before the guild had got proper supplies laid in ; so food was abnormally scanty, and our party was too large to justify our risking its detention for several days without food—a thing that might easily have happened had we been caught between two flooded rivers. If the next traveller starts in March from Moukden, crosses the Lao-ling to T'ang-ho-k'ou by the direct bridle-path from Hsin-min-pu or T'ung-hua-hsien, taking a month's supply of flour with him, and goes on to Hung-chi Ho either by the Ta-sha Ho route or by the White Mountain, he will make his way to Hun-ch'un easily enough between the melting of the snow and the commencement of the rains.

After our return we looked at the famous work of Père Du Halde, compiled from Jesuit accounts of China, published at Paris in 1735. We there found the following account of the White Mountain, which, it will be seen, our visit corroborates almost exactly. I quote the English translation :

The mountain from which the Sungari derives its source is likewise the most famous in Eastern Tartary. It lies much higher than the rest, and may be seen at a vast distance. One part of it is covered with wood, and consists only in a soft gravel which looks always white. Therefore it is not the snow that whitens it, as the Chinese imagine, for there never is any, at least in summer. On the top are five rocks, which look like so many broken pyramids exceeding high, and are always wet with the perpetual fogs and vapours that condense around them, and in the middle they enclose a deep lake, whence issues a fine fountain that forms the Sungari. The Manchus, to make the mountain still more wonderful, have a curious saying that it is the mother of their great rivers, the Toumen, the Yaloo Oola, and Cihou Oola,[1] which, having coasted the borders of Corea, unite and fall into the sea of that kingdom.

But this is not exactly true, as may be seen in the map, nor can the origin of the rivers be attributed to the Ch'ang-pai-shan, unless you include the neighbouring mountains that separate the kingdom of Corea from the ancient city of the Manchus.

This description is quoted from Père Regis, who, with Pères Jartoux and Fridelli, surveyed Manchuria for the Emperor Kanghi in the year 1709, and whose original report I have endeavoured to trace, but without success. I was at first inclined to think, in spite of the general accuracy of the account, it was physically impossible for the Jesuits to have seen the White Mountain itself, for they began their work in

[1] I have not been able to identify this river. Perhaps it is the Erh-tao-chiang, the second or eastern branch of the Upper Sungari.

Manchuria on May 8; they went to survey another province, Pechihli, on December 10 of the same year; they appear to have travelled together, and it is difficult to believe they could have had time in the interval, not only to visit places so widely apart as Hun-ch'un, the country north of the Amur and the river Usuri, but also to penetrate to this remote mountain. Other circumstances pointed to the same conclusion. The Jesuits call the mountain one of the highest in the world, which it certainly is not; they did not calculate its latitude and longitude (the nearest observations taken being at Fêng-whang-ch'êng, or the 'Corean Gate,' and at Hongta Hoton, or Yongta Hoton, at the bend of the Tumen, the one three hundred, and the other nearly a hundred and fifty miles away); and its position is not marked upon their map. Indeed, the map which D'Anville ultimately produced from their surveys shows the boundary of Corea, not, as they describe it and as it actually exists, following the course of the Yalu and Tumen, but considerably north of those rivers. They state also that the Emperor did not approve of their entering Corea, so an envoy was sent the next year with a mandarin of the mathematical tribunal, who surveyed the eastern and inland parts, and brought back a map made by the Coreans. Again, a writer in the 'Chinese Repository' for 1851 (vol. xx. p. 299) states positively—I do not know on what authority—that none of the Jesuits who saw the mountain ascended it. But in another place Du Halde distinctly states that the whole of the boundary between Tartary and Corea was measured geometrically, and the White Mountain is close to the frontier. The Jesuits, therefore, must have been the first foreigners to look down on the blue waters of the Lung-Wang T'an;

certainly they were the first to reveal its existence to Europe.

An interesting account of a visit paid to the White Mountain, more than thirty years before the Jesuits, by a Chinaman named Oumoune, will be found in Klaproth's 'Mémoires relatifs à l'Asie;'[1] a translation is given in the notes.[2] This narrative, it will be perceived, tallies with ours, especially as regards the agreeable meadows and flowers. Oumoune, like Père Régis, singles out five pinnacles for special mention, and characterises the mountain as being always covered with fog, so possibly Père Du Halde's account was borrowed from this source. Appended to his account will be found extracts from such very different authors as the Archimandrite Palladius, the Emperor Kienlung, and the learned Père Amyot. Any of my readers who are interested in Chinese legendary lore will learn from these that the Long White Mountain, whose solitude we have dared to violate, has enjoyed a grand mysterious fame for many centuries past. It is the scene of the miraculous birth of the progenitor of the Manchu dynasty narrated in Chap. II. And even as late as fifteen years ago, in spite of the Jesuits' specific statement to the contrary, Mr. Delmar Morgan was not satisfied whether the whiteness of the mountain was due to perpetual snow or to the greyness of limestone rock. This point has now been definitely cleared up.

During our progress through the hills we made a collection of flowers and plants, the preservation of which was a source of difficulty and anxiety, owing to the constant rain. The Director of the Royal Gardens, Kew, has kindly favoured me with the following observations upon it:

[1] Paris, 1824.   [2] Note F, p. 451.

It comprises upwards of 500 species of flowering plants, 32 ferns, and 10 lycopods and horsetails (Equisetum). Unlike the vegetation of the mountains of the Peking region and the neighbouring provinces, this specimen of the flora of Manchuria contains a very small endemic element, and less than half-a-dozen absolute novelties. Among the genera characteristic of the flora of North-eastern Asia, *Stenocœlium, Eleutherococcus, Platycodon, Glossocomia, Metaplexis, Brachybotrys, Siphonostegia,* and *Funkia* are represented; but with few other exceptions the genera are dispersed all round the north temperate zone, and many of these have a very much wider range. In short, it is a part of the same floral region to which the British Islands belong, and no fewer than 160 of the species collected, or nearly a third of the total, are identical with the species inhabiting these islands. These species are almost all herbs or very dwarf alpine shrubs. As in temperate Northeastern Asia generally, the proportion of arboreous and shrubby species to herbaceous species is relatively high. They include three limes, six maples, one pear, one mountain ash, one cherry, one bird-cherry, two thorns, one elder, one dogwood, one ash, five conifers, three willows, two poplars, two hazels, and one oak.

The predominant natural orders are:—Compositæ, 65 species; Rosaceæ, 30 species; Liliaceæ, 28 species; Ranunculaceæ, 27 species; and Leguminosæ, 20 species; and conspicuous genera are *Aquilegia* (columbine), *Pœonia, Dianthus, Potentilla, Lathyrus, Spiræa, Aster, Artemisia, Senecio, Saussurea, Adenophora* (Campanula), *Polygonum* (knotgrass), *Lilium,* &c.

Otherwise noteworthy plants:—*Papaver alpinum, Vitis vinifera, Trifolium lupinaster, Saxifraga* (a new species with large peltate leaves), *Linnæa borealis, Phyllodoce cœrulea, Utricularia intermedia, Pinus mandshurica, Lilium* (various species).

A supplementary collection was also made in the autumn on the Mongolian steppes and on the eastern frontier, which proved of the same phytogeographical character as the preceding one. Note G, p. 455, contains a list of the plants as identified, for the benefit of future collectors.

We also preserved a number of bird-skins, though the rapidity of our movements and the obstacles we met with greatly impeded our ornithological efforts. The fact is, it is extremely difficult to discover birds in the tops of lofty forest trees, and, when found, they are often out of shot. On the march, too, it was unsafe to leave the convoy; and though I have often stayed behind for a quarter or half an hour trying to secure a new species, on most occasions I was disappointed, and the trouble of catching up the mules was considerable. Mr. Bowdler Sharpe, of the British Museum, has obliged me with the following observations on our specimens:

The following are amongst the most interesting species in the collection: Black grouse (*Tetrao tetrix*), a grey shrike (*Lanius sphenocercus*), Dybowski's bustard (*Otis Dybowskii*), white-headed long-tailed titmouse (*Acredula caudata*), Chinese nuthatch (*Sitta villosa*), Naumann's thrush (*Turdus Naumanni*), Siberian partridge (*Perdix barbata*), chestnut-headed bunting (*Emberiza castaneiceps*), Eastern hawk-owl (*Ninox scutulata*), and red-rumped accentor (*Accentor erythropygius*). The black woodpecker (*Dryocopus Martius*) is identical with a species found in Sweden.

The commonest bird in Manchuria is the ordinary magpie, the sacred bird, which goes in large flocks and is very tame. They were fond of teasing Rattler, settling down and hopping about just in front of him, and behind him, and all round him, croaking loudly and fluttering away just as the dog thought he had got one, and driving him perfectly wild. There is also a lovely bird called the Corean magpie, with black head and its back and tail a lovely shade of blue. The golden oriole is common in inhabited tracts, and beautiful paradise fly-catchers with extraordinarily long delicate tails (I believe they are identical with the Indian

whydah-bird) and woodpeckers are also found.   Eagles
and hawks are very numerous, and so are all aquatic
birds.   Partridges are not so common.   One of a species
greatly resembling the British bird was killed near Kirin,
and two kinds of mountain partridges, one with a crest,
are tolerably plentiful.   We did not see the magnificent
Crossoptilon Manchuricum, the ordinary pheasant being
the splendid *torquatus*.   Ravens, carrion crows, and
white-breasted crows were common.

Throughout the mountains we saw numbers of very
beautiful butterflies.   The most common is a splendid
dark-green swallowtail with blue ocelli, which is not
uncommon at Simla.   They collect in fifties and sixties,
settle down together in a dense mass on a moss-grown
stone in a ravine, and remain for hours in that position, quivering their gorgeous wings and making a
very pretty effect.   Younghusband was an entomologist,
and he pointed out to us various rare English kinds,
swallowtails large and small, purple emperors, tortoise-
shells, rare clouded yellows, and others, most of them
very plentiful.   The only place where I ever saw so
many lovely varieties at once was on the top of Mount
Senchul, near Darjeeling.

CHAPTER IX.

T'ANG-HO-K'OU TO KIRIN.

A snake story—Wild and cultivated ginseng—Useful trees—Another flood down the Sungari—Rapacity of Chinese boatmen—A fine heronry—Difficulties of the road—The Erh-tao-chiang—Gold-washing—Murder on the highway—Rural theatricals—Kirin—Unpleasant quarters—Vegetables and fruit—Père Verbiest's account—Situation of Kirin—Diagram for averting fires—Filthy market-place—Telegraph office—Chang San sent to the coast for supplies—Arsenal—Machinery and arms—Powder-mill—Selecting recruits—Dinner with Mr. Sung—Smart young signaller—Town magistrate—Fictitious letters of introduction—Temples at Lung T'an Shan—Mahommedan families at Kirin—Absorption of isolated religious communities.

WE returned to T'ang-ho-k'ou by the way we came, without adventure, unless I may count a snake story as one. We had been sleeping with our followers in a deserted Corean hut, and, on getting up in the morning, one of us saw the head of a snake peering out, between the wall and the bit of matting on which we were lying. We lifted up the matting, and there lay four big brown adders. They were sluggish brutes, and made no attempt to escape. After killing them, we found all had poison fangs in their jaws, so, if they had crawled over us in the night, the consequences might have been unpleasant. The day was Sunday, and it seemed scarcely a mere coincidence that afterwards we read in the Psalms for the day, 'There shall no harm happen to thee; thou shalt go upon the young lion and adder.'

On our way back we stayed, as before, at the ginseng plantations, one of them situated, as we now found, in the basin of an old crater like the White Mountain, but this volcano must have been extinct for many ages, and is filled now with luxuriant forest and vegetation. Ginseng, which I have mentioned before, is the long fleshy root of a plant, *Panax ginseng*, which grows wild in the mountains of Manchuria and Corea. It is so highly valued by the Chinese that the bulk of the Corean King's revenue is derived from the export duty levied upon it, and in one of the principal streets of Peking they sell nothing else. The plant grows from twelve to eighteen inches in height, with five long leaves on each stalk like a horse-chestnut. In spring it bears a cluster of purple flowers on the top of the stem, replaced in summer time by bright red berries, which the searchers for the root look out for. The wild plant is rare, but we were shown one or two in our travels, carefully fenced round and left to grow, for, like diamonds, their value increases in geometrical proportion to their size. Only emperors and millionaires can afford the genuine article, for a root four or five inches long realises perhaps 10*l*., but plantations for growing it artificially are pretty numerous. The seed is sown as thickly as possible in long narrow beds of the finest pulverised loam, and the plants are protected from the heat of the sun by a roofing of thatch or white sheeting. They are not considered fit to gather till seven years old, and then the roots fetch about 5*s*. a pound, less than one-hundredth of the price of the wild article. The uninitiated, however, can detect no difference between the two.

We saw companies, twelve or fifteen young men in each, scouring the valleys and glens in search of the wild plant, one or two roots of which are sufficient to repay them for a season's labour. Extraordinary virtues are attributed to it, and I am not sure they are altogether moonshine. A friendly innkeeper once gave us a little, chopped into fine shreds, of which we made tea, and it proved very useful in case of stomach-ache. Supplies of wild ginseng are forwarded occasionally from Kirin to the Emperor by special messenger, and particulars of the consignment are duly given in the 'Peking Gazette.' From one of these announcements we learn that, in January 1884, twenty roots, costing 1,260 taels, were sent for his Majesty's use, which makes a rate of between 14*l.* and 15*l.* a root.

The timber in the inner Ch'ang-pai-shan forests is very fine, a tree with a cork-like bark growing to an immense size. Amongst the trees most valued by the hunters are the birch, out of the bark of which pretty little boxes and plates are made, and a pine, the wood of which is so inflammable, that a lighted splinter burns away like a candle.

After our return to T'ang-ho-k'ou the Sungari again came down in flood, detaining us nearly a week, and Mr. Yen announced that it was impossible for us to reach Hun-ch'un that year. I cannot help thinking the old man could have shown us the way if he had liked, as, by the route he subsequently took us, we got over all the awkward parts of the Hun-ch'un journey except two or three stages. But the supply difficulty stood in the way, and we were tired of detentions, so we agreed it would be better to make for Kirin, which lay about fifteen days' journey to the north. Mr. Yen had got so fond of us that he agreed to accompany us, for a still heavier consideration than before; and as it was his slack season, and his ancestral home was close to Kirin,

T

the arrangement suited him very well. I am bound, at the same time, to say he was a capital guide, and took us across a very difficult country in a masterly way; only he failed to protect us from the rapacity of some other Chinamen, who looked upon the foreigners as fair game. The first case occurred the very day we left T'ang-ho-k'ou. We crossed the river Sungari by a dug-out belonging to the guild, and then found there were two crossings lower down, for which the boatmen refused to lend us their boat, except on payment of an extravagant sum. Yen would not interfere, saying the boat was not his; so there we were, stranded—for a precipitous spur ran down to the river's brink, and there was no possibility of passing between them. We inquired if there was not a route right over the main range, and Yen replied 'Yes,' but it was impracticable. Rather than give in, we resolved to try it, and we succeeded in climbing safely up a steep glen, although the going was so bad that at one place a mule tumbled backwards over, very nearly knocking me over with him, and he turned three complete somersaults, pack and all, before reaching the stream at the bottom. He ought to have been killed, but he was not a bit hurt, and went on again as if nothing had happened. Once at the top, we found a track grown over and almost obliterated, which we followed for about fifteen miles along the crest of a ridge, at the end of which we saw the Old White Mountain far away in the distance, clear against the sky, no other hill approaching it. This was the last time we saw it.

Descending from the ridge, we passed through richly cultivated valleys till we reached the Sung-chiang, one of the largest affluents of the Sungari. Near the junction was the finest heronry I ever saw.

Thousands of herons and cormorants were nesting together in the willow-trees. At this place also the owner of the boat demanded exorbitant terms. We agreed to pay seven taels (more than thirty shillings) for half an hour's use of his canoe, but when we had crossed our baggage he demanded three taels more, seized one of the mules, and not only tried to prevent our going on, but threatened to send our things back again. Fortunately, his friends and neighbours would not support him, seeing we had guns and were prepared to resist, so we eventually got on our way, and then, although he had behaved so badly, we gave him his seven taels. For fifteen days we continued crossing ravines and climbing ridges. Twice we had to camp out in the swampy forests, the heavy rain damaging a quantity of botanical specimens, and a mule strayed away in the woods and gave us an infinity of trouble to recover. The state of the track in places beggars description. The marshes were full of water, and eight or ten mules at a time might be seen floundering on their bellies and sides. Imagine a wet moorside in Scotland, with a boggy old birch plantation running down the burn-side; choose the very uncanniest bit of it, and you have a Ch'ang-pai-shan bridle-path in the rains. Once, while the procession was halting, owing to a stoppage in front, a quiet old pony near me began to kick as if possessed. I wondered why, but did not wonder long, as an agonising bite on my neck made me caper too. A nest of large black ants had been disturbed in a tree above, which dropped down and bit so venomously that the places swelled up like the sting of a hornet. Accommodation in the settlers' huts was scanty, though cordially given. One evening we slept on the floor of the tiny little room, while ten Chinamen lay together on the k'ang, packed like herrings in a barrel. On another occasion we had to thread our way along a narrow valley, in the midst of which was a hill-torrent several feet deep, called the Yü-shih Ho; and this stream we forded no less than twenty-four times in the day's march, for it wound from side to side under the scarped walls of the ravine. There were no mules to spare for riding, so we had to plunge in—there was no shirking.

After a week's journey we came upon the Sungari again, at a place called Yü-shih Ho-k'ou-tzŭ, a short distance from the place where the Erh-tao-chiang, or eastern branch, joins it. The Sungari is here a splendid stream, 300 yards broad, and the scenery at the confluence is grand. The Erh-tao-chiang rushes down a narrow ravine with lofty precipitous sides, crowned with forests, and a tall cliff, or rather rock—for it is an isolated mass 800 feet high—hangs frowning over the meeting of the waters. The Erh-tao-chiang, though hitherto shown on the maps as the main stream, is, as its name implies, the second. It is not very much more than half as broad as its fellow, though very deep. Beyond this point we came on extensive gold-washings, where we were warned to look to our guns, as the diggings were situated in a kind of no-man's land, out of the jurisdiction and protection both of mandarin and guild, and upwards of three hundred outlaws had assembled there to wash the sand for gold. However, though we spent a night close to them, they did us no harm.

Beyond was an extensive swamp, I think the worst of all. We crossed it, fortunately, without accident, and then came to the Hua-pi Ho (the Khu-i-fa River of the maps), a very large tributary, and found ourselves

at last outside the forests amidst regular cultivation.
The road onwards was a cart road, muddy and heavy,
but it was a great relief to be out of the eternal trees,
and no longer to hear the constant chop, chop of the
axe clearing the way for the mules, and to see waving
corn and millet instead of rank ferns and brushwood.
Forty-five miles south of Kirin we crossed the last pass,
called Ching-ling.   Here was ocular demonstration that

OUTSIDE A PAWNSHOP.

we had come once more under the inefficient rule of the
mandarins.   A large roadside shop close by was regularly fortified, and its master told us that, though so
near to the capital, the pass itself had been the scene
of a terrible massacre only the year before.   Three
carts laden with opium and deer-horns were plundered
in open day, and nine persons in charge of them were
killed.   We met several heavily-laden vehicles going
up the pass, and the carters were all armed to the

teeth. Farther on, the country became better cultivated and more and more populated. In one large village, called Hêng-ta-ho, theatricals were going on, to fill up, said the people, the slack time between the coming into ear and the ripening of the grain, when the cultivator has but little to do. Fancy a set of British farmers chartering a troop of actors to amuse them, while waiting for the harvest to commence! A day's march from Kirin we parted from old Yen, paying him the full sum agreed upon. We told him, however, he did not deserve it for neglecting to protect us from extortion at the ferries, as he had expressly agreed to see us through all such difficulties, but we would not give him an excuse for saying in the future that Englishmen did not keep their word. I am afraid he did not profit by our lecture, for he only smiled a sour smile and took himself off. Next day, the fifteenth from leaving T'ang-ho-k'ou, we arrived at Kirin, all well except Fulford, who was suffering from an attack due to fatigue and the long marches in the heat and rain, and I am sorry to say he did not thoroughly recover till the cold weather set in.

It was the 12th of August when we reached Kirin. None of the inns would receive us, as they were full of recruits for the new regiments which the Imperial Commissioner was raising. Eventually, as a great favour, we were admitted to the inn where our muleteers were wont to put up. It formed one side of a large quadrangle, through the centre of which ran a large open drain ; and as long as we stayed there the yard was a lake of mixed mud, mule-dung, and house sewage, a foot or eighteen inches deep. Another sewer passed outside the inn immediately under our windows, and a little farther off there was a third—the main drain

of the town. With the aid of stepping-stones and
boards we could get outside the yard, but that was of
little advantage, as the streets were filthier still, the
mud, without any exaggeration, being up to our knees.
We had a little room sixteen feet by eleven, one of
three opening into a common veranda. On our right
was a carpenter's shop, and on the left a lumber-room.
There was the usual k'ang at the end, a small table,
three wooden chairs with perpendicular backs, and a
wooden box meant for charcoal in winter, which served
as a washing-stand. This comprised all the furniture,
In this detestable prison we passed three weeks and a
day; but we made ourselves as comfortable as circumstances would admit. We hung waterproof sheets over
the doors and windows to keep out prying eyes, and
made the room neat and tidy. Our time was chiefly
spent in reading, writing letters, or arranging dried
flowers. It rained as if it had never rained before,
till the officials went in state to pray to the Dragon
King to stop it. But their prayers were in vain. A
Catholic priest at Yingtzŭ had warned us that where
we found ourselves at the beginning of August, there
we should remain to the end, and never came prophecy
more disagreeably true.

In some respects, perhaps, our detention was beneficial, as it enabled us all to recruit after the somewhat
fatiguing journey in the mountains, and we could get
a sufficiency of plain good food. The beef at Kirin was
very fair (we never got mutton, and seldom or never
saw a sheep); sometimes we had fish, and there were
plenty of fresh vegetables and fruits, such as plums,
haws, melons, and dried apricots, which we found
very palatable. In the woods we often saw wild pears
and grapes; but they were not cultivated so far north;

and wild raspberries and filberts also, which were extremely good all along the road, were so little appreciated by the Chinese, that they never came to the
market at all.   But on the whole we fared very well.

We had also to be thankful for one advantage which
our inn, the Yü Fa Tien, possessed ; it was close to
the north wall of the city.   It is true, to get to the
wall, we had to execute a sort of Blondin performance
for two hundred yards along a slippery piece of bank
a few inches wide, covered with abominable filth, with
a deep sewer on one side and a high wooden paling
on the other.   Still, when we reached the wall—a
broken-down earthen mound with a path over it—
there were market gardens, and beyond them hills,
where we could get a breath of fresh air without the
population pestering us ; and for that we had reason
to be thankful.   On the apex of one of the hills,
almost overhanging the town, so to speak, stands a
very conspicuous monument, consisting of a brick wall
about ten feet high, with four oblong pieces of granite
(of which stone there are excellent quarries in the
neighbourhood), let horizontally into its face, something
after the following fashion.

As long ago as 2730 or 2850 B.C. it occurred to
a philosopher, called Fu Hsi, to represent the nume-
rical proportions of the universe by diagrams composed

of combinations of a line and a divided line, taken from the quaintly-marked devices on the back of a tortoise, or, as some say, a 'dragon-horse,' whatever that may be. There were eight diagrams at first, signifying earth, air, fire, or some other element, but subsequent combinations have raised the number to sixty-four. Two whole lines with a broken one between them, as depicted above, signify fire, or rather the influence in the cosmos which produces fire, and the object, in this instance, is to preserve the city from conflagration by the display of the mystic symbol. The diagram faces south, as that point of the compass is the most auspicious, and has some peculiar influence upon the devouring element. The view from this monument was charming: in the background a circle of mountains with bold irregular outlines; in the middle distance the city of Kirin, with the mighty Sungari rushing past it; and in the foreground numerous grassy knolls and undulating ground, with little wooded dells, and here and there a group of quaint temples. We tried to hire rooms at a temple, as the legations do every year at Peking, but the priests thought we should be troublesome lodgers, and refused to take us in. A hill on the west of the town is called the Small White Mountain, and is supposed to reflect the benign influences of the Great Pai-shan. According to both Mr. Meadows and M. Palladius, the Military Governor solemnly prays there once, or else twice, a year, looking towards the true Pai-shan, the sacred mountain of the dynasty; but the priests forgot to mention the fact to us.

The famous Père Verbiest visited Kirin in the train of the Emperor Kanghi in the year 1682, and the following is an extract from his account:

'Kirin stands on the great river Sungari, which

takes its rise in the Pai-shan, or White Mountain, 400 miles off. This mountain, so famous in the East, from having been the ancient habitation of the Man-chu Tartars, is said to be always covered with snow, whence it takes its name. When the Emperor came within sight of Kirin, he alighted from his horse, and, kneeling on the bank of the river, bowed thrice to the ground by way of salutation. He then mounted on a throne glittering with gold, on which he made his entrance into the city, all the people running in crowds to meet him, and weeping for joy to see him. These marks of affection were highly acceptable to the Prince, who, in token of his favour, condescended to show himself to everybody, forbidding his guards to hinder his people from approaching him, as they do at Peking.' —(I may add, as they do at Peking to the present day.)

Kirin is now better known as Ch'uan-ch'ang, or the 'Dock-yard,' from the number of river-going craft which are built there. Père Verbiest mentions that a particular sort of barge was kept at Kirin, of which a number were always in readiness to repulse the Russians, who often came up the river to dispute the pearl-fishery. In fact, it was just about that time that the Emperor removed the head-quarters of the Governor to Kirin from Ninguta, where he had previously been stationed, in order to secure the Sungari from trespassers. The situation of the town is undeniably fine. The Sungari, on emerging from the hills, sweeps abruptly round from west to east, making a great bend for about four miles, and then turns northward again. It is upwards of four hundred yards broad. The town, which contains, I should estimate, from 75,000 to 100,000 inhabitants, extends for about two miles along this bend, so close to the bank that the street along the river front

is constructed of wooden flooring raised on piles, in
many places rotten and unsafe. A circle of low hills,
springing beyond the west end of the town, curves
right round behind it, so that, with the river in front
and rising ground behind, it might be made a very
strong place. The streets in the rainy season are a
quagmire, except one or two which are paved with
stout wooden logs, and the market-place is one of the
most loathsome spots in the whole inhabited earth. A
long stagnant cesspool divides it from end to end,
wherein float dead pigs and dogs and every kind of
filth, and along the margin of it are located the
butchers' and greengrocers' stalls; not a square foot of
ground but reeks with ordure and every kind of abomi-
nation both to see and to smell. The shops are very
poor, and there is scarcely a temple or public building
worth looking at. The western part of the town is
built on a swamp, and is under water a great part of
the year, and the inhabitants boat from one place to
another just as they do at Venice.

We paid off our mules at Kirin, as the next part of
our tour was through country fit for carts. When
settling up, the sergeant gave some trouble, denying
the receipt of a sum paid through him for the purchase
of animals at T'ung-hua-hsien. But he quarrelled with
everybody, thereby courting punishment, till at last one
of his fellows rolled him in the unsavoury lake of mud
before our door. A telegraph office had been just
opened at Kirin; so, thinking our supplies of money
might run short, we telegraphed for more to be sent.
But the rains washed down the line, and an answer
never came; therefore, after waiting a fortnight, we
sent off our servant Chang San to Yingtzŭ to bring
back both the money and our letters. We took the

opportunity of sending back some guns and superfluous baggage.

The principal thing of interest at Kirin is the arsenal, which has recently been established under the management of a gentleman named Sung, who received his training under foreigners in the arsenals of Tientsin and Shanghai. He was exceedingly courteous and friendly, and showed us over the place. It was very interesting to see a large establishment filled with foreign machinery, some German and some English, with boilers and engines and steam hammers, just such as one might see at Woolwich or Elswick, all erected and managed by Chinese without foreign assistance of any kind. It would open the eyes of those Europeans who think that Western nations have a monopoly of mechanical and administrative ability. Most of the artisans were from Ningpo, and had also practical experience before they came. They can turn out anything, from a gingall to a repeating rifle. The Chinese verdict on English compared with German machinery was that the latter worked more quickly and did delicate work better, but the English was more solid, and could always be depended upon for accuracy. Amongst other curiosities, Mr. Sung showed us a machine-gun invented by one of his foremen, perhaps it would be more correct to say adapted, from a Western model. It was so portable that two men could carry it, and the tripod on which it worked, with the greatest ease. We saw it at work, and it could fire eighty shots a minute smoothly and without any symptom of obstruction. On the opposite side of the river to the arsenal a powder-mill has also been put up, just what one might see at Erith or Kirkee, in which gunpowder is manufactured on approved scientific principles. The fact that the Chinese apply the mechanical knowledge they learn from foreigners in the first instance to the better destruction of their fellow-creatures, affords food for reflection.

The establishment of the arsenal and powder-mill leaves no doubt of the earnestness with which the military strength of Manchuria is now being looked to; and throngs of young Manchu recruits, whom the imperial commissioner had selected, testified to the same thing. As we entered the town for the first time, we saw numbers of them passing in procession before a severe-looking old man standing in a gateway, who wielded a fan with great vigour, opening and shutting it sharply and slapping it on his open palm in a manner indicating great decision of character. And later on several thousand passed us coming from parade with many bright banners galore. They were dressed in rather an untidy uniform, consisting of a long blue apron with a white border, and a waistcoat or sleeveless blue coatee above it, with the name of the regiment and the colour of the banner inscribed on a circular patch let into the front. On their heads they wore neat dark turbans. One of the men remarked to a runner who had accompanied us, ' What do they think of us? We are thirty thousand; I don't suppose they'll ever come here.' Asking if the recruits were free or conscripts, we were told they could not dare to disobey the Emperor's orders and must serve when called upon. They were, in fact, members of the Manchu militia being turned into regulars. They looked fine, healthy lads—just the stuff to make soldiers of.

Mr. Sung invited us all to dinner, which proved, as an American would say, quite sumptuous. I hope, if our kindly host ever reads this, he will forgive the breach of hospitality I make in recounting the good things he gave us.   First there was placed in the middle of the table a collection of *hors d'œuvres* in saucers—shrimps and pickled cucumber, cold pickled hairy beans, which were meant to be resorted to at intervals during the repast, to restore the flagging appetite, cold morsels of chicken, hard-boiled egg in green aspic (very good indeed—fortunately we did not discover for a long time afterwards that it was composed of stale eggs), mayonnaise of different kinds, sliced ham, tongue, and cold pork.   After tasting these, there followed a series of *grosses pièces*, each in a large china bowl, out of which we helped ourselves, interspersed with a be-wildering succession of smaller and more delicate *plats*, of which a separate bowl was given to each guest. The first series included roast chicken, stewed beef, stewed mutton, pickled carp with sweet sauce (un-commonly good), stuffed egg-plants, and roast mutton with suet dumplings—the last, unlike the stolid British article, were airy and melting in the mouth, and con-structed, like oysters, with a hinge at one side, so that slices of mutton could be put inside, and the whole eaten like a sandwich.   The smaller pieces comprised sea-slug soup (super-excellent, though the creature itself is hideous to look upon, something like a huge black caterpillar, all covered with warts and excrescences), bean-curd soup, *crème aux haricots verts*, truffle soup, dumplings stuffed with mince, and shark-fin soup fla-voured with seaweed.   The last was delicious.   There were no sweets, and the grand *finale* was plain boiled rice and mutton broth.   Fortunately, we were not expected to finish every course, or nature would have succumbed at an early stage.   Some of the dishes were really fit for the gods.   The wine was a weak spirit dis-tilled from rice, tasting exactly like weak warm sherry.

Excellent as the banquet was, the warm greeting and *bonhomie* of our entertainer were still more delightful. Fortunately, we had not to depend on chop-sticks, or we should have been badly off (though I am sure the use of these implements would come with a little practice), and Mr. Sung had provided knives and forks. Mr. Lo, a young gentleman from the telegraph office, who had been trained at Tientsin, and could talk English, had been invited to meet us, and he began by asking us to ' make ourselves to home,' and we did so, never minding the preposition. Mr. Lo came to lunch with us one day, dressed in a long coat of rich black silk, covered with geometrical patterns, and the sleeves turned up with a delicate pale blue satin. His continuations were fine French-gray, below which came top-boots of black velvet, with thick white soles. On his head was a mandarin's hat with a white button and a pearl in front, so altogether he was a very smart figure indeed.

The only other Chinese gentleman who showed us any politeness was the town magistrate. As he was also president of the local board of works, we asked him how the streets came to be so bad, and his reply was something like the inscription on the Highland road, ' If you'd seen these roads before they were made, you'd have held up your hands and blessed—the present administration.' His explanation amounted to this, that the town had been built on a swamp originally, that till lately the streets had been wholly impassable in wet weather, and that we might be thankful any corduroy tracks had been constructed at all. Our visit to Kirin also brought to light a good instance of that mock-politeness with which Chinese will treat people to avoid the appearance of being disobliging.

Just before leaving Calcutta I met a Chinese clerk who
said he came from Kirin, so I asked if he could give
me any letters of introduction there. Oh, yes, he would
be delighted; and he gave me two, addressed to officials
who, he said, would be very useful to us. On making
inquiries, we learned that no such people existed, and
the letters were mere waste-paper. The town magistrate, too, was disobliging when we asked him to assist
us. We had brought plenty of fishing-tackle, and, finding
the rains did not abate, we tried to procure a boat large
enough to live in and fish. There were many such to
be seen, but the magistrate kept putting us off and off,
till we gave up the idea. On Mr. Sung's suggestion,
we made an excursion to a hill on the right bank of
the Sungari, called Lung T'an Shan, on the Mountain of
the Dragon's Pool, situated about five miles below the
city. It was a pretty quiet spot, with quaint temples,
prettily disposed amongst the trees. The Dragon's Pool
itself, supposed to be fathomless, was a small pond only
a few yards in breadth, at the bottom of a bosky dell.
The priests, however, were ignorant and stupid, and
could tell us nothing about their gods, whose very
names they scarcely knew. There was also a solitary
elm-tree, surrounded by a paling, which was treated as
sacred by visitors, but no one could tell us the reason
why. The priests' chief treasure was an autograph of
one of the Emperors, I think Kienlung. Unfortunately,
the temples were undergoing repair at the time, and
the place was so crowded with workmen that we could
not get a comfortable room. We returned, therefore,
to Kirin.

There are a thousand families of Mahommedans
in Kirin. The principal mosque can hardly be distinguished from a Chinese temple, except for a few

Arabic sentences upon the walls, and on the back of the pulpit a mass of texts from the Koran. The moulvie told us he had been to Mecca by way of Hongkong and Singapore, and displayed some neatly-written Arabic and Persian books which, he said, came from Candahar. He could read but not understand them. To outward appearance there is but little to distinguish Mahommedans from Chinese, and unless a religious revival takes place I suspect their faith will gradually deteriorate. Shortly after leaving China I went to Jamaica, where a number of Mahommedan coolies from India are settled, and I gathered from them that, for want of an environment of the Faithful, they are now giving up Islam and call themselves Jews; and Dr. Williams, in the ' Middle Kingdom,'[1] gives an account of an ancient colony of Jews in the province of Honan who gradually dropped their faith and became absorbed amongst the Chinese. In 1700, when the Jesuit Gozain visited the colony at K'ai-fêng, there was a large establishment of Jews with a fine synagogue, and various buildings enclosed for residence, worship, and work. In 1866, when a missionary revisited them, he found that the synagogue had been pulled down for sale as building materials; only a stone was left recording the erection of the synagogue in A.D. 1183 and its rebuilding in 1488; all ritual and worship had ceased; and some of the Jews had begun worshipping at a mosque, while others had become Buddhist priests or literary graduates, so that by this time their existence as a separate sect has probably been quite obliterated. These instances show that even Islam and Judaism will disappear, when there is want of vitality within, and pressure, social, intellectual, or religious, from outside.

[1] Vol. ii. 271–274.

U

CHAPTER X.

KIRIN TO TSITSIHAR.

An obliging banker—Gold ingots—Engage carts—Piece-work *v.* daily wages —Obstinacy of mules—A bad start—Timber at Chiachan—Wuluk'ai— Temple to the phœnix—Hsi-la Ho—Gateway through palisades—The old bed of the Sungari—Brigands on their way to execution—Arrival at Petuna—Illness of Chu-hsiu—Painful remedies—Temple and frescoes at Petuna—Mosquitoes—Manchurian cranes—Difficulties in crossing the Sungari—Island—Shui-shih Yingtzŭ—Accident to Younghusband— Antelopes—Jerboa rat—Bustards—A Mongol palace—Road to Tsitsihar —Buddhist tombs—Chinese aversion to milk—Nai-p'i, or cream-cheese— Lama form of religion—Check against over-population—Couriers— Anecdote of the Russian police—The Archimandrite Palladius—Ancient fortifications—First view of Tsitsihar—A p'ailou—Neglected coffins— Concrete flat roofs—Gabled roofs—Scene in a banker's parlour—A disagreeable inn—Convicts—An unpleasant custom—Soldiers drilling— A funeral—Change of plans—Country north of Tsitsihar.

ON the 3rd of September it had cleared up sufficiently to justify us in making a start for Tsitsihar. The Kirin people were much divided as to the business that had brought us there, one party saying we were going to start a bean-cake business, and others that we had taken a contract to mend the road. The telegraph was still out of order, and we could not expect our servant back for several months, so, although, as it turned out, we could really have done without it, we determined to be on the safe side, and to borrow some money locally. A civil banker, who managed a branch of a famous firm, Tsun-I-Kung of Peking, agreed to lend us 200 taels on condition we deposited security. We had brought some watches and rings to give away as

presents, and these we left as pledges. We took
the opportunity of inquiring what became of the gold
found in the hills, and learnt that it was melted up
into beautiful little ingots and forwarded to Peking.
It so happened that the manager of the branch of
the Hongkong and Shanghai Bank at that place had
showed me some exactly similar, which were supposed,
he said, to come from Thibet. I have little doubt some
of them came from Manchuria, the trade being conducted in secrecy, for fear of the Government. The
banker's parlour was a neat quiet room, hung round
with moral texts in all styles of picturesque calligraphy.
Here, as at every other respectable place we ever called
at, we were treated to tea—almost always delicately
flavoured green tea made *à la Chinoise*—that is to say,
the tea-leaves put into the cup and boiling water
poured on them, an inverted saucer being placed on
the top of the cup (in addition to that underneath), and
held in its place when the cup is raised to the lips, so
as to strain the liquor from the tea-leaves.

We now hired four light carts, each drawn by
three mules, for one tael a day each. This payment
was higher than the market rate, but the heathen
Chinee justified it by saying that there was a great
demand for carts owing to the projected journey of the
Imperial Commissioner Mu to the north. The bargain
turned out a bad one, as the cartmen, after we once
started, used purposely to loiter on the road, and the
man who was chosen to lead would deliberately drive
into a quagmire and delay the procession for hours.
Changing the leader made no improvement, and, instead
of doing thirty-five miles a day, or even more, we only
averaged twenty-five or thirty. I should recommend
future travellers to make bargains by piece-work, what-

ever it may cost them to do so, and change their carts if necessary at every large town. It will be far cheaper and less troublesome in the end, the journey will be got over more quickly, and the constant irritation which the intentional loitering gives rise to will be avoided. The leading cartman had a fine set of mules, but all three of them were obstinate—in fact, mulish to a degree. There was one of them which, on feeling the ground a little soft under his feet, would calmly lie down, and, even though all his harness might be removed, could not be induced to rise by the most severe beating ; and, what was worse, when once he went down, the others would follow his example. On one occasion the wheeler prostrated himself calmly in about a foot and a half of mud and water, and declined so persistently to move that even his master lost patience with him; so, after undoing his harness, two other mules were attached to his cart, making with the original leaders four, and they dragged it triumphantly over their prostrate comrade. Fortunately, from rolling in the mud, his body presented so slippery a surface to the wheels that they glided over him—stomach and legs and head—without having time to do any damage. When all was over he rose with an abstracted air, as if he had quite forgotten he was keeping us, and in a short time he was on the road again as if nothing whatever had happened.

Cart-mules in Manchuria are bitted with a piece of whipcord put over the upper gums, the only tender part of their mouths. They are often vicious, so that, when they are shod, they have to be trussed up tightly —hand and foot, so to speak—to a kind of gallows to prevent their kicking. But, on the whole, they are docile and very enduring, and their masters treat them very well, attend to their feeding the last thing at night, again during the night, however hard the frost may be, and again at midday. The result is that they stand any amount of hard work, and suffer nothing when left out at night, as they always are, even when the thermometer is 40° below zero Fahr. Except for their resolve to lag on the road, our carters were good enough fellows. They worked hard when needed, and their patience under difficulties was inexhaustible. They generally addressed their beasts as 'Wang-pa kao,' a somewhat coarse term of abuse, which means the spawn of a turtle.

Our start from Kirin did not augur well. The road through the great northern gate of the town, this capital of a province, was so much out of repair that the carts stuck in it for a couple of hours, and one was upset in a lake of black mud. The fact is, the road had once been paved with large blocks of granite, fragments of which protruded like islands out of the mire, and were calculated to upset any vehicle. Such sights, however, are not uncommon even at the gates of Peking, and are not entirely unknown in Europe—at least, I once nearly stuck in the mud in driving to the railway station at Madrid. Once started, the roadway was not very bad, though travelling was very monotonous between fields of lofty millet and hemp. For about twenty-four miles we kept along the left bank of the Sungari, passing Chia-chan, where rafts of huge trees, floated down from the Ch'ang-pai-shan Mountains, were being dismembered, and the logs hauled up the bank by a team of twenty-four ponies. We crossed the river in a flat-bottomed ferry-boat to a place called Wuluk'ai, which, in ages gone by, was the chief town of the district. Père Verbiest,

who went there on a fishing excursion with the Emperor Kanghi in 1682, describes it as the first city in
all the country, and formerly the seat of the Tartar
emperors. When the Military Governor of Ninguta
was moved to Kirin, the local officials were moved
from Wuluk'ai at the same time. It was evidently
once a place of importance, as there are the remains
of giant walls outside it, all grass-grown now, which
Consul Meadows assigns to the Ketans nine hundred
or a thousand years ago. The Jesuit surveyors who
visited it nearly thirty years after Père Verbiest called
it Pou-tai-oula-hotun, from the Pou-tai-oula, or Sungari.
They believed it was built by the Manchus in the
twelfth century, who, under the name of Chin, conquered the north of China. Nothing was then to be
seen of it but a 'pyramid indifferently high, with the
ruins of the walls, without which are some houses inhabited by Manchus.' They called it also the fourth or
last city, 'for there are but four in the government of
Kirin, of which this is the least, as not having an equal
jurisdiction, but in other respects it is much more
agreeable, being situated in a fertile plain and better
inhabited.' It is evident that 200 years ago the present
province of Kirin was nearly a desert.

Twelve miles farther on we crossed the Shih-chia-tzŭ
river, a fine stream 120 yards broad, not far from
which is a forest-clad hill, crowned by a temple dedicated to the phœnix, which can be seen for many miles
round. It reminded one oddly enough of the monument to the first Earl of Durham, that smoky copy of
the Parthenon in the most coal-beridden part of England.
We were now bidding good-bye to the last spurs of the
Ch'ang-pai-shan ranges. The next place was Hsi-la-ho,
where we found a manufactory of great stoneware jars,

such as Morgiana found the robbers in. Then we passed under the Fa-ta-ha Mên, or Great Gateway, now a rickety wooden affair, representing the passage through the palisade erected to keep out the Mongols. Hardly a trace of the palisades now remains. Then the road descended into a very singular depression, evidently the old bed of the Sungari. The stream has gradually been working westward, leaving behind a bottom of rich marshy land, which, as rounded fragments of pumice testified, is still occasionally overflowed. When we again ascended a bluff overlooking the river, there was a splendid view of the Sungari creeping tortuously through the plain by various channels, like the Ganges or Brahmaputra in the hot weather. Finally, we emerged upon extensive prairies, and, though the autumn had begun and leaves were falling fast, we found lovely skyblue larkspurs, purple anemones, bluebells, and other flowers. One day a consignment of brigands passed us, chained together in carts, who were being carried to Kirin for execution.

A week after leaving Kirin we arrived at Petuna, or, in Chinese, Hsin Ch'êng, a town containing about 30,000 inhabitants, prettily situated on the Sungari, here very wide and shallow. Younghusband and I went for a walk in the streets and promptly got mobbed. I note for future travellers that it was a mistake not taking riding horses. All over the East 'a walking buccra,' to use a Jamaica term, is looked down upon, more or less. Riding on the carts had its advantages, no doubt: one could easily jump off to gather botanical specimens or take an observation; our guns were always handy in case we came across game or robbers, and, more important than all, we ran no risk of losing sight of our servants or baggage. But, when all is said and done, it is a way of travelling that I cannot recommend.   At Petuna, Chu-hsiu, the bird-stuffer, was taken ill.   It was a bad bilious attack, with severe headache and high fever.   A native physician was called in, who kneaded up the skin of his poor burning forehead, his cheeks, ears, temples, and the back of his neck, then pinched up the flesh and pricked each place vigorously with a needle till he had squeezed out a few drops of blood.   As this operation did not give the relief expected, I tried my hand with some tartar emetic, followed by paregoric elixir, and the results surpassed all expectation.   There is a temple at Petuna with a series of frescoes representing the tortures in hell, as painfully realistic as those in the Campo Santo at Pisa: women being ripped open, men being sawn asunder, boiled in oil, frozen, or burnt, or flayed alive. It is a favourite subject for Chinese temple-decoration. On the other hand, we saw pictures as frequently representing miracles of mercy achieved by the Queen of Heaven, Kuanyin.

Beyond Petuna we came to a vast swamp where the Sungari and Nonni join, the only place where we got any snipe shooting.   Here the mosquitoes were more vicious than any I have ever heard of.   It is no exaggeration to say that they bit through thick cord breeches as if they were a pair of silk stockings.   We saw quantities of ducks and geese, and, I think, swans, and the superb Manchurian crane (*Grus montignii*) was pretty numerous; but they were all so wild that we could not get near them.   A guide took us over the swamp, which was about twelve miles across.   The ferry-boat was lying on the south bank of the Sungari, far away from any house or village, and the ferrymen declared they must dine before starting.   Meanwhile it began to rain and blow furiously. The ferrymen took refuge in a hole dug in the ground, roofed over with hay, while we waited patiently in the open. The storm grew worse, till after several hours the ferrymen announced they could not start, and recommended us to go to a house on the marsh which they pointed out in the distance and declared was an inn. But the water had been rising all the time; the marsh we had crossed was like a sponge, and, when we tried to drive a cart back the way we had come, it stuck in the mire and took nine mules and two hours' hard work to extricate. Fulford waded across the creek, which still separated us from the house, and he found the water was by this time up to his middle, but the house was quite full—not a corner to creep into; so we again attacked the ferrymen, and, with a great deal of coaxing, we at last induced them to start. There was no shelter on board, and the wind whistled through our dripping garments and chilled us to the marrow. The river was ten miles across; darkness came on, and it looked like our spending, servants, cartmen, mules, and all, an extremely moist and unpleasant night on the bosom of the mighty Sungari. Luckily we spied a tiny island about twenty yards long by ten broad, on which some fishermen had built a hut. We asked them to take us in, and, like good fellows, they consented. It was a tight fit, but we made ourselves comfortable, and soon forgot our miseries. Next day we spent another two or three hours in the wet, punting and rowing alternately, till at last we landed on the left bank of the Nonni at an inn called Shui-shih Yingtzŭ. This was indeed a miserable piece of journeying, and it ended up by a singular, and what might have proved an ugly accident. Younghusband, who was reclining on the k'ang, suddenly jumped off it, upsetting a pair of scissors which were lying upon his bedding ; his foot caught them before they reached the ground, and he ran the points, which were slightly open, more than an inch perpendicularly into the sole of his foot. He at once got on his back again and we bandaged him up, but it was a fortnight before he could put his foot to the ground.

We were now, for the first time, fairly on the Mongolian steppes, and outside the government of Manchuria. For the palisades on the south form the boundary, outside of which, and a line drawn from a point near Hulan to a point a little south of Tsitsihar, it is Mongolian soil, and the people say, 'We are the subjects of the Emperor, but the land is the King's '— i.e. the Mongol chief's. There are said to be forty-eight of these chiefs altogether, and taxation and administration is in their hands. From the Nonni to Tsitsihar only a little cultivation, and that very poor, was to be met with. Vast undulating plains stretched before us as far as the eye could reach, covered with succulent grass, affording pasture for fine herds of sheep and ponies. Large numbers of antelope (huang-yang, literally 'yellow sheep') galloped across our path, and a remarkable jerboa-rat, with hind-legs a foot long and rudimentary fore-legs like a kangaroo, and a tuft at the end of his tail like a lion, went skipping through the grass. There were prodigious numbers of a fine bustard (*Otis Dybowskii*), undistinguishable except by ornithologists from the ancient British bird. We shot some specimens and found them excellent eating. About fifteen miles from the junction of the Nonni and the Sungari is the residence of the Chief of the Northern Korlos tribe of Mongols, who bears the first-grade title of nobility. We did not visit it, but Mr. Meadows states that he has seen few country seats of wealthy Chinese landed proprietors, and still fewer yamens of mandarins in Chinese cities, that could compete with it, whether in style, size, or the condition in which they are kept. It has groups and avenues of oaks around it, which, in a country where trees are rare, give it an imposing appearance. It consists, according to the Northern Chinese plan, of successive rows of buildings facing the south, with courtyards between them, and a large outer court in front of the most southerly row. The whole occupies some five or six acres of ground, and standing apart on one side is a handsome temple. The Chief is the hereditary judge of his tribe, and exercises his jurisdiction without control in all but capital cases, which he has to refer to certain superior courts at Moukden and Peking. The Chief of the Southern Korlos resides about two miles back from the left bank of the Sungari, about fifty miles above its junction with the Nonni.

The road to Tsitsihar runs generally parallel to the left bank of the Nonni, but floods had converted all the intervening country into a succession of lakes, on the banks of which were great flocks of the common and demoiselle crane, and another magnificent black crane with long drooping plumes. The region is very thinly populated, and we generally found shelter at nights in Mongol farms, which are very clean and comfortable. We only saw two youarts in the whole steppe, for the Mongols in this part of the world are giving up their nomad life and settling down in houses. At a place called Chiu-shan Mên is a group of prettily ornamented Buddhist tombs exactly like those in La- dakh, but not so large, shaped like a dagoba, with an orifice in the dome through which the ashes of the deceased are inserted, and ornamented with tiles moulded in beautiful patterns. At a little Mongol house called Hao-têng-kai by the Chinese, is a real Buddhist stupa made of earth, of considerable size, surmounted by an umbrella which can be seen from a great distance. In

A MONGOL LAMA'S TOMB.

their houses the people have neat little shrines of carved black wood, which, when opened, disclose a little brass image of Buddha, just such as one might buy at Khatmandu or Leh. Even the brass lamps which burned before them had exactly the same shape and ornamentation. From the Mongols we got the first fresh milk

we had tasted since we left Newchwang, and delicious
it seemed. It is an odd thing that the Chinese, who
will eat unsavoury food such as dogs and cats and
rotten eggs, and who are also the most economical
husbandmen in the world, letting nothing go to waste,
will not, as a general rule at least, touch good cows'
milk, considering it an unclean product. The Mongols also gave us curds and cheese of their own
called *nai-p'i*, or milk-skin, which is very good. It is

ORNAMENTAL TILE FROM A MONGOL LAMA'S TOMB.

made by simmering a bowlful of cream for hours
together till the residuum is left in the shape of a cake
about half an inch thick. When fresh and soft it is
very like Devonshire cream, and, when dried, it will
keep for any length of time. At one place we found
a great treasure, a potful of fine clarified butter. In
India the sahib turns up his nose at 'ghi,' but he is
glad enough to get it in Mongolia. We met some
Lamas riding about, dressed in red coats, and their
caps with three-cornered lappets, again just the same as

in Ladakh—nay, in one house there was a female Lama with shaven head, coarse yellow robe, and hempen girdle, telling her beads with all the fervour of a Catholic penitent.

The Lama form of Buddhism differs from that in China in being much purer—that is to say, it has no ad-mixture of Confucian philosophy or Taoist spirit-worship. The Lamas believe in heaven and hell as well as in the efficacy of prayer and thanksgiving, though both are mechanically rendered, being usually the repetition of some Thibetan phrase which the worshipper does not understand. We did not see any prayer-wheels, but here and there, on the top of two long poles, bits of calico might be perceived fluttering in the breeze, with texts inscribed upon them, exactly as in Sikkim or Ladakh. The Mongols have great faith in Lamas, some of whom they credit with supernatural powers, going so far as to reverence one or two as Gigens, or living incarnations, or rather repetitions of Buddha. The Rev. Mr. Gilmour [1] estimates that sixty per cent. of the male Mongol population are Lamas, having been dedicated as boys to a life which binds them to celi-bacy, but which ends in extensive immorality. The same gentleman describes them as a very grasping and oppressive class. Most writers fail to perceive—at least so it seems to me—that the Lama system, which prevails from the Amur to the Indus, and is in some places supplemented by polyandry, though objection-able in a thousand ways, is in reality nothing more than a rough, though efficient, device for preventing the population of those vast and sterile regions from out-growing the means of subsistence.

From Kirin to Aigun, every fifteen miles or so there

[1] *Life amongst the Mongols.* London, 1883.

is a postal stage, at each of which twenty-five mounted couriers are stationed for carrying the Government despatches. A certain number must always be on duty in turn. They are given quarters rent free, and divide the small sum of thirty taels amongst themselves every month. Attached to the station is a house like an Indian dak bungalow, where Government officials put up on journeys. Two or three couriers were detached every day to show us the road, which would have been difficult to find across the flooded country. The great attraction was the Military Imperial Commissioner Mu, who passed us with his escort on his way to Tsitsihar, to reorganise the forces at that station. His Excellency travelled in a sedan chair—how the early Manchu heroes would have laughed at him!—accompanied by about two hundred troopers. He was an early riser, and, no matter what time he went to bed, he was always on the road again by 2 A.M., so that his attendants looked very weary and wobegone.

Half way to Tsitsihar we met a Danish gentleman employed in the Chinese Telegraph Department, who had been surveying a new line to the northern frontier and had spent a week at Blagovaschensk. As we had received no news for four months, we eagerly questioned him, but the only information he could give us was that King Ludwig of Bavaria had drowned himself. Of the fate of Mr. Gladstone's Home Rule Bill he was absolutely ignorant, but he told us one amusing anecdote. When visiting Hun-ch'un, on the south-east frontier, he went from Possiet Harbour by steamer to Vladivostock; his passport was quite *en règle*, but shortly after his arrival two Russian officers in full uniform, helmets, swords, and all, marched into his room and told him they had orders to transport him by sea to Shanghai. He remonstrated, and, after much trouble, as a great favour they permitted him to return the way he had come, on giving his parole that he would land nowhere. He supposed they had taken him for an English spy. Russophobia is ludicrous enough in England, so it is pleasing to find a little Anglophobia on the other side.

In his map of the road between Petuna and Aigun the Archimandrite Palladius constantly notes 'remains of ancient fortifications.' At first we concluded he had mistaken for old earthworks the remains of old cattle and horse corrals which are constructed in the form of a square, with a deep ditch and a mound. But near a place called Hao-têng-kai we came on a real old fort, the walls crumbled and overgrown with grass. The Jesuit surveyors noticed such fortifications on their way to Aigun, and they were told that when the Yuen (Mongol) dynasty was expelled by the Mings, even after they had retreated into their own country, they were attacked with such vigour by the Chinese that, after retreating to this, the remotest part of it, they were obliged in their turn to draw lines and raise fortifications, the ruins of which the Jesuits themselves saw. At that time the province of Tsitsihar was inhabited by Manchus, Solons, and by the ancient inhabitants of the country, called Tagouri (Daurians); and the only towns in existence were Saghalien and Merguen (both of which in their turn had been capitals of the province), and thirteen li higher than Saghalien were the remains of an ancient city called Aykom (Aigun), which the greatest of the Ming Emperors, Yung-lo, built, to prevent the return of the Mongols, whom he had driven across the Amur.

The first view of Tsitsihar is very agreeable. The most conspicuous object is a handsome painted wooden p'ailou erected in honour of a late Military Governor. The eaves and exterior of the arches bristle with handsome, quaintly carved wooden spicula, which completely line the ceiling and cause it to resemble a gigantic piece of frilling. Adjoining is a fine marble slab which gives a history of the p'ailou, and which will assuredly outlast it. On the right lie two sets of barracks, neat buildings ranged round three sides of a square, each set with accommodation for 750 men; and on the left, in an enclosure filled with trees, is the Mahommedan cemetery. There is also a temple to Lao-yeh. Farther on, and just outside the city gate, is the dreadful but common spectacle of a number of coffins lying neglected and rotting on the surface of the ground. These contain the bodies of strangers or of those whose relations are too poor to buy them a grave. The town is supplied with water from a lake which connects with the Nonni, nearly three miles off. It is surrounded by a low mud wall, and laid out in the usual fashion of two long main streets, which cross one another in the centre of the town, with parallel lanes to correspond. It is filthier even than Kirin. Many of the houses have flat concrete roofs as in many Oriental countries, and we had noticed the same thing at Petuna. The Chinese are naturally such bad engineers that they will not build any gabled roof unless they can support it with massive beams and uprights, far in excess of what is necessary, and timber is so scarce in the north that they cannot afford to waste it. Any gabled roofs there are carry thatch, not tiles, and to prevent the high winds from carrying them away an arrangement of spars like a series of St. Andrew's crosses is fixed along the topmost ridge, giving them a picturesque appearance.

x

With the aid of a runner from the Military Governor's yamen, we obtained room in an inn, where the people were civil, though some other guests had to be turned out to make way for us. We went first thing to visit the banker on whom we had a bill for between five and six hundred taels. He expressed his readiness to cash it, if we procured a guarantee from the yamen, but the officials not unnaturally declined to have anything to do with our money matters. However, the innkeeper, after some deliberation, agreed to certify to our respectability. An English banker would laugh at the scene which his Chinese brother's back parlour presented. All the riffraff of the town poured in after us, squatted themselves down comfortably on the banker's best cushions, smoked and spat and listened carefully to all that went on, leaning their heads forward and joining in the conversation as the spirit moved them. We did not half like the idea of these ruffians knowing that we were going away with considerably over 100*l.* in cash, and hearing exactly how we were going to 'take' it. But the banker only simpered when we remonstrated with him and made no attempt to turn the fellows out. The reason is, he dared not offend his fellow-countrymen merely to please three 'foreign devils.' In one respect our inn was the worst we had ever experienced, for all sanitary conveniences were conspicuous by their absence.

Tsitsihar is a regular Botany Bay, and there must be several thousands of exiles there from all parts of China, who have to report themselves to the police once a month. These are the gentry who supply the brigand chiefs with recruits. Yet society was not, to outward appearance, more villainous than at other places. People at Tsitsihar have one disagreeable trick,

which we afterwards found common all over the north,
of carrying, grasped in one hand, a couple of large
cornelian marbles, or else two walnuts, which they are
for ever twiddling and grinding one against the other
in a way eminently calculated to set one's teeth on edge.
The theory is that it is good for old people to keep
their fingers supple; but here everyone did it, and
very irritating it was. Even our ruffianly little servant,
Chiang, thought he would be in the fashion, but I soon
put a stop to that. Even American gum-chewing is not
so objectionable.

There was little to see at Tsitsihar. The officials,
as usual, would not receive us. Most of the troops
were brigand-hunting in the neighbourhood, but we
saw a few on parade with flags and the usual paraphernalia. The gun drill is apparently trusted to boys, and
the guns were little brass howitzers. Most of the soldiers
were Manchus, and they treated us more civilly than
usual. A funeral here was interesting. The coffin,
painted red and of enormous size, was carried on a huge
litter, and followed by a band of music and a crowd
of women in carts. They were dressed in their best,
their heads one mass of silver combs and ornaments.
They chatted and laughed and smoked, and evidently
enjoyed themselves. It is singular what pleasure old
women take in funerals, no matter what part of the world
one may go to. The first traces of Russian proximity
were visible in a shop full of Russian fabrics, chiefly a
rough kind of serge, dyed in bright colours, purple and
blue, and they gave us a longing to go on to Blagovaschensk. But we had had enough of Mongolia. We
had been looking forward to first-rate snipe and duck
shooting, and had even dreamed of swans and other
majestic birds; but, north of the Sungari, we had been

x 2

bitterly disappointed. Occasionally we came across a
few ducks, but they always kept out of shot. There
were quantities of rooks mixed with white-breasted
crows, but they were of no use, and, with the exception
of an occasional lapwing, a shrike, or the cranes, which
were too wary to let us near, and the bustards, which
were almost as wary, the absence of bird life was conspicuous. Then the Mongol boys on ponies were always
chevying the antelopes, so these animals were unap-
proachable. The advance of autumn had killed the
flowers, and there was no more botanising to do. A
journey to the Amur, a march of at least three weeks
on the road, with the possibility of the Russians refusing
to let us cross the frontier, did not present many attractions, and for several days past we had all found
the road somewhat wearisome. We made up our minds,
therefore, to strike across a new line of country and
go by a direct route across the steppe to Sansing.

Readers who are interested in this region should
peruse the account of the Archimandrite's journey
already alluded to. Suffice it to say that he describes
the country north of Tsitsihar as just what it is to the
south of it, a boundless rolling plain, dotted with postal
stations, and inhabited by Solon Manchus or Dahurs
(Daurians),[1] a Tungusian tribe. Mergen is more like a
village than a town, lying in an open desolate country,
bare of trees. Beyond is a steep pass over the range
which forms the watershed between the Nonni and the
Amur, covered with dense forests at the top. Hei-lung-
kiang, called by the Jesuits Saghalien (the first is the
Chinese, the other the Manchu word), is now only a
post station. Beyond that lies Aigun, the main Chinese

---

[1] *Vide* page 23, footnote.

outpost on this part of the frontier. Seventy li[1] farther on comes Sakhalin, and opposite to that, on the left bank of the Amur, stands Blagovaschensk, the principal Russian station on the Upper Amur.

[1] So says the Archimandrite. A gentleman who did the journey told us it was only thirty or forty. The Jesuits call it thirteen li; perhaps they meant miles.

ORNAMENT FROM A TILE ON A MONGOL LAMA'S TOMB.

CHAPTER XI.

TSITSIHAR TO SANSING.

The steppe—Artemisia plant—Soda and other salts—Primitive method of
extracting soda—Wolves—A sad story—A Mongol cottage—Mongol
children—Hsiao-chia-tien—Hulan—Manufacture of cart-wheels—Donkey's flesh—A terrible massacre—Pei-lin-tzŭ—Wild-goose shooting—
Brigands in the road—The Chrétienté—The priest's room—A victim of
opium smoking—Deep wells—Fortifications against brigands—A curious
weapon—Harvest—Pa-yen-shu-shu—M. Raguit—M. Card—Home-
made wine—Hsiao-shih Ho—M. Riffard—Experiences of brigands—Our
escort—Extortion—Verdict of Europeans on the Chinese—Sport near
Pa-yen-shu-shu—An ancient plate—Low degrees of temperature—Wise
colonists—Good pheasant-shooting—Fowls of the mist—Our landlord
and the brigands—Arrival at Sansing.

WE had arrived at Tsitsihar (locally known as Pu-k'uei)
on September 20—that is to say, on the seventeenth day
after quitting Kirin, from which it is distant about
360 miles. We left on the 23rd, steering south-east
across the downs towards a place called Hulan, lying
north of the Sungari about 200 miles away. We heard
that in that neighbourhood a great area of country
had been recently reclaimed, and that large towns were
springing up, the names of which had not found their
way into European maps, so we determined to see
them for ourselves.

It took us a week to cross the steppe. Near Tsitsihar it is very wet, and for a mile or more in one
place the water was over our axles, ending in a deep
w‛   the passage through which drenched our
          ‛e mules in Fulford's cart commenced by

lying down, and, to all appearances, we might have
stayed there for weeks; but some empty carts came
up and relieved us of some of our heavy things, and
so we got through safely. Farther on, the ground lay
higher, the undulations of the surface forming a regular
series of ridges about four miles apart, from the top of
which the prairie could be seen for miles, rolling away
like a sea of giant billows. The steppe was mostly
covered with high grass, or with very dense artemisia,
several varieties of which grow profusely, and which is
cut in the autumn and piled up for use as fuel during the
winter, making the whole face of the country seem dotted
with haycocks. In some places the steppe was barren,
the soil being full of soda and other salts, which are
extracted by primitive methods, like borax at the works
near Leh. The efflorescence is scraped up from the
edge of brackish pools, mixed with water, and boiled.
In the case of soda suitable for making bread (mien-
chien-tzŭ), the strained mineral deposits itself in crystals
at the bottom of the pot, and is taken out in large
cup-shaped masses several inches thick. For making
another kind, called chien-tzŭ, the deposit which collects
at the bottom of the caldron is ladled out into a
wicker-work basket and allowed to drip through. The
result is a fine, moist, brown substance, which is put
into moulds and pressed into bricks, each weighing
55 catties, or about 75 lbs. Soda, delivered at the
works, costs about 3s. for 50 catties, or about 66 lbs.
The other substance fetches 1s. 6d. per brick of 55 catties.
Fifteen men were engaged on the work, who earned
about 3s. a day amongst them; but the work only goes
on in the winter and in dry weather, as for want of other
fuel the fires are only kept up with dried grass. The
steppe otherwise was almost uninhabited, a house or

inn being only met with at intervals of twenty or thirty miles. In winter, when the snow lies deep, large packs of wolves frequent it, and one of our cartmen told us he was once beset by a small number. They followed his cart, and he kept shouting at them in mortal terror, till, fortunately, two horsemen rode up and the wolves took to flight. Autumn was by this time advancing rapidly, and, though the days were bright and sunny, the nights were cool. On September 25 the thermometer registered 37° Fahr. in the morning, and at noon 102° in the sun, almost as great a difference as in the Himalayas in spring. On September 28 it froze for

AN OIL-CART.

the first time—the thermometer showed 25° Fahr.—bringing the leaves off the dwarf birch-trees which occur sparingly over the steppe. A number of oil- and wine-carts passed us going to Tsitsihar, each with a huge wicker-work basket, lined with oiled paper and quite water-tight, constructed to fit into the cart. The Mongols are very bad farmers, their scanty cultivation being full of weeds, so they depend on the Chinese, as far as they can, for luxuries and even the necessaries of life. Were they more industrious, there would not be so much need perhaps for celibacy on a large scale. But they are naturally nomads, or the descendants of nomads, and ingrained national characteristics cannot be dropped in a moment.

At a house used as an inn we met an old man who had a sad story. He had been to Hulan with a horse and cart to buy grain and stores. On his road back he lost his way and had to camp out in the open. His horse escaped from him, and he spent two days trying to catch it. Then he found his way to the inn, where assistance was given him; but, when they returned to the place, the cart, containing all his worldly wealth, had disappeared. In wandering about he ran a thorn into his foot, which festered until both foot and leg became one deep ulcerous sore. The people of the inn knew him well, and there was no doubt that his tale was true, but he bore his lot uncomplainingly.

One tiny little Mongol cottage at which we stopped was a model of neatness and cleanliness, contrasting greatly with Chinese houses. It contained only two rooms. The first was the kitchen, where nai-p'i was always kept simmering. The inner room served both as parlour and bedroom. A k'ang with a nice clean mat occupied three sides of it, so that there was only a yard or two of floor-space in the centre. On entering, the wall to the right was piled up to the ceiling with chests and boxes of lacquered wood ornamented with pretty brass handles and locks kept scrupulously bright. Facing the door was a large cheerful window, next to which stood an elegantly carved black cabinet containing an image of Buddha, in front of which, on a projecting shelf, a series of bright brass lamps and incense-burners was arranged. The screen, for it was little more, dividing the living room from the kitchen was made of prettily designed lattice-work, and over the door hung the

master's matchlock and powder-horn. The mistress
of the house, a buxom, good-looking dame, invited
us in. While we were discussing the milk and nai-p'i
which she offered us, some neighbours, with their wives
and families, came in to see us. The children were
pretty, engaging things, and it was pleasant to see a little
girl nestling up to her mother to be kissed and have
her head stroked, for one seldom sees the undemon-
strative Chinaman indulging in such tokens of affection.
One young girl of about seventeen was remarkably
pretty, her great brown eyes and olive complexion
recalling one of Murillo's Madonnas. The men had
good-humoured, pleasant faces, and heads shaped exactly
like a plover's egg, with prominent cheek-bones and
pointed chins. The Chinese are great smokers, but the
Mongols beat them hollow. Even their babies enjoy
the pipe. While we were at lunch an old gaffer came
in to pay the strangers a visit, and it amused us to see
him tap a little girl, not more than six years old, on the
head and give her his pipe to light. The little maid
ran nimbly to the fire, put the pipe to it, and puffed till
the pipe was fairly under way, and then she handed
it to her old grandfather, but not without taking one
long final pull at it herself, showing how much she
enjoyed it. And a little later we saw the lady of the
house and a gossip from next door settling themselves
comfortably on the k'ang for a confidential chat, smoking vigorously, and expectorating at intervals with a
copiousness and accuracy that would have done credit
to Mr. Hannibal Chollop.

As we got farther south the soil and vegetation of
the steppe improved, and herds of fine ponies and sheep
became very numerous. At last we emerged upon
cultivation again at a place called Hsiao-chia-tien. The

change from prairie to ploughed land was very abrupt, and marked the border between Mongolia and Manchuria. From the limit where the Chinese farmer began the fields were as carefully cultivated as in Lombardy. We had now entered upon a strip of country, varying in breadth from 100 to 200 miles, between the Sungari and the mountains. Most of it has been reclaimed in the past twenty years, and the crops are worthy of the virgin soil. After leaving the steppe twenty miles behind we came to the river Hulan, a sluggish stream about 150 yards broad, across which we were ferried. A young married couple with an infant were crossing at the same time, and the way they wrapped up their treasure to keep the cold wind off its face, crooning over it and singing to it—in fact, worshipping it—was delightful to behold. Half-way across, the mother carefully handed over her charge to the father, and went herself to the stern of the boat, where she solemnly dropped a few cash into the water —an offering, I suppose, to the genius of the river for a safe passage across to her baby. The young parents seemed quite pleased when I noticed the child and played with it, though most Chinamen would not care for a foreigner doing so.

The town of Hulan is situated at a bend of the river, ten miles beyond the ferry, and about eight or ten miles from the junction of the river with the Sungari. It contains about 30,000 inhabitants, as far as we could judge, and consists chiefly of a long broad street, about a mile and a half from end to end, running away from the river. The shops are as good as any in Manchuria, with the single exception of Moukden, and there was every sign of a thriving trade, articles of luxury as well as in the necessaries of life, such as lacquered furniture, mirrors, china and pewter ware, furs, cloth, and, of course, coffins. The principal branch of industry is the manufacture of cartwheels and vast quantities of stoneware pots, which are exported by boat all over Northern Manchuria. In the river several good-sized boats and junks were

A CHINESE CARPENTER.

moored. They ply principally between Kirin and Sansing. Heaps of very fine logs proved that the forests in the hills to the north are now being worked. Hulan is the place where a French missionary, Père Conraux, unfortunately shot a mandarin a few years ago; but I shall give an account of that regrettable incident farther on. The market was well supplied with donkey's flesh. This delicacy is very popular in Northern Manchuria, and the unfortunate ass's tail is always displayed erect on the butcher's stall, so that the buyer may feel certain that common beef or mutton is not being palmed off upon him.

While we were at Hulan an incident occurred which proved how close we were to barbarism. A few weeks before, a party of twelve men went into the hills to the north to dig a medicinal root called huang-chi. While so employed they were attacked by a party of wild Solons, who killed them all except three and took away all their property. The three survivors owed their escape to being absent from the camp at the time. They heard the firing, and, advancing cautiously behind the brushwood, were witnesses of the massacre of their companions, so they turned and fled for their lives. They had just come back to Hulan and were engaged in offering up incense and thanksgiving to the gods for their preservation, which shows they were grateful, at any rate. We inquired what measures would be taken to punish the murderers, and the answer was, 'None. How can the mandarins go into the mountains to attack the wild tribes?' The Chief Superintendent of Nomads, who receives an annual tribute of furs from these hunters, apparently has no control over them as far as keeping order or repressing crime is concerned.

From Hulan we turned north-west, across a rich country, to a new town called Pei-t'uan-lin-tzŭ, or Pei-lin-tzŭ. The harvest was by this time in a forward state, and the air resounded with the cries of wild geese which came to feed on the grain. There were two sorts, *Anser albifrons* and another much larger. Fulford led off by stalking a party and dropping three at a shot, and this led to our wasting a good deal of ammunition, firing at them flying overhead. But we soon learned to judge our distances, and every day we bagged a few. They were very good eating, and, as for sport, there is hardly anything to equal the pleasure of pulling a fine old goose going about sixty miles an hour out of the skies. It may be cruel, but the thump with which he comes down is undeniably gratifying, and the birds were a valuable addition to the larder. They were very difficult to stalk, for a wary old gander would mount on the top of a stook, and keep as sharp a look-out as an old buck ibex or oorial. Pushing on, to reach Pei-lin-tzŭ by nightfall, we passed the river Ni, a stream flowing through the centre of a swamp, and were then still a few miles from our destination. Just as night came on we saw in the shade of a millet-field five gentlemen, who our cartmen at once said were brigands. They were standing by the roadside and each carried a gun. We always kept our own guns handy, and as we drew near we held them quietly across our knees. I, for one, marked the man I intended to fire at if they came near us, but we were going at a good pace downhill, and, as they showed no signs of attacking us, we did not meddle with them. They were strong young fellows, all dressed alike, and I could not help wondering if they were a police patrol, but the Chinese knew better. The fact is, we had just reached the thick of the brigands' preserves. Gentry of the kind like the edge of the backwoods, where the administration is weak, and the mountains which border this region on the north afford them excellently secure retreats.

Pei-lin-tzŭ itself is a rapidly growing town, surrounded by a moat and mud wall, with little guns at the four main gates. This is the place I mentioned in a previous chapter as having been sold to the brigands by the military officer in charge. Like the Pindaris of India in the early part of the century, the banditti occasionally torture people who are suspected of concealing money or opium, by burning their fingers or hanging them up by the thumbs; and a less cruel but equally effective way is to keep chopping gently on the back of the victim's neck with a sword, just drawing blood, until he at length confesses. The uncle of one of our cartmen had emigrated to Pei-lin-tzŭ a few years before, and was kidnapped, being thought well to do. He could not pay the ransom demanded, and lost his head in consequence. But, in spite of it all, Pei-lin-tzŭ flourishes, and the shops are remarkably good for so out-of-the-way a place. The day after we arrived we went for a walk in the town, and were soon pursued by a howling and jeering mob. They crowded round us, trod on our heels, peered into our faces, and at last one very dirty fellow came behind and caught hold of my coat between his finger and thumb. Instinctively I whipped round and 'caught him one' on the nose with my fist. He instantly dropped to the rear, making such a horrible wry face that the rest of the people roared with laughter, so no harm was done. After that they did not come quite so close, but when we turned into a distillery to see native whisky being made they pressed in after us, trampling over everything, till the owners begged us to go away and make inquiries about distilling somewhere else.

Pei-lin-tzŭ is the most northerly station of the 'Société de la Propagation de la Foi.' The priest, M. Card, was not at home, but we visited the Chrétienté, which is situated in an enclosure surrounded by a lofty boarded paling. The chapel is a small room,

neat and unpretentious as a 'Little Bethel' in England.
Its windows are filled with glass, not paper. The
altar is of plain stained deal, with pewter candlesticks,
and a few sacred pictures decorate the walls. On
the other side of the yard was the priest's own room,
which the sacristan invited us to enter. It was neatly
furnished, the bookshelf being full of standard works,
theological and scientific as well; while an aneroid,
telescope, and other instruments showed the owner to
be a civilised being. There was no fireplace or stove,
which appeared strange at a place where the thermometer falls to −49° Fahr. We learnt that the priest
had run a series of flues under the brick floor, which are
heated like a k'ang, and they warm the room perfectly
with a singularly little expenditure of fuel.

Our quarters were in the common room of the inn,
where we saw one of those rare specimens, a victim
to immoderate opium smoking. He was a commercial
traveller, and smoked all night long and part of the
day besides. His frame was like a living skeleton, at-
tenuated and cadaverous; he scarcely ever ate, and
only occasionally drank cups of tea. He was truly a
miserable spectacle, only less repulsive than the confirmed drunkard.

The wells in this neighbourhood are 100 to 120 feet
deep, a marked contrast to the rest of swampy Manchuria, where water bubbles up to the surface.

From Pei-lin-tzŭ we turned towards the south-west
again. All along the road the farms and hamlets were
fortified against brigands with high walls and bastions.
The distilleries were really formidable places, with
strong brick walls, eighteen feet high, surmounted by
terre-plein and parapet all complete, the gate fortified,
and at each angle flanking towers armed with small

carronades, which are protected from the weather by
picturesque cupolas or pavilions. The doors and door-
frames are of sheet iron, ornamented with massive studs,
and strengthened with heavy locks and bars. Groups
of buildings in the inside are often gaily ornamented, a
proof that the trade is flourishing, and the lofty chimney
reminds one of an English factory. These distilleries represent the capital and wealth of the district, which
can only export its surplus grain in the form of liquor,
owing to its distance from the sea and the badness of
the roads. In the fields and along the roads the
country people were armed with matchlocks and swords,
and some travellers carried a curious life-preserver like
a flail, made of bolts of iron four or five inches in
length, joined to one another by iron rings. The
handle was of wood, and at the end of the lash a long
and heavy piece of iron was attached. Wielded dexter-
ously it would give a fatal blow, but it would be useless
at close quarters. It is an ancient military weapon,
and some of the banner-men at Peking are still armed
with it. Except for these disquieting signs the aspect
was that of an industrious and peaceful community.
The fields were carefully tilled and the crops splendid.
Pedlars might be seen hawking their wares about the
farm-houses, or a blind fiddler or flute-player discoursing sweet music in front of a roadside inn, or
at the village well, as if brigands and crime were
things unknown. The harvest was half over, and the
grain was being trodden out by oxen or ponies, generally not muzzled, or else a light stone roller, such
as is used in spring-time for crops sown in ridges,
was dragged over the ears on the thrashing-floor.
Then the chaff and grain together were thrown into
the air with a spade, and the wind blew the chaff to

Y

one side. This primitive mode of cleaning the grain
was rather a surprise, as even at T'ang-ho-k'ou we had
found winnowing machines exactly the same as in
England.

Thirty miles from Pei-lin-tzŭ is the fine village of
Chao-hu-wu-pu, surrounded by a low mud wall and a
wet ditch, the head-quarters of the field force on duty
hunting brigands. All told, 600 men were so engaged,
and they had succeeded in catching and putting to
death a large number of the enemy (a missionary put
the figure as high as 600 in the two previous years).
Beyond Chao-hu-wu-pu, the rich dead level changed
into an undulating tract, much cut up by water-courses,
with here and there copses of poplar or willow. Thirty-
five miles of this brought us to Pa-yen-shu-shu, the
third and last of the Hulan group of towns. It also
contains about 25,000 inhabitants. The mud walls are
seven miles round, and so weak that all bankers' and
important merchants' houses are separately fortified.
The inhabitants hope for an imperial grant to surround
the town with a wall of stone. Père Raguit, another
Roman Catholic missionary, is stationed here, and we had
the great pleasure of finding him at home, as well as
M. Card, from Pei-lin-tzŭ. Both gentlemen were attired
in the garb of ordinary French priests, and looked right
worthy specimens of the Caucasian race. M. Card in
particular displayed so superb a beard that, compared
with the Chinese around him, he appeared like a lion
amongst jackals. They received us with the greatest
cordiality.

The Chrétienté at Pa-yen-shu-shu is older and the
buildings more elaborate than those at Pei-lin-tzŭ. The
church is much larger, though, I am glad to say, it
requires an additional aisle already. M. Raguit has a

beautiful garden, which even at that late season of the
year (October 4) was still gay with flowers. It also
grows very fine vegetables; and when we left M. Raguit
filled our carts with cabbages, carrots, potatoes, and
lettuces, equal to anything in Covent Garden. The
versatility of the French is well exemplified in various
ingenious measures which M. Raguit and his *confrères*
adopt to save themselves expense and make life tolerably comfortable. They manufacture capital claret
and eau-de-vie from the wild grapes, hardly bigger
than black currants, which grow in the hills, and
good sound liquor it is. We half hoped the fathers
might have some news of Europe, but they had received none for a long time past. M. Raguit had not
even heard of the fall of Khartoum in the January
of the previous year (1885). Far from the madding
crowd's ignoble strife, getting news and supplies perhaps once a year, these good missionaries toil at their
Master's work and heed not the great world outside.

I went into M. Raguit's school, but in consequence
of an epidemic fever only half-a-dozen children were
present. One little lad came forward and repeated
his catechism at lightning speed, *comme un perro-
quet*, standing Chinese fashion with his back to his
master, a position designed to prevent him looking
over his master's book, and to enable the latter to
box his ears soundly without the little victim knowing
what is coming.

We spent two days very pleasantly with M. Raguit
and his *confrère*, and gained a great deal of information
from them as to the state of the country and administration. Our next halt was at Hsiao-shih Ho, ten miles
off, close to the Sungari, where resides a third missionary,
Père Riffard. M. Raguit and M. Card were both fine

specimens of Europeans, but no more stalwart figure than M. Riffard's ever came to the East. He also greeted us with much kindness, and took us into the woods adjoining his house, where, in a short space of time, we bagged thirteen pheasants. M. Riffard[1] himself is a good shot, though, like a courteous sportsman, he allowed his guests to take all the shots. He had trained a great Chinese dog, named Pickwick, and it retrieved several winged birds very successfully.

As might have been expected, we heard a good deal from the missionaries about the brigands. All three had had their experiences. M. Card was in Pei-lin-tzŭ when the brigands were repulsed the year before. And he was once surrounded by a mounted party while travelling, but *cantabit vacuus coram latrone* Sacerdos, and when he showed his beard out of the cart the villains incontinently made off. In Pa-yen-shu-shu itself the yamen had been burnt down by robbers a few years before; and a few months, almost a few weeks, before our arrival M. Riffard had been a spectator of two different attacks on shops at Hsiao-shih Ho. The first time, the merchant capitulated without striking a blow, and a great deal of money and opium was carried off. But the second place attacked was defended by a watch-tower, from which the inmates fired on the brigands and drove them away. To hear all the stories it is difficult to decide whether the people who are robbed, the brigands who rob, or the troops that pursue the robbers, are the most cowardly. The soldiers catch a good many, it is true, but cases are of frequent occurrence when brigands caught inside a building have shown a bold front and forced their way out. The authorities, solicitous for our safety, sent

[1] Alas! M. Riffard is since dead—a victim to typhoid fever.

a mounted escort with us, but they were not of much use. After leaving Pei-lin-tzŭ, for instance, they all dropped behind. They turned up at Pa-yen-shu-shu the day after we did, and coolly asked for a certificate that they had efficiently protected us. Beyond Pa-yen-shu-shu the road was considered especially dangerous, and fifteen men and two sergeants followed us about for several days. The first thing they did was to jump off their horses and plunder the cart of an old man who was bringing a cart-load of wild grapes; and, as they were always either a long way behind or a long way ahead, the protection they afforded was only nominal. At the same time, we felt grateful to the authorities for the interest they took in our safety. The soldiers were a picture, reminding one of an impecunious rajah's following in India. They carried a perfect museum of arms—Brown Bess muskets dated 1858, and carbines of German and American make. One who had a bayonet permanently fixed to his musket enlivened the proceedings by riding a race with a friend, when both their horses came down, and it was a marvel that neither man nor beast was impaled. Some of these soldiers act as police, and, being under-paid, prey on the people in many ways. One mode of extortion is not unheard of in India—the threatening, in default of a little palm oil, to carry off to the court as witnesses a number of persons unconnected with the case. Corrupt as mandarins are generally allowed to be, in this out-of-the-way province they appear unusu-ally bad. The same tale is told of them from highest to lowest. Sometimes the worm turns and higher authorities are appealed to. The chief mandarin at Pa-yen-shu-shu itself, a man of much influence at Court, had been dismissed a short time before; and with the aid of an enormous bribe sent to Peking itself, to which all the traders in the country subscribed, a still higher official had been got rid of.

It is a significant fact that I did not meet with one single European, even amongst the missionaries of the different churches who have cast in their lot with the Chinese for good, who did not give them an unpleasant character. *Menteurs, orgueilleux, lâches,* was the laconic verdict of one priest, and all describe them as so saturated with a love of material prosperity as to be but little sensible to the finer feelings. Some even assert that, in spite of the exaggerated deference enjoined by law and custom to parental authority, there is little real natural affection amongst them ; while in gross immorality they are said to surpass Persians or even Afghans. Sweeping accusations necessarily imply large deductions, and, I doubt not, many of my informants would themselves readily point out numerous exceptions from the general condemnation, so much easier is it to descry national faults than national virtues. I simply repeat the verdict as it was given to me, and I particularly noticed it because, in India, when a discussion takes place amongst Europeans about natives, the number of those who uphold the natives for their good points generally exceeds that of their detractors. Unquestionably the Chinaman has not many lovable qualities on the surface. Englishmen ought, properly speaking, to sympathise with his intense national pride ; but with this fine quality he develops so much superciliousness and selfishness, that he necessarily makes himself disliked.

In M. Raguit's yard was a noble stag, and M. Riffard offered, if we would prolong our stay, to get us some good tiger, bear, or deer shooting close by, with the aid of the Solon Tartars, who, said he, were included in his parish. Winter was approaching very rapidly,

and, as delay would have imperilled our journey on the
eastern frontier, we were compelled to decline. But
I feel sure that splendid sport awaits the traveller
who has time to go hunting in these hills. M. Riffard
mentioned that a tigress and cubs had just been killed
near one of his Christian villages, and a bear, which
seemed to have lost its way, was killed not far from
his own house. Wolves, he said, were very numerous,
and boys herding pigs were constantly carried off by
them.

I ought not to forget that M. Raguit gave me at
parting a curious old porcelain plate, which had been
dug up by one of his converts at a place where an
ancient city is believed to have stood, probably an old
Ketan town, even the ruins of which have perished.
Connoisseurs pronounce it to belong to the Sung
dynasty; in other words, it is as old as William the
Conqueror. It is now in the British Museum.

We inquired particularly how far the thermometer
fell in winter, as Mr. Ravenstein throws doubt on M.
de la Brunière's accuracy in stating that he had felt a
continuous cold of $-51°$ and even $-65°$ Cent. M. Raguit
had a thermometer, by Negretti and Zambra, gradu-
ated down to $-38°$. This, he said, failed to register the
extreme cold, which he had known as low as $-47°$ Cent.,
and M. Riffard had registered $-46°$. M. de la Brunière
appears, therefore, not to have exaggerated.

After leaving Hsiao-shih Ho the road runs parallel
to and not far from the Sungari, and the views afforded
of the mighty river were very fine. On our left were
the spurs of the Chingan range, which in places run
down to the water's edge, and south of the river rose a
chain of mountains which divides the valley of the Mai-
Ho from the Hurka or Mu-tan-chiang. M. Raguit told

us that the colonists in the Mai Valley have been wise
in their generation, and foiled any outsider settling
there who could not give a good account of himself
and his belongings. We passed through a wood, well
known as a lurking-place for brigands, where a fight
had taken place a short time before, in which some
of our escort were engaged. According to their own
account, twenty-four soldiers had routed thirty-two
brigands, of whom twelve were killed. We saw no
more bad characters, although a band was said to
infest the low grounds near the river, occasionally
plundering junks and river boats. Beyond, as far
as Sansing, the country was mostly uncultivated, the
annual tide of immigrants not having reached so far.
Great stretches of low oak scrub afforded splendid
cover for pheasants, and in the neighbourhood of
cultivation the quantity of birds was perfectly ridiculous. I have often seen a couple of hundred rise
off one little patch of stubble and go down in the
rough stuff close by, where they lay till we almost
had to kick them up. We killed as many as we
wanted, and very pretty shooting it was, and for two
or three months we lived almost exclusively upon
them. *Toujours faisan* is rather pleasant diet than
otherwise. Geese kept flying over us in countless
numbers, occasionally giving us a shot. One day we
saw two or three birds, jet black, like large grouse or
wood-pigeons, flying in the distance. They circled
round and we could see they were game birds of some
sort. The Chinese called them 'Wu-chis,' or Fowls of
the Mist. We could not make them out, and though
we saw specimens on one or two occasions, sometimes
sitting on the top of a stunted oak or else on a stook of
corn, they seemed very shy, and we did not get a shot.

It was not till we nearly reached Hun-ch'un that the mystery was cleared up.

Winter now began to show signs of approach ; in ordinary years it would have come much sooner. The thermometer at starting fell to 23° Fahr., and one day a snowstorm detained us. Fortunately the landlord of the inn was an intelligent man, who gave us much useful information. Asked if he had ever suffered from brigands, 'Oh, yes, frequently,' was his reply. 'Seven years ago I was carried off, and had to pay 2,000 taels (say 500*l.*) ransom.' We suggested as politely as we could that there were no outward and visible signs of his being worth a tithe of that sum. But he stuck to his tale, and did not appear to be hurt at our disbelieving him. He had probably told the story very often.

At Pai-yang-mu, a comparatively large village, we joined the main road from Kirin to Sansing *viâ* Asheho. Sansing is on the right bank, but the road crosses the river twice, as the cliffs on the Kirin side are impracticable. From this point onwards we were again under the jurisdiction of Kirin. The high road has been bridged, but many of the bridges are broken down, and some of the larger streams were just as deep as the carts could manage. Finally, on October 13, we arrived opposite Sansing. The wind was high and we crossed with difficulty, and then, after fording various lakes of black mud, in the high street, we reached a comfortable inn.

CHAPTER XII.

SANSING TO NINGUTA AND HUN-CH'UN.

Situation of Sansing—Population—Fort and barracks—Gold-mining by the
Government—Theatricals in the market-place—Fish at Sansing—
Sturgeon—Difficulties of the road—Accident to a cart—Scenery up
the Hurka—Tamaba salmon—Curious modes of fishing—Cantonment
at Yeh-ho—Ninguta—'Mr. Gladstone'—Theatre at Ninguta—Start for
Hun-ch'un—Cold weather—Edible pines—Lao-sung-ling—Black game—
Valley of the Tumen—Mi-chiang—Lieutenant-General I.

SANSING, the principal town of North-east Manchuria,
is situate about 180 miles above the junction of the
Sungari with the Amur, and 300 from Khabarofka, the
head-quarters of the Governor of the Primorsk. The
only communication with that place is by river, as the
Chinese do not care to be on too intimate terms with
their neighbours, and colonisation farther north is
discouraged, if not prohibited. There is, however, a
growing traffic in grain, which is sent down by junks
to Khabarofka; and Russian merchants occasionally
visit Sansing. By the treaty of Aigun, concluded in
1858, the navigation of the Sungari was conceded to
Russian merchants and travellers provided with a proper
passport by their Government. General Ignatieff's
treaty of 1860 omitted the provision, but the treaty of
St. Petersburg in 1881 revived it. Shortly afterwards,
a steam-launch ascended the Sungari as far as Hulan,
but the inhabitants stoned it, and the experiment does
not appear to have been repeated. The Russians pro-

bably consider it wiser not to force matters on, but to
allow the trade to expand gradually from the Chinese
side. In this way, every year, the *entente cordiale* between the two places and peoples is likely to improve.

The town, which contains between 15,000 and
20,000 inhabitants, does not seem to be flourishing, and
the shops are very poor. It is surrounded on three sides
by rivers—the Sungari on the north, the Hurka (called
by the Chinese the Mu-tan-chiang or Peony River,
but I shall use the shorter Manchu name in prefer-
ence) on the west, and the Wu-kung on the east.
The Hurka at Sansing is about 200 yards broad, and
for a mile below its confluence its clear blue waters can
be seen flowing side by side with those of the muddy
Sungari. The town is in the angle made by these two
rivers. The Wu-kung falls into the Sungari nearly a
mile to the west, flowing at the base of a precipitous
range of hills, and is about 100 yards broad at its
mouth. Sometimes it is sufficiently shallow to ford,
but at the time of our visit it was ten feet deep.
Looking down from a lofty eminence, the town appears
the centre of an amphitheatre of hills, which shelter
it from the wind and keep off the cold. In spite of
the advanced state of the season, the thermometer went
up to nearly 95° during our stay.

The fort and barracks are about six or seven miles
to the east. We told a sergeant who had been sent to
wait upon us that we were going to see them, and he
went away at once to tell the Lieutenant-Governor.
Back came a message to beg us not to go till we had
seen him. We were afraid there might be some objection, but another message came permitting us to go ; so
off we started. We swam our ponies across the Wu-kung,
and then climbed a steep hill overlooking the Sungari.

Beyond was a badly cultivated plain some three or four miles across, then a climb over another spur, and then eight barracks of the ordinary pattern—i.e. surrounded by a lofty earthen wall with a parapet.   A mile beyond stands the fort, a few hundred yards distant from the bank of the river.   The gate was wide open and we rode in, finding a petty officer on duty, who was very polite, showed us all that was to be seen, and afterwards gave us some tea.   The fort, which completely commands the approach up the river, is armed with large Krupp guns of the latest scientific pattern. That the Chinese Government should have gone to the trouble and expense of importing first-class artillery from Europe, and sending it over 400 miles of the worst road in the world to Kirin (beyond Kirin the passage was by boat), to defend a place like Sansing, shows a determination to make their frontier as impregnable as modern science can make it.

The soldiers of the Sansing garrison are not allowed to idle.   They were busily employed on various works at the fort, and at other times they dig gold—at least so we were told—in a Government mine in the vicinity.   We had seen in an inn a notice that mining of all kinds was prohibited, and a man was executed for infringing the rule only two days before our arrival. It is generally supposed the Chinese Government does not want to excite the cupidity of the Russians by letting it be known there is gold to be had, but perhaps the fact that it digs gold on its own account is the true explanation.   In theory, the digging of metals out of the bowels of the harmless earth is sacrilege according to strict Chinese notions, so the miner can always be punished for a breach of religious law.   But the Government itself is now giving up the pretence.   It has coal-mines of its own near Peking, and employs foreign geologists prospecting for metals in several pro vinces, so perhaps it will make a revenue some day out of gold-mines in Manchuria; it would be wise to do so, as its proclamations against mining are generally dis regarded.

One day we were fortunate enough to find a thea trical entertainment going on in the market-place, given by some merchants in honour of the God of Wealth. It really was very good, though of course we could not understand a word. A lean, sour-faced old woman, dressed in black, with hair plastered down like a prim old duenna on the English stage, was lecturing with uplifted finger a pretty girl in a fine embroidered frock, who with agonised face and clasped hands was listening to the harangue on her knees. An elderly father, with long grey beard, who evidently sympathised with the girl, was looking on ruefully, not daring to interfere, while a gay young lover, with a wobegone look, was timidly peeping round the corner. If only the actors had not, *more sinico*, spoken throughout in falsetto, the scene would have been perfect.

Sansing is a very good place for fish. The huang yü (literally 'yellow fish'), or sturgeon, is said some times to weigh 1,300 lbs., and many fine varieties of fish abound. But the season was late for all except the tamaha, or salmon, of which I shall have more to say farther on. We tried to make the acquaintance of the Yü p'i-ta-tzŭ, or Fish-skin Tartars, who wear clothes made of salmon-skin. They have now retreated a hundred miles down the Sungari, and only come up to Sansing in the winter to make purchases, so we did not see them.

We rested a couple of days at Sansing. Then, as

the thermometer was getting gradually lower, and the rivers were freezing across, we acted on advice given us by the French missionaries, and bought long sheepskin coats reaching to the feet, with the fleece inside and sleeves extending beyond the fingers' ends. Later on we found them invaluable. Then we turned our faces south, and followed the right bank of the Hurka till we reached Ninguta, about 170 miles from Sansing. There are eight stages on the road, with ten to twenty soldiers at each, who furnished escorts for our protection. These posts are garrisoned, partly from Sansing, and partly from Ninguta. The men have a variety of arms—Brown Bess muskets marked 'Tower' and 'Windsor,' Enfields, Winchester repeating rifles, and others. Their duties are to carry the post and occasionally hunt brigands. There are no inns, but the soldiers took us into their own quarters.

The road we now took was only made fit for cart traffic a few years ago, but we had our misgivings about it, which proved only too well founded. If we had known what it really was like, I doubt our attempting to take carts along it. The Hurka runs through a mountainous country, and the hills in many places overhang the water. Thus the road has to cross a never-ending succession of ridges from 200 to 1,000 feet high, the intervening valleys being simply swamps. As in Devonshire, the engineers made no attempt to lessen the gradients or improve difficult places, but simply followed the old bridle-paths, with the result that carts have to go straight up hill-sides, which in any other country but China would be considered absolutely impassable. And though some of the worst bits of bog had been rudely embanked or bridged in many places, the bridges, which were only oak saplings and turf, had in many cases collapsed. The second day

it rained, and the hill-sides were simply a succession
of morasses. Over and over again we had all to collect,
and shove behind, or to lift a cart out of a hole. One
bridge had a great chasm in the roadway, which the
leading cart managed to avoid, but the second fell
through, and we had to unload before the cart could
be righted. The day ended with a pull up a hill that
seemed almost perpendicular, and the carts could go only

A BRIDGE.

a yard or two at a time. Another day, going down a
steep descent to the river, two carts upset, and the shaft
of one was snapped. Then, after they were righted
and the shaft mended as best we could, the road took
us along the river-side between the cliff and the water,
in so narrow a place that we had to turn to and build
up temporary revetments of stone, and then the carts
could only just squeeze past. A mistake of an inch
and they would have toppled into the river, at that

place very deep. After that we thought we must be over the worst, but the soldiers shook their heads, saying, 'Wait till you come to the sky-scraping range.' This was the loftiest and steepest climb of all. One cartman, who fancied himself as a whip, declared he could do it with no assistance but men to scotch the wheels; but the gradient was too stiff. One of the mules staggered over the edge, the wheel of the cart followed, and over they all went down the hill-side, the cart turning two complete somersaults, and there they lay. The baggage was scattered far and wide, the hood of the cart was smashed in, but even the shaft mule was not hurt, and no serious damage was done. The rest of the carts we brought up one by one, with six mules harnessed to each and soldiers pushing behind, and at last they got safely up. But another time I think I should take pack-mules along this route. Indeed, had not the first frosts of winter begun, and the surface of the morasses become tolerably hard, we might have been compelled to turn back. Part of the way along we noticed telegraph poles lying by the roadside, destined for a line from Ninguta to Sansing. The soldiers said they had been distributed along the road in carts, and that the casualties to both carts and mules had been innumerable.

The scenery up the Hurka must be very lovely in summer. The river winds about in a deep valley between hills covered with dwarf oak, which come down to the water's edge, while on the east rises a chain of fine mountains, the tops of which are covered with lofty pine forests; these form the watershed of the Hurka and the Usuri. Much gold is found in the adjacent glens. The fall of the Hurka is very gradual; nor did we notice rapids anywhere. Its average width is about 100 to 150 yards, the depth varying from five to ten feet, so that there are no fords.

Forty miles from Sansing we stopped at Wei-tzŭ Ho, from which place starts the mule-track that was taken by the heroic M. Venault in his memorable journey to search for the murdered M. de la Brunière in the year 1850.[1] At the present day even carts find their way across the mountains as far as the junction of the Moli with the Usuri. Up to Wei-tzŭ Ho cultivation is pretty general, but south of it the valley narrows, and population almost ceases.

Around each stage there are a few fields of maize or millet, which attract pheasants in large numbers, and we got capital shooting. Had we been murderously inclined, our bag might have reached a startling figure. Here and there grey quail abounded also, and the hillsides swarmed with roe-deer. The soldiers gave us some heads, one of which is now in the British Museum. It is finer than any head I ever saw from Scotland. We also flushed a few woodcock. Again we saw the strange Fowls of the Mist, and once, when we were busy negotiating a rotten bridge, upwards of a hundred flew slowly over our heads, like a flock of tame pigeons. They settled on some willow-trees the far side of the river, so we could not pursue them. With my glass I could see that the males were deep blue or black and the females rich mottled brown ; but they sat crowding together on the branches like hens in a poultry-house, and we could not guess what they might be. Partridges were rare in the Hurka Valley. We only shot one.

Between Sansing and Ninguta the Hurka has four principal affluents, two on each bank, out of which

[1] *See* Note D, p. 423.

z

we saw tons of a salmon called 'tamaha' being taken.
This species travels in shoals, and the season had
come for their going up to spawn. Many devices are
used by the people to intercept them. Across the
Wu-su-hu Ho, a stream about thirty yards broad and two
and a half to three feet deep, a weir had been constructed of willow twigs, pierced with two small holes
at the bottom, on the far side of which was a coop.
The salmon pass through the holes, and, unable to get
beyond the coop, rise helplessly to the surface and are
then pulled out with a gaff. We must have seen
upwards of a hundred salmon collected in this way in
the space of a few minutes, the wretched fish, burst-
ing with spawn, being pulled out as fast as the gaff
could be put into the water. It was an extraordinary
sight. The salmon are split open and dried in the sun,
and they constitute a valuable and most palatable
article of diet during the winter. They are also netted
in large quantities, or pulled out with what is known in
Cumberland as a click-hook. Old men and boys sit all
the day long at points where a stream crosses a shallow
bed of gravel, with poles eighteen or twenty feet long,
at the end of which is a hook. The pole is placed in
the water, reaching halfway across the stream. As it
slowly floats or rolls down towards the bank, some
stray salmon swims up against it, and, instead of leaping
over, it follows along the pole till it reaches the hook.
Then the fisherman strikes, and the fish is hauled out.
The quantities taken are prodigious. At one place
alone we must have seen thousands drying. This
species is darker in colour and wants the silvery appearance of *Salmo salar*. There are two large teeth
in each jaw, and the sides are marked with extensive patches of pink. One remarkable feature in con-

nection with them is that their size scarcely ever varies. You might take a hundred, and it would be difficult to select by the eye one conspicuously smaller or larger than the rest. M. de la Brunière mentions the 'Tamaha' fishing in the Usuri. (*Vide* Note D, p. 435.)

On the ninth day after leaving Sansing the valley widened, and for the last fifty miles into Ninguta we had a fair road, with numerous flourishing villages and a wide extent of cultivation. Twenty miles north of Ninguta, at a place called Yeh-ho, there stands an important cantonment, containing seven sets of barracks ranged in a semicircle. Only four of them are now occupied, the garrison having been reduced. This post guards the head of the pass which leads across the hills to the Chinese outpost San-chia-k'ou, close to Poltavskaya, about 100 miles from Yeho, whence a road leads to the Russian station Nikolsk, about thirty-five miles on the south-east. The ancient city of Furdan, mentioned in 'Lettres édifiantes et curieuses' as the place to which the Manchu princes who accepted Christianity were exiled preparatory to being imprisoned and tortured to death, was probably near Nikolsk.[1] We halted a day at Yeh-ho, and went to visit the barracks, blocks of huts in rectangular enclosures, surrounded by lofty earthen walls. But on our way a message arrived from the commandant to say he had orders to help us on our journey, but had heard nothing about showing us his barracks, and enter we

[1] Mr. Grinnell, an American traveller, describes the remains of an old fort at Nikolsk as a rectangular fortress, with walls thirty or thirty-five feet high, covering six acres of ground. It had four gates, and was protected outside by a moat and two ditches. Mr. Grinnell also saw stone statues and elaborately carved fragments of columns. Like forts in the south of Fêng-t'ien, it is now attributed to Coreans, but probably dates from the Bohai kings.

z 2

should not. We returned a polite message that we had visited barracks at Tientsin and Yingtzŭ, and thought there must be some mistake This brought out the brigadier himself in full uniform, riding a fine horse, with an exalted button and a two-eyed peacock's feather in his hat. He was very polite but firm. Fulford explained to him that we did not care very much to see his barracks, as we had seen many like them elsewhere, but that, as we were passing, we thought it would be discourteous not to pay them a visit. We then bade him 'good morning' and went for a ride in the country. A meek little pony which Younghusband was riding signalised itself soon afterwards by suddenly kicking up behind and shooting the bold dragoon, who never dreamed of such effrontery, clean over his head into a muddy ditch. It was a startling and beautiful spectacle, and even the victim roared with laughter. Next day we crossed the Hurka by a ferry, and after seven miles more, on October 26, we arrived at Ninguta. Between the ferry and the town the river sweeps round in a great curve, and, though its general direction is north and south, at Ninguta it runs east and west like the Sungari at Kirin.

Ninguta is a flourishing place. When Mr. Adkins, formerly Consul at Newchwang, visited it in 1871, it had only 3,000 inhabitants. It now contains upwards of 15,000 to 20,000, and is growing daily. The country round is open and well cultivated, and there are numerous fertile valleys in the neighbourhood. Commanding the highway to Kirin and also to Hun ch'un, and furnishing an abundance of supplies in an otherwise sterile and mountainous region, it is a place of considerable importance; and it is said the Russians would have occupied it, as well as Sansing, if war had been declared

on the Kuldja question in 1880. It has no fortifications, the yamen only being enclosed by a lofty stone
wall. It is well situated close to the edge of the Hurka,
a clear stream three to four feet deep in the middle.
Though it is navigable all the way to Sansing, there
was not a single boat upon it besides the ferry. In
the summer, boats are said to come from Sansing for
melons, garlic, and other vegetables; but there is no
river traffic to speak of. On the bank near the ferry
were the heads of some brigands hung in cages to encourage law-abiding citizens.

Just after we arrived a card was brought in, bearing
in English the well-known name of Gladstone. When
the owner was shown in we were astonished to see a
Chinese telegraph signaller, who informed us he had
been given this appellation by his European instructors at Tientsin. He was a gentleman of varied accom-
plishments, including the Chinese violin, on which he
was good enough to play us a tune. I regret to say
that on our return we learned that 'Mr. Gladstone'
had been found wanting in his duty to his country—he
had forgotten the distinction between his own and his
country's cash, I believe—and he had been sent away
under guard with a heavy wooden collar round his
neck.

The telegraph office had just been opened. We
sent a message to Yingtzŭ, and learnt that the servant
whom we had sent there from Kirin had started on his
return on October 15. So we telegraphed to him at
Kirin to come on to Ninguta, and await our return from
Hun-ch'un.

At Ninguta, as at Sansing, the sight most worth
seeing was a theatre. (Chinese theatrical performances
in the country, be it remarked, are open free to the

public, the performance taking place on a stage in the market-place.) It was evidently a mythological piece, very like plays of the kind in India. The male performers wore masks, with great gilt helmets, ferocious moustachios and gigantic beards, just like the gods out of a temple, and one of them displayed a superb plume made of the tail feathers of Reeves' pheasant. They swaggered and ranted just like the Kurus and Pandus on an Indian stage, and the attendants, bravely got up with swords and daggers, mouthed it as well as the rest. Our advent drew the attention of the entire audience from the stage to our humble selves, and the pushing and shoving to inspect us was so great that we were glad to make our escape.

On October 29 we started for Hun-ch'un. The days were shortening fast, and from this time we had to get up by candlelight, and, after swallowing a plate of hot porridge and a cup of tea, start at the first streak of dawn. The thermometer, too, was getting lower and lower, and had now fallen to 11° Fahr. in the morning. The streams and bogs were freezing and the roads drying up and hardening. This made travelling easier, except at first, when the ice was just not thick enough to bear. Our sheepskins were now invaluable when riding on the carts. When walking, a thick English greatcoat, a Cardigan waistcoat, and a knitted woollen waistcoat below that sufficed to keep out the cold, except when the north wind blew, and then nothing short of fur or sheepskin was of any use. We crossed the Hurka, following up the valley of a small stream called the Hama (there is a better road to the right along the rich valley of the Ma-lian Ho). The second day one of the leading mules lay down, as was his wont, in a mixture of ice and mud, and it really looked as if

we should have to leave him, as, even when hoisted into
the air, the beast declined to put its legs to the ground.
He cared nothing for being beaten, and in the intervals
of torture calmly stretched out his neck and munched
mouthfuls of the frozen grass. As on the road from
Sansing to Ninguta, inns were conspicuous by their
absence; so at night we put up at the postal stages.
The third day we reached a forest of birch, spruce, and
pines. Amongst the latter was the edible pine, bearing
cones six inches in length, with seeds the size of
almonds packed tightly in rows at the base of each
layer of leaves. When the skin outside is cracked
and stripped off, the kernel is good to eat, though
perhaps a little tasteless. I counted 146 seeds in one
cone. The fourth day we ascended a very steep pass,
between two banks ten feet high and scarcely six feet
apart, so narrow that a cart could hardly pass. Just at
the worst place a huge tree had been cut down by the
telegraph people, which had fallen across the road, and
was just a few inches too low for our carts to pass
underneath. There was no possibility of getting round,
so we had to dig away at the ruts with a pickaxe to
deepen them and shave away the under surface of the
tree with an adze. It was cold, tedious work, as the
ground was as hard as a rock and the pickaxe un-
commonly blunt, so that it took us several hours'
patient toil before we could squeeze through. We
then crossed the top of the ridge called Lao-sung
Ling, or Old Pine Pass, 1,400 feet elevation, and descended into the vale of the Tumen.

On November 2 we arrived at Ssŭ chan, the fourth
stage, garrisoned by troops from Hun-ch'un. It was
situated on the banks of a rivulet, on the other side of
which was a grove of willow-trees about a mile in

length. What was our joy to see these trees full of
Fowls of the Mist !¹ We instantly crossed by a narrow
rickety bridge, in a way that would have done credit to
Blondin, and found them crowded fearlessly in the boughs.
So we opened fire on them sitting. The noise at first
was only sufficient to make them fly a few yards to the
next tree and wait to be shot at again, but eventually
they began to get scared. We then found what we had
for some time suspected—they were no other than
genuine black grouse. The black-cocks especially were
very fine birds, though not nearly such good eating as
pheasants. None of us had an idea we should find
black-game in Manchuria, much less sitting upon trees
as tame as barndoor fowls.

After that we crossed a series of ranges, amongst
fine wild scenery, striking in one place the Kaya River.
Here and there there was a little cultivation. We heard
various tales of brigands, a party of whom had carried
off the proprietor of a pawnshop not long before and held
him to ransom; not money, but 700 ounces of opium
was the price demanded for his release. One day we
met another European belonging to the telegraph department, who had been constructing a line from Kirin
to Hun-ch'un. The marshes made his task extremely
difficult, but he had completed it most successfully.

On November 5 we entered the main valley of the
Tumen, at a point which appeared like the bed of an
ancient lake. All around the base of the hills were the
gravelly relics of a primeval beach, just what one sees
in the valley of Cashmere. We reached the bank of the
river at the mouth of a very narrow, precipitous gorge,
through which during the lapse of ages the river has
forced its way. The Tumen is a very disappointing

¹ A friend suggests that Wu-chi means Black-fowl and not Fowl of the
Mist. It is a matter for Chinese scholars to decide.

river. We expected to see a fine stream like the Yalu, but here, close to its mouth, it is scarcely more than 100 yards across, and full of rocks and boulders. Tumen is a Corean word, and the Chinese only know it as the Kaoli-chiang or Corean River. On the opposite bank was a walled Corean town called Ta-wen-ch'êng, and the country around it appeared comparatively flat and well cultivated. The Jesuit Fathers have recorded their sensations on reaching the banks of the Tumen, ' with nothing but woods and wild beasts on one side, while the other presents to the view all that art and labour could produce in the best cultivated kingdom. They saw walled cities, and determined the situation of four of them, which bounded Corea on the north.'

A few miles below the defile the road leaves the river on the right and passes the affluent called Mi-chiang and the village of the same name. Twenty miles farther on stands the town of Hun-ch'un. It consists of an enclosure about 800 yards long by 400 yards broad, surrounded by a lofty stone wall, inside which are the General's yamen and some inns and shops. The barracks are all outside, and so is the principal part of the bazaar. Everything is very spick and span, and avenues of young trees have been planted all about, quite like an Indian cantonment. We recognised with pleasure that we were now within a measurable distance of civilisation, for the shops were full of foreign goods imported from Russia, such as kerosene lamps, clocks, glycerine soap, comfits, biscuits, chintz, English teacups, American canned fruit, and a quantity of miscellaneous goods. Three parts of the things, I am glad to say, were English, and to a Cumbrian like myself, the sight of ' Ainsworth's Best Cleator Moor Thread ' in this far-distant place was most welcome.

Hun-ch'un is essentially a garrison town, though there are a few dealers in seaweed, toadstools, and medicinal roots, large quantities of which are sent to Ninguta and Kirin, and thence to all parts of China. There is also a considerable trade in deer-horns. Shortly after arrival we went to call on the General (Fu-tu-t'ung) I, an officer of distinguished service in the Taeping war. He was a most aristocratic-looking old man, and received us with great politeness in his room of state, the best furnished apartment we had seen in Manchuria. We complimented him on the cleanliness of the town and its surroundings, which contrasted greatly with the places we had visited. He replied deprecatingly that he had been there only six years and had not been able to do all he wanted; but he had made it a rule that each householder should, every evening, clean up that part of the pavement and street in front of his own shop. Previous to coming to Hun-ch'un, General I commanded at Aigun, on the northern frontier. After some conversation he gave us each a glass of madeira, and then opened a bottle of Heidsieck's champagne, which was very enjoyable. When we took our leave he promised to return our call, and said he would send us a dinner. Just before leaving we made an unfortunate mistake. We heard there was going to be a review next day, and remarked we should be glad to see it. He replied that it grieved him to say that foreigners were on no account allowed to be present on such occasions. This was a disappointment, as, if we had said nothing about it, we could have gone unasked, but after what had passed it would not have been courteous to do so, and for all we knew there might really be a rule on the subject for the benefit of Russian officers.

CHAPTER XIII.

NOVO-KIEVSK.

Forts at Hun-ch'un—Weapons of the garrison—Huge banners—Russian
frontier—Cossack outpost—Colonel Sokolowski—Service and pay of
Cossacks—Russian and Chinese Frontier Commission—Russians and
brigands—Russians, English, and Orientals—Novo-kievsk—Possiet
Harbour—Colonists—Coreans—Greek church—The pope—M. Methuen
—*Diner à la Russe*—Russian alarmists.

THE day after our arrival we walked round Hun-ch'un,
which is garrisoned at present by about 3,000 men,
and we visited a new fort, one of two that have been
built lately in the plain to the south-east of the town
and are to be armed with Krupp guns. The troops
passed us coming home from the review, some armed
with Brown Bess, and others with Winchester repeaters,
which apparently is to be the weapon of the future
throughout the Chinese army. There were a good
many lancers and gingall men, and around the General,
who travelled in a cart drawn by mules, was a forest
of banners—huge banners, chiefly red and blue, each
of which took a powerful man to carry. I suppose
this one garrison displays more flags than the whole
of the armies of Europe put together, from which it
may be gathered that the Chinese frontier force has
not yet adopted every modern European improvement.
Should they ever come to a conflict with their neigh-

bours across the border, one cannot help speculating whether the fate of the Assyrians will be repeated :

Like the leaves of the forest in summer are green,
That host with their banners at sunset were seen ;
Like the leaves of the forest when autumn hath blown,
That host on the morrow lay withered and strown.

The Russian frontier, which has only recently been demarcated afresh by a Chinese and a Russian Commission, is not more than eight or ten miles from Hun-ch'un. The road passes for five or six miles over an open plain, on which the Chinese have built the two forts I spoke of, and ascends a low range, an outwork of a lofty chain forming the watershed between the Tumen and the Suifun, a river which runs into the sea a little beyond Possiet Harbour. Scarcely a mile from the crest of this ridge there is a brass pillar, with an inscription stating that, by imperial command, Wu Ta Ch'êng, senior vice-president of the Court of Censors, and I-k'o-t'ang-a, lieutenant-general of Hun-ch'un, surveyed the frontier and set up the pillar in the fourth moon of the twelfth year of Kuang Hsü ; and about three miles farther on the Russians have constructed an outpost for 200 or 300 Cossacks. We were not provided with passports, as we had no intention of travelling in Russian territory, but we wrote to the officer commanding, asking leave to pay him a visit, in order to hear the news from Europe, and buy some stores and provisions. We received a most courteous answer, offering us the cordial but frugal hospitality of a Cossack. The letter was brought by a couple of his men, mounted on good ponies, who looked exactly like pictures out of the 'Illustrated London News,' dressed in long and warm brown frieze coats, sheepskin shakos, swords strapped to their saddles, and rifles slung across their backs ; with

their fresh, fair faces, and clear grey eyes, they looked
like beings of a world we had forgotten during the
months we had passed amongst Chinamen. We rode
across, and found Colonel Sokolowski busy with the
construction of the new outpost. The Chinese call
the place Hêng-ta-ho-tzŭ, or Swanka. In spite of the
bitter freezing cold, the whole place was like a beehive, for the Cossacks have to house themselves; and
a fine barrack-room, together with subsidiary buildings,
stables, hospitals, bakery, married quarters, officers'
houses, and last, but not least, a great Russian bath,
were under construction. We were told that the
grant for the entire station was only 20,000 roubles,
and I am sure a British Royal Engineer would consider
that ridiculously inadequate. The Colonel was himself
his own architect, engineer, and clerk of the works,
and his house was a miniature arsenal. On one side
were ranged the carbines of his men, and around the
room were nails, hinges, rope, twine, stirrup-irons,
leather—in fact, every kind of miscellaneous article
required by his men for their houses, their horses, or
equipments. He showed us all over the station, and
then gave us a capital dinner and a shake-down on the
floor.

Swanka is not, I should say, a very favourite Russian
station, situated as it is on a desolate hill-side in a very
out-of-the-way corner of the world. Perim, or Aden, or
Thul Chotiali are cheerful, sociable, and civilised in comparison. The Cossacks are only kept four years on
foreign service, and are then sent back to their homes,
though liable to be called out again with the reserves.
Their pay is 20 roubles, say 50 shillings, a month, but,
with the exception of a trifle allowed them for tobacco
and pocket money, all is expended for them by their com-

manding officer. They are allowed to use their Berdan rifles for sporting, those weapons being strongly made and not liable to break ; so that they are always bringing in a deer or a bear, for the hills abound with game. Occasionally a lucky Cossack kills a tiger, whose skin fetches as much as 150 roubles. They are mounted on trans-Baikal mountain horses, as Chinese ponies are not up to the work. But those beasts are difficult to acclimatise, and a large number have been lost by an unaccountable epidemic of blindness. The Colonel thought this might possibly be due to dust storms during the summer, or to the grass of the swampy hill-sides not agreeing with them.

The Colonel told us that he got on very well with the General over the border, and that he and some of his officers were going to spend a few days with him shortly, on the occasion of the dedication of a fine new temple. We told him how the old General had prevented our seeing the review. He laughed and replied: ' You should not have noticed the prohibition. You should always repay a Chinaman's courtesy by courtesy ; but when you have made up your mind that something is to be done, mere polite phrases should not stop you, as you cannot tell whether their objection is real, or merely put on to see the extent to which you will yield ;' which shows that the Colonel understands Oriental character. I replied that what he said was very true, but we did not know how far the prohibition might not be genuine, so we could not take the law into our own hands. The Colonel gave us an interesting account of his dealings with Imperial Commissioner Wu when settling the boundary, which had been revised from Lake Hinka downwards. He treated him, he said, as the representative of a great nation ought to be treated, gave him a guard of honour, and the rest of it, with the result that the whole business had gone off smoothly and satisfactorily. We heard afterwards that the Russians did not get everything they wanted, as they contemplated building their outpost on a ridge five miles nearer to Hun-ch'un—in fact, on a hill over-looking the new forts; but no doubt there was give-and-take on both sides.

I asked Colonel Sokolowski how the Russians dealt with brigands. He said that, properly speaking, they were brought in, tried, and imprisoned; but it now and then happened in the fight or pursuit that one or two Cossacks' rifles accidentally went off, and the brigand fell pierced with bullets. Such accidents were unfortunate, no doubt, but they had had the merit of absolutely clearing the Russian hills of the pest. I told him such accidents occasionally happened in India.

We met at Colonel Sokolowski's table a Chinese officer who spoke Russian, and who proved to be inter-preter to the Fu-tu-t'ung. He was quite at his ease, and kept up an animated conversation with Fulford. Incidents like this help one to realise the mistake which native gentlemen of India commit, in not making efforts to enter English society on friendly and reciprocal terms. .It is the fashion to blame British exclusiveness, but if, as I believe, social intercourse between natives and Europeans ought to be on a much better footing, the fault is the natives' own. In other countries an Englishman soon finds himself on friendly terms with people in society, but in India, though he may receive an advanced native gentleman at dinner, he will not be asked to his guest's house in return, unless to a 'nautch,' or similar dreary entertainment; and some of the most advanced natives systematically hold aloof. This social estrangement, if it be an evil, native gentlemen alone can cure.

Next morning we rode off to the principal military station, Novo-kievsk (called in Chinese Yen-Chi-Ko), fifteen miles farther on, on the north shore of Possiet Harbour. The road is rough and hilly and not very good. The telegraph wires were mounted on short crooked oak saplings cut in the hills, which contrasted unfavourably with the fine straight pine-trees invariably used by the Chinese Telegraph Department, though no doubt they cost less to put up. We soon reached an eminence, and obtained a beautiful view of Possiet Harbour flaming like a sheet of gold in the sun, with a circle of hills towering over it. The harbour, which resembles a long narrow lake more than an arm of the sea, is about twelve miles long by three or four broad, with mountains on all sides of it, and communicates with the sea by a long narrow inlet.

In summer, Novo-kievsk must be a lovely spot, surrounded by lofty mountains, with the ocean close by; but in winter its aspect is very desolate. (This is partly owing to the system of burning the dry grass on the hills at this season, with the object of improving the pasturage, and also of gathering hazel-nuts, which grow in abundance on dwarf trees. After the fire the mountains look very black and repellent.) Novo-kievsk bears a strong family likeness to a small Indian station; its shops, barracks, offices, and picturesque Greek church are scattered here and there, with quite the Indian want of system. The shops were just as good as the ordinary Parsee establishments in India, and we got all the luxuries we wanted. Possiet itself, a settlement of only thirty houses, is about two miles off as the crow flies, on the seaward side of the harbour, but by road round the head of the harbour the distance is ten miles. Novo-kievsk is situated on the edge of a small stream. Two or three miles to the north, up a valley, is a colony of farmers, but they were not doing very well. The Colonel informed us they did not grow enough food to support themselves, and the Government had to import flour to save them from starvation. The main object of these colonies is to assure communication between the various military posts, and to develop local resources. A good many Coreans have taken up land in the vicinity, and the Russians consider them docile, industrious, and well behaved. So much in favour were they till recently, that, according to a French missionary, a large number were brought to Khabarofka, and a colony of them formed on the left bank of the Amur,

A COREAN CART.

opposite the embouchure of the Sungari. Now, however, this is forbidden. We watched a party of young Cossacks being drilled, and others being instructed in gymnastics, and it was difficult to realise one was not back again in India. But the men go about dressed much more shabbily than would be allowed in an English cantonment. On the banks of the stream were a number of soldiers' wives, dressed in scarlet petticoats and brightly-coloured caps, who, in spite of the severity of the weather, were washing their clothes in

A A

the water. West of the harbour, at the point near the mouth of the Tumen, where the Corean, Chinese, and Russian frontiers join, is another Russian outpost.

We went over the Greek church, which is painted green outside, the roof with the usual steep conical bell-tower and dome. The pope was a man of rather effeminate appearance, with long soft flowing hair and beard. He could not speak Latin or French, nor we Greek, so the landlord of the Chinese inn interpreted for us in Russian. The entrance is by the west door. The nave is bare of seats, the only furniture being a kind of counter in one corner. A few pictures hang on the walls, and from the ceiling depends a large corona for lighting. The chancel is completely shut off from the transept by a panelled wooden screen, on the face of which are paintings, fairly well done, representing our Lord, the Virgin Mary, and the four Evangelists. The pope showed us in the transept a miracle-working picture (of St. Nicholas, if I recollect rightly), opposite which stands a massive silver candelabrum. We were allowed to go behind the screen and enter the chancel. The altar stands in the centre, not up against the wall as in Anglican churches. A book of the Communion office in Church-Slavonic language, handsomely printed in black and red, was standing open, and I asked to be allowed to see it. The priest misunderstood me, and, lifting up another book which lay upon the table, disclosed a sort of parcel wrapped up in cloth which was lying underneath. He untied the parcel, discovering inside a silk handkerchief, and inside that another. After he had opened several, he came to a piece of silk of a deep golden colour, into which was woven a picture of the Last Supper after Leonardo da Vinci. Inside that lay a lump of black bread resembling dirty wax—evidently that used for the celebration of the Holy Eucharist. It was shocking to see such a thing being displayed as a curiosity. The pope exactly resembled a Mahommedan moulvi in India, who unties wrapper after wrapper, to disclose at the end a page of the Koran written by Ali's pen, or a hair from the Prophet's beard.

We bought some coffee, biscuits, and other eatables to which we had long been strangers, and started back the next day, stopping to dine again with Colonel Sokolowski, who had invited several friends to meet us. One gentleman, M. Methuen, who spoke English, gave us the important news that Mr. Gladstone's bill for Home Rule had been defeated and that Lord Salisbury had become Premier. The conversation was a little mixed, being carried on in French, English, Russian, and Chinese, but we all got on capitally. The English idea of a *dîner à la Russe* differs somewhat from the reality. The meal began by drinking a glass (one or more) of vodka, accompanied by morsels of dried Kamschatka salmon, at a side table. After that we sat down, and the guests were told to help themselves out of a big dish placed in the centre of the table and changed at every course. The roast beef was equal to any found in 'Old England,' and the Crimean claret was excellent. After dinner we rode back to Hun-ch'un.

A correspondent of the *Times* recently[1] raised a cry of 'Russian encroachment' because the recent convention relating to the revised frontier line contains a proviso that only Russian, Chinese, and Corean vessels may ascend the Tumen. The correspondent represents the Tumen as navigable into the heart of Manchuria, and the only outlet to the sea except the

[1] *Times,* February 19, 1887.

A A 2

distant port of Yiṇgtzŭ, on the Yellow Sea. The cry is quite unfounded, for the rocky Tumen issues from pathless and uninhabited mountains, and I wish the Russians or any other nation joy of the trade they may find upon it. It is satisfactory that the alarmists are not all on one side. Colonel Sokolowski mentioned that our own China squadron had visited Possiet the preceding summer, and that Russian *gobemouches* were promptly on their legs declaring that Great Britain had designs on it. '*Ma foi*,' said he, 'what is it that you'd get if you did take the place? A few old mud and log barracks, some ponies and harness, and these barren hills. I wish you joy of them.'

A COREAN BRACELET

CHAPTER XIV.

HUN-CH'UN TO PA-CHIA-TZŬ.

THERE is a short cut from Hun-ch'un to Omoso, a place halfway between Ninguta and Kirin, but scarcely fit for carts. Like the rest of our route from Moukden up to this point (with the exception of two pieces of road between Kirin and Tsitsihar and Pei Yang-mu and Sansing), it had never been described, so we agreed that I should go alone and explore it, while my two companions returned to Ninguta, picked up Chang San with our letters, and caught me up at Kirin. Accordingly, I arranged to accompany a convoy of pack-mules which were going that way to Kirin, with loads of sea-weed, mushrooms, deer-horns, and the medical root previously mentioned, huang-chi. The muleteers stipulated that I should always get up and start at the same time they did, to which I assented, hardly realising at the time the responsibility I was undertaking. Just before starting, a small mandarin arrived to say that the Fu-tu-t'ung was coming to call. This was a surprise, as he had already returned our cards with a civil message that he was too busy to come in person. Before we had time to make any preparations for his reception, in the great man walked, dressed in his smartest clothes. His round winter hat was turned up with sable, with an opaque red button in the centre, the highest but one that he could wear, and a peacock's feather behind, set in a jade tube. His coat was lined and trimmed with beautiful sable, and over that came a black silk pelisse, or Inverness cape, lined with sable, the edges and cuffs trimmed with the finest white Astrachan fur. His petticoat was of dark maroon-coloured silk outside and Astrachan fur inside. I confess we felt very humble in the presence of so much magnificence, as our tweed shooting-coats were by this time just a trifle shabby, and, with greater regard to comfort than appearances, we had just bought ourselves each a delightfully comfortable, but very plebeian, cap of long soft fox-skin.

The General's object was to dissuade me from taking the hill route, as it was much infested by brigands. I assured him I felt quite certain no brigands would dare to touch anyone in a district where he commanded. He rejoined that, although every means had been taken to extirpate the pest, still there were great forests in which robbers lived like wild beasts, and that, in spite of all exertions, they would occasionally rush out and cut travellers' throats. I replied, with much deference, that after his warning of course the responsibility was on my own head if I got into trouble, but that a Russian gentleman had told me he had travelled that road. The General would, therefore, see it was impossible for me to abandon my intention, or I could not face my friends, much less the Russians, afterwards. The General gave in with a bad grace, would not stop till tea was brought, and went away.

We left Hun-ch'un on November 11, travelling together as far as the first stage, Mi-chiang, and there we parted company. To prevent any mistake about the early rising, the muleteers called me the first morning at half-past one. I got up accordingly, and marched with the mules some ten miles to an inn, which we reached before daylight. Then we breakfasted, and went on slowly over hill and dale for twenty more miles, getting in just at dusk; and the same sort of programme was repeated daily. The moment we arrived we had our dinner and went to sleep at once, about seven or eight P.M. The cold was becoming more severe. The first day, at starting, it was 7° Fahr., a day or two afterwards it fell to zero, and for several days in succession it was −6° and −7° Fahr. I carried a thermometer, and observed that the coldest half-hour of the day was just before sunrise. Between dawn and sunrise it invariably fell four or five degrees, sometimes more, and a few minutes after the sun had risen the mercury rose rapidly too. I walked most of the way, for, though I had brought a pony, my feet got so frightfully cold I could only ride for short distances. The Catholic priests had warned us that English boots would be of no use in winter, and recommended us to buy thick ones of Chinese felt, but these were so clumsy to walk in that I preferred Hoby's. It was somewhat tiring work, as, including the halt for breakfast, we were on the road for fifteen or sixteen hours daily, the mules being heavily laden and marching very slowly. Sometimes it snowed and blew, and then it was very miserable. Rattler went with me, wrapped in a little sheepskin coat. Luckless dog! he twice tumbled through broken ice into the water when the cold was below zero, and had to be wrapped in my sheepskin until he got warm again. Fortunately it was the bright half of the month, as a Hindoo would call it, and the moon was beautiful. The sensation was weird and solemn, as we went winding slowly up the ravines, through sombre forest—the silence of the night broken only by the regular tramp of the mules or the bark of a deer on the hill-side above, while a torrent roared below and the moonlight gleamed through the trees—till the top of the hill was gained, and the flood of light displayed the dim outlines of range upon range of hills with dark valleys between, and in the distance the snow-capped top of some monarch of the mountains. Nature seemed dumb with the intense cold, and when the mandarin significantly tapped his rifle and pointed gravely towards an approaching glen, there was a sort of feeling that, if the brigands were lurking near, instinct would betray their presence, no matter how quietly they might advance. Fortunately, we were not molested. By the General's orders I had a small escort, but they seldom took the trouble to get up in the morning, and trotted after us in daylight, a thing I should have liked to do myself, only my bedding was too bulky to carry on my saddle, and a pack-animal could not have caught the others up. To share our protection several other sets of mulemen, with forty animals or more, attached themselves to our rear, and the mandarin, whom I have already mentioned, and a respectable merchant took advantage of the same opportunity. I always carried my gun, and Chu-hsiu, who could shoot a little, was given a rifle. When day dawned we all presented a very curious appearance. My beard was a mass of

solid ice, and so were the fur lappets of my cap
and the woollen comforter I wore round my neck.
Mutatis mutandis, the Chinese were in the same plight.
The mules were all covered with hoar-frost and ice,
and from the muzzles they carried to prevent them
stopping to graze depended two or three thick icicles a
foot long or more. Sometimes a mule would stumble
in fording a rough stream, and then the wretched
animal would march on, cut and bleeding, a mass of ice
from head to foot; but they are very hardy beasts, and
the exposure seemed not to harm them.

The route I was now taking branches off from
the Ninguta road at a place called Liang-shui Chien-
tzŭ. The first day brought us to the Ka-ya Ho, not far
from its confluence with the Tumen. The next day
we crossed a ridge into the valley of the Wei-tzŭ Ho,
after which we climbed a long and lofty range, descending on the other side upon a river called the
Yang tzŭ Ho, which, so I was informed, was identical with the Wei-tzŭ Ho. At a village called Nan
Kang-tzŭ, on the banks of this stream, are situated
two barracks full of soldiers—a detachment from the
Hun-ch'un garrison stationed here to keep the hills
quiet. The big Krupp guns for the Hun-ch'un forts
were lying here. It affords a good illustration of the
difficulties of transport in Manchuria that they had
arrived so far the previous winter; but the thaw came
on prematurely, so they had to lie for a year till the
marshes and streams should be frozen once more. The
path continued up the valley of the Yang-tzŭ Ho,
past places notorious as the resort of brigands, right up
to the river's source, a distance of about seventy miles.
It then climbed a pass called Ha-la-pa Ling, crossed the
main chain of the Ch'ang-pai-shan Mountains, and de-

scended on to an elevated plateau, where rise the head waters of the Hurka and its numerous affluents. This plateau is divided into a series of fertile but very swampy plains, separated from one another by low ranges 1,000 to 1,500 feet in height, which, on the south, are covered with fine forests, while in the midst of them isolated hills occur, 200 to 500 feet high, rising abruptly like islands in a lake. In the winter it is a tolerably fair route for carts, but in summer the bogs must be almost impracticable, even for pack-mules. M. Methuen told me that when he once travelled this way a number of his transport animals stuck in the swamps, and tigers came down at night and devoured them. Throughout all the region, however, signs of increasing peace and prosperity were visible. Farms were fairly numerous, and the waste land in the valleys is being rapidly ploughed up.

The eighth day after leaving Hun-ch'un we reached a considerable village called Tung-o-kang-tzŭ. Twenty miles west of this is the principal town of the district, called Autun, or T'un-hua-hsien, where a magistrate resides, and which maps have hitherto put on the wrong side of the mountains in the Tumen basin. This is the place I have already mentioned [1] as the possible site of Odoli, which the Jesuits put exactly in this locality, and the next traveller should certainly go there. It lay out of our way, and I could not reach it myself. Tung-o-kang-tzŭ is situated on the river Sha Ho (by some called the Ta-sha Ho), near its confluence with the Hurka. This stream winds about more frequently and more grotesquely in a short space than the Wye itself, and its channel is sunk so deeply below the surface of the plain, that an incautious horseman might easily ride

[1] Page 32 *ante*.

over the cliff without the least suspicion a river was near. I took compass bearings of the route, in order to try and locate with some approach to accuracy the rivers and villages I came across, and, though I cannot say much for my success, I persevered under considerable difficulty. First, I had to take my gloves off and hunt for the compass in an inside pocket; then, to wait patiently till the needle had done swinging, with a bitter north wind blowing and my fingers rapidly freezing; then, to extract my pencil and note-book and record the observation, so that when I had finished my hands were numb and painful to a degree. As long as the air was calm the cold did not matter much, but when the north wind blew it was cruel.

On the ninth day from Hun-ch'un I crossed the Hurka at a place called San-chia-k'ou, a little below where the Sha Ho falls into it, and at its confluence with another river, the Chu-erh-tao Ho, the left bank of which the road then follows, till Omoso, a large village nearly 200 miles from Hun-ch'un, is reached. Ninguta lies about ninety miles to the east, and that represents pretty nearly the distance saved by the short cut. We now turned along the Kirin high road up a beautiful wooded glen, and another march brought us to the foot of one of the most important passes in Manchuria, the Chang-tsai Ling, over the watershed between the Hurka and the Sungari. It is about 4,000 feet high, covered with dense forest and very steep; in fact, when covered with snow or ice, traffic over it is stopped. A little below the top, on the Kirin side, there is a barrack, where a detachment of soldiers is stationed for the safety of travellers. In 1871 Consul Adkins reported that the pass was the terror of the Chinese trader who seeks to convey money or valuable

produce between Kirin and Ninguta.   No better place
could be found for an ambush of banditti than the
forest through which the road passes.   A very daring
act of brigandage was committed there on a rich convoy
coming from Ninguta a few days before Mr. Adkins
passed the spot, and he saw the bodies of the men who
were killed while trying to defend their property from
plunder.   This state of affairs is only a little improved
at the present day.   When our party passed, a gang of
twelve brigands was 'out,' as they say in India, and the
authorities at Omoso sent a strong guard with me in
consequence.   Soldiers were then busily scouring the
hills in search of the gang, whose house had been found
and burnt, though the birds themselves had flown.
The views on the pass were very fine, the noble forest-
clad range contrasting vividly with the dull frozen
plains and insignificant hills of the upper valley of the
Hurka, and recalling memories of the Long White
Mountain itself.

My convoy of mules followed the high road for
about twenty miles beyond the Chang-tsai Ling, and
then turned off again to the right by the base of a
curious hill, called La-pa-la-tzŭ, to the pass of Hai-
ching Ling, over another range.   The regular cart road
crosses by a pass farther south, called the Lao yeh
Ling; but the Hai-ching Ling, though about ten miles
longer, is so much less steep that even heavily-laden
carts sometimes prefer it.   Springs, however, abound in
places, which in winter convert the road into one sheet
of ice, and in summer it becomes a bog for hundreds of
yards together.   I had no means of gauging its height,
but I guessed it at 2,000 feet.   Both the ascent and
descent are made through pine-clad valleys, not so fine
as the Chang-tsai Ling, but still very beautiful.   The La-

pa-la-tzŭ, or Trumpet Hill, is very conspicuous for miles round. Pyramidal in form, with a bold rough sky-line and craggy precipitous sides, its formation resembles the Ch'ien Shan, or ' Hill of a Thousand Peaks,' east of the road between Yingtzŭ and Moukden, and ranges of the same character are found all through the Kuan-tung peninsula. It abounds with roe deer and yeh-yang, or wild sheep, an animal like a chamois, and several fine specimens were lying frozen at the cottage of a hunter, who was making a good trade in the meat. Not far from this hill, at a place called La-pa Ho-tzŭ, excellent coal is found, which is used in the Kirin arsenal.

On November 24, the fourteenth day from Hun-ch'un, I arrived at the banks of the Sungari below the powder-mills. The mighty stream had contracted its waters since we left it at the beginning of September, and was one marble sheet of ice over a foot thick. We marched straight across, and once again I found myself in Kirin. Two days afterwards, Younghusband and Fulford re-joined me. They had only spent one day in Ninguta, but had seen a good deal. When approaching that place they had taken the Ma-lian Ho route, and visited an ancient town called by the people Tung-ching-ch'êng, or ' Eastern Capital.' It was once a large city, with lofty stone walls and good houses, which have now fallen into complete ruin. The country folk believe it has been deserted since the Coreans held the country 1,000 years ago. Mgr. Boyer, whom we met shortly afterwards, told us that in his opinion this was the real Odoli. Consul Adkins, who reached as far as this point in 1871, believes it was the capital of the confederation of Tungusian tribes I have referred to in Chapter II., under the name of the Bohai State. Mr. Adkins's graphic description of the city I will quote in full: ' An earthen rampart, which is still in good preservation, forms an *enceinte* of fourteen or fifteen miles, in the north-west corner of which is an inner city of two miles in circumference. In the inner city the stone platforms of halls and pavilions are still to be seen, with the stone basements on which rested the wooden pillars that supported the roof. The plan of these buildings seems to be the same as that with which we are familiar in Peking, a series of pavilions built on lofty stone platforms and facing the south. Blocks of lava form the building material. In the courtyard of a temple, which stands in the south-east corner of the outer city, there is a very ancient and curious incense burner, carved from a mass of lava. It is about twenty-five feet high, in the shape of a pagoda, with its base resting on a lotus flower. A tablet erected forty years ago states that the site has been occupied by a temple ever since the days of Wufi, of the Han dynasty, B.C. 140. A scattered hamlet containing a few poor shops is all that now constitutes the city.'

On the road between Ninguta and Kirin, Fulford and Younghusband also passed over the remarkable 'Plain of Stone,' of which I subjoin a description, also in Mr. Adkins's words, only adding that my companions thought the film of lava very thin, as the water from the swamp below could be seen gurgling and forcing its way up through fissures in the rock. 'A broad valley, perfectly adapted by nature to become the bed of a lake, has been inundated by a lava stream coming apparently from the mountains lying on the north-west, and in place of a morass or body of water there is now a body of solidified lava of vast extent and volcanic characteristics, so well preserved that it seem as if the convulsion of nature which pro-

duced it occurred within a period of which a record
might have been left to us. For about three miles the
road traverses the "Plain of Stone" along its northern
edge. That portion of its surface is somewhat uneven,
rising and falling in undulations. In some places the
lava crust has fallen inwards, forming deep pits with
ragged, precipitous sides; in others the pent-up gases
have forced their way upwards, leaving masses of lava
piled up in conical heaps. But these irregularities of
surface are as nothing when compared with the southern
part of the plain, where tremendous rents and fissures
and loose masses of lava render walking a matter of
difficulty. In places where soil has collected, there is
a growth of stunted shrubs or tall rank grass. The
plain is sixty or seventy miles in circumference. The
source of the lava flood which overwhelmed it is said
to be in the mountains 100 miles to the north-
west. The Hurka River forms the southern boundary
of the plain, debouching from a fine lake called Piltan,
having a maximum width from north to south of six
miles and a long diameter of twenty miles from east to
west. It must have been the very centre of the convulsions which at some time or other rent the "Plain of
Stone." About three miles from the *débouchement* of the
river from the lake, the bed of the stream has been,
as it were, torn asunder and depressed some hundred
feet. Into the stream thus formed, which is oval in
shape and surrounded by precipices of lava 100 feet
high, the river leaps at a bound from above. The
falling waters raise a column of spray visible—the only
cloud of a bright still morning at sunrise—from a distance of twenty miles.' Unluckily my companions had
not this account with them, and the Chinamen in the
neighbourhood described the waterfall as so insignificant that they did not go out of their way to visit it.

The temperature and weather, too, were not the best possible for sight-seeing.

With my companions also arrived Chang San. His journey from Kirin to Yingtzŭ during the rains had taken him twenty-three days, but he had done the return journey in eleven, so great is the difference between ways that are mire and ways frozen like iron. On his road back he was waylaid by thirteen mounted robbers, who searched his cart. Chang San told them that they would not care for Scotch oatmeal or jam, which was all he had to give them; adding, rather meanly, that there were three heavily-laden carts coming up behind him. Off went the robbers and on went Chang San, and by the time he had finished his breakfast the three carts arrived, having been plundered of 150 taels in silver and a quantity of merchandise. The robbers made up their spoil into bags, and then proceeded to pick out the best mule of each team, slung the bags across them, and drove them away. This happened in broad daylight on the greatest highway in the land, the imperial high road between Moukden and Kirin. The robbers' retreat was well known to be inside the Emperor's hunting park. Life also as well as property is not very secure. My companions saw between Ninguta and Omoso the dead body of a murdered man lying by the roadside. The authorities had covered it with boughs, pending the inquest, but how the man met his death we could not exactly ascertain.

Chang San brought with him the first letters we had received for more than six months, and, joyous though they made us, they were accompanied by one great disappointment. My agents in London had not sent us a single newspaper, in spite of clear orders given them before we started; and as no one noticed the mistake in Yingtzŭ, we had to construct the great political

conflict of 1886 as best we could from scattered allusions in our letters. However, it gave us more to read
when we got back to civilised parts again. Chang San
also brought a bill for a considerable sum of money,
which, like a wise man, he had preferred to carrying
silver, and which, still more wisely, he cashed as soon
as he got to Kirin, depositing the shoes at our old inn.
For, as he shrewdly remarked, the Chinese new year
was approaching, when accounts are balanced and firms
are apt to fail, and there was nothing like having the
money safely lodged.

We paid another visit to Mr. Sung at the arsenal,
who was very glad to see us. He returned our call,
and again asked us to dinner. This time the gentleman whom we had met on our way to Hun-ch'un, who
proved to be a Dane, made a third foreign guest,
and there were three agreeable Chinese gentlemen—
Mr. Yao, the Superintendent of Telegraphs, brother of
a gentleman who was three years in London as an
attaché to the Chinese Legation; Mr. Fang, Advocate-
General to the Governor, and a Mr. Fêng. We had a
pleasant and jovial banquet, of which I subjoin the bill
of fare.

Hors d'œuvres.
Shrimp Mayonnaise.   Candied Fruit.
Apricot Kernels.   Melon Seeds.   Morsels of Ham.
Morsels of Mutton.   Eggs in Aspic.

Poissons. Entrées. Rôts.
Garlic Salad.   Crême de Sharks' Fins.   Rolled Beef.
Soup of Young Bamboo Shoots.   Fried Trout.
Puffs with Garlic Stuffing.   Potage à la Holothurium.
Grilled Bones.   Soup à la Toadstools.   Chicken Curry and Rice.
Stewed Beef in Soup.

Dessert.
Pears.   Grapes.   Roots of Rushes.

Vins.
Champagne du Pays Jaune.   Champagne Moët and Chandon

B B

The garlic rolls were delicious, as were the shark-fins, sea-slug, and toadstool soup. The roots of rushes were sweet and tasted like apples. Certainly Chinese gentlemen, when they wish to be kind and hospitable and to make you feel yourself at home, are eminently successful in doing so.

I must also render testimony to a capital remedy an innkeeper gave me for toothache, from which I had begun to suffer. Rinsing the mouth with it afforded instant relief. The innkeeper said it was not meant to be swallowed, and it was just as well he told me, as I found out afterwards that it was highly poisonous, being compounded of roots of aconite and *Iris floren-tina*, leaves of *Heterotropa asaroides*, and another vege-table substance, called Pi-po, which I could not identify.

The next place to visit was K'uan-ch'êng-tzŭ, pro-nounced Kwanchungza, eighty miles to the north-west of Kirin, the greatest place of commerce in Northern Manchuria. Before starting we redeemed the articles which we had left in pawn with Messrs. Tsun-I-Kung. We then each of us caused to be manufactured a pair of huge top-boots of sheepskin with the wool inside, reaching up to our knees. We had tried native shoes, but they were not comfortable, while if we sat on a cart in English boots our feet got frozen. Our new top-boots we could pull on over our old ones, so that, whether walking or riding, our feet were kept warm. We left Kirin on November 30 by the west gate, passing over the same wooden gallery on the river front by which we had entered the city on August 12. A few miles from the city the road traverses a low pass called, like one on the Ninguta road, after Lao-yeh, the God of War. The good folk of Kirin think it a most diffi-cult and dangerous pass, though it is only 540 feet

high, and we should not have noticed it when travelling
on the eastern frontier. The neighbouring hill-sides are
still covered with woods, and therefore, though almost
adjoining the gates of Kirin, it is still a favourite haunt of
highwaymen. During the previous summer a caravan
was plundered near the top, not half an hour after two
missionaries had crossed it. The crest of the hill has a
greater collection of p'ailous and monuments in memory
of distinguished officials than any I have seen in Manchuria. What monument would he not deserve who
put down once for all the scourge of brigands? It
would certainly be *ære perennius.*

How busy a sight are the roads just now, in the
full flow of winter traffic! Strings of carts a quarter
to half a mile long, each vehicle drawn by eight or
nine animals, and carrying upwards of a ton and a
half of goods, speed lightly over the frozen ground in
never-ending succession, laden with every conceivable
thing. There are mushrooms, and coffins, and wine,
and oil, and furniture, and deer-horns going south;
while great piles of piece-goods (mostly American, very
few English), dyeing stuffs, tea, and pickles (let no
man scoff at pickles, for the Chinese consume them
largely) are travelling north. Occasionally we meet a
melancholy procession of emigrants, driven by poverty
or floods from their homes to seek fresh and cheap
land in the north—their carts piled with furniture
and boxes and covered with extempore awnings, inside
which the wives and infants huddle together out of
the cold, while the young and stalwart walk bravely
on, though sometimes driven by hunger to ask for
a meal. Or a courier goes past with his bag of
letters, striding along at a steady pace of fully five
miles an hour, eating his meals as he goes, and doing

a good seventy miles in a day. How would not a
light American railway pay in a country like this!
Like ourselves, every convoy starts long before daylight,
in the keen freezing air, and trundles along till dark
again, only halting a short while at midday. The
carters wield long whips of twisted cane, the crack of
which sounds like a rifle-shot, and a number of which
from a distance look like a forest of masts on the
horizon. The supercargoes make a bold show against
brigands, with great gingalls, and matchlocks, and
swords and spears, and on each cart by the driver's
seat there waves a flag, so that the world may know
whence he comes and whither going. The shops in
the villages and stalls in the market towns are hung
with fur caps, car gloves, fur stockings, and shoes made
of felt an inch thick, all suitable to the season. Grain
dealers have piled great heaps of millet on the edge of
the road, so that purchases can be made without
stopping the train of carts. All the inns have been
painted afresh, the windows outside made air-tight
with new clean paper, and the feeding troughs for the
horses repaired. Outside, touts are standing at the
inn-gates, or they travel a mile or two up the road,
praising the cheapness and accommodation of their
inns and inviting the cartmen to enter; in the inn-
yard are tethered rows upon rows of beasts, so closely
packed there is scarcely room to pass between them,
eating sweet millet-stalks and kaoliang, bought cheap
from some road-side huckster, who has an underground dwelling, dug by himself for protection from
the cutting wind. The beasts stand nearest the house;
beyond them are the carts, so tightly ranged it seems
a mystery how they are ever to be disentangled and
harnessed again. And inside the inn sit groups of jolly

carters on the k'ang, devouring with good appetites
bowls upon bowls of boiled millet or rice soup, stewed
pork or mutton, ending with a glass or two of hot
wine, and then, whilst they are putting the horses to,
the supercargo takes just a single whiff of opium, to
prepare him for going out again into the cold. The
waiters bustle to and fro, filling up the bowls and
fetching the wines, full of zeal and importance. Along

A CORNER OF AN INN YARD.

the road, troops of men and children stand ready,
from two in the morning till dark, to collect the
horse-droppings that fall as the carts pass, and great
heaps are gathered, to be afterwards mixed with earth
or peat for manure. It is a busy time indeed, and
so determined are the Chinese not to idle, that young-
sters who cannot get other employment are put to
spend the day in the fields, dragging behind them long
fan-shaped rakes made of springy pieces of cane or

kaoliang rind, strung together with string and hooked at the end, which they trail over hill and dale, over plough and waste, collecting every dried blade of grass, every dead weed, every fallen leaf. The collected rub - bish is piled in heaps and taken home, to be used as fuel or manure. Now, too, that the roads are smooth and hard, sledges are brought into general requisition, on which weighty goods, such as massive gravestones, bundles of iron rods, and baulks of timber, are whirled about with ease and speed.

To reach K'uan-ch'êng-tzŭ it was necessary to pass through the palisade, but the whilom barrier has so utterly disappeared that we did not even notice it. Not far from our destination we met, for the second time in our travels, thirteen brigands, chained together in threes, being taken on carts to Kirin. They were decently clad, but looked thorough ruffians. The soldiers said they had been in pursuit of them for three months, and that others had got away, one of them wounded. According to the Jesuit surveyors, both Ninguta and Petuna were repeopled with exiles after the Manchu conquest of China; so the brigand-pest may be due to ancestral taint. K'uan-ch'êng tzŭ lies close to an important stream called the I-tung Ho, in the middle of a very fertile plain, somewhat broken up by watercourses, resembling a piece of the Tapti valley. It is surrounded by a ditch and low mud wall, with a rusty gun on a worm-eaten carriage mounted at each gateway. A few years hence, Hulan and other towns in the north may reduce its importance; but trade-centres are difficult to shift, and at present it is by far the largest emporium in the north. A busy, bustling place it is. The Chinese here have forgotten their steady, solemn gait, and hurry about their work as if their lives depended on their speed.

The main street, which runs north and south, is nearly three miles long, extending from one end of the town to the other. It is really a splendid thoroughfare—a bewildering vista of sign-posts, and obelisks, and gilt inscriptions, and lamps. The four cross streets are also prettily decorated. The first time we went out the mob pursued us, but afterwards we got runners from the yamen, who kept them off and answered the old, old questions they kept putting about us—How old are they? What are their boots made of? Aren't their clothes very cold? How many carts have they got? What do they pay them? How many servants have they? What are their wages?—and so on *ad infinitum*.

There is a temple at the east gate to Lao-yeh, in the inclosure of which is a two-storied building dedicated to some star or mortal who has been raised to the skies, beautifully carved in brick with elephants' heads projecting from the corners. Except a temple on the road between Moukden and Tieh-ling, this is the only piece of modern ecclesiastical architecture we noticed worth looking at in Manchuria. On the other side of the town is a temple to Buddha. In the portico at the gate are four giant guardians, gorgeously got up, with eyes in their knees and foreheads, and carrying different weapons. The first has a sword for defence, the second a rosary for prayer, the third a fiddle to make all the world listen, and the fourth an old red umbrella, which, when raised, makes thunder, rain, and darkness, to terrify mankind. Buddha himself holds a bowl in the left hand, coloured red, while the right hand is raised as if in the act of teaching. Doubtless it represents the sage addressing Sujâta, as the 'Light of Asia' records. In another direction, also outside the town, is the mosque, with a three-storied pagoda as a minaret, and the usual animals on the angles of the roof. On the door is painted a decree of the thirty-third year of the great Kanghi, announcing toleration to the Mahommedan religion so long as the followers of it do not conspire against the state. Mahommedans in all countries seem fond of displaying the decrees of Government in their favour; at the great mosque at Hughli, in Bengal, a resolution of Government is given *in extenso*, permitting, if I recollect aright, processions under certain circumstances. But what gave us more pleasure than either temple or mosque was a humble mud house, in which a native deacon from the Irish Presbyterian Mission has opened classes for teaching the Gospel. One thing I have observed is that, while the Roman Catholics adorn schools or places of worship with pictures of Our Saviour, the Virgin Mary, the Crucifixion, and scenes from the New Testament, Protestant missionaries, no doubt from the best motives, most frequently display pictures from Old Testament story, such as the history of Joseph, or Daniel in the lions' den, or the naming of the beasts by Adam, or the ark sailing over the Flood. The point is not one of importance, but, seeing that the main object of missionaries is to teach the history of our Lord and the work He did for mankind, surely Roman Catholics in this matter are the more sensible of the two.

K'uan-ch'êng-tzŭ borders so close upon Mongolian territory, that we expected to find Lamas, and Buddhist images in the shops, but we were disappointed. It is a Chinese town, pure and simple. We now turned off in a north-westerly direction to Hsiao Pa-chia-tzŭ, about 'wenty miles off, where a Roman Catholic Mission has

existed for many years. From a great distance over
the flat plain we could espy the lofty tower of the
church, and the sacred edifice itself is the first object
to be seen on entering the great gate. It is a good substantial building, dedicated to the Blessed Virgin, and
behind it stands the vicarage, a two-storied brick
building. On the ground floor is the refectory, a
sparely furnished chamber with whitewashed walls and
no carpet, though the thermometer was below zero outside. At a little distance is a row of buildings where
seventeen scholars, whose ages vary from eight to
seventeen, are boarded and educated. Cut off by a high
wall from the rest of the premises, is a girls' school,
superintended by a Chinese lady teacher, attached to
which is a community of Chinese Sisters of Mercy working under the superintendence of the coadjutor bishop.
Two of the priests—Père Litot and Père Maviel—came
outside to welcome us, and to introduce us to Mgr.
Boyer, the bishop coadjutor, a kindly venerable gentleman, who has served his Master in Manchuria for
thirty-two years.[1] The whole establishment at Pa-chia-
tzŭ has grown up under him, and the church was built
by himself and Mgr. Dubail in 1868. I have already
narrated his adventure with pirates when first arriving
in Manchuria, but that is not the only occasion he
has been in danger. Once he was waylaid by brigands
and stripped of everything, even of his clothes; and
another time, a band of 1,000 robbers came to the
settlement after murdering the neighbouring mandarin.
But the chief was very polite and only asked for any
guns or saddles they had got, and, seeing the women
crowding and praying in the church, told them they

---

[1] Since this was written, I have heard of the lamentable death of Mgr.
Boyer, which occurred at Pa-yen-shu-shu, March 9, 1887.

need not be afraid, as he and his followers had wives
and children of their own.

Next day was Sunday, so we all attended mass in
the morning. The church was crowded—men on one
side, and women on the other. There were a few com-
municants, and it was a pleasure to see the intelligent
and devout interest the congregation showed in the
service, joining in the responses and canticles throughout. Then we visited the college. Its object is to
train the children not only in Christian doctrine and
morals, but also in Chinese learning and philosophy, so
that they may meet their heathen compatriots on an
equal footing. They appeared bright lads, though not
very far advanced in learning.

CHAPTER XV.

PA-CHIA-TZŬ TO PORT ARTHUR.

An inn on fire—The Ma-t'ien-tai Mên Gate—A frozen fog—The Kai-yuan pagoda—A bridge—A coffin in transit—Curious superstitions—Tieh-ling—Floods in Liao-tung—Chinese service at the Mission House—Père Conraux's affray with soldiers—Massacre at Tientsin—Residence of the Presbyterians—Hospital of the Medical Mission—Mongol idol's temple —Shopping—Delicacies—Long finger-nails—College at Sha-ling—Hot-springs at T'ang-kang-tzŭ—Hai-ch'êng—Christmas Day in China—The party breaks up—Manufacture of salt—Result of Fêng-shui—Sha-k'ou—Buddhist cave—A silk filatory—Invasion by pirates—Firewood planta-tions—Oysters—Ancient forts—Tiger Mountain—Port Arthur—Naval and military establishments—Foreign policy of the Chinese—Return to Shanghai—Conclusion.

WE had by this time visited typical portions and seen the most important towns of the entire province. No doubt we had omitted the outlying district of Pe'rh, or Buir, on Lake Dalai Nor, south-west of the Russian station of Argunsko; but, though subject to the Governor of Tsitsihar, it is geographically a part of Mongolia. We now determined to turn southwards and reach Ying-tzŭ by Christmas, and we left Hsiao Pa-chia-tzŭ on December 6. Shortly after starting, brigands were re-ported in the neighbourhood, who had lunched gratis at an inn close to where we were stopping; so we took care to sit with our guns ready by us, like a party of Irish landlords. We soon joined the main high road from Petuna to Moukden, along which there were capital inns. One night some one nearly set the house on fire by putting a candle in an angle of a latticed window,

where the flame caught the woodwork. It went on
smouldering after we had gone to sleep, but, fortunately,
a woman saw it, or the window would have been in a
blaze before long and lives would almost certainly have
been lost, as the inn was crowded with people, and the
roof was composed of inflammable millet straw.

The road passed through a succession of fine villages, or rather towns--Ta Pa-chia-tzŭ, Hsiao-ch'êng-
tzŭ, Mai-mai-kai, Ssŭ-ping-kai, Yü-shih-ch'êng-tzŭ—all
flourishing and increasing, and distilleries also were
frequent. Twice we met on the road large consign-
ments of foreign machinery and arms, destined for the
arsenal at Kirin. Now and then it snowed and blew,
and the country exactly resembled a miserable bit of
fen-country at home, all melancholy stubbles and willow-
trees. On December 10 we passed the Palisades again,
through a gate called Ma-tien-t'ai Mên, which is kept in
good repair, and the line of the barrier is still to be
traced by a row of trees. The cold that morning was
the greatest we had felt, the thermometer going down
below $-20°$ Réaumur, equivalent to about $-14°$ Fahr.
As day dawned we found ourselves in a frozen fog, and
the air filled with myriads of lovely little spicula, which
powdered us over like hoar-frost, while the trees presented a most exquisite appearance, every twig seem-
ing covered with frosted silver. Some miles farther
we came to Kai-yuan, an ancient town, whose name
is familiar to students of early Manchu history. It
is surrounded by a magnificent old wall six miles in
circumference and thirty feet high, now out of repair.
There is a good deal of vacant ground inside, but the
place shares in the general prosperity, and has, besides,
a plethora of temples. The wall to the south is washed
by the river Ching, here 100 yards broad, but not very

deep, and in the corner overlooking the river is a fine old-fashioned pagoda, probably ninety or a hundred feet high. For the first thirty feet the base is without ornament, and upon it rises a lofty shaft divided into circular rings, like a mass of great quoits piled one on the other, and finished at the apex with the usual Buddhist

PAGODA AT KAI-YUAN.

umbrella-shaped pinnacle. This and the town wall showed we had now reached the old settled Chinese part of Manchuria. The Ching was crossed by a long primitive bridge, the roadway made of bundles of kaoliang stalks, and the framework resting on wooden piles. Rough and unsubstantial as these structures seem, they answer their purpose admirably. The millet stalks are very tough, and last out an enormous amount of traffic. They are so light that the weight of the roadway counts for nothing, and so inexpensive that when worn out the whole roadway can be remade for a trifling sum. A long train of carts was crossing, so we drove over the ice, but, though our carts got across safely, Fulford unfortunately tumbled through a hole up to his knees. He walked as fast as he could to the nearest inn, though his garments were frozen like wood long before he got there; he was fortunately no worse, though an immersion with the thermometer below zero is not a pleasant experience.

In the courtyard of the inn was the coffin of a Chinaman on its way from K'uan-ch'êng-tzŭ to the tomb of his ancestors at a village within the Great Wall. The cart which carried the coffin was decorated with a yellow flag to denote that the deceased was a person of rank, and with a red flag to avert all evil influences that might be hovering in the air. On the top of the coffin in a cage was a common domestic cock. One of these birds is invariably sent in company with a corpse. We asked why, and found people divided in opinion. Some thought that, if the cock were absent, only the body would be transported, and not the spirit. Others thought that without it the spirit could not pass the Great Wall. 'However,' said one, 'cock or no cock, it's no use—no spirit can pass the Wall. When the great Emperor Kienlung died, they wanted to send him to Moukden to be buried with his ancestors, but even his spirit could not get through, and they had to bury him at Peking.' The authoritative explanation is that the soul which accompanies the coffin becomes apprehensive and is apt to lose itself, and the crowing of the cock acts as a guide to the wandering spirit. Palladius states that it is also customary in Manchuria to obtain from the Ch'êng-huang-miao, or temple to the tutelary deity of the town where the deceased lived, a supply of tickets, one of which is burnt every time a barrier is passed or a river crossed, and the Good Genius of the place then allows the spirit free transit.

We were now travelling with redoubled speed, but our carts were now and then impeded by huge droves of pigs going south to Moukden for consumption at the Chinese New Year, the greatest national anniversary. Fat and sleek they looked, though the idea of eating them is repulsive, for they live on the foulest garbage.

The next important place was T'ieh-ling, also an old-fashioned walled town with a pagoda, situated on a branch of the river Liao, which at times overflows and damages the suburbs. The name is literally, Iron Hill, derived from a mountain close by where iron abounds, and the town is celebrated for its blacksmith's work. We were now fairly in the lower valley of that river, which is much subject to periodical inundations. The heavy rains of the past season, which had destroyed the telegraph line when we were first at Kirin, had spread desolation far and wide, and the loss and misery were extreme. In some places the cultivators had seen not only their houses destroyed, with all their little property inside, but considerable tracts of good land were damaged by sand and gravel left upon them by the floods. Many of the emigrants we had passed going north belonged to these poor ruined peasants. The English and other foreigners at Yingtzŭ subscribed liberally to alleviate the distress, and it was in distributing their alms that a missionary—the Rev. Mr.

c c

Westwater—lost his life. He died of an epidemic fever, which attacked the starving people like typhus after the Irish famine.

December 19 saw us at Moukden, having covered the last ninety miles in two days. During the latter part of the journey we saw the best portion of Liao-tung. In spite of the floods it is very carefully culti-vated, and covered with flourishing towns and villages. Whatever the merits or demerits of Chinese rule, this province certainly has, as already described in Chapter III., improved enormously in the last two centuries. Still, though the country has improved, the highways have not. Even in the Emperor Kanghi's time there was no royal road to Kirin. Père Verbiest writes on this subject even more feelingly than I can: 'The fatigues of this journey were almost inexpressible, the roads being spoiled and almost rendered imprac-ticable by the waters. They (the Emperor and his retinue) marched without resting over mountains and valleys, passing most dangerous rivers and torrents, where the bridges were broken by the current or covered with flood. In some places they met with deep pools and sloughs, which they had the greatest difficulty to get out of. The beasts that carried our baggage could not move forward, but remained sticking in the mud or dead for faintness on the road. Men fared no better, and all went to wreck for want of provisions and necessary refreshments for so long a journey.'

At Moukden we halted several days with our good friends the missionaries. On Sunday we attended a Chinese service at the Mission House, at which there was a congregation of some seventy persons of both sexes, and in the afternoon we went to a chapel in the town, which, in deference to Chinese prejudices, is only attended by men. One of the elders, a Chinaman with a fine intelligent face, opened the service with prayer, and old familiar hymns, translated into Chinese, were sung to old familiar tunes. The singing was rude but hearty, and it was touching to see these quondam heathens, from one of the most thoughtful of uncivilised nations, raising their voices in praise of the One God and His Son the Redeemer.

I met Père Conraux, the gentleman who was nearly killed by soldiery at Hulan. He told me that he had been negotiating for the site of a residence, a proceeding which made him very unpopular with the mandarins, and was sitting in his quarters one evening when a band of soldiers rushed in through both door and window. Very injudiciously (but all men have not the same presence of mind) he snatched up a revolver and fired amongst them, killing their leader, a petty mandarin. He was seized, tied to a cart with his head hanging over the tail, a shot was fired at him which pierced his leg, and he was treated in the most brutal manner, beaten with sticks over his defenceless head and face, filth forced into his eyes and mouth, and his body scored with the soldiers' redhot pipes. Still, the only wonder is that he was not killed on the spot. After being kept in this state for some hours, the sport of the soldiers at the police station, he was released. The French Consul at Tientsin was despatched in the winter of 1882–83 to investigate the affair and obtain compensation. He visited both Hulan and Tsitsihar, but nothing was gained. It has often been remarked that the French Government, which loses no opportunity of insulting its priests at home, takes every care to uphold them abroad, even if they exceed the limits of discretion or good behaviour. In the interests of true Christianity, incidents like that which I have related are greatly to be regretted. An excitable, headstrong spirit unsuits men for dealing with Orientals, and sometimes brings about a positive catastrophe, such as occurred at Tientsin in the year 1870. The mortality in the Catholic orphanage was great, owing to the enormous number of famine-stricken children received in a moribund state; the people became excited, and a ridiculous rumour got about that the children were being put to death for the sake of the juices of their eyes,[1] which it was thought were needed for photography. It was suggested, as the best means of calming the excitement, that the Chinese officials should be invited to go over the orphanage and see the excellence of the arrangements; but the Consul flew into a rage and said, 'No! it would be an indignity.' The consequence was that the mob attacked the orphanage, massacred the Sisters of Mercy in the most horrible way, and the French Consul himself and some other Europeans were killed.

The Presbyterian missionaries at Moukden have chosen a capital healthy site for their residence, on the outskirts of the town, overlooking the river and open to the breeze. There are three houses adjoining one another, with spacious courtyards attached. A little chapel, a schoolroom, and a boarding school for girls, daughters of members of the church, form part of the premises. At my visit there were sixteen girls present, of different ages, bright eyed and with rosy cheeks. One lassie read a chapter of the Bible and

---

[1] This is an old accusation against Christians. In 1844, the celebrated minister, Keying, in a memorial to the Emperor Tao-kuang, requesting toleration to be extended to Christianity, said that, of course, if the converts were caught puncturing sick people's eyes or seducing women, both offences habitually charged against them, they would still be liable to punishment.

answered questions upon it, and they all sang a hymn nicely. The little ones had the front part of their heads shaven, but the elder ones let their hair grow, plaiting it behind into a long tail.

Not far from the mission colony is the Medical Mission's hospital and dispensary. It contained fourteen in-patients, who looked comfortable and well cared for.

BABY FRIENDS.

Two were soldiers, wounded by brigands' bullets. One man was shown me who had been brought in so ill that his coffin had been bought and his funeral ordered, when it occurred to his friends to try the 'foreign devils' as a last resort, and an operation had saved him. Another of the patients rose from his bed, and, speaking very earnestly, asked Dr. Christie to assure me that the preservation of his life was due to the grace of God. A hospital for females does not exist as yet, as a site has not been obtained. It was at this hospital that the blind man of T'ai-ping-k'ou [1] first heard the Gospel preached.

On the west of Moukden is the Lama temple of Pan-shen-shi, built in 1638 by the Emperor Tai Tsung for the reception of an idol which he took from Lindan, chief of the Chahar Mongols.[2] Palladius describes this idol as follows :

It is called Makha-Hala, the defender of the faith, and was cast during the time of Kublai Khan by the celebrated Pakba Lama for the temple of the hill, Wu-t'ai-shan, in Shantang, one of the oldest historical hills in the world. Thence it was removed to the north of Mongolia. Khutukhta Siarbà brought it to Lindan; and when the Manchus invaded his territory and defeated him, a Lama named Morgen gave it to the Manchu chief. It was carried into Moukden with great ceremony, a building worthy of it was commenced, and a large quantity of gold and silver was lavished on the decoration of the temple. Such is its history inscribed in four languages on a monument in the temple.

At K'uan-ch'êng-tzŭ we had heard of this temple, but, unfortunately, when we got to Moukden, we omitted to go and look for it.

The streets of Moukden were very busy and the shops full, in anticipation of the New Year. At an old curiosity shop I made a few purchases of old china at much more reasonable rates than at Peking ; but a bottle of a rare colour, called Lang-Yao, or, in French, *sang-de-bœuf*, a marvellously rich purple red, with a narrow white lip, was perhaps the only real bargain. A sketch of this piece will be found at the end of the chapter. The fishmongers' and poulterers' shops displayed nume-

[1] See Note E, p. 440.   [2] See *ante*, p. 41.

rous quaint fishes and birds, sent frozen from all parts
of the country, the most novel item being sets of little
bears' paws, which are esteemed a delicacy, while bears'
gall is used in medicine. Another article popular in
Manchuria, and also in China, is not unknown in Europe
—I mean frogs' hind-legs. This batrachian is called
' hashuma,' and Mr. Ross describes it as having a brown
back and very long hind-legs, which are divided by
two joints into three equal parts, terminating in an elon-
gated foot with five webs. The hind-legs are considered a great delicacy and the peculiar property of
the Emperor. A sign of respectability in shopkeepers,
here and elsewhere in China, is to grow the finger-
nails to an inordinate length, as evidence that they do
not depend on manual labour for their livelihood. One
young fellow had the nails of both hands quite like
bird's claws, and must have found great difficulty in
maintaining them unbroken. Fakirs in India follow
the same practice for ascetic reasons, and so do a few
Bengalee Baboos, sometimes as a vow, but generally
for vanity.

On the 15th we left for Yingtzŭ. The second day
we arrived at Sha-ling, another Roman Catholic station
with a lofty tower rivalling the Liao-yang Pagoda, which
is visible a few miles away. We received the usual
cordial welcome from the pro-vicaire of the province,
Père Hinard, M. Choulait, and M. Sandrin. They
showed us over the college, where thirty lads are being
educated for the priesthood, and taught Latin and
theology. One rule is that no convert in the first generation shall be admitted to priest's orders. All was neat
and substantial as usual, and the Spartan absence of
luxury very conspicuous. A few months previously the
whole country had been under water, and the flood was

several feet deep in the priests' rooms; fortunately, the masonry was good, or all would have been swept **away.**

We then rejoined the main road, keeping on our left the Ch'ien-shan, or 'Hill of a Thousand Peaks'—a rugged, picturesque range. Then came T'ang-kang-tzŭ, where there are hot-springs 112° Fahr., over which bath-houses have been constructed. Inside, the water wells out into deep circular pits lined with stone, and at the bottom, through clouds of steam, the dim forms of nude Chinamen may be discovered enjoying the unwonted luxury of a bath. There is a similar hot bath near Chin-chou-fu. Then on to Hai-ch'êng, a fine old walled town frequently mentioned in history. In the centre of it are to be seen the remains of an old fort, once occupied by the Coreans, and taken from them by the T'ang dynasty in A.D. 645. Mr. Ross considers them the only genuine Corean remains now existing in Liaotung. Outside are the foundations of a massive wall built by the Ming dynasty, which extended two miles each way. The present wall is of Manchu construction and of smaller dimensions. At Hai-ch'êng is the tomb of Kosi, also called Shang, one of the three famous princes I spoke of before.[1] He was Viceroy of Canton and Southern China. In his old age his son Chusin took part in Wu San-kuei's rebellion, but, although in China a man's treason involves punishment to his living and desecration to the tombs of his dead relations, Kosi's services had been so eminent that in 1681, after order had been re-established, the Emperor Kanghi ordered his body to be brought to his native place with extraordinary marks of honour. There is now a beautiful temple over his grave, and a large stone tablet declares his faithfulness and worth. Two hereditary Tsoling,

[1] See p. 41.

or Captains, look after the tomb, the temple, and the estates with which the Emperor endowed it; and on certain stated days, the descendants of Kosi, in and in the neighbourhood of Hai-ch'êng—a large number of people—meet together to pray at the tomb of their great ancestor.

A WAYSIDE MONUMENT.

Along this part of the road were numerous monuments, of which I give an illustration. The Chinese much resemble ourselves in desiring to record the memories of deceased worthies. Sometimes the testimonial is based on singular grounds, and takes the form of a p'ailou, for the construction of which the imperial sanction must be conveyed by an edict in the 'Gazette.'

A virtuous widow, who has cried herself to death in an inordinately short time, a dutiful daughter who cut a piece out of her arm or liver to make broth for a sick parent, has her piety rewarded after this fashion, and the monument is erected in the most conspicuous place possible.   At Hsiu-shui-tien-tzŭ, between Kirin and Petuna, where the high road to Asheho and Sansing diverges, there is one—to a widow, if I remember aright—and near the entrance to Tsitsihar is another, but they are not uncommon in any well-peopled part of Manchuria.

We spent a day at Hai-ch'êng with the Rev. J. Mac-Intyre, whose mission is making great progress.   On December 19 we arrived at Yingtzŭ once more, exactly seven months from the time we started, and met with a warm welcome.   We stayed till Christmas Day, on which festival, in the absence of an English clergy-man, one of the Presbyterian missionaries read the English service, and we sang the old Christmas hymns. Certainly, Christian tolerance and charity are developed by travelling abroad.   Points of ritual and even dogma, which are fiercely discussed at home, are quietly allowed to drop out of sight.   On Christmas Eve Mr. Allen, the Consul, and I attended the midnight mass at the Roman Catholic church, which was crowded to suffocation.   At the elevation of the host, fireworks were discharged outside, the triumphant sound doubtless cheering the Chinese converts and stimulating their devotion.   The 'Adeste Fideles' was sung with great fervour.   We also visited the Roman Catholic orphanage.   The children were gaily dressed in red and blue frock sand looked very happy, expecting their Christmas dinner.

At Yingtzŭ our party broke up, and we had to

exchange farewells. Younghusband, who had more leave than myself, and Fulford, with Chu-Hsiu and the cook, went leisurely back by land to Tientsin, passing through the Great Wall. Rattler and I, attended by Chang San, continued journeying south, as I was in a hurry to return to Shanghai, and, the river at Yingtzŭ being closed by ice, I had to seek the port at the extreme end of the peninsula which divides the Gulf of Liao-tung from the Yellow Sea—the same which, as I have mentioned before, was christened by H.M.S. 'Alceste' at the time of Lord Amherst's Embassy the 'Regent's Sword,' and is now called on the Admiralty charts Kuantung. Leaving Yingtzŭ, the road passes over a mud flat, where salt is extensively manufactured. The water is conducted by long trenches into shallow pits, and the salt forms by evaporation in the usual way. After twenty-five miles came the fine walled city Kai chou, or Kai-ping. I had to go round to the south gate, as those on the north and west of the city were both blocked up: one because a fox used to haunt it, a kind of *loup-garou*, who carried away maidens, and the other because it was frequented by scorpions, or, according to another version, because a fox and a scorpion were seen entering the two gates simultaneously. Suffice it, the 'Fêng-shui' was spoilt and the traffic had to be diverted. It is singular that Fêng-shui, now so univer-sally venerated, was at one time known to be and treated as a gross superstition. Only a century and a half ago, the Emperor Yung-chêng ordained that belief in the false stories of necromancers and geomancers (*yin-yang*, *fêng-shui*) should be punished with death.

Beyond Kai-chou, on an eminence, stands a little cast-iron pagoda, a most elegant monument. Farther on, low ranges of hills take the place of the level plain. We crossed a low pass called the I-êrh Ling and followed the river Pi-li Ho up a barren stony valley, passing Wan-fu-chuang, or the 'Village of Ten Thousand Happinesses.' Once more I was amongst the mountains, and on all sides were seen rocky ranges upwards of 1,000 to 2,000 feet in height, remarkable for their rugged and picturesque outlines. Two more passes, called the Sing-kai Ling and Ta-la Ling, brought me to Sha-k'ou, the first missionary station in Manchuria, to which I have previously alluded. It stands on the bank of the Ta-chuang Ho. There is a pretty little church, with the usual tall steeple and a beautiful white marble altar. On either side of it rise two fine mountains, whose names, translated into French, are 'Crête du Coq' and 'La Montagne de la Gloire.'

My chief object in going to Sha-k'ou was to visit a celebrated Buddhist cave-temple, and the priest, M. Guillon, kindly accompanied me there. The cave is situated in a mountain called Hsien-jên Shan, or 'Mountain of the Sages,' about ten miles from Sha-kou. We dismounted at a temple near the entrance of a noble gorge, disclosing to view a series of precipitous crags, very wild and rugged, fringed at the top with evergreen pines. The path winds up this ravine. After passing some ancient monuments which date from the time of the Mings, the defile becomes gradually very narrow and steep, and each turn in the road reveals fresh glories of mountain scenery. At last the dark mouth of the cave is perceived high up on a lofty scarp near the apex of the principal peak. A long and steep stair, made of stones, perhaps 500 feet high, is then climbed, till it reaches a narrow rift in the living rock through which the pilgrim passes; and beyond comes another stair hewn

BUDDHIST CAVE TEMPLE IN THE MOUNTAIN OF THE SAGES.

out of the mountain side, which at this point is almost perpendicular. At last the gloomy portal is reached. Two huge idols guard the entry. Yet another ascent by a dimly-lit stair of some forty or fifty steps, and the pilgrim finds himself facing a recess, in the depth of which stand three or four shrines. There are Buddha and his eighteen apostles; Lao-yeh, the Rain God, the God of the Ten Diseases, and the Queen of Heaven in the character of Lucina; there is an eighteen-armed Buddha, something like the eighteen-armed Kali, the goddess beloved in Orissa, and a god whom the ignorant bonzes could not name, exactly like the figure in the great temple at Canton, which travellers are told represents Marco Polo. Certainly the face, moustache, and headdress appear European. Two dirty priests are always on duty, who use for a charcoal brazier a splendid old bronze basin that looks 1,000 years old and is said to date from Corean times. In one respect the cave is disappointing. It does not penetrate nearly as deep into the hill as the cave-temples of India; but it has the advantage of being left exactly as Nature made it, and for wild grandeur of scenery it rivals Ajanta. Père Guillon and I ascended the peak above, and the sun shone so warm and bright that, winter though it was, we rested awhile on a bed of fragrant pine-needles, feasting on the view and getting glimpses of the sea in the far distance.

On leaving the cave, Père Guillon showed me, growing in a patch of soil a little below it, a singular pair of trees. They were male and female, with elegant fan-shaped leaves, and the female bore a fruit like a plum, which the Father believed to be poisonous. He added that there were no others like them in the whole country. Here, thought I, is a grand botanical *trou-*

vaille. I carefully collected some dead leaves, dried fruits, and stones, and, after returning to England, took them with pride to Kew. 'Oh,' said Mr. Thiselton Dyer, 'it is the Salisburia, or Jungo tree ; there is one growing outside the window.' It was too mortifying.

At the mouth of the ravine which leads to the cave was a silk filatory. The district is noted for the production of tusser silk, a name derived from the Chinese *tŭ-ssŭ*, meaning 'local,' or 'native.' The worms are fed on the dwarf oaks[1] with which the hill-sides are covered, and the cocoons are gathered and wound off in winter. At this filatory upwards of thirty or forty young men were engaged in winding silk. They were crowded together in a dark, unwholesome room, some of them being obliged to use candlelight all through the day. The atmosphere was fetid, and they all looked very wan and emaciated. The machine in use consisted of an octagonal skein-winder, worked with a treadle, which also turned the bobbins on which the silk is wound in the first instance. Ten cocoons were used for one thread, and in most cases three skeins were being wound simultaneously. The silk is of a rich grey colour, but very coarse. The value annually exported from Yingtzŭ now amounts to 150,000*l.*, and it bids fair to become a most important branch of trade. About 10,000 bales were exported in 1886, and it is estimated that the production would have been at least 18,000, had not the heavy rain destroyed a large number of

---

[1] *Quercus Mongolica*, Fisch., and *Q. dentata*, Thbg., or *Q. oborata*, Bunge, which is closely allied to *Q. robur*. Mr. Meadows states that there are three kinds of oaks, called in Chinese tsing-kang-lew, large and small, and hoo-pŏ-lŏ, and that the worms also feed on another bush, not an oak, called tsin-tsŭ-tzŭ, with long and narrow leaves, which when plucked have a faint agreeable smell. This tree yields the best silk, and after that the tsing-kang-lew.

the worms which were then feeding. Many immigrants from Shantung are annually attracted to the silk country, and much waste land has been planted with success. Mr. Edgar, the Commissioner of Customs, informs me that some eight years ago, a foreigner connected with the filatory at Chefoo visited this district, and took much pains to instruct some of the natives in the art of reeling off the cocoons, instead of spinning as heretofore. Since then, southern experts have also instructed the natives from time to time, and gradually, but surely, the improved style of reeling and the attention which has been bestowed upon the rearing of the worm, and the healthy preservation of the cocoon, have changed the rough-grown floss originally produced, which could be bought for 100 taels per picul, into a valuable silk, worth from 200 to 300 taels a picul.[1] In making purchases great judgment must be exercised in order to avoid loss by adulteration, as there is not unfrequently introduced into the packages a kind of floss so closely resembling the genuine article that only experts can detect the fraud.

From Sha-kou I followed the course of the river to Ta-chuang, a pretty little village on the sea-coast, which carries on a small trade with Chefoo. But in winter they told me junks can come no nearer than Ta-la-yun-tzŭ, eighteen li distant, which perhaps may mean Ta-lien-hoang Bay. Here, and at others of the small ports on the coast, small detachments of troops are stationed, a by no means useless precaution; for in 1867, just two months before the Rev. Mr. Williamson visited the neighbourhood, 200 red-bearded robbers landed from a junk and levied blackmail with impunity from all the small ports. At a little place like Ta-chuang

---

[1] Picul = 133 lbs.

they got 8,000 taels, upwards of 2,000*l.*, and much more elsewhere. They finally sailed away, and were never caught.

In this part of Manchuria the supply of firewood is kept up by the planting of special little plantations for

A GRAVE STONE.

the purpose, independent of the cemeteries, which are always filled with trees. Here is another example of the practical Chinese mind. An Indian ryot scarcely ever dreams of voluntarily surrendering any of his land for growing sticks. But we noticed the same thing in the plain between Pei-lin-tzŭ and Hulan, although forests are comparatively close to that region.

Beyond Ta-chuang the road skirts the sea shore, crossing the Chin-chang, or ' Plain of Gold,' the diggings in which are now closed; and it then passes over frozen marshes, from which vast quantities of excellent peat are dug. Two rivers, the Sha Ho and the Pi-li Ho, must then be crossed, and the quaint but flourishing little port of Pi-tzŭ Wo is gained. It is situated like a Devonshire fishing-village, partly on the overhanging cliff, with a long street leading down to the beach, along which runs the main parade, with the shops and principal inns. The water of the bay was frozen for half a mile out, and six or eight junks were moored in the floe, waiting for the end of the winter. Here, and all along the coast, first-rate oysters are to be had, as small as natives and quite as good, very plentiful and ridiculously cheap. The shops also were full of frozen fish of all shapes and kinds. Outside Pi-tzŭ Wo may be seen a really good specimen of a fort, attributed, like all antiquities in the neighbourhood, to Coreans. It is about 100 yards square, with square flanking towers at the corners and in the middle of each side. The walls are twenty-five feet high, composed of stone at the bottom and fine large bricks above, similar to those which may be seen in the Great Wall of China. The gate is very strongly fortified. This fort, which is still in perfect preservation, was probably built as a protection for the port of Pi-tzŭ Wo against pirates. Moreover, on the top of every conspicuous hill in the vicinity is a watch-tower composed of a solid pyramid of masonry, forty feet square at the base, tapering off gradually to a rounded top about forty feet from the ground. There is no staircase, and no apparent means

D D

exist for climbing to the top. Around it is a wall about
fifteen feet high. The natives informed me that these
were used as watch-towers and beacons, and that in
former times signals were exchanged by means of them
from the end of the promontory as far north as Moukden,
some 300 miles.

There is a similar series of circular forts, but made
of brick and with crenellated parapets, like lofty
martello towers, about three miles apart from one
another, along the road between Chin-chou Fu and
Hai-ch'êng, on the north and west of the Liao-tung
Gulf. Mr. Ross[1] states that the bricks are precisely the
same as those made by the Manchus at the beginning
of their rule, and unlike the only ancient bricks which
he can attribute to Coreans. He suggests, therefore,
that they were built by the Manchus as beacons to give
notice of the approach of Ma Wên Lung (*vide ante*,
Chapter II. p. 40), and summon the Army of the North.
According to Mr. Williamson, when danger appeared,
fires were lit upon them at night and intelligence was
thus conveyed rapidly to Shan-hai-kuan and thence to
the capital. The device for daytime was to make fires
of dried wolf's dung, which the Chinamen declare has
the peculiar property of emitting a dark volume of
smoke, so peculiarly dense, that, wind or no wind, it goes
straight upwards, making a dark perpendicular column
discernible at a great distance. The Archimandrite
Palladius, however, who calls them Duntai, or beacons,
relates a still more wonderful tale, affirming that in the
latter days of the Mings they were called Lu-tai, or
round-sided towers, and were built for the relief of travellers attacked by Mongol robbers, who fled to them for
protection and were dragged up by ropes to the top!

[1] *The Manchus*, p. 64.

A direct road exists from Sha-k'ou to Pi-tzŭ Wo, about twenty miles shorter than that which I followed; but Père Guillon dissuaded me from taking it, as the track was difficult and the inn accommodation bad. From Pi-tzŭ Wo I turned through a rocky sterile country across the peninsula. At a place called Liao-chia-tien, in a shrine near the inn, is a very ancient stone idol, the only one of that material I remember noticing in Manchuria. It has an Indian rather than a Chinese appearance, for, in China, the worshipper is quite content with a god of either clay or wood. The road then follows the sandy bed of a river for ten miles to Chin-chou T'ing, a fair-sized town with a wall in good repair, and strongly-fortified gates. Its situation is fine, at the head of a deep bay, the entrance to which is flanked by rocky cliffs. Above it, to the east, towers a lofty isolated mountain, with grand crags and precipices, called the Tiger Mountain. South of the town the isthmus is barely a mile broad, and here the Chinese Government have stationed a strong military force, while the construction of parallels and ditches shows they do not mean Port Arthur to be attacked from the rear. Upwards of 1,000 men, neatly dressed in black coats and blue trousers, were being drilled in European style, and the familiar bugle was heard resounding. From the narrow neck of land the view of the cliffs and sea on both sides is very striking. On the east lies Ta-lien-wan Bay, the rendezvous of the British fleet in 1859. It still bears the reputation of being a capital harbour.

At Chin-chou I visited the Temple of the Fox, and found Reynard represented by an old gentleman, with a venerable white beard, dressed as a mandarin, with a first-class red button in his hat, and carrying a sceptre in his hand. He is called Hu-shên, or Fox-spirit. In an adjacent niche, sharing half the honour of the temple, was Yao Wang, the God of Medicine, similarly attired, but bearing a phial of medicine. At an inn close by was a curiosity in the way of a bellows. Through one of the ends of an oblong wooden box a piston was fixed, which worked a valve inside with a horizontal motion. Inside, a space of about an inch was partitioned off from one angle along its whole length, communicating with the rest of the box by small orifices at each end, and also with a nozzle outside. The machine was, in fact, a primitive air-pump. As the piston worked backwards and forwards, the compressed air was forced into the compartment, and through that into the fire. It was an efficient, but a noisy implement.

About thirty-five miles south of Chin-chou I came to my journey's end. The last piece of road passed through very rough country, where I narrowly escaped spending a night in the snow. The weather had been changeable for some days. On January 1 it thawed, on the 2nd it was 13° Fahr.; on the 3rd, zero Fahr. at daybreak, and 58° in the sun at 11 A.M. On the 4th it was 5° Fahr. at daybreak, and at noon on the same day it was 25° in the shade and 56° in the sun. On the evening of the 4th a few inches of snow fell, and next morning it looked very threatening. I was so near my destination that I determined to push on, though I had been warned against doing so when snow was falling. After going some miles, it began to snow heavily, and the track was soon buried a foot deep. We regained it several times by making a cast across country and feeling about with our feet for the cart-ruts, but at last we came to a standstill; no house was in sight, and the tracks behind us were long ago obliterated.

After some delay I was preparing to strike across country to find a telegraph post, meaning to follow the line down till I came to a house—a rather forlorn hope —when fortunately a cart drove up belonging to a neighbouring farmer. He knew the landmarks and led the way, and at last we got safely to a wretched little inn, wet through and miserable, but thankful for a roof over our heads. Till then my impression had been that Chinese servants were not quite equal to Indian, but on this occasion Chang San worked well. He plodded through snow-drifts like a man, hunting for our lost track, he taking one side and I the other; and when we got under shelter he gave me as good a dinner as man could wish, cooked in a little wigwam a few feet square, crowded with the innkeeper's family, carters, and idlers, the kitchen range being represented by an earthen pot, and fuel by roots of millet and husks of maize.

Lu-shun-k'ou, or Port Arthur, as it was named by our naval officers over thirty years ago, is a small oval-shaped harbour about a mile and a half long by a mile broad, surrounded on all sides by hills and connected by a very narrow inlet with a fine bay outside about eight miles across. The approach to this inlet from outside is protected by two reefs, and inside a spit of land runs diagonally across the entrance and so hinders any rough water from coming inside. It is a model of a naturally protected harbour, its main defects being its bad water supply and the shallowness of the upper part of the basin. It has been chosen by the Chinese Government as the first line of defence for the capital—it is scarcely seventy miles from Chefoo—and it has been constituted the headquarters of the northern fleet. The hills to seaward are crowned with a series of forts, thirteen in number, armed with very powerful Krupp guns, and manned by artillerymen, who are drilled and instructed by Captain Schnell, a German officer. The garrison consists of 7,000 foreign drilled troops armed with the Mauser rifle, and there are field batteries besides. During the war with the French 25,000 men are said to have been massed at this place, which is in communication by telegraph with Newchwang and Peking. The hills on the landward side, which have not yet been fortified, are covered with barracks, magazines, and other offices, all connected by telephones, and on the far side of all lies the native bazaar. A graving dock and a refuge dock are now under construction, at an estimated cost of 250,000*l.* sterling. On the eminence overlooking the entrance of the port an electrical search-apparatus is mounted, to illuminate the sea and prevent an enemy approaching under cover of darkness. There are factories for submarine mines and torpedoes, with a supply of torpedoes in stock ; in fact, Port Arthur is like a good suburban villa—fitted with the latest modern improvements. The Germans have the credit for what has been done till the present time, including the drilling of the garrison; but in accordance with the policy, which the Chinese thoroughly understand and enjoy, of pitting the different Western nations against each other in turn, using all as they want them, and turning them out just when they think they are firmly established in favour, only a short time before I arrived they had dismissed their German engineers and appointed a Frenchman to finish the docks. The German instructors in torpedoes and mining have been also dispensed with, and these departments have been made over to the English, who already command the

navy. But let not those English think they are for ever
settled in comfortable berths. Their turn will come,
and then perhaps the Americans or the Russians will
have a chance.

It is, indeed, impossible not to admire the imper-
turbable calmness with which the Chinese, looking—and
I do not want to blame them—absolutely and entirely to
their own interests, play off against one another the
disinterested European nations who only want to benefit
the poor dear Chinese. The Chinaman is thoroughly
wide-awake, and means to do precisely what will be to
his own advantage, and, whenever it suits him to do so,
he will remorselessly cut every one of his foreign friends
adrift, without a spark of gratitude or thanks for service
rendered. In the matter of railways, or roads, or guns,
or telephones, he will not allow China to be exploited
for the benefit of any but himself; and nothing pleases
Chinese officials better than to have a German syndicate
offering thirty millions, a Frenchman outbidding them
with fifty, an American firm going up to two hundred,
or an English house an unlimited amount, if they only
may be allowed to develop the resources of the country.
Certainly I believe, from all I could gather in China, and
the wish is not father to the thought, that the English
do stand high at present with the Chinese for honour
and truthfulness. Our representatives and merchants
do not stoop to curry favour or custom by intrigues
and undignified shifts. And the concessions we have
made, in giving up Port Hamilton to China, and agreeing to send decennial presents from Ava (though the
last-named may be open to comment on other grounds),
have had a material effect in strengthening the friendly
feeling which some of the leading officials are disposed

to accord to us. It is well, however, that there should be no misunderstanding, and the English people should know that the Chinese are a proud, self-contained, and selfish nation, looking on all foreigners with aversion, and that, should a conflict arise between any of the Western nations, their assistance, if they give any, will be sold to the highest bidder, or, at all events, to the nation from which they have reason to fear the most. And who will say they are wrong?

To return to Port Arthur: no men-of-war were to be seen there, though it is the head-quarters of the northern fleet. The little ice which forms on the shore of the harbour is supposed to be too much for the delicate skins of the torpedo-boats, which had, therefore, been taken across to a place on the opposite coast called Wei-hai-wei, near Chefoo, and the fleet itself was at Shanghai, so that only a despatch steamer, a small gun-boat or two, and some dredgers, represented the naval power of China. Not very long before my visit, the place had been very gay, as Prince Ch'un was deputed by the Empress to inspect the troops and defences, and, by all accounts, he put every one concerned through his facings right well. His ancestor, Nurhachu, little thought, when he first attacked the Ming, that his de-scendants would conquer China and neglect Manchuria, and that the first visit of a Manchu prince, after a very long interval, to the land of his ancestors should be to the remotest corner of Fêng-t'ien, to inspect weapons and armaments brought there by foreign nations, of whose existence the 'great ancestor' had never heard.

On January 9, I left Port Arthur in the transport 'Li-yuan,' commanded by Captain Sims, one of those Englishmen whose capacity and resource contribute to make his country stand not least in the respect of the Chinese. In about seven hours I landed at Chefoo, on the Shantung coast, where I caught a steamer for Shanghai. About the same time, Younghusband and Fulford arrived safely at Tientsin, and so our journey through Manchuria was ended. I, at least, shall never regret having made it, not only because it was a real rest after prolonged desk-work, but because travelling in China acts as a wholesome corrective to the some-what despotic tone which service amongst Hindus is apt to impart to the Anglo-Indian. I am only sorry we have such a poor record of sport to show. But, our main object being to see the country and people, and ascend the mythical snowy peaks, we were obliged to sacrifice something, and, after all, scarcely any sport is comparable to what can still be obtained in India.

Many of my friends have asked me since my return whether I believe the Chinese will eventually overrun the world. I know that a six weeks' tour in India justifies a Member of Parliament in passing a verdict on every important Indian question, but I am not so sure that a slightly longer journey in China justifies anyone in posing as a prophet. Still, a man has a right to his opinion, and mine is decidedly in the negative. In the first place, the Chinese would find it difficult to combine together, as they cannot understand each other's dialects; and in the second, a rusty repeating rifle is almost as useless as a bow and arrow. In other words, until Chinese habits and ways of thought are changed, a pro-cess that will take many generations, they will not attain to that pitch of discipline, purity of administration, and self-control, which alone will enable them to use European methods and appliances of war effectively.

When they have attained to it, they will not want to devastate the world. Should they try to do so in the meantime, they will be vanquished with the greatest ease.

BOTTLE OF LANG-YAO PORCELAIN.

APPENDIX.

———◦◦◦———

NOTE A.

INDIA, CHINA, AND NEPAL.

THE wars of the upstart and aggressive Ghurkas, first with the Chinese and then with the British, gave rise on two occasions to interesting correspondence between the Government of India and the Chinese, of which I may give a brief summary. The reason assigned by the Ghurkas for attacking Thibet in the first instance was that the Lamas would not assent to a reform of the debased Nepalese currency, which was the common medium of exchange in Thibet as well as in Nepal. But the invasion was mainly due to the instigation of Sumhur Lama. This man was brother of the Teshu Lama, who died at Peking, and for some reason or other had fled to the Nepalese Court. The Nepalese defeated the Lhassa troops, and the Dalai Lama consented to a treaty providing for a reform of the currency as well as for the payment of a tribute to Nepal of three lacs of rupees (30,000*l.*) annually. The Dalai Lama, however, only meant to gain time, and applied to the Governor General of India, with whom communications of friendship had previously taken place, for assistance. This was declined. Meanwhile the Ghurka Rajah attacked Teshu Lumbo, the seat of the Teshu Lama, and plundered it. The result was that, in Sir George Staunton's words, the Emperor Kienlung determined to avenge the repeated aggressions against the spiritual fathers of his faith and against countries under his protection, and an army of 70,000 men was sent, which reached the southern border of Thibet in 1791. Both the Rajah of Nepal and the commander of the Chinese forces then sought for British assistance; the latter writing in a lofty style to the Governor-General of India, and desiring, in the name of his master, 'the flower of the imperial race, the sun of the firmament of honour, the resplendent gem in the crown and throne of the Chinese territories,' that British troops should be sent to seize and chastise the Rajah as he deserved. The Governor-General replied to the Rajah of Nepal, that he would send an officer to his country with the object of settling his dispute with Thibet and China, if possible, in an amicable manner; and he wrote in similar terms to the Dalai Lama, stating that friendship had long subsisted between the English and the Rajah of Nepal, and also between the Emperor of China, whose protection extended over the Lama, and the East India Company. The second letter, however, did not reach Sun Fo, the Chinese General, in time. He advanced into Nepal, and when Major Kirkpatrick, the Governor-General's agent, arrived at Khatmandu, the Chinese were at Nayakot, within striking distance of the capital, before him. The Chinese General afterwards wrote a courteous letter to the Governor-General, saying that he need not put himself to the trouble of sending an envoy to him in Thibet, and that doubtless the Governor-General's letter had induced the Rajah of Nepal to submit to the Emperor. But the General, annoyed at not receiving sooner either a letter or military assistance from the British, or from some other cause, reported at Peking that English troops had assisted Nepal. Whatever the reason, it is certain that he took a violent dislike to the British, of whom he knew a little, having been Viceroy of Canton, and he represented them as an encroaching people, whom it was dangerous to encourage. He was present at Jehol, the Emperor's country seat in Mongolia, at the time of Lord Macartney's embassy, and to his evil influence the failure of the mission—for, in spite of the Emperor's gracious reception, it ended in nothing—is principally attributed.

About twenty-five years after the invasion of Nepal by China, the Ghurkas' aggressiveness south of the Himalayas rendered their subjugation by the British a necessity. On this occasion it was the Governor-General of India who warned the Chinese, in common with other Powers, against aiding or abetting the enemies of the British Government. The letter reached the Ambans (Umbas) at Shigatsze (otherwise called Diggurchi, or Teshu Lumbo), and they sent on the communication, together with the Nepal Rajah's appeals for assistance, which had been previously disregarded, to Peking. The Emperor Chia Ching was very indignant, and ordered a Tsiang-kun, (Tartar General) with two Ta-jên, or Commissioners, to proceed to the frontier with an army to follow, and a force did arrive on the Chinese frontier in 1816.

The three Chinese officers then addressed the Governor-General of India, through the medium of the Rajah of Sikhim, who was closely connected with the Deb Rajah of Bhutan and the Dalai

Lama of Lhassa, calling on him to state if the insinuations as to the ulterior views of the British were well founded, and to submit a suitable explanation to the Tsiang-kun. The Sikhim Rajah, in forwarding this letter, stated that the Ghurkas had been trying to impose on the Chinese, by representing that the British were going to attack both Nepal and China, and that this was the sole foundation for the Chinese letter. In reply, the Governor-General stated the real facts of the case, and when the Nepalese went to Shigatsze, the Chinese (who did not like being asked if the Emperor of China meant to leave one of his tributaries to its fate, but saw no way of helping them), scolded them for their misbehaviour, which had brought on the war. The Nepalese then complained against the British for posting a Resident at Khatmandu, so another Chinese letter was sent to India through the Rajah of Sikhim, in the following terms : 'His Imperial Majesty, who by God's mercy is well informed of the conduct and proceedings of all mankind, reflecting on the good faith and wisdom of the English Company, and the pure friendship and constant commercial intercourse which has so long existed between the two nations, never placed any reliance on the calumnious imputations put forward by the Ghurka Rajah. You mention that you have stationed a Vakil.[1] This is a matter of no consequence. But as the Rajah, from his youth and inexperience, and from the novelty of the circumstances, has imbibed suspicions, if you should, out of kindness to us, and in consideration of the ties of friendship, withdraw your Vakil, it would be better, and we shall be inexpressibly grateful to you.' The Governor-General replied that the late war was due to the want of a Resident, but that, if there were an accredited agent of the Chinese to whom the Governor of India could with confidence recur in matters of dispute with the Nepalese, the Government of India would be saved the expense of a Resident. As matters stood, the Resident would be directed to preserve harmony between the two states, and to abstain from all interference in the internal and foreign affairs of Nepal. The Commissioners acknowledged this letter with much satisfaction, adding, however, that China did not keep Residents at the Courts of her tributaries. They could not, therefore, forward the Governor-General's proposal to Peking. The Ghurka Rajah, they said, had long been a tributary of the Chinese Government, and referred himself to it when occasion offered. And there the matter dropped.

Missions from Nepal to China, provided for after the war of 1792, if not regular, were not infrequent until 1852. In that year the envoys were exposed to gross insults and indignities, both in

---

[1] Ambassador, or delegate.

Thibet and China. One member of the mission was imprisoned, another had his nose cut off, and several died from the hardships to which they were subjected. Remonstrances to the Umbas of Lhassa were treated with contempt, so in 1854 Jung Bahadur, the celebrated Maire du Palais, declared 'that the subjection of Nepal to China had from that time ceased, and that the Ghurkas would thenceforth neither pay any more tribute nor acknowledge the supremacy of that country.' Nay, more, he declared war against Thibet itself, and after a year's preparation invaded it. He carried Junga and occupied the Kerong and Kutti passes, but his troops greatly suffered; they were reduced to eating yaks, which the Brahmins were induced to declare were deer for the nonce, and not bovine animals, whose flesh the pious Hindu may not touch; and the war was so costly that the temples in Nepal were stripped of the bells which hung from them as votive offerings to cast into guns. Jung Bahadur could not effect a lodgment in the interior of Thibet, while the Thibetans found they were unequal to Ghurkas as fighting men, and could not oust them from the positions they had occupied, though at one time they nearly succeeded; so a peace was made, after frequent references to the Chinese Umba at Lhassa. The Nepalese were to receive 10,000 rupees annually on condition of their evacuating the passes, import duties on Nepalese goods were to be remitted, and a Ghurka official was to reside at Lhassa to look after the interests of Nepalese merchants. After the conclusion of peace, the missions to China continued to be withheld; but the Umbas promised honourable treatment for future missions, and the Nepalese had made such a good thing in 1852 by smuggling opium into China, and the Envoy had also received such handsome presents, that Jung Bahadur resolved to send another. It started in 1866, but got no farther than Thindafu, fourteen miles beyond Chentu, in Sszchuen. There it was stopped because the Chinese would not provide carriage for the merchandise, and the members of the mission were not well treated. The party, therefore, returned in 1869, and Jung Bahadur determined to send no more. But in 1877 his brother Runodeep Sing, who had succeeded, despatched another mission, with a view to receiving a much-coveted title which the Chinese Government had conferred on Jung Bahadur. It reached Peking in 1879, left in the summer of 1880, and arrived back at Nepal in 1882. In November 1885, a revolution took place in Nepal, in which Runodeep Sing was murdered, and as his successor, Bir Shumshere, coveted the same title as his uncle, another mission was sent in October 1886.

But although the missions to China have been fitfully resumed, with an inferior Nepalese official at their head, the ruler of Nepal never omits to send one to each new English Viceroy ; and even if he be the highest personage in the State, as occasionally is the case, he is not received at Government House as an equal. Owing in the main to her geographical position, Nepal fully realises the fact of her dependence upon her British suzerain. And freely and right loyally has she come forward, both in the mutiny and since, to display her fealty. The British, on the other hand, have ever respected her independence. They have never even insisted on the admission of British travellers or traders within her borders, and, beyond bringing pressure to bear on her rulers for the abolition of suttee and similar barbarous practices, which they have done successfully, they have ever refrained from interference with her internal affairs.

It may be noted that when Thibet was attacked in 1854 the Chinese did not interfere. Probably their hands were too full with the Taeping rebellion. But from the time of Kanghi, who was the first Emperor to interfere effectually in Thibetan affairs, even from the time of Kienlung, who took the opportunity of the Nepalese war to garrison many Thibetan towns, the control of China over Thibet has been only nominal. As late as 1886 she was compelled to draw back from an engagement she had made with the British Minister at Peking, that she would facilitate the journey of an English envoy to Lhassa for the purpose of opening out trade between India and Thibet. For the Chinese Amban declared himself powerless to assist the Envoy, and the Thibetans themselves, suspicious of British designs, prepared to resist his entry by force. And, shadowy as the power of China is over Thibet, it is still more unsubstantial in regard to Nepal. Only four or five years ago the quarters of the Nepalese merchants at Lhassa were attacked and plundered by Thibetans, and the Nepalese threatened war. Fortunately, matters were arranged amicably, the Chinese Government issuing directions that the Nepalese were to receive compensation. But had hostilities broken out, it is a curious speculation whether the Government at Peking would have tried to interfere or not.

Note B.

OPIUM.

There is a good deal of ignorance afloat about the responsibility of Britain for the opium trade with China.

So far from the drug having been introduced into China by the British, as some think, it has, according to the 'Encyclopædia Britannica,' been known there for many centuries, possibly before the Christian era. It is described in a Chinese herbal 200 years ago, and in the history of Yunnan, republished in 1736, it is mentioned, as being then, as now, a common product of that province. In India, on the other hand, the cultivation of the poppy was not started by the East India Company; for opium was an imperial monopoly of the Great Mogul, and after Clive's victory at Plassy it passed with the dewanny of Bengal to the British. In 1773 the East India Company, then a trading as well as a civilising body, determined, like honest stewards, to develop the revenues of its newly-acquired provinces, and the opium export trade to China, till then in the hands of the Portuguese, was taken by the Company under its own management. The export was said at first to be only about 200 chests, but in about twenty years it increased to 400, and, as the article was good and to the taste of the Chinese, it developed in half a century to 50,000 chests. The Indian ryot profited, and the East India Company was enabled, by the revenues which opium brought in, to conquer tyrants like Tippoo Sahib and marauders like Holkar, to repel the Nepalese invasion and disperse the hordes of Pindarees, besides improving its civil administration and giving the people of India peace, justice, and prosperity.

The Emperor Chia Ching, in 1796 or 1797, issued a proclamation against the drug, which, to judge from the inaction that followed it, was a mere formal protestation like the English royal proclamation against vice and immorality, or the Chinese edict quoted at page 171, which was published in 1883, a well-meaning parade of moral sentiments not worth the paper it was written upon; for the trade in opium was allowed by the mandarins at Canton, where the East India Company's factory was situated. Chia Ching's son, the Emperor Tao-kuang, also published edicts against it. But Tao-kuang also had reigned nearly twenty years before taking active steps to enforce his wishes, and he was then as powerless to deprive his people of the luxury they desired, as the East India Company was to stop its export from India. The question, indeed, is sometimes asked whether, at the time when the Emperor Tao-kuang insisted on making opium contraband, the East India Company and the British Government ought not, as representing a Christian and civilised nation, to have seconded his well-meant endeavours. The answer is, first, that up to the time he took the law into his own hands, menacing and confining British subjects and forcibly confiscating their property, he not only made no effort to address the British Government on the subject, but, whatever his own private sentiments may have been, he allowed, through his officers, so much uncertainty to prevail as to his real wishes, that well-informed people actually thought the trade would shortly be legalised. Consequently, England's duty to India did not admit of her checking a valuable trade, which there was reason to expect might shortly be put on a proper footing. Next, even if the East India Company had tried to prevent Indian-grown opium being sent to China, their efforts would have been fruitless—they might have injured the revenue, but they could not have profited the Chinese ; for at that time the Punjaub and Sind were both independent, and the opium traffic would have been merely diverted to Kurrachee from Calcutta. These considerations alone would have prevented the Company from taking action in the direction indicated, wholly apart from the further question of their right to interfere with the cultivation of a profitable staple by the ryots of Bengal.

There is also much misapprehension as to the fundamentally evil effects which opium is supposed to entail upon the consumer of the drug.

Turning to the most recent standard work that deals with the subject, Dr. Garrod's 'Materia Medica' states that opium is perhaps more extensively used than any other drug, and of such value is it, that it has been called the gift of God. Pain, from whatever cause arising, is advantageously treated by it. It is both a stimulant and a sedative : in inflammation it not only assuages pain and spasm, but combats diseased action ; it cures fever and ague ; in short, it is invaluable in every kind of illness. The abuse of opium, like alcohol, impairs the digestive organs, and, although used as an aphrodisiac, persons indulging in it to excess become afflicted with debility. Still, it does not excite to wife-beating like gin, or running a-muck like *Cannabis Indica*. Indeed, Dr. Garrod quotes cases in which enormous quantities have been taken without any evident effect being produced.

Dr. W. J. Moore, again, a very eminent physician in the East, one of whose works is a text-book in every family in India, and who

has had unusually favourable opportunities of observing the effects
of opium upon the native races of India, says: 'The only malady
opium-eating in Rajpootana tends to foster is the minor ailment of
constipation. . . . Daily evidence sufficiently proves that it is often
or continuously administered to children without the latter being
very much the worse for it, and that grown-up people may take it
without injury for years—may even under certain circumstances, and
at certain times, consume it with advantage. The physiological fact
appears to be that opium, when taken into the system, acts in some
respects very much like alcohol, and the use of stimulants in some
shape or other always has been and always will be a desideratum, it
may even be said a necessity, to the human race. Those using opium
do not, as a very general rule, indulge in alcohol.' 'He must be,'
Dr. Moore goes on to say, 'a bold man who dare fling the stone at
the majority of persons using opium, at least in Rajpootana. When
taken by the camel-feeders in the sandy deserts, it is used to enable
the men far away from towns, or even from desert villages, to sub-
sist on scanty food, and to bear without injury the excessive cold of
the desert winter night and the scorching rays of the desert sun.
When used by the impoverished ryot, it occupies the void resulting
from insufficient food, or from food deficient in the necessary alimen-
tary substances ; and it affords the ill-nourished cultivator, unable
to procure or store liquor, not only a taste of that exhilaration of
spirits which arises from good wine, but also enables him to undergo
his daily fatigue with far less waste of tissue than would otherwise
occur. To the courier, again, obliged to travel a long distance, it is
invaluable.' Dr. Moore is personally acquainted with natives of
India who have taken opium from boyhood, and who at forty, fifty,
or even the grand climacteric of sixty-three, are hale and hearty as
any of their fellows. He once had a servant who had been an opium-
eater from 'his youth upwards.' This man contracted the habit in
the first Afghan war, and he marched with his master many thousand miles year by year over the semi-desert districts of Rajpootana.
Although the opium pipe was this man's nightly solace, he never
neglected his work, or failed to appear at that unpleasant hour in
the very early morning at which long marches through heavy sand
rendered riding a necessity ; and he never forgot to have every
article required in its proper place. 'The fact is,' adds Dr. Moore,
'that opium only shortens the lives of those who (in the same manner
as many Europeans consume gin) use the drug excessively, or as a
substitute for food. It therefore follows that, as a rule, it is the
lives of the poor and needy which are shortened by opium. Doolittle
tells us that well-to-do Chinamen smoke opium in moderation all

their lives without injury, which indeed accords with experience in other countries.'

At the present day opium is produced in nine or ten at least of the eighteen provinces of China, and the southern provinces alone produce more than twice the entire export from India. It is more lightly taxed than Indian opium, and there can be no question that the Chinese confidently look forward to the time when home-grown opium will entirely supplant the foreign drug. About 55,000 chests of Bengal opium, and 40,000 of Malwa opium (grown in native states) are now exported from India to China annually, bringing in a net revenue to India of between six and seven crores of rupees, or 4,500,000*l.* to 5,250,000*l.* sterling.

NOTE C.

DECREE ON THE SUBJECT OF OFFICIAL CORRUPTION.

(EXTRACT FROM THE 'PEKING GAZETTE' OF AUGUST 5, 1885.)

A DECREE calling the attention of Provincial High Authorities in emphatic terms to the prevalence of corruption and abuses in every department of the Government Administration.

It is to the agency of the Provincial High Authorities that the Sovereign has to look for the successful carrying out of the beneficent system of Government which it is his unceasing desire to administer. The cessation of popular distress, the flourishing condition or the reverse of the finances of the Empire, and the proper administration of its laws, depend entirely upon these High Authorities. With such grave responsibilities placed upon their shoulders, how energetic ought they to be in their efforts to ensure their labours being productive of genuine success! While it is not denied that there are some amongst them who apply themselves conscientiously to the performance of their duties, there are others who have not succeeded in purging themselves from the taint of perfunctoriness. Express commands and emphatic injunctions from the Throne are considered by such Governors-General or Governors as these to be done with when they have been communicated to their associates or subordinates. No pains are taken by them to ascertain actual facts by the test of searching inquiry, with the result that benefits do not permeate to those for whom they are destined, and abuses spring up like weeds. Others even go so far as to smooth away charges or facts which they receive the special command of the Throne to inquire into, or intentionally postpone the investigation of them.

The Army of the Green Standard has long been in an effete and useless condition, and so the numbers of irregulars that are enlisted go towards the maintenance of a useless force. Pay and rations, too, are wasted, and in every province more men are returned than are actually enrolled. Unless the army be purified from these abuses, how is it possible to obtain an efficient and well-drilled. army ?

So, again, with taxation, which is the stay and support of the Administration. False returns of disaster and applications for remission of taxation have become the rule, while the taxation on the productive lands never resumes its assessed amount. Customs duties are regarded as a rich preserve in which to hunt, personal gain being all that is considered, and not the public good. *Lekin* is a tax which is imposed by the State under the pressure of unavoidable circumstances, and the abuses which it has created are especially numerous. It is looked upon as a means of lending a helping hand to subordinates, who fatten upon it and sweep gains into their net in a manner which has attained the force of usage that cannot be broken through. So, again, with the manufacturing departments of the State, where expenditure is incurred on an enormous scale, the services of incompetent agents are employed, false returns of expenditure are sent in, and deception is practised upon a scale that renders these departments one of the most fertile sources of waste.

The same is true of other items of expenditure over and above that sanctioned by law, which are a drain upon the revenue of the Empire as well as upon the earnings of the people, and are hedged about by long-standing abuses of so many sorts and kinds that they defy classification.

If Provincial High Authorities would act uprightly and verify their expenditure, considering the interests of the State as though they were the interests of their own families, and, regardless of hard work or of contumely, maintain an attitude of independence and impartiality, how could there fail to be sufficient to meet the needs of the State or to enrich its subjects, and effect an improvement in the condition of the Empire, the growth of which would be daily marked ?

All the Provincial High Authorities are ministers who have been specially selected for their posts, and in whom confidence has been reposed. Let them all, then, rouse their consciences into activity, and, reverently furthering the burning anxiety which consumes the

Head of the State by day and night, bring true devotion of heart to bear upon all matters which pass through their hands. The trammels of favouritism must be absolutely broken through, capable and intelligent agents only be employed, commands and warnings be regarded as something more than mere empty words, and representations to the Throne not as a formal fulfilment of an allotted task.

From the issue of this emphatic injunction henceforward a continuance in the beaten track of corruption and perfunctoriness will be met in its lightest form by instant dismissal, and in more aggravated instances by the unsparing punishment of the offender.

In sum, in the employment of proper individuals and the administration of Government, the Court has no other standard than that of truth. All the Provincial High Authorities concerned are hereby called upon to give the general question of reorganisation and its requirements their thorough consideration, and to submit a detailed exposition of their views to the Throne. There must not be the slightest suspicion of perfunctory obedience to this call, or any attempt to screen matters from view under pain of punishment and tribulation.

EXERT YOURSELVES AND TREMBLE!

NOTE D.[1]

JOURNEYS OF M. DE LA BRUNIÈRE AND M. VENAULT
in 1845 and 1850.

SHORTLY after 1841, M. de la Brunière proposed the conversion of the Chang-Mao-tse—i.e. long-haired people—on the banks of the Amur, but could not be spared before 1844, when the number of missionaries was increased. In May 1845 he left Kai-Cheu, with the understanding of not extending his journey beyond three months. His further progress may be seen from the following letter, dated from the banks of the Usuri, and addressed to the Directors of the Seminary for Foreign Missions:[1]

'Manchuria, on the river Usuri: April 5, 1846.

'. . . On July 15, after some retirement wherein I had consulted the will of God, I departed from Pa-kia-tze, a Christian district of Mongolia, accompanied by two neophytes quite unaccustomed to

[1] *Annales de la Propagation de la Foi*, vol. xx. 1848.

travelling. They were the only guides I could then find. We directed our course eastwards, keeping a little to the north. Seven days' journey sufficed to reach the town of A-she-ho, recently founded, and settled by successive emigrants from China, as had been the case to the deserts of Mongolia. A-she-ho is situated forty leagues north of Kirin, and twenty-five west of the Sungari. Its population, estimated at 60,000 souls, increases every day; a mandarin of the second class governs it. It has within its territory some Christian families, which were visited the preceding winter by our dear brother the Rev. Dr. Venault. I preferred to stop this time with a rich pagan, a friend of one of our neophytes, hoping that his generous hospitality would afford me the opportunity of announcing to him Jesus Christ. Great was my surprise to find that this man had the faith already in his heart, and sincerely despised the vain superstitions of paganism. And still he remains chained down to that belief; he is insensible to every exhortation, inasmuch as, directing a large establishment of carpentry, if he were a Christian, he could no longer make idols for the temples, from which source he derives a considerable profit. In return for my zeal, he eagerly tried to dissuade me from the journey I had undertaken, representing to me the troops of tigers and bears which filled these deserts; and whilst relating these things he sometimes uttered such vehement cries, that my two guides grew pale with horror. Being already a little accustomed to the figures of Chinese eloquence, I thanked him for his solicitude, assuring him that the flesh of Europeans had such a particular flavour, that the tigers of Manchuria would not attempt to fasten their teeth in it. The answer was not calculated to reassure my companions; and they did not partake of my confidence when we resumed our route.

'Eight leagues from A-she-ho, the country, hitherto sufficiently peopled, suddenly changes to an immense desert, which ends at the Eastern Sea. Only one road traverses it, conducting to San-sim (in the Manchu language Ilamhola), a small village situated on the right bank of the Sungari, twenty-four leagues from its confluence with the Amur. The forests of oaks, elms, and fir-trees, which bound the horizon on all sides, the tall thick grass, which oftentimes reached above our heads, were convincing proofs of fertility of the soil, as yet untouched by the hand of man. At every ten leagues you find one or two cabins, a kind of lodging-houses, established through the care of the mandarins for the Government couriers, which also as a matter of course lodge other travellers. There you need not ask for a bill of fare. If simplicity be one of the best conditions of a dietary regimen, it cannot be denied but that in this respect the fore-mentioned hostelries deserve to occupy the first rank. You have millet boiled in water, and nothing else. Two or three times the master of the house, in consideration of my noble bearing, brought to me a plate of wild herbs gathered in the neighbourhood. I do not know what these plants were, but I suspect strongly that gentian, an infusion of which is often drunk as a medicinal tea, was a chief component. The choicest dainty in these countries—which, however, is never served up in the hotels—is the flower of the yellow lily, which abounds on the mountains and is very palatable to the Chinese.

'Meantime no tigers appeared. But other kinds of animals, no less ferocious in my opinion, awaited us on our journey. I have not words to express to you the multitude of mosquitos, gnats, wasps, and gadflies which attacked us at every step. Each of us, armed with a horse's tail fixed on an iron prong, endeavoured to strike them, and this weak defence only served to render the enemy more vicious in his attacks. As for me, I was completely beaten, without strength either to advance or protect myself from the stinging of these insects ; or if, at times, I raised my hand to my face, I crushed ten or twelve with one blow. Two wretched horses, which carried the baggage and occasionally our persons, lay down panting in the midst of the grass, refusing to eat or drink, and could by no means be induced to march. They were all covered with blood. We had been already three days on our journey, and four still remained before we could reach San-sim. We therefore changed our system of travelling, converted night into day, and reached the inn an hour before daybreak. By this procedure we avoided two terrible enemies, the gadflies and wasps ; the mosquitos alone escorted us, in order that we might not be altogether without annoyance.

'Those who know the country best never go out without a mosquito cloth—that is to say, without a thick, double wrapper, covering the head and neck, and having two holes cut for the eyes. As to beasts of burden, to make them travel in the deserts five or six days in succession, under the noon-day's sun, is to expose them to almost certain death. These insects swarm particularly in moist, marshy places, and on the banks of the rivers by which Manchuria is intersected. Beyond San-sim they grow to a monstrous size, particularly the gnats and wasps. As to others, as far as regards the punishment they inflict, it matters not whether they be small or large. The houses are somewhat preserved from them by the cultivated districts which surround them, and by their being fumigated with horse or cow dung : but they are not completely rid of them till the end of September, the time of the severe frosts.

'Another difficulty in these journeys consists in the immense deposits of mud which intervene on the route, and frequently compel a deviation of three or four leagues . . . At last, towards the evening of August 4, San-sim displayed to us its wooden walls and houses. This city presents nothing remarkable but its great street, inlaid with large pieces of wood, six inches thick and joined together with much precision. Its population is reckoned at ten thousand souls. The Manchu mandarin who governs it is of the second class (dark red button), and has under his jurisdiction the banks of the Usuri and the right side of the Amur as far as the sea.

'The city of San-sim, the last post of the mandarins in the North is to every Chinese or Manchu traveller the extreme limit which the law allows him to reach. To travel beyond is considered and punished as a great infraction of the laws of the state. About ten merchants protected by imperial passports, which cost each of them one hundred taels or more annually, have the sole privilege of descending the Sungari, entering the Amur, and finally ascending the Usuri, in the forests of which is found the celebrated ginseng root. Any other traveller is beaten without any form of law, and his baggage, even to his clothes, taken from him. Evasion, moreover, is difficult on account of the small barges which are continually plying on the river in all directions day and night. The Government of San-sim despatch annually three war junks in succession, carrying no guns, and having only a few sabres on board. The first of these goes to·Muchem, on the right bank of the Amur, in 49° 13′ N. lat. This Muchem (Dondon of the Tunguzians) is neither a town nor a village, nor even a hamlet, but simply a building of deal, which during three months serves as a court-house for the mandarins of the boat. Their business is to receive the skins and furs which the tribe of the Sham-mao-tze (" Long-hair "), so called because they never shave the head, furnishes to the Emperor, in exchange for a certain number of pieces of cloth. The second barge collects the same imposts from the Yupitatze (or " Fish-skin "), from the skins of fish which they make use of for clothing. The third boat has jurisdiction over the Elle-iao-tze (or " Long-red-hair "), a wretched and almost extinct tribe, occupying two or three small inlets of the Usuri, and dwelling under tents made of the bark of trees.[1]

'It often happens, however, that the mandarins and soldiers of these boats take more care of their own affairs than of those of the Emperor. Not content with the skins of sable, they exact large

[1] The 'Long-hairs' of the Chinese are the Mangun or Olcha, the 'Fish-skins' the Goldi, and the 'Long-red-hairs' the Orochi of the sea-coast.—R.

sums of money before delivering the promised cloth ; and in spite of all the natives may urge, they are no less bound down, under pain of being scourged, to this arbitrary impost. Many families, on the approach of the boat, leave their huts and fly to the mountains. But even this is of little avail ; for during their absence everything belonging to them is pillaged, and the cabin itself burnt down.

'For my part, after a few days of rest spent in procuring information and laying in the necessary provisions, I sent back to Leaotong one of my two Christians, whom the experience of the previous journey had disinclined from proceeding further. When we arrived at San-sim it was just the time when the Manchu Yupitatze and Sham-mao came to exchange the produce of fishing and the chase for cloth, millet, and especially Chinese brandy. I learned from them that about forty leagues below San-sim, also upon the banks of the Sungari, was situated one of their principal villages, named Su-su. They added, at the same time, that we Chinese were prohibited entrance, and no one would venture to conduct us thither. This double obstacle was no reason why I should abandon my project. Having then implored the Divine aid, and celebrated for that purpose the holy sacrifice at my hotel, the master of which, a man of the tribe of Xensi, took me for a sorcerer, I directed my way at an early hour of the morning towards the eastern range of mountains. If Providence permitted us to wander on our route, we always did it in such a way, that, meeting with some lonely cabin, we were able, either by inquiring or by conjectures more · or less correct, to keep without too many deviations the straight road to Su-su. We journeyed full of confidence in the invisible Guide who alone directed our steps, when, in the middle of the fourth day, we were met by two horsemen, who bore an air of haughty nobility. It was a military mandarin attended by an inferior officer. He stopped, alighted from his horse, and saluted us very politely. We sat down on the grass and smoked a pipe together. The European countenance, more masculine than the generality of Chinese physiognomies, puzzled him for a moment. He addressed himself to my Christian, and desired to know from him the object of our excursion into a country severely interdicted. The latter replied, in accordance with instructions given beforehand, that, as a simple man and labourer by profession, he had followed me as a domestic, without having any power to take a part in the important affairs which had brought me into these parts. On hearing this answer the mandarin immediately suspected that I was a ministerial agent, charged with examining into the state of the country and the conduct of the officials. This is in reality a common practice of the Government, when they have conceived any prejudice against the functionaries of a city or a district. It should also be remarked that the Manchu mandarins are in general illiterate, and very little skilled in business. He therefore turned to me with increased caution, entered into conversation upon the name of my family, the province in which I was born, the products of the south of China, the state of commerce, &c. During all this time there was no inquiry after the object of my mission. He dreaded to compromise himself and lose my favour. Two hours having thus passed in exchanging compliments, we parted well pleased with each other. He had the kindness to point out to us the best route to Su-su ; and the next day, at an early hour, we were reposing in the cabin of a Yupitatze.

'My sudden appearance occasioned great alarm to these poor people ; my unusual look ; the dress, which in that country denoted somewhat of a high rank ; the breviary, and the crucifix, formed the subjects of a thousand conjectures. Little presents made to the principal persons of the district soon established a familiarity of intercourse, which enabled me to speak openly and with authority of the Gospel. My hearers found the religion very fine ; but the new doctrine, and the new preacher who announced it, stopped them short at once. One day—it was, I believe, the fourth of my arrival —I was sitting on the bank of the river conversing with one of the natives, and just beside us were his two sons engaged in fishing. In despair of catching anything they pulled in their long lines and were going away, when I said, assuming a jocose tone :

' "You do not understand ; give me one of your lines."

'I threw it about ten paces further, not without much laughter from the spectators. Providence willed that a large fish should bite at the very instant ; and I drew out my prey, more astonished myself than those who laughed.

' "This unknown," said they among themselves, "has secrets, which other men have not ; and nevertheless he is not a bad man."

'In the evening, at supper, there was much talk about the wonderful capture I had made. They wished to know my secret. Instead of an answer, I contented myself with one single question :

' "Do you believe in hell ?"

' "Yes," answered three or four of the best informed ; "we believe in hell, like the bonzes of San-sim."

' "Have you any means of escaping it ?"

' "We have never reflected on that point."

' "Well, then," I replied, "I have an infallible secret, by means of which you can become more powerful than all the evil spirits, and go straight to heaven."

' The first secret gained credence for the second. Thus Divine
Providence disposes of all things.

' The next day, three long-beards of the village made their appearance in my chamber, armed with a jug of brandy and four
glasses.

' " Your secret," said they, " is of awful consequence. If our
importunity does not hurt your feelings, we would wish to know in
what it consists. Let us begin by drinking."

' Notwithstanding the natural repugnance which I have for
Chinese brandy, I thought it necessary to accept the invitation, in
order to avoid incurring the aversion of these poor people, who could
be made to know or understand nothing but through this channel.
I then commenced to develop my " secret," by explaining the dogma
of original sin, of hell, of the salvation wrought by Jesus Christ, and
the application by the sacraments of the merits of the Saviour. It
was in the simplest manner, and by familiar comparisons, that I
proceeded. But, unluckily, my interrogators, taking ten or twelve
bumpers to my one, became in five or six minutes incapable of understanding anything. However, I gained favour. They lodged
me and my Christian in a very spacious house, which had become
vacant by the death of the proprietor. One of the most intelligent
men of the village was appointed to teach me their Manchu language, which is more pleasing to their ear than Chinese, although
they speak the one as well as the other. The Manchu has become
a dead language in Manchuria Proper. The natives glory in
abandoning the language of their ancestors in favour of that of the
new comers—the Chinese. It is not the same with the Yupitatze,
whose language is to the Manchu much the same as Provençal
patois is to the French or Italian.

' A week had elapsed when in the middle of the day the sharp
sound of the tam-tam was heard on the river. Fear was immediately depicted on every countenance.

' " It is," said they to me, " a large boat from San-sim, bearing
two mandarins and twenty soldiers, who at this moment are assem-
bling all the inhabitants of Su-su."

' In addition to the ordinary apprehension caused by the sudden
appearance of the functionaries, the people saw themselves seriously
compromised by my presence, which would bring down upon them
the wrath of the mandarin. After a mutual understanding with
me, they simply declared me to be an unknown person, who transacted no commercial business, and who, in opposition to their
resistance at first, had forced himself upon their hospitality. An
officer, followed by seven or eight soldiers, came directly to the house

where I was ; and, the first usual compliments being passed, demanded of me what business brought me into a country, the entrance of which was strictly forbidden by law.

' "My business," I answered, "calls me not only to Su-su ; I must go further, and push on even to the Usuri."

'The officer, without daring to follow up his inquiries, gratefully accepted a cup of tea, and retired, inviting me to visit the boat. To anticipate the mandarin, and pay him the first marks of politeness, was a decisive step ; this indication of confidence would remove all suspicion. I went, therefore, on board, attended by my Christian, and was received almost with open arms.

'On the evening of the same day he returned my visit. I offered him some pu-cha, the much-esteemed tea of Seshwan, the glutinous leaves of which form a roll as hard as wood.

' "My lord," said he on retiring, "your presence here causes no inconvenience ; I allow you to remain ten or even twenty days, if your business require it."

'Nevertheless, the crew of the boat exacted from fourteen poor families of Su-su a sum equivalent to two hundred francs. The whole amount of money in possession of the Fish-skins did not amount to more than seventy-two francs. Three days passed in parley. My presence evidently annoyed the collectors. I had become an object of suspicion, and thought it best to return to San-sim, on August 23, where I lodged with a Mohammedan.

'My beard and my eyes induced my host first to imagine that I was one of his co-religionists. His conjectures vanished completely before a plate of pork, which he saw me eat with a great relish. But what was his surprise when he heard me relate the history of the creation ; the fall of our first parents ; the travels of Abraham, &c. !

'The Mohammedans of San-sim are numerous, and form about one-third of the population ; they own a mosque, which is guarded by a kind of Marabut, called Lao-she-fu. The duty of this man is, every day at sunrise to give the first stroke of the knife to the beast or cow, which is sold in the Turkish shambles. He also opens the school for the young persons who wish to study the Koran. I received the unexpected visit of a superior officer, a confidant of the chief mandarin. His mission was not to interrogate me judicially, but by means of certain captious questions and counterfeit politeness to extract my confidence. After a long conversation the officer retired just as wise as he came, but only to return in a short time to the charge. He paid me as many as three visits in the space of six days ; so that the Turk, not being able any longer to repress his fears, came to me to humbly ask how much longer I counted on a shelter under his roof. It was, therefore, necessary to consider anew about my departure.

'I remembered having heard it said by the Fish-skins of Su-su that towards the east, a little to the south of San-sim, there was a narrow path by which the ginseng dealers annually went to the Usuri. The distance by the long winding caused by the rivers and mountains is reckoned at one hundred and twenty leagues. The Turk, to whom alone I had confined my project, cheerfully assisted my little preparations; and on September 1, 1845, we once more quitted San-sim, without knowing when we might return.

'This time the mule carried along a complete kitchen—namely, a small iron pot, a hatchet, two porringers, a bushel of millet, and some cakes of oaten bread. Whoever makes the journey from San-sim to the Usuri need not look for any other bed than the ground, any other covering than the heavens, nor any other food than what he may have taken the precaution of bringing. The journey, on account of the autumn rains, took us fifteen days. I confess that, in comparison with these, former fatigues appeared as child's play. You must cut and drag trees, light fires, necessary against the cold and the tiger, prepare your victuals in wind and rain, and all this in the midst of a swarm of mosquitoes and gadflies, who do not suspend their attacks until about ten or twelve o'clock in the evening. Water and wood were in abundance during the first days of the journey; but thirty leagues from the Usuri the springs became so scarce, that we were compelled to do like the birds of heaven, and eat the millet raw. The forests of this wilderness have scarcely any other trees than an oak, of poor growth in consequence of the rigorous climate.

'At last, towards the evening of September 14, the river Usuri came in view; it is as deep but not as broad as the Sungari. We were then forty leagues north of the Lake Hinka (Tahu). Our first asylum was a lonely house built by the Chinese merchants, serving as a warehouse for the ginseng trade. Two days had scarcely passed when, yielding to the invitation of one of the merchants, I availed myself of his bark to descend the river for a distance of twenty-four leagues, to a miserable cabin, situated ten leagues from the confluence of the Usuri with the Amur.

'This cabin belonged to a Chinese, a native of Shan-tum. With him were ten of his countrymen, from different provinces, whom he employed for six months in the year to traverse the mountains and forests in search of that celebrated root of Zu-leu, about which I will say something farther on. The first interview made me imagine myself far from savage districts, and within the pale of Chinese urbanity. But when they learned my quality of Christian priest, then were verified the words of the Teacher, " The servant is not greater than his Lord " (John xiii. 16). Aversion and disdain were succeeded by wrath, when, profiting by the many questions they addressed me, I openly announced Jesus Christ. In return for the words of salvation and love they heaped maledictions on me.

'I had been there fifteen days, when a strange accident broke up our meetings. This happened about the middle of October. The trees already bare, and the high grass parched and turned yellow, announced the approach of great cold. At mid-day, there appeared in the horizon above the forests an immense cloud, which completely intercepted the light of the sun. Suddenly, all hurried out of the house, crying " Fire! fire! " They took hatchets, and destroyed all the vegetation which bordered on the dwellings. The grass was burned and the trees dragged into the river. The cloud kept fast approaching. It opened, and disclosed to us the focus of a raging fire, as rapid in its course as a horse spurred to the gallop. There were concussions in the atmosphere, in violence resembling the shock of a tempest. The flames at hand, as soon as seen, passed a few paces near us, and plunged like an arrow into the forests to the north, leaving us in a sad state of consternation, although we had not suffered any loss. These fires are caused by hunters coming from the banks of the Amur, who find no easier means of compelling the game to quit their retreat.

'A few glasses of brandy having dissipated the late impressions of fear, the conversation turned anew upon religion. The greater part of my hearers agreed that my doctrine was good and true. But the Ten Commandments were universally deemed an insupportable burthen. You will not be astonished at this when you are made aware what kind of people I had to deal with.

'The entire population of the Usuri and its tributary rivers does not amount to eight hundred souls. It is divided into two classes, the first of which comprises the Chinese, to the number of two hundred, and the second about five hundred Manchu Fish-skins, subdivided into eighty and some odd families.

'The two hundred Chinese, two upright merchants excepted, are vagrants, felons guilty of murder, highway robbers, whom crime and the fear of punishment have compelled to exile themselves into these deserts, where they are placed beyond the reach of the law. I only judge them from their own account. How many have avowed to me their daring robberies, the number of men whom they had killed or grievously wounded, and the excesses of every kind to which their appearance bore testimony! "No," said they, "misery and poverty alone could never have made us voluntarily undergo such dreadful exile." And the aspect of the place induced me to believe them without difficulty. Would, at least, that the sufferings of banishment inspired some salutary remorse to these depraved hearts! But they preserve even now, as in their past life, an ardour for crime, to develop which opportunity alone is wanting. Each year is marked by two or three murders. But a very short time ago, even an old man of sixty-eight killed another of seventy-six, on account of some debt which the latter could not discharge on the instant. Four days afterwards I saw the murderer, and he related to me the bloody scene with an air as tranquil as if he himself had taken no share in it.

'These men, wretched in their entire being, have here no other means of sustaining life than that of giving themselves up, with incredible fatigue, to the search of the ginseng. Picture to yourself one of these miserable carriers, laden with more than twenty-four pounds weight, venturing without any road across immense forests, climbing up or descending the mountains; always left alone to his own thoughts, and exposed to every distemper; not knowing if to-day or to-morrow he may fall a victim to the wild beasts which abound around him, supported by the modicum of millet he brings with him, and a few wild herbs to season it. And all this during five months of the year, from the end of April to the end of September.[1]

'I will now give you some details about the Yupitatze, or Fish-skins. This tribe, formerly numerous, at present scarcely counts from seventy to eighty families, who trade from the Lake Hinka as far as the Amur. The Yupitatze inhabit houses differing little from those of the poorer Chinese. In winter the chase, in summer the fishing, comprise in two words the history of their arts, sciences, and social state. No government, no laws among them; and how could there be any for scattered members who have not even the appearance of a body? Their whole religion consists in a debasing worship, which in Chinese is called *Tsama* or *Tsamo*. This super-stition, equally in favour with the lower class of people in Leao-tong, has for its object the invoking of certain good spirits in opposition to the devil, whom they dread. With the Yupitatze, a tribe fond of

[1] M. de la Brunière here gives a description of the ginseng plant from hearsay. He also encloses some seed, with directions how to propagate it. The medicinal virtues of the ginseng M. de la Brunière can speak of from his own experience; he was cured in a short time of a weakness in the stomach, which had resisted the treatment by Peruvian bark-wine and other infusions. I also can testify to the excellence of tea made from ginseng, as we found it very comforting and effective in slight cases of diarrhœa.—H. E. M. J.

the chase, three spirits—that of the stag, that of the fox, and the spirit of the weasel—stand highest in public estimation. If a member of a family fall sick, it is ascribed to the agency of the demon. It is then necessary to call upon one of these genii, which is performed by the following ceremony, which I witnessed twice. The great Tsama, or evoker of the Tia-shen (spirit), is invited by the family. At a distance of half a league the sound of the drum announces his approach. Immediately the master of the house issues forth with a drum of the same kind to receive him. It should be well understood that brandy is always at the reception ; and I may as well tell you beforehand, the sun has hardly set before they are all dead drunk.

'When the hour of the Tia-shen has come, the great Tsama clothes himself in his sacred robes. A cap, from which streamers of paper and thin stripes of the bark of trees flutter, covers his head. His tunic of doe-skin or cloth, variegated with different colours, descends to the knees. But the girdle is what seems most necessary for his occupation. It is composed of three plaits, and attached to it are three rows of iron or brass tubes, from seven to eight inches long. Thus accoutred, the exorciser sits down, the drum in one hand, a stick in the other. Then in the midst of solemn silence he intones a lamentation, the music of which is not disagreeable. The drum, which he strikes at regular intervals, accompanies the voice. This lamentation, or invocation of the spirit, has many stanzas, at the end of each of which the face of the Tsama assumes a fearful aspect. Gradually the sounds of the drum become stronger and quicker. The Tsama contracts his lips, and, emitting two or three dull whistling sounds, he stops. Immediately the spectators respond in chorus with a prolonged cry, gradually dying away, the sound of which is that of our open é.

'The invocation ended, the Tsama rises quickly, and with hurried steps and frequent bounds he makes the circuit of the chamber repeatedly, crying out like a man in a transport of frenzy and multiplying his contortions, which cause the tubes of brass to re-sound with a frightful noise. The spirit is then at hand and shows himself, but only to the exorciser, and not to the spectators. The Tsama I saw called upon the spirit of the stag. It was the commencement of the hunting season. He paused in the middle of his performance and uttered such a cry, or rather howl, that the Chinese merchants, who at first had laughed at the farce, fled the house and sought shelter for the night elsewhere. An old cook, a native of Peking, assured me he had felt the spirit ; but what was his terror when the next day on rising he found an iron pot empty, which he had left full of millet the evening before ! It became known some time after that the spirit, in a generous fit of conviviality, had awarded the dish to the great Tsama and his companions as a recompense for their labours.

'The natives hunt only during the winter. The snow, which covers the mountains and plains to the depth of six feet, offers no impediment. Two planks cut from the pine tree, a quarter of an inch thick and at most five inches broad and six feet long, sloping upwards at both ends, covered underneath with a deer-skin, and bound tightly to the foot by two straps ; such are the snow-shoes used by the hunter. Equipped with these, he will skim lightly over the snow, follow the track of the stag and deer, and go twenty to twenty-five leagues in the shortest winter's day. Should a mountain lie in the way, he climbs it without difficulty by the aid of his snow-shoes. The hair of the deer-skin, with which they are covered, is put on so as to slope backwards, and, sinking in the snow, serves as a means of support.

'The dexterity of the Yupitatze is no less exhibited in fishing. Furnished with a simple iron-pointed javelin, he sits in a skiff made of the bark of a tree, and manages it with the same ease on the water as the snow-shoes on land. The Chinese call this skiff Kuai-ma—i.e. 'swift horse.' A few strokes of an oar, shaped like our *battoirs de lessive*,[1] cause it to glide up the river with extreme rapidity. The Chinese dare not venture in it, for the least motion would upset the venturesome navigator. When the Yupitatze strikes the fish with his dart, the arm alone moves, the body not losing its equilibrium for an instant. The Usuri and its small tributary rivers abound in fish. That which ranks first is the Iluam-yu, unknown in Europe. I have seen some which weighed more than 1,000 lbs., and was assured there were some of 1,800 to 2,000 lbs. It is said to come from the Hinka Lake. Its flesh, perfectly white and very tender, makes me prefer it to all other fresh-water fish. Entirely cartilaginous, with the exception of three small bones in the neck, it has lips formed like those of a shark, the upper protruding much over the lower. Like the shark, it turns itself to seize its prey or bite the hook ; and, like it, swims slowly and clumsily. The cartilage and bones are the most esteemed portions of the fish, and sell at San-sim for one and a half tael of silver the pound. The mandarins annually lay in a supply for the Emperor's table.

'Towards the end of September, at the approach of winter, another kind of fish called tamara appears in the Amur and Usuri. It comes from the sea in shoals of several thousands, and weighs

---

[1] An oar with a blade at either end.

from ten to fifteen pounds. Its shape, and especially the flavour of its flesh, give me reason to suppose it a kind of small salmon. God, in His paternal providence, mindful even of those who do not glorify Him, gives it to the poor inhabitants of this country as an excellent preservative against the rigours of winter. I state what I found by experience. Without wine and without flour, supported by very little millet, and a morsel of this dried fish, I have suffered less from a continual cold of 51°, and which during many days reached 65°, than I did in the south of Leao-tong, with better food and a temperature of some four degrees below zero. To the Yupitatze the fishing of the tamara is of the same importance as the gathering in of the harvest is to our rural districts and cities ; a deficiency in one or the other will bring a famine along with it. The two fish I spoke of are more frequently eaten raw than cooked. I followed this custom without any very great repugnance, and scarcely believed I might become a savage at so small a cost. You can conceive, gentlemen, that this exclusive regimen of fish, like everything else exclusive, has its inconveniences. The heat which it imparts to the blood, so beneficial in winter, is the cause of severe diseases during spring and summer. Among these maladies I would particularise the small-pox. Its ravages are horrible. The most aged persons dread its attacks as much as infancy and youth. The same individual may suffer from it four or five times in the course of his life.

'But, though dangerous as a constant article of food, the fish of these rivers are invaluable on account of the imperishable garments made of their skins. In boots made of such fish-skins you may wade through rivulets and walk in the snow as on the dry ground, equally protected against the cold and moisture.

'The swan, the stork, the goose, the duck, the teal, appear each year in the month of May in numberless flocks, attracted by the prey which is easily had and in abundance ; and the birds are the more daring, as no one disturbs their repose. The natives do not seem to value wild fowl.

'I will conclude with a word on the mode of travelling practised in the winter season. The great and only road during summer or winter is the river or lake. A very light sledge made of thin oaken laths, five or six feet long, a foot and a half high, convex in the lower part, whilst the upper part is level, serves as a general mode of conveyance. Here the dog discharges the same office as the reindeer with the Russians. Every family keeps a pack of fifteen or twenty of these animals. The master eats the flesh of the fish ; the dog has for his share the head and the bones. During winter the latter feeds entirely upon the tamara, which produces such heat that he sleeps on the snow during the most severe cold without seeking a more comfortable berth. A team of eight dogs (they are of middle size) draws a man and two hundred pounds of luggage during an entire day with the swiftness of our best coaches. These journeys in winter, and the chase to which the Yupitatze are addicted at this season, bring on here as elsewhere in cold countries where no precautions are taken against it many cases of ophthalmia, which at an advanced age terminates in blindness.

'About the 13th or 15th of May I will buy, if it please God, a small bark in which I may descend the Amur to the sea to visit the Long-hairs. I shall go alone, because no one dare conduct me, and my companion, a poor Christian from Leao-tong, returns to his home sick from fear and melancholy. I am well aware how difficult it will be to avoid the barges of the mandarins who descend the river from San-sim; but if it is the will of God that I arrive where I design going, His arm can smooth every obstacle and guide me there in safety; and if it please Him that I return, He knows well how to bring me back. Whatever this future may be, to proceed appears to me in the present circumstances the only duty of a missionary, who in the prayer which the Church enjoins him says often with his lips and in his heart the words of the sacred canticle, "Shall I give sleep to my eyes or slumber to my eyelids or rest to my temples, until I find out a place for the Lord, a tabernacle for the God of Jacob?" (Ps. cxxxi.)

'Have the kindness, gentlemen, to remember me at the holy altar and before the sacred hearts of Jesus and Mary.

'DE LA BRUNIÈRE, *Missionary Apostolic.*'

M. de la Brunière did actually descend the Usuri and Amur, but met his death at the hands of predatory Gilyaks. Two messengers were sent to seek him, but they only got as far as San-sim, where the swollen state of the river put a stop to their progress. Further researches were not made, as the situation of the Christian communities in the south of Manchuria did not permit of it. But eventually, M. Venault, who had been active at Asheho, a newly-founded town in Northern Manchuria, resolved to start from there upon an exploratory journey to the Lower Amur. One of the objects of this journey was to clear up the fate of M. de la Brunière, still enveloped in mystery. In this he perfectly succeeded, as the following letter will show:

'My Lord,—As soon as the wishes of your Lordships had become known to me I prepared to proceed to the kingdom of Si-san, said to exist in the north. I left my residence at Asheho on the 6th day of the first month of 1850 on a sledge drawn by three horses and accompanied by the Christian converts, Ho, Cheu, and Chao.   During the first three days of our journey we met with several hostelries on the road, but after we had passed the river Son-hoa-kiang (Sungari) these became scarcer, and the traveller is obliged to seek hospitality amongst the few colonists dispersed on the western bank of that river—a demand never refused.   Numerous military stations are distributed on this western bank of the Sungari, each of which has a mandarin and a tribunal.   The distance from Asheho to Sansin is about fifty leagues, and we passed five days on the road.   Sansin is situated at the confluence of the Sungari and the Mutan, on the eastern bank of the former, and to the north of the latter.   M. de la Brunière had stayed in this town in 1845, and his assassination by the "Long-hair" still formed the subject of conversation.   In order to render my journey as secret as possible, I thought it prudent not to stop here.   In haste I supplied the deficiency occasioned in our provisions, made during a five days' march, and, though night had almost set in, proceeded with my sledge across the snow.   It was almost midnight when we arrived at a small tavern.   The intense cold, or perhaps rather copious libations after supper, rendered our landlord for a long time deaf to our appeals for shelter.   At last, however, the door opened and a place was assigned us on the *khang*. Two took their turn in resting here, whilst the third watched the horses and the sledge on the roadside.

'In order to avoid the military station built by the Emperor at the confluence of the Sungari and Amur to prevent all intercourse between Sansin and the Hei-Kin district, we directed our course towards the Usuri (Utze-kiang) and crossed that river where it receives the Imma (Ema), above its confluence with the Moli.   Our first station was Wei-tze-keu, ten leagues from Sansin.

'Wei-tze-keu consists of a group of villages situated within a radius of six leagues.   Some agriculture is still carried on here, and the population is pretty numerous.   But going east, hostelries, cultivated lands or roads are no longer met with ; only now and then we encounter in the midst of the wilderness the solitary hut of a ginseng dealer.   Between Wei-tze-keu and Imma-keu-tze (Ema), a distance of a hundred leagues, there are only a few solitary huts in the mountain gorges.   They are inhabited by old men—a woman is never seen here—whose occupation it is to fell trees which they leave to decay, when a kind of mushroom grows upon them which at Sansin forms the object of a lucrative traffic.

'Scarcely ten leagues beyond Wei-tze-keu the paucity of snow compelled us to abandon our sledge, place the baggage on the backs of our animals, and travel on foot. We continued crossing the wilderness for twelve days, lodging sometimes in one of the huts just mentioned, but more frequently in the open air. On our arrival at our stopping-place in the evening we cut down some wood, cooked our millet, and after supper peaceably fell asleep surrounded by an immense circle of burning embers, which protected us equally against the piercing cold and the teeth of the tiger. Thanks to God, we had not yet met during the whole of our journey with a single beast of prey, but scattered bones still covered with pieces of human flesh, and clothing recently torn and besmeared with blood, reminded us of the precautions which it was necessary to take against the dwellers in the forests.

'Imma-keu-tze merely consists of a few houses inhabited by ginseng seekers. These men are homeless adventurers, gallows-birds who live here *en famille*, with the proprietor of the house as chief. Gains and expenses are shared alike among all. Such a house is not a tavern, but a homestead of which you may become a member by presenting yourself; a republic where anyone may acquire the rights of citizenship by participating in the labour of all. In such a community I was obliged to stay for two months; it scarcely needed so long a time to make me desire to leave it. But I had neither guides nor a sledge, and, nilly-willy, was compelled to wait until the thawing should enable me to continue my journey in a canoe. During these interminable months we frequently spoke to these ginseng seekers and Chinese or Manchu travellers, who, like ourselves, sought shelter under the same roof, of God and our holy religion. But we spoke to men who had ears and would not hear, who had eyes and would not see. May the Lord deign to send down upon these vast regions a fire—not to destroy—but to enlighten the stultified understanding of these men, a fire to purify their hearts so profoundly degraded!

'At last the thaw came. I had purchased a small canoe made of the trunk of a tree, about twenty-five feet long and two wide. I engaged a pagan Manchu as pilot, and paid him at the rate of ten taels of silver (3*l.* 12*s.*) a month. I gave him the helm, my people and myself took to the oars, and on the 19th day of the third month (April 31) we departed for the country of the "Long-hairs." Notwithstanding the ten taels which we had paid to our Manchu, he only accompanied us with repugnance and ill grace.

'The many absurd rumours afloat regarding me—I was said to be a Russian in command of a large army, which I was about to rejoin for the purpose of pillaging the country, or a sorcerer having power over life and limb—these rumours made my pilot singularly unwilling and ill-humoured. To these were added the statements of the merchants on our arrival at the Hai-tsing-yü-kiang about the ferocity with which the " Long-hairs " had murdered M. de la Brunière ; their rapacity, which would induce them to treat us the same, and rob us of our effects. Fear exasperated our Manchu's naturally irascible temperament, and God knows we had daily to suffer from his violence.

' Apprehensive that he might desert us on the first opportunity, we engaged a second pilot, a Chinaman who had previously visited the " Long-hairs " and spoke their language. But instead of one tormentor we had now two. Not a day, not an hour, passed without some altercation, and of so satanic a kind that it scarcely is possible to imagine. Remonstrances would only have still more irritated them, and possibly put a stop to our further journeying, so promotive of the glory of God and the salvation of souls. I therefore held my peace and suffered in silence the insults of these leopards. *Ecce ego mitto vos sicut agnos in medio luporum.*

' Towards the end of the fourth moon we arrived at Mucheng (Dondon). This is neither a town nor a village, but simply an enclosure of palisades in the centre of which stands a wooden house, which serves as a residence to the mandarin, who comes here annually to collect the tribute in furs from the Tatars, and give them in return a few pieces of silk. This official, in attending to the interests of his master, neglects not his own. He, as well as the armed satellites, who accompany him to the number of thirty, traffic on their private account. Woe to the natives upon whom he lays his hands when ascending or descending the river ! Having thoroughly exhausted them in pulling the barge, with cudgelling at discretion, he compels them furthermore to purchase his merchandise, and always at the highest figure.

' As stated above, the Emperor has established several military posts on the confluence of the Sungari and Hei-long (Amur), to prevent all communication between Sansin and the tribes to the north. A flotilla of from twelve to fifteen barges is sent down the river under the mandarin spoken of, and in addition bodies of armed satellites commanded by sub-officers are sent annually to Mu-cheng to prevent the higher functionaries themselves from favouring smugglers. Nevertheless, any one on paying a heavy bribe, which the officials divide between them, is allowed to pass. But the Son of Heaven may rest assured that these military posts, this flotilla, these armed men, maintained at a large expense, only serve to fill up the coffers of the mandarins. In order to obviate paying for the right of passage, a great many barges descend to the sea previous to the arrival of the mandarin at Mu-cheng, and only ascend to Sansin after his return. I did the same. After travelling twenty-four leagues we came to Aki, the first village of the "Long-hair." This hamlet, though said to be the largest of the Chang-Mao-tze, is inhabited by only seven or eight families. I observed here with pleasure much more manly features than among the Twan-Moa-tze (Tatars who shave the head), and almost European physiognomies. I also saw them embrace each other in sign of friendship, which I had seen nowhere in China. When brandy expands their hearts they are particularly prodigal in signs of affection. I made a small present to each family, but they received it without any sign of pleasure. Had it been a bottle of brandy, they would no doubt have better appreciated it.

'Since our departure from Asheho we had generally travelled alone. But from Aki the number of barges following the same route increased much in number, and we were always in company. Great pains were taken to make me give up my intended journey to the sea; all arts of rhetoric were employed to describe the terrible tortures which M. de la Brunière had been subjected to. At last, when they saw I would not yield to the fear of undergoing the same fate, they came to menaces, fearing perhaps that the business which took me to these regions would injure their commerce. Notwithstanding these little friendly disputes, we kept inviting each other to dine on each other's boats. I took advantage of such opportunities to speak eternal truths and to distribute good books.

'In this way we came to Pulo, opposite Uktu (Ukhtr), the last village of the "Long-hairs." There my Manchu, whose fears had kept increasing the further we advanced, declared roundly he had had enough of this voyage, and nothing in the world should induce him to go further. My other companions did not refuse to remain with me, but I could plainly see their hearts began to fail. In my embarrassment, I begged one of the merchants to take me on board his barge and conduct me to the sea; but in vain. Not knowing what to do, I visited Pulo. I there found a man just returned from Sisan (Sakhalin): seven barges had foundered in the bay in a gale of wind, his alone escaping. Great rejoicing consequently took place in the family of this merchant during my stay. I was obliged to share in them, and, when the feast terminated, availed myself of the goodwill of my entertainer to interest him in the success of my journey. A nephew of his agreed to conduct me down the river for ten taels. I left part of my merchandise as security, and we were again *en route*, not even excepting my Manchu pilot, who had taken fresh heart. We entered the country of the Ki-li-mi.[1] But scarcely had we advanced five

[1] Gilyaks.

leagues [1] when our progress was stopped by a new alarm.   We were told that the first village, Hutong, we were about to approach was the one near which M. de la Brunière had been murdered, and that eight barges were lying in wait for us a little above it to make us share the same lot.   The whole of my men refused to go any further. I sought an interpreter who understood the language of the Ki-li-mi, and I sent him forward with three of my companions to ascertain what was going on, and collect precise information regarding the melancholy fate of my former fellow-labourer.   They were gone six days.   The two men whom I had kept with me augured evil from the delay, and were about to abandon me, when I perceived two Kwai-ma [2] rapidly rowing towards us.   They brought back to me my messengers, dripping wet, soaked to the skin.   In the joy of the happy termination of their mission, the unlucky fellows had got drunk, quarrelled, and upset themselves in the river.   They confirmed the report of M. de la Brunière's death, and in corroboration brought several things which the murderers had taken from his barge.   I abstain from giving the numerous versions of the cause of this act of ferocity, and restrict myself to the statement of one of the murderers as most worthy of credit.   When my messengers arrived at Hutong, all persons concerned in the murder, one excepted, had fled.   This one remained in the village on the assurance of a merchant that I was not come to take vengeance.   My people saw and interrogated him.   According to his statement, M. de la Brunière was engaged preparing his meal in a small bay, where he had sought shelter against a violent storm, when two men, of whom the narrator was one, attracted by the prospect of booty to be expected from the strange priest, went towards him armed with bows and pikes.   When they arrived at the bay seven of them landed, the others kept on their boat.   Having hit M. de la Brunière with several arrows, the seven Ki-li-mi went on his boat and struck him with their pikes.   The last stroke fractured his skull and proved mortal.   During the whole of this tragedy, M. de la Brunière remained seated quietly in his boat, without speaking a word ; no complaint escaped his lips.   In silence he offered himself a sacrifice before God, in the conversion of the people, whose salvation had constantly occupied his thoughts from his first entrance into Manchuria.   It is currently reported among Chinese and Tatars that after his death the Ki-li-mi wrenched out the teeth of their victim, tore out his eyes, and mutilated the corpse most frightfully.   The body was thrown ashore, and after a few days washed away by the river.   The natives pre-

---

[1] Fifty leagues in the original.   [2] Swift boat, made of birch bark.

tended to have seen the stranger walking the scene of the outrage since, an apparition which caused them much fear.

'This crime consummated, the assassins divided the booty. I have since then seen many children wearing miraculous medals and small crosses. The silver was converted into earrings for the women. The murderer whom my messengers saw appeared to repent of the deed. Of his own will he restored his part of the spoils, consisting in an ornament, a holy stone, a silver cup for mass, the remains of a thermometer, and two compasses. Besides this, my messengers, in concert with three headmen of Ki-li-mi villages, imposed a fine upon him, which he submitted to without much difficulty. It consisted of five pots, two spears, two Mang Pao (dresses embroidered in various colours, such as are worn by the mandarins), a skin dress, a piece of satin, and a sabre. The spears will remain in the hands of the interpreters as a memento of the peace concluded between us and the murderers. When these objects had been delivered to my messengers, in presence of the three chiefs, an act of reconciliation was signed, of which one copy remained with the Ki-li-mi, and the other was forwarded to me. It is as follows :—

'" In the thirtieth year of the Emperor Tao Kwang, Shien-Wen-Ming (M. Venault) and Chen-Tu-Chu (one of the Christians) came to demand satisfaction for a murder committed in the twenty-sixth year upon the person of a missionary called Pao (M. de la Brunière) by men belonging to the villages Arckong, Siöloin, and Hutong, and peace has been restored between both parties. The above villages engage not to incommodate for the future any travellers who may come on barges during the summer, or on sledges during the winter ; but promise to treat them as brothers. The relatives and friends of the priest Pao promise on their part not to revenge the assassination of the twenty-sixth year of Tao Kwang. But as the spoken word passes away and is forgotten, these engagements have been put on paper by both parties, in presence of the interpreters, who are charged with seeing them properly carried out.

'" The witnesses : Chen-Tu-Chu and Shang-Shwen.

'" The interpreters : San In Ho and I Tu Nu of the village of Ngao-lai, Tien-I-Tee Nu and Shy Tee Nu of Kian Pan, Hu Pu and Si Nu of Hutong."

'But whilst peace was being thus concluded on the one hand, strife broke out on the other. I had promised to distribute among my guides the fine paid by the Ki-li-mi. They did not, however, wait for my decision ; each took what suited his fancy, they quarrelled, and from words they came to blows and knife-thrusts. Disheartened by so many disasters, my two neophytes refused to go any further,

and I was obliged after all to give up my journey to Sisan. I therefore returned to Pulo, and prepared to proceed home, as soon as the
mandarin should have quitted Mucheng with his flotilla.

'I had been there about a month when the news spread that the
Chinese were coming to surprise us. We hastily concealed our
baggage in a store-house, and with my two Christians I retreated to
the neighbouring forest. It was the night of Assumption. Our
only provision consisted of some rice-wine, but Providence ordained
that we should meet at the skirt of the forest two women, carrying
millet and dried fish, part of which they gave us in exchange for our
wine. On the following day, towards evening, pressed by hunger,
we cautiously ascended a small hill, where I saw on the river, not
far from the wood, a solitary canoe with a man in it. He took my
belt in exchange for some rice, which we cooked in a hollow where
the rising smoke would not easily betray us. Our meal was not
very copious, and soon finished. Before lying down to sleep, I went
aside to pray, when I heard several men advancing towards our retreat, and impatiently calling upon us. I feared the mandarin had
received information of our whereabouts, and that he desired a
nearer acquaintanceship. I therefore let them shout and beat the
bush, concealing myself in the dense shrubs covering the ground.
After a time all was silent and I fell asleep. On the following day
our first care was to procure food. We walked a long distance
without encountering any habitations, but at last came to a village
where we heard the good news of the mandarin's return to Sansin.

'Whilst hidden in the woods, my two pilots and the man in
whose house I had lodged had been flogged on suspicion of knowing
about my evasion, and only got out of the hands of the mandarin
on giving up to him their dresses, furs, &c.—in short, all they were
possessed of. I was obliged to indemnify these unfortunates, not
only for their loss, but also for the cudgelling. To increase my misfortune, the Chinese pilot had remained on the spot when I concealed my effects in the store-house on the day of my flight. My
trunk had become an object of affection to his heart, and previous
to flying himself he wanted to have a last peep into it; and on
my return, my watch, a silver cup, a compass, and a pair of scissors
were missing.

'Notwithstanding this accumulation of obstacles, I still thought
of Sisan. The refusal of all parties to accompany me obliged me,
however, to forego this journey—one of the principal objects of my
voyage—and to return to my station at Asheho. I arrived there on
the sixth day of the ninth month, nine months after my departure.
I only brought back with me skin and bones; more than two hun-

dred and forty taels had been expended on the journey ; I had sold my clothes and even lost my breviary.

'Throughout, I was taken for a Russian. Russians frequently make their appearance among the Ki-li-mi and "Long-hair," with whom they carry on trade. I have seen with these tribes various objects of European origin, such as pots, hatchets, knives, buttons, playing-cards, and even a silver coin of recent date, which they had obtained in this way. At Pulo I was told that in April 1850 several Russians had come to select the site for building a town. Six days after I had left the Ki-li-mi village of Heng-kong-ta, on my return to Pulo, a boat with seven Russians arrived there. Had the difficulty of ascending the river not detained them, they would have met me at that place. Ki-li-mi, Long-hair, and Chinese, all assert that the Russians are going to build a town and take possession of the country. May not Divine Providence have appointed them to open to us the islands north of Japan ?

' A few words now on the chances of success which these regions offer to the propagation of the Gospel. Between Asheho and Sansin, few families are met with ; there are only soldiers and vagabonds, whose life is passed in gambling, in orgies, in excesses of the most disgraceful debauchery. Sansin, with its environs, is a second Sodom.

'The Yupitatze of the Usuri are big children, affable and hospitable ; but unfortunately they have adopted the vices of the Chinese, with whom they are constantly in contact. Their superstition on commencing the respective seasons for hunting and fishing, as well as their long and frequent journeyings, present obstacles which the missionary would find it difficult to surmount.

'The Yupitatze of the Amur are gross, more cruel, and addicted to drink.

'The Long-hair and Ki-li-mi surpass all other tribes in ferocity, lust of plunder and thirst for blood, especially when they are drunk, which happens every day. A missionary desirous of converting them would be sure of much suffering : but if the difficulties are great, the power of God is still greater. Courage, therefore, and confidence ! The blood of the righteous which the ungrateful earth has drunk calls for mercy towards it ; it renders it fertile and makes it bring forth fruits of salvation.

' I have stated to your Lordships the reasons which prevented my going to Sisan. But I will at least give the result of the inquiries I have made respecting it. The Chinese barges which descend the Amur to the sea never visit Sisan, which is separated from the continent by a narrow strait which they dare not cross. The more hardy Yupitatze, however, go there annually. They depart in the fifth moon, pass the winter on the island hunting or trading, and return in the spring of the following year. Their cargoes consist of millet, spirits, and silks, which they exchange for furs. A Long-hair of Heng-kong-ta proposed to take me there in the following year, and a similar offer was made to me by a merchant of Sansin. The shortest route would be to leave the Amur at Cha-She, sixty leagues above Pulo. The country thence to the sea may be traversed in sledges in four days, and another day, with a favourable wind, would suffice to cross the strait.

'From all information Sisan appears to be identical with the island of Karaftu or Tarakai, half of which is subject to Japan, and for this reason the Chinese call it indifferently Sisan or Shepen (Japan).'

NOTE E.

ACCOUNT BY THE REV JAMES WEBSTER OF CONVERSIONS TO CHRISTIANITY EFFECTED BY A RECENTLY CONVERTED BLIND MAN AT T'AI-PING-K'OU.

'In the evening of October 7, 1886, accompanied by Mr. Chang, one of our native agents, and by my teacher, I reached Mai-Mai-Kai (lit. Market Street), the common name of a populous market town, situated about one hundred and thirty miles north of Moukden. About six years ago it was raised to the rank of a Hsien, and as such bears the name of Fêng-hua, or the "transformed." In former times I am told it was infested with troops of "catarans," a wild and lawless horde, who at one time overran the entire province. They have died out, or rather have been killed out, and a quiet industrious population have taken their place. Mai-Mai-Kai, from a missionary standpoint, I regard as an important place, chiefly because of the intimate connection it has with the villagers in the surrounding neighbourhood. We were to break off the main road at this point, and seek out a man living in one of those villages a few miles to the east. Some time in the early summer—the month of May, I think—this man, who is almost totally blind, was a patient in the Moukden hospital, and at the end of a month came forward as an applicant for baptism. He belonged to the "Hwun Yuen" religion, a sect of the Taoists, among the most impressible of this unimpassioned people, and generally regarded as zealots in matters religious. The account he gave of himself, and the knowledge he evinced of the simple truths of salvation, were all that could be desired; but I hesitated to admit him, a man of whose antecedents we knew nothing, whose home was far distant, and whose knowledge of Christianity had been gathered in a month. So we gave him some books, and bade him return, promising after a space to visit him, and if he was of the same mind towards Christianity he would, *cæteris paribus*, be admitted to the Church. This man we visit to-morrow.

'*Saturday, October* 8.—After spending the greater part of the forenoon floundering in the mud, we reached the neighbourhood where we hoped to find our blind friend. When within a mile of the village we reached a place where it seemed impossible for the cart to cross. The carter growled, and talked of giving it up, so I dismounted and proceeded on foot. The driver wasted a great deal of eloquence in a vain attempt to induce me to return; but "a wilful man must have his way," and on I went, well assured the cart would not return without me, and that it would follow some-how. By-and-by I came to the village where I hoped to find the man, and inquired if they knew a blind man named Ch'ang who lived in the neighbourhood. "Oh, yes, over the hill yonder, at a village called T'ai-ping-k'ou." Arrived, and was again met with a disappointment. He was at another and more distant village still. By this time the cart was completely lost sight of; if it had suc-ceeded in crossing the swamp, it had followed another road, and, weary and hungry, I began to despair of meeting either man or cart, and not the shadow of an inn was to be seen. When at last I reached the village, they directed me " to follow a narrow path for about a mile, till I reached the next village (I wondered how many more), and there to ask for a man named Li, who would be able to supply me with all information as to the whereabouts of blind Mr. Ch'ang." " He is of the same religion," they added, as I left—a remark which I took to mean that they were both of the " Hwun Yuen," the sect before mentioned. At the end of the footpath at the entrance to the village two men were standing, and, accosting the elder of the two, the following conversation took place :—

'(*I.*) " May I borrow your light ? Do you know anyone of the name of Li who lives here ? "

'(*He.*) (Very eager and knowing) " Where do you come from ? what is your honourable surname ? "

'(*I.*) (Indignant and dignified) " Will you please tell me where this Mr. Li lives, if you happen to know ? "

'(*He.*) (Bowing profoundly) " I am Li, the man you ask for, and I am glad the pastor—for I take you for the pastor—has at length arrived."

'Then he led me with much ceremony into his house, where I found sixteen boys on the k'ang, for Mr. Li was the village schoolmaster. We drank a cup of tea, he telling me, the while, tidings which made me forget all hunger and weariness, to the effect that when blind Ch'ang came home from Moukden he began to tell them about this religion of Jesus, going from village to village, and into as many houses as received him, and in the evenings preaching sometimes to hundreds under the shade of the willow trees ; how at first everybody laughed at him, or thought him crazed and pitied him ; how, when he still went on preaching and giving practical proofs of having undergone a change, people got divided about him. Some were for him, some against him ; some blessed him, some cursed him ; and, in short, the whole country-side was in an uproar. Week after week passed, Ch'ang daily praying his prayer for help from on high, and singing his one hymn learned in Moukden, and then sallying forth alone, groping his darkened way with his staff, to tell of Jesus, the Son of God, who was born in Bethlehem, and died upon the cross for the sins of the whole world. "And the upshot of all this," said Mr. Li, "is, that there is a large number earnestly inquiring about his doctrine, and several are thoroughly convinced and heartily believe and desire to become members of the religion of Jesus." But where was the blind man all the while ? He had gone to visit one of the inquirers and I had missed him on the way ; Mr. Li left his school and accompanied me. We had proceeded but a little distance when we learned that the cart had arrived at the very house where the blind man was, and that, in his eager joy, he had started in search of me. At last we met, and I accosted him. He stood stock still for a moment, resting on his staff, as if to assure himself, and then his face became perfectly radiant with joy, and great tears dropped from his blind eyes as he said, in a voice quivering with emotion, "Oh, Pastor, you promised, and I always said you would come ! " Then in company we directed our steps to the inquirer's house, talking as we went of all that had taken place. At the house of Mr. Yin, the inquirer afore-mentioned, we met with a cordial welcome, the "best room " was placed at our disposal, a poor-enough place according to our Western notions, but given with hearty goodwill and many apologies that it was no better. The few remaining hours of light were occupied in speaking to the houseful of old and young who had gathered, answering questions and instructing inquirers. Then, when it was time to retire, the head of the house, the blind man and the evangelist, began to talk, and what a night of it ! All manner of questions were started and discussed, knotty subjects explained, almost every point in the whole range of theology touched upon.

Midnight, the small hours of the morning passed, and at last I fell asleep in the midst of an elaborate discussion of Confucianism in its relation to Christianity, in which Confucius is made to assume the character of a man standing at the mouth of a deep pit, discoursing on the advantages of walking circumspectly to an unfortunate wayfarer who has stumbled into it ; and another—Jesus—comes along, throws a rope, and draws him out, telling him, when his feet are on the rock, to go and sin no more.

'*Sunday and Monday, October* 10 *and* 11.—Whether the three ever slept I do not know, but the first thing I was conscious of in the morning was shrill voices in earnest converse, as on the previous night.

' Heavy rain fell in the early morning, and the roads were very muddy ; but we had a crowded house all day. I made arrangements to meet privately with each applicant, and it was late on the Sabbath night before I had seen and examined the fifteen individuals who came forward of their own accord. On the whole, one has seldom had more satisfaction with candidates than with those men. What pleased me most was not the amount of their knowledge as *their way of knowing.* Without art, with an utter absence of technicalities, each in his own way declared his faith in God the Father, and in Jesus Christ His only Son our Lord —a faith, we trust, as sincere as it was simply expressed.

' On Monday forenoon, in a house crowded to the door, I preached from Christ's farewell command, explained the ordinance of baptism, and nine whom I had seen my way to admit were baptized. Seldom have I witnessed a more interesting scene, or joined in a more solemn and joyful sacramental service. It was an occasion for singing the 126th Psalm. Nine men, headed by their blind guide, who had to be led by the hand to receive the sacred rite, professing to come to Christ, and to believe in Him, and to venture their all both here and hereafter in thus believing, forsaking the idolatry of their fathers, casting it forth root and branch, expressing the desire through grace to turn from evil and serve the living God, and all this with a warmth of feeling and an earnestness of purpose impossible to describe.

' One could not but wish that all the friends of missions had seen it. They would, I am sure, have shared in my joy.

' But that could not be ; and it may be that some who read this account of the work in T'ai-ping-k'ou will have their doubts about the reality of it, because missionaries, they think, are so apt to deal in bright colours. Be it so ; I have not coloured this narrative in the least, so far as I am aware. I speak that I know, and testify that I have seen. Believe if you can, and doubt if you like. Either way, it really matters very little. There is one thing of which I am well assured, however, and it is this : Blind Ch'ang of T'ai-ping-k'ou, with little knowledge of Divine truth, but with a heart thrilled to its centre with the truth he knew, has done more work and better work for the kingdom of heaven in a couple of months than half-a-dozen foreign missionaries, brought up from their youth at the feet of Gamaliel, would have done in as many years. And this is only one of many instances that might be given to show that China must be evangelised by the Chinese.

'One other observation it occurs to me to make in connection with the foregoing narrative. This work among the villages, long desired, and now so providentially opened up, must call forth not merely gratitude but effort. It must be followed up. There is every encouragement to hope that, if wise measures are taken now, we shall speedily see many hundreds embracing Christianity. And let it not be said that all this is the mere vapourings of an enthusiast. Forty miles from that very spot the Jesuits have a following of over five thousand, and, think you, is our Protestant Gospel less worthy to be believed, or our Protestant Christianity less likely to succeed ?

'The people inhabit a rural district, unsophisticated by the materialising influences of city life. They have hitherto, as I have said, belonged to a sect peculiarly open to religious teachings, and susceptible of religious impression. From personal observation I am convinced of a widespread feeling of discontent with the old religion ; they are tired of it, and cling to it only for want of something better and more satisfying. It may be that a transition period has set in, and that the movement above narrated is but the coming event casting its shadow before. Be that as it may, there can be no doubt that a rare and most favourable opportunity of extending the Gospel among the villages has arisen, and I trust we shall be enabled to devise such means as, by the Divine blessing, will ensure not only that the opportunity is not lost, but that the fullest advantage is taken of it.'

NOTE F.

THE LONG WHITE MOUNTAIN.

ACCOUNT of a Visit by a Mandarin to the Long White Mountain in 1677 :

'In the year 1677 Kanghi sent a courtier named Ou-mou-ne, a connection of the imperial family, to visit the Pai-shan and describe it. The Emperor said in his order that the mountain was situated in the blessed country which was his native land and the theatre of the glory of his first ancestors, and, as there was no one at Peking who was well acquainted with that country, he despatched Ou-mou-ne, not only to bring back a description of it, but to sacrifice to his ancestors. Ou-mou-ne was instructed at the same time to describe the country of Ninguta. He left Peking in the month of June and travelled by Moukden to the town of Kirin. There and in the whole country of Ninguta he sought for some one who could guide him to the Great White Mountain, but could only find an old man born in the country of Ekké-Neïen, who in his youth had heard from his father that the White Mountain was not far off that country. He remembered also that they used to hunt stags there, and that a hunter who killed one of those animals had brought it on his back to Ekké-Neïen.

'Ou-mou-ne left Kirin the second day of the sixth moon (July), and after a troublesome journey arrived at Ekké-Neïen. From that place he sent men ahead with axes to hew him a road through the impenetrable forests, and desired them to let him know how far off the White Mountain proved to be. Ten days afterwards they sent word to say that they had reached a small hill thirty li off, from which, on climbing a high tree, they had discovered the Great White Mountain, and which did not appear very far distant, probably 160 or 180[1] li from that place. Later accounts said that they had climbed a high mountain, from which they had seen the White Mountain much more distinctly than before, but that it was covered with cloud and fog. It seemed then 100[2] li off.

'On receiving this information Ou-mou-ne and his attendants started on the thirteenth day of the sixth moon for the mountain from which the second report had been despatched. They made their way along for two days. On the third, early in the morning, some cranes began to call, and at the same time a thick fog covered

---

[1] Fifty or sixty miles.   [2] Thirty or thirty-five miles.

the neighbourhood, so that the travellers could see neither mountain nor even objects quite close to them. Obliged to go in the direction from which the cry of the cranes proceeded, they soon found a deer-path, which seemed likely to bring them to the White Mountain. They were not mistaken.[1] Near the mountain they entered on an agreeable wood, in the midst of which was a little meadow of circular shape. Half a li from this wood they saw a space surrounded by trees which appeared to have been planted by the hand of man. They were intermingled with sweet-scented shrubs. Yellow flowers covered the ground. At this point Ou-mou-ne left his horses with more than half his attendants, and pursued his way on foot with only a few of them. The clouds and fog prevented them from seeing the White Mountain, so he resolved to repeat a prayer to the tutelary gods of the place. He had scarcely commenced doing so when the fog was dispelled, and the mountain revealed itself to him in all its beauty. He then discovered a path to the top. The air was pure and agreeable. They could see perfectly all the outlines of the mountain, on the summit of which rested only a few slight clouds. At first the ascent was not very difficult, but the further he climbed the more troublesome it became. The travellers went on for more than 100 li.[2] As they got higher and higher, they were obliged to hold up their garments, as they walked continuously along snow encrusted with ice, which appeared to have lain a whole year without melting. On reaching the top they found a plain[3] surrounded by five very high peaks, between which was a lake filled with water, the circumference of which might be thirty or forty li.[4]

'Ou-mou-ne, when approaching the lake, discovered on the north shore, on the side opposite to him, a bear which at that distance seemed very small. The tops of four of the peaks bent at such angles that they seemed almost as if they were going to tumble. The fifth, on the south side, was very straight and not so high as the others. They saw, at several spots on the mountain, springs and fountains, which flow to the left towards the Sungari, and on the right to the great and small Neïen.[5]

'Ou-mou-ne spent some time in exploring the mountain, and then, after offering a fresh sacrifice, commenced to descend. He had scarcely gone a few yards down when he saw on a sudden on the

[1] By this calculation Ou-mou-ne reached the Pai-shan in fourteen days from Kirin.

[2] Probably not more than twenty li by measurement, but the Chinese mode of describing a difficult road is by magnifying the number of li in it.

[3] It is a sharp knife-edge. [4] Fifteen or twenty would be more accurate.

[5] Probably the Yalu and the Tumen.

heights a troop of deer which were running towards him, and, what appeared more surprising to him, these animals precipitated themselves, one after the other, from top to bottom of the rocks, so that seven were killed.[1] Ou-mou-ne regarded this extraordinary occurrence as a mark of the tutelary deities' special favour to him. In short, this was their way of making a valuable present to the envoy whom his Majesty had sent, and who was without provisions. When he had descended the mountain he caused the deer to be prepared, and, to show his gratitude, sacrificed some of the meat to the spirits. Then, having finished his task, he left the spot. On his departure the mountain disappeared again in clouds and mist.

'Ou-mou-ne returned to Ninguta, made an account of that country, and returned to Peking on the twenty-first day of the eighth moon. The Emperor was delighted with the success of his mission, and ordered the Board of Rites to give a new honorary title to the tutelary spirits of the White Mountain who had accorded to his representative so good a reception.'—*Translated from the French of Klaproth (Mémoires relatifs à l'Asie, iii. 66).*

The mythological history of the White Mountain will be gathered from the following extract from a paper by the Archimandrite Palladius, translated by Mr. Delmar Morgan, F.R.G.S. :[2]

'The sacred importance of the White Mountains has been recognised in the Far East for ages. They are first heard of under the name of Bukhian-shan ; a name not of Chinese origin, but reminding one of the Mongol Burkhan, as the Gentehi Mountains in Mongolia (according to some, Khan-ola at Urga) were called in ancient times. Formerly there was greater similarity between the Mongol and Manchu languages than at present. The actual name of Chang-pŏ-shan (Long White Mountains) was given them during the Kin or Churchi dynasty ; before which time they were generally called Tai-pŏ-shan (Great White Mountains), or simply Pŏ-shan, and under this name were known for ages to the Coreans. Both ancient and modern writers describe these mountains to be unwooded, with flora mostly white, and white-haired fauna, never injuring or injured by man. During the Kin dynasty they were reputed to be the abode of the merciful Poi-hwan-in—i.e. the White-robed Hwanin, who is represented as a woman bearing a child in her arms. The word Poi, white-robed, is in this instance

---

[1] Our guide showed us the path by which deer occasionally descend to the edge of the lake to crop the narrow rim of herbage on one side of it. We tried to descend by this track, but it was broken away and impracticable.

[2] *Palladius' Expedition through Manchuria.* By E. Delmar Morgan, F.R.G.S. (*Proceedings R.G.S., 1872.*)

only a play on words ; it is applied to Hwan-in in the sense of a lay
divinity (lay priests were called white-robed, in contradistinction to
the monks), and not to express a symbolical white colour as the
peculiar attribute of the deity. At that period—i.e. during the
Kin dynasty—there was a temple in Corea dedicated to the spirit of
the Chang-pŏ-shan Mountains (symbolised as a maiden), and pre-
sided over by a *shamanka*, or sorceress. The Corean Buddhists
assigned the Chang-pŏ-shan as the home of their miraculous deity
Manchushri. And here we are reminded of the legend of the name
of the Manchu dynasty having been derived from this deity. The
similarity between the names must, however, be accidental, as the
word Manchu occurs in the nomenclature of the Churchi long before
the time of the Manchu Tai-tszù. All the pathetic descriptions of
the Chang-pŏ-shan Mountains refer altogether to their principal
peaks or group of peaks, and convey no accurate information about
the physical character of the range ; indeed, they seem hardly
reliable, and the only information to be derived from them is, that
at a considerable altitude in the main group of the range there is a
lake surrounded on three sides by naked rocks, which rise to the
height of 2,500 feet (760 mètres) above its surface. The dimensions of the lake are given differently by the several authors ; according to some, it is 80 li in circumference, others say 40, and some
only 25 li. Vu-tchjao-tèhu, in his verses on the Chang-pŏ-shan,
describes the lake to be 5 li in breadth and 8 in length, and in shape
like a pig's kidneys. According to the description given of it, this
depression in the mountains is probably the crater of an extinct
volcano sloping towards the south. With regard to the whiteness
of the Chang-pŏ-shan, it is difficult to decide whether it is caused by
the perpetual snows or by the white limestone rock which was
quarried in the Corean spurs of the range. Besides the Girin
branch of the Chang-pŏ-shan, another range extends to the south-
west, along the west side of the Yalu-kiang river, as far as its
confluence with the Tunga-kiang.'

The Emperor Kien-lung, in his poem on Moukden, refers to the
mountain in the following terms (I rely on Père Amyot's translation) :

'To ascend to the primitive source of the August Race which has
founded our Tai-tsing (Great-clear dynasty), we must carry ourselves
to that mountain, distinguished in like fashion (with the dynasty)
for its size and for the colour with which it shines. The famous
Lake Tamoun occupies part of its summit ; the rivers Yalu, Hountoung, and Ai-hou' rise from its bosom, carrying fertility over the
fields which they water ; and the fragrant mists which for ever rise

in this charming spot are, without contradiction, those of true glory and solid happiness. On this blessed mountain, a celestial virgin, a daughter of heaven, tasted a fruit to which she was attracted by the brightness of its colour above all others, ate, conceived, and became the mother of a boy, heavenly like herself. Heaven itself gave him the name of Kioro, to which it added, by way of distinction, that of the precious metal, and ordained that he should be called Aisin Kioro, or Golden Kioro.'

Père Amyot adds to the above that in the 'Chan-hai-king,' or book treating of seas and mountains, it is called Pan-hien-chan. In a book written on the Tang dynasty, it is called the Tai-po-shan, and sometimes Tou-tai-shan. In the 'Y-toung-chi' of the Mings it is said that 60 li S.E. of this mountain is the ancient town of Houi-ning. The book treating of the customs of the Manchu dynasty says that the mountain is 200 li (73 miles) high, and more than 1,000 (333 miles) round. But when a Chinaman speaks of the height of a mountain, he means the total distance to be traversed from the foot of the most outlying spur to the summit.

Père Amyot states that the Hountoung rises on the north side of the mountain, and flows into the sea to the north, and that the Ai-hou, after a northern course, discharges itself into the Eastern Sea. There is an Ai-ho, a large affluent of the Yalu, which joins it close to Sha-ho (Autung-hsien), and the Hwun or Hunchiang also joins the Yalu higher up. Can these be the rivers the Emperor speaks of? They are in the immediate vicinity of Shing-king.

NOTE G.

PLANTS COLLECTED BETWEEN MOUKDEN AND KIRIN.

Clematis (Atragene) alpina, L.
    fusca, Turcz.
    paniculata, Thunb.?
    recta, L.
    angustifolia, Jacq.
Thalictrum tuberiferum, Maxim.
    aquilegifolium, L.
    simplex, L.
    minus, L.
Anemone chinensis, Bge.

Anemone dichotoma, L.
    nemorosa, L.
Caltha palustris, L.
Ranunculus aquatilis, L.
    repens, L.
    pennsylvanicus, L.
    sp.
Trollius chinensis, Bge.
    patulus, Salisb.
Aquilegia sibirica, Lam.

Aconitum Lycoctonum, L.
    tenuifolium, Turcz.
    Kusnezoffii, Reich.?
    Fischeri, Reich.
Delphinium elatum, L. (D. Ma-
    ackianum, Regel.)
Cimicifuga simplex, Wormsk.
    dahurica, T. and G.
Pæonia albiflora, Pall.
    obovata, Maxim.
Magnolia conspicua, Salisb.?
Schizandra chinensis, Baill.
Menispermum davuricum, D.C.
Nuphar intermedium, Ledeb.
Epimedium macranthum, M.
    and D.?
Leontice microrhyncha, S. Moore.
Berberis vulgaris, L.
Papaver alpinum, L.
    somniferum, L.
Chelidonium majus, L.
Corydalis decumbens, Pers. var.
    longiloba.
    ochotensis, Turcz.
    pallida, Pers.
Dontostemon integrifolium,
    Ledeb.
Lepidium ruderale, L.
Brassica juncea, Hk. f. and T.
Capsella bursa-pastoris, Moench.
Arabis pendula, L.
    Halleri, L.
    perfoliata, Lam.
Cardamine amara, L.
    macrophylla, Willd.
Nasturtium palustre, D. C.
Barbarea vulgaris, R. Br.
Draba nemorosa, L.
Viola biflora, L.
    Patrinii, D. C.
    sylvestris, Kit.
Gypsophila perfoliata, L.
Cucubalus baccifer, L.

Lychnis laciniata, Maxim.
    fulgens, Fisch.
Silene repens, Patr.
Sisymbrium sp.
Silene aprica, Turcz.
Potentilla chinensis, Ser.
    fruticosa, L.
    fragarioides, Willd.
    centigrana, Maxim.
    cryptoteniæ, Maxim.
Pyrus communis, L.
    sambucifolia, C. and S.?
Prunus sp.
    Maximowiczii, Rupr.
    avium, L.
    Padus, L.
Cratægus pinnatifida, Bge.
    sanguinea, Pall.
Rubus sp.
    cratægifolius, Bunge.
Rosa davurica, Pall.
Geum strictum, Ait.
Spiræa chamædrifolia, L.
    salicifolia, L.
    digitata, Willd.
    sorbifolia, L.
    Aruncus, L.
Saxifraga, n. sp. (large peltate
    leaves).
    Rossii, Oliv.
    stellaris, L.
    rotundifolia, L.
Chrysosplenium sp.
    alternifolium, L.
Parnassia palustris, L.
Astilbe chinensis, Maxim.
Deutzia parviflora, Bge.
Philadelphus coronarius, L.
Ribes grossularia, L.?
    alpinum, L.
Sedum sp.
    Rhodiola, D. C.
    kamschaticum, L.?

Sedum Fabaria, Koch.?
    Aizoon, L.
Circæa alpina, L.
    lutetiana, L.
Lythrum Salicaria, L.
Epilobium angustifolium, L.
    roseum, Schreb.
Pleurospermum austriacum,
    Hoffm.
Anthriscus sylvestris, L.
Stenocœlium divaricatum, Fisch.
Heracleum dissectum, Ledeb.?
    barbatum, Ledeb.?
Bupleurum ranunculoides, L.
    falcatum, L.
    longeradiatum, Turcz.
Sanicula rubriflora, F. Schmidt.
Angelica anomala, Lallem.
    ? sp.
Cicuta virosa, L.
Eleutherococcus senticosus,
    Maxim.
Aralia sp.
    quinquefolia, L.
Viburnum davuricum, Pall.
    Opulus, L.
Sambucus racemosa, L.
    sp.
Linnæa borealis, Gronov.
Triosteum, n. sp. (will be figured
    in Icones Plantm.)
Cornus alba, L.
Galium sp.
    sp.
    trifidum, L.
    Aparine, L.
    boreale, L.
    verum, L.
Rubia cordifolia, L.
Patrinia scabiosæfolia, Fisch.
Scabiosa Fischeri, D. C.
Valeriana officinalis, L.
Lonicera sp.

Lonicera near chrysantha, Turcz.
    cærulea, L.
Boltonia (Calimeris) incisa (D.C.)
Carpesium sp.
Leontopodium sibiricum, Cass.
Inula britannica, L.
    salicina, L.
    linariæfolia, Turcz.
Erigeron canadensis, L.
    alpinus, L.
    acris, L.
Siegesbeckia orientalis, D. C.
Chrysanthemum sibiricum, Fisch.
Siegesbeckia sp.
Eupatorium Kirilowii, Turcz.
Matricaria limosa (Maxim).
Bidens tripartita, L.
Lappa major, Gœrtn.
Aster striatus, Benth.
    trinervius, Roxb. ?
    scaber, Thunb.
    ageratoides, Turcz.
    tataricus, L. f.
Ptarmica mongolica, D. C.
Artemisia vulgaris, L.
    Sieversiana, Willd.
    desertorum, Spreng.
    scoparia, W. and K.
Syneilesis aconitifolia, Maxim.
Cacalia sp.
    hastata, L.
Senecio nemorensis, L.
    near nemorensis.
    argunensis, Turcz.
    campestris, D. C.
    flammeus, D. C.
Ligularia sp.
    sibirica, Cass.
Atractylis ovata, Thunb
Carduus crispus, L.
Cirsium arvense, Scop.
Serratula coronata, L.
Saussurea sp.

Suassurea sp.
    sp.
    sp.
    multicaulis, D. C.
    grandifolia, Maxim.
    ussuriensis, Maxim.
    alpina, L.
    sp.
    pulchella, Fisch.
Cnicus sp.
    sp.
    Wlassovianam (Fisch).
    pendulum (Fisch).
    near kamschaticum.
Lactuca sp.
    sp.
    (Ixeris) ramosissima (A. Gr.).
    (Ixeris) versicolor (D. C.).
    (Mulgedium) sibiricum (Less.).
Crepis tectorum, L.
Taraxacum officinale, Wigg.
Picris hieracioides, L.
Hieracium umbellatum, L.
Scorzonera macrorhyncha, Turcz.
Adenophora sp.
    denticulata, Fisch.
    sp.
    sp.
    trachelioides, Maxim.
    verticillata, Fisch.
Glossocomia ussuriensis, R. and M.
Campanula punctata, Lam.
    glomerata, L.
    Trachelium, L.
Platycodon grandiflorum, A. D. C.
Lobelia sessiliflora, Lamb.
Moneses grandiflora, Salisb.
Pyrola secunda, L.
    rotundifolia, L.
    minor, L.

Ledum palustre, L.
Phyllodoce cærulea, Salisb.
Rhododendron Chamæcistus, L.
    chrysanthum, Pall.
Oxycoccus palustris, Pers.
Vaccinium vitis-idæa, L.
Syringa amurensis, Rupr.
Fraxinus mandshurica, Rupr.
Androsace filiformis, Retz.
Primula cortusoides, L.
Trientalis europæa, L.
Physalis Alkekengi, L.
Hyoscyamus niger, L.
Solanum nigrum, L.
Cuscuta japonica, Choisy.
Calystegia sepium, R. Br.
Vincetoxicum acuminatum, Maxim.
    volubile, Maxim.
    near volubile.
    atratum, Bunge.
Metaplexis Stauntoni, R. and S.
Gentiana near Moorcroftiana.
    prostrata, Hænke.
Polemonium cæruleum, L.
Menyanthes trifoliata, L.
Lysimachia barystachys, Bunge.
    davurica, Led. (vulgaris var.).
    thyrsiflora, L.
Orobanche sp.
Utricularia intermedia, Hayne.
Brachybotrys pardiformis, Maxim.
Myosotis sylvatica, Ehrh.
Eritrichium pedunculatum, A. D. C.
Lithospermum officinale, L.
Veronica serpyllifolia, L.
    alpina, L.
    longifolia, L.
    spicata, L.
    sibirica, L.

Siphonostegia chinensis, Bth.
Mazus rugosus, Lour.
Melampyrum roseum, Maxim.
Euphrasia officinalis, L.
Plantago major, L. vars.
Phryma leptostachya, L.
Amethystea cærulea, L.
Pedicularis resupinata, L.
Nepeta Glechoma, Bth.
Primula vulgaris, L.
Ajuga genevensis, L.
Stachys baicalensis, Turcz.
Leonurus sibiricus, L.
Lophanthus rugosus, F. and M.
Plectranthus glaucocalyx, Maxim.
Dracocephalum sinense, S. Moore.
Scutellaria sp.
    galericulata, L.
    japonica, M. and D.
Mentha sativa, L.
Phlomis sp.
Lycopus lucidus, Turcz.
Calamintha chinensis, Bth.
Lamium album, L.
Polygonum sagittatum, L.
    Thunbergii, S. and Z.
    perfoliatum, L.
    sp.
    minus, Huds.
    nodosum, Pers.
    Convolvulus, L.
    aviculare, L.
    polymorphum, Led.
    Bistorta, L.
    viviparum, L.
Fagopyrum esculentum, Moench.
Rumex Acestosella, L.
    crispus, L.
Kochia sp.
    scoparia, Schrad.
Chenopodium glaucum, L.
    album, L.
Viscum album, L.

Urtica dioica, L. var. angustifolia.
Euphorbia near Esula, L.
Croton ?
Geblera suffruticosa, F. and M.
Humulus japonicus, S. and Z.
Abies sibirica, Ledeb.
Larix dahurica, Turcz.
Pinus mandshurica, Rupr.
Juniperus communis, L. type and
    var. nana.
Taxus baccata, L.
Salix myrtilloides, L.
    Caprea, L.
    daphnoides, Vill.
Populus balsamifera, L.
    tremula, L.
Corylus heterophylla, Fisch.
    mandshurica, Maxim.
Quercus mongolica, Fisch.
Juglans sp.
Betula davurica, Pall.
Eulophia, ? sp.
Habenaria sp.
    sp.
    sp.
    (Perularia) fuscescens
        (Lindl.).
    (Platanthera) hologlottis
        (Maxim.).
    linearifolia, Maxim.
    chlorantha, Cuss.
Microstylis monophylla, Lindl.
Pogonia ophioglossoides, L.
Herminium sp. = Wilford 1168.
Cypripedium macranthum, Sw.
    guttatum, Sw.
Iris sibirica, L.
    sibirica var. orientalis
        (Thunb.).
    lævigata, Fisch.
    ensata, Thunb.
Dioscorea sp.
    sp.

Dioscorea quinqueloba, Thunb.
Smilax herbacea, L.
Veratrum Maackii, Regel.
    nigrum, L.
    album, L. var. viride.
Asparagus officinalis, L.
    schoberioides, Kunth.
Hemerocallis Middendorfii, F.
    and M.
    flava, L.
    Dumortieri, Morren.
Polygonatum officinale, All.
    verticillatum, All.
Smilacina japonica, A. Gray.
Convallaria majalis, L.
Maianthemum bifolium, D. C.
Funkia ovata, Spreng.
Allium lineare, L.
    Grayi, Regel.
    angulosum, L.
Paris obovata, Led.
Trillium erectum, L. var. japoni-
    cum, A. Gr.
Clintonia udensis, F. and M.
Disporum smilacinum, A. Gr.
Lilium tenuifolium, Fisch.
    concolor, Salisb.
    avenaceum, Fisch.
    Hansoni, Leicht.
    davuricum, Gawl.
    tigrinum, Gawl.
Sagittaria sagittifolia, L.
Calla palustris, L.
Potamogeton nutans, L.
Alisma Plantago, L.
Typha latifolia, L.
Scheuchzeria palustris, L.
Juncus acutiflorus, Ehrh.
    effusus, L.
Luzula campestris, D. C.
Monochoria Korsakowii, R. and
    M.
Commelyna communis, L.

Cyperus glomeratus, L.
    Monti, L.
    Eragrostis, Vahl.
Scirpus near Wichurai, Bœck.
    (Isolepis) Micheliana (R.
    and S.)
    Tabernæmontani, Gmel
    sylvaticus, L.
    radicans, Schk.
Eriophorum latifolium, Hoppe.
Heleocharis palustris, R. Br.
Carex ampullacea, Good.
    near acuta, L.
    sylvatica, Huds.
    atrata, L.
    leiorhyncha, C. A. M.
    loliacea, L.
    vulpina, L.
    rupestris, All.
Chloris barbata, Sw.
Alopecurus fulvus, Sm.
Phragmites communis, Trin.
Calamagrostis Epigejos, Roth.
    sp.
Setaria verticillata, P. B.
    glauca, P. B.
Panicum Colonum, L.
    mandshuricum, Maxim.
    Crus galli, L.
Arrhenatherum avenaceum, P. B.
Elymus sibiricus, L.
Melica nutans, L.
Spodiopogon sibiricus, Trin.
Phalaris arundinacea, L.
Phleum alpinum, L.
Agrostis laxiflora, R. Br.
Festuca sp.
Eragrostis ferruginea, P. B.
    pilosa, P.B.
Poa nemoralis, L.
    pratensis, L.
Kœleria cristata, Pers.
Onoclea germanica, Willd.

Onoclea sensibilis, L.
Davallia Wilfordii, Baker.
Woodsia manchuriensis, Hook.
   polystichoides, Eaton.
   ilvensis, R. Br.
   Hancockii, Baker.
Pterisaquilina, L. var. caudata.
Adiantum pedatum, L.
Cheilanthes argentea, Hook.
   Kuhnii, Milde.
Asplenium Filix-fœmina, Bernh.
   spinulosum, Baker.
   crenatum, Rupr.
Cystopteris sudetica, Milde ?
Scolopendrium sibiricum, Hook.
Aspidium craspedosorum,
   Maxim.
   aculeatum, Sw.
   tripteron, Kze.
Nephrodium Thelypteris, Desv.
   Filix-mas, Rich.
     var. elongatum (Sw.).
   spinulosum, Desv.
Polypodium near punctatum ?
   (Perhaps new, but ma-
   terial too incomplete to
   describe.)
Polypodium Phegopteris, L.
   Dryopteris, L.
   Lingua, Sw. var.
   lineare, Thunb.
Gymnogramme javanica, Bl.
Osmunda cinnamomea, L.
Botrychium virginianum, Sw.
Lycopodium alpinum, L.
   obscurum, L.
   annotinum, L.
   clavatum, L.
   complanatum, L.
Selaginella involvens, Spring.
Equisetum hyemale, L.
   arvense, L.
   pratense, Ehrh.

Equisetum palustre, L.
Climacium japonicum, Lindb.
Thridium cymbifolium, Dz. and
   Mlkb.
Mnium rostratum, Schwägr.
   lycopodioides, Schwägr.
Marchantia polymorpha, L.
Cladonia rangiferina, Hoffm.
Arenaria (Moehringia) lateriflora,
   L.
Cerastium trigynum, Vill.
   near dahuricum.
   pilosum, Ledeb.
Stellaria graminea, L.
   aquatica, Scop.
Cerastium triviale, Link.
Dianthus chinensis, L.
   superbus, L.
Hypericum Ascyron, L.
   perforatum, L.
Actinidia callosa, Lindl.
   Kolomikta, Rupr.
Hibiscus Trionum, L.
Tilia mongolica, Maxim. ?
   cordata, Mill (parvifolia,
   Ehrh.).
   mandshurica, R. and M.
Geranium davuricum, D. C.
Linum stelleroides, Planch.
Geranium Thunbergii, S. and Z.
   eriostemon, Fisch.
   pseudo-sibiricum, Mey.
Dictamnus albus, L.
Impatiens Noli-me-tangere, L.
   sp.
Oxalis stricta, L.
   obtriangulata, Maxim.
Vitis vinifera, L.
Rhamnus davuricus, Pall.
Euonymus europæus, L.
   pauciflorus, Maxim. ?
Rhus succedanea, L.
Acer tegmentosum, Maxim.

Acer spicatum, Lam.
 tataricum, L.
 truncatum, Bge.
 Sieboldianum, Miq. ?
 barbinerve, Maxim.
Melilotus suaveolens, Led.
Trifolium Lupinaster, L.
Indigofera macrostachya, Bge.
Astragalus dahuricus, D. C.
 chinensis, L. f.
 adsurgens, Pall.
 sp.
 sp.
Desmodium Oldhamii, Oliv.
 podocarpum, D. C.
Agrimonia Eupatoria, L.
Dryas octopetala, L.

Sanguisorba cfr. canadensis.
 tenuifolia, Fisch.
 officinalis, L.
Amphicarpœa Edgeworthii,
 Benth. var. japonica, Oliv.
Vicia unijuga, A. Br.
Lathyrus vernus, Koch. var. ?
 palustris, L.
 sp.
 sp.
 Davidi, Hance
Vicia Cracca, L.
Lespedeza sericea, Miq.
 bicolor, Turcz.
Fragaria collina, Ehrh.
Potentilla pennsylvanica, L.
 norvegica, L.

PLANTS COLLECTED BY THE AUTHOR BETWEEN KIRIN, TSITSIHAR, AND HUN-CH'UN.

Clematis angustifolia, Jacq.
 recta terniflora ? (Too imperfect for determination.)
Anemone Pulsatilla, L.
 chinensis, Bge.
Delphinium grandiflorum, L.
Aconitum Anthora, L.
 barbatum, Patr. B. Gmelini.
Cimicifuga dahurica, Torr. et Gr. ?
Capsella bursa-pastoris, L.
Viola phalacrocarpa, Maxim. ?
Dianthus Seguieri, Vill. (D. dentosus, Fisch.).
Gypsophhila perfoliata, L.
Silene tenuis, Willd.
 sp.
Arenaria formosa, Fisch. var.
Portulaca oleracea, L.
Malva verticillata, L.
Hibiscus Trionum, L.

Linum stelleroides, Planch.
Tribulus terrestris, L.
Erodium Stephanianum, Willd.
Geranium sp.
Impatiens noli tangere, L.
Medicago lupulina, L.
Trifolium lupinaster, L.
Astragalus dahuricus, D. C.
 adsurgens, Pall.
Lespedeza bicolor, Turcz.
 juncea, Pers.
Vicia pseudo-Orobus, F. Mey.
Geum striatum, Ait.
Potentilla bifurca, L.
 anserina, L.
 chinensis, Ser.
Lythrum Salicaria, L.
Bupleurum falcatum, L.
Seseli (Stenocœlium divaricatum, Fisch.).
Peucedanum terebinthaceum, Fisch. ?

Patrinia heterophylla, Bge.
Scabiosa Fischeri, D. C.
Eupatorium Kirilowii, Turcz.
Aster fastigiatus, Fisch.
    scaber, Thunb.
    tataricus, L. f.
    (§ Calimeris) sp.
Brachyactis ciliata, Led.
Xanthium Strumarium, L.
Leontopodium sibiricum, Cass.
Tanacetum sibiricum, L.
Achillea sibirica, Ledeb.
Siegesbeckia orientalis, L.
Bidens parviflora, W.
Inula japonica, Thunb.
Artemisia palustris, L.
    annua, L.
    anethifolia, Stechm.
    lavandulæfolia, D. C.
    sp.
    sp.
    sp.
Senecio argunensis, Turcz.
Echinops dahuricus, Fisch.
Cirsium segetum, Bge. (C. arvense var. setosum).
Saussurea japonica, D. C.
    japonica, D.C. ?
    ussuriensis, Maxim.
Saussurea ?
Atractylis ovata, Thunb.
Hieracium ? (scrap without leaves).
    sp.
Lactuca (Mulgedium sibiricum, Less.).
    denticulata, Houtt. (two forms).
    squarrosa, Miq.
Sonchus arvensis, L.
Scorzonera radiata, Fisch. ?
Codonopsis (Glossocomia) lanceolata ? S. and Z.

Adenophora polymorpha, Led. forma.
    sp. (foliis angustissimis).
Statice bicolor, Bge. (of Hb. Paris, David coll.) an S. sinensis ?
Androsace filiformis, Retz.
Vincetoxicum atratum, Bge. ? (only in fruit).
Gentiana triflora, Pall. ?
Limnanthemum nymphæoides, Lk.
Convolvulus arvensis, L.
    Ammanni, Desv.
Ipomæa obscura, K. ?
Cuscuta reflexa, Roxb. var.
Solanum septemlobum, Bge.
Hyoscyamus niger, L. forma.
Linaria vulgaris, L.
Siphonostegia chinensis, Bth.
Phtheirospermum chinense, Bge.
Euphrasia officinalis, L.
Melampyrum roseum, Maxim.
Incarvillea sinensis, Lam.
Fragment Leonurus ? aff. L. macrantho.
Plectranthus glaucocalyx, Maxim. ?
Elsholtzia cristata, L.
Calamintha near C. Clinopodium.
Nepeta lavandulacea, L.
Mentha arvensis, L. var.
Amethystea cærulea, L.
Scutellaria macrantha, Fisch.
Phlomis dentosus ? Franch.
Stachys palustris, L. var.
Brunella vulgaris, L.
Dracocephalum moldavicum, L. (D. fœtidum, Bge.).
Thymus Serpyllum, L. var.
Chenopodium album, L.
Atriplex sibirica, L.

Chenopodium (Teloxys) arista-
  tum, L.
Axyris amarantoides, L.
Corispermum an C. hyssopifolium
  L. ? var.
Salsola soda, L.
  sp.
  collina, Pall. ?
Polygonum aviculare, L. forma.
  orientale, L. forma.
  polymorphum, ? forma.
Euphorbia (not in fruit : near E.
  adenochlora, Dcn., and E.
  Rochebruni, F. and S.).
  humifusa, W.
Humulus japonicus, S. and Z.
Urtica cannabina, L.
Gingko biloba, L. (Salisburia
  adiantifolia, Sm.).
Pinus (fragment without cones :
  P. koraiensis, S. and Z.,
  or P. mandshurica, Rupr.).

Spiranthes australis, Lindl.
Hemerocallis flava, L.
Asparagus sp. *Cf.* A. davuri-
  cus.
Allium Bakeri, Reg.
  odorum, L.
Monochoria Korsakowii, Reg.
Cyperus Eragrostis, Vahl.
Scirpus triqueter, L.
Eriochloa villosa, Kth.
Panicum Crus. Galli, L.
  miliaceum, L.
  (Digitaria humifusa, Pers. ?)
Setaria viridis, P. de B.
  glauca, P. de B.
Stipa sibirica, Lam.
Chloris barbata, Sw.
Saccharum officinarum, L. ?
Phragmites communis, Trin.
? Chrysopogon (= Maingay, N.
  China, 81).

NOTE H.

ITINERARY.

(NOTE.—Three *li* = one English mile.)

1886	Place	Distance in Chinese *li*
May 19 . .	Left YINGTZŬ.	
	Kun-tzŭ Pao	45
„ 20 . .	NEWCHWANG	45
	Chiang-chia T'un	60
„ 21 . .	Sho Shan	55
	Chang-chia T'ai	48
„ 22 . .	Chang-shing T'ai	45
	MOUKDEN (Hsên-yang) . .	50
		348
„ 29 . .	Hsing-lung Tien	50
„ 30 . .	Fu-shun Ch'êng	30

ITINERARY—CONTINUED.

1886	Place	Distance in Chinese li	
	Tê-ku	40	
May 31 .	Ku-lou (*via* Sarhu)	50	
	San-chia Ho	20	
June 1 . .	Mu Chi	35	
	Yung Ling	40	
			265
,, 3 . .	Hsin-minpu (*via* Shing-king)	40	
	Pai-chia Pu	15	
,, 4 . .	Wang-ching Mên	35	
	San-ko Yü-shu	20	
,, 5 . .	Kan-shan Ling	25	
	La-fêng'rh	35	
,, 6 . .	Kuai-ta-mao-tzu	35	
	T'ung-hua Hsien	45	
			250
,, 15 . .	Jê-shui Ho	35	
,, 16 . .	Ssŭ-tao Chiang, Lo-chuan K'ou Valley	20	
,, 21 . .	Yung-cha Tien·	60	
,, 22 . .	San-tao K'ou	40	
,, 23 . .	Over Hang-lung pass to Tso-chiao K'ou	60	
,, 24 . .	Hsiao Li-shih K'ou . . .	40	
,, 25 . .	Bark hut on the Ya-lu bank .	30	
,, 26 . .	Mao-erh Shan	10	
			295
,, 29 . .	Erh-tao K'ou	35	
,, 30 . .	*via* Lao-ling to Tan-chia Ching K'ou-tzŭ	60	
July 1 . .	Camp in forest	70	
,, 2 . .	T'ang Ho K'ou	25	
			190
,, 4 . .	Corean hut	10	
,, 5 . .	Nai Shan *via* Shih-t'ou Ho .	60	
,, 6 . .	Hsiao Shan	35	
,, 7 . .	Hei Ho	40	
,, 8 . .	Hei-li Ho	20	
,, 9 . .	T'ou-i-pi-ho	40	
,, 10 . .	Hua-pi Ho *via* Shih-t'ou Kang	30	
,, 11 . .	Erh-li-pan Mu-li	50	
,, 12 . .	Shui-pi-li-tai	20	
	T'ang Shan (foot of the White Mountain)	20	
			325
Return, July 15	Hut	60	

H H

ITINERARY—Continued.

1886	Place	Distance in Chinese *li*
July 16 . .	Hua-pi Ho	30
	T'ou-i-pi Ho	30
„ 17 . .	Hei-li Ho	40
	Hei Ho	20
„ 18 . .	Hua-pi Ho	20
„ 19 . .	Hsiao Shan	20
„ 20 . .	Nai Shan	35
	Corean hut	60
„ 21 . .	T'ANG-HO K'OU	10
		325
„ 27 . .	Cross Sungari	3
„ 28 . .	Ta Tien-tzŭ	60
„ 29 . .	Wan-li Ho	20
„ 30 . .	Ta Huang-t'ing-tzŭ camp . .	40
„ 31 . .	Ch'ang-kang camp . . .	15
Aug. 1 . .	Huang-shû Tien-tzŭ . . .	30
„ 2 . .	Yü-shih Ho K'ou-tzŭ (Sungari ferry)	25
„ 4 . .	Pi Chou	50
„ 5 . .	Wang's Inn, at Chin-ch'ang .	40
„ 6 . .	Hua-pi Ho	80
„ 7 . .	KUAN-KAI'RH	3
„ 8 . .	T'ien-p'ing Ling	40
„ 9 . .	Sha-hsi Wan	30
	HÊNG-TA HO-TZŬ . . .	8
	Ma-fêng K'a-la	12
„ 10 . .	Ching Ling	20
	Chao-yang Pu	15
„ 11 . .	SAN CHIA-TZŬ	40
	Kou-chin	40
„ 12 . .	Shan K'ou-tzŭ	34
	KIRIN (Ch'uan Ch'ang) . .	6
		611
„ 27 . .	Lung-tan Shan	15
„ 28 . .	Kirin	15
		30
Sept. 3 . .	San-tao Ling	25
	San Chia-tzu	10
„ 4 . .	WU-LU K'AI	40
	Shih Chia-tzŭ	40
„ 5 . .	Hsi-la Ho	10
	Pai-chia T'un	25
	Fa-ta Mên	30
	Huang-shan Tsui-tzŭ . . .	25
„ 6 . .	Hsiu-shui Tien-tzŭ . . .	35
	Ka-li Ho	20

ITINERARY—Continued.

1886	Place	Distance in Chinese *li*
	Mêng-ku Chan	25
	Wu-ku Shu	12
Sept. 7 . .	Tao-lai Chan	45
	San Chia-tzŭ	20
	Wu-chia Chan	30
„ 8 . .	Lia-li T'un	36
	Shih-li Shu	44
„ 9 . .	Kuan-ti	35
	PETUNA or SHING-CHÉNG . . .	40
		547
„ 11 . .	Pe-tu-na Chan	25
„ 12 . .	Ferry	35
	Island	15
„ 13 . .	Shui-shih Yingtzŭ	15
„ 15 . .	Mo-sing	45
	Hsin Ch'ang	45
„ 16 . .	Ku-lu	45
	Shih-li Tien	10
„ 17 . .	Pai-pai Tien	50
	Ta-la-ha	18
„ 18 . .	Hao-têng Kai	40
	Po-po-li	15
	Chiu-shan Mên	15
„ 19 . .	Ka-la Fan-tzŭ	40
	Wan-ta Hun	10
	Shu-lu Mu	40
„ 20 . .	Ta-mo-ho T'un	35
	Yü-shih T'un	15
	San Chia-tzŭ	15
	TSITSIHAR (Pu-ku'ei) . . .	15
		543
„ 23 . .	Lang-chia Tien	50
„ 24 . .	Ta Hao-tzŭ	25
	Wu-t'ai-rh	40
	K'o-shih-k'o	50
„ 25 . .	Lama Tien	40
„ 26 . .	So'rh-tu Tien	40
	An-ta Tien	50
„ 27 . .	Ching Kên	50
	Wu-lu-mu	40
„ 28 . .	Hsien-chia Tien	50
	Hsin Yü Shu	30
„ 29 . .	Hu-lan R. Ferry	30
	HU-LAN	30
		525
„ 30 . .	T'ai-p'ing Shan	60

R H 2

ITINERARY—Continued.

1886	Place	Distance in Chinese *li*	
Oct. 1 . .	Shih-yuan Ch'êng-tzŭ . . .	30	
	Chao-ying Pu	15	
	Ssŭ-chia-wo Pu	20	
	Chi-pao Shan	15	
	Pei-t'uan-lin-tzŭ, or Pei-lin-tzŭ	35	
			175
,, 2 . .	Pa-pao Shan	35	
,, 3 . .	Chao-hu-wo Pu	25	
	Lung Wang Miao . . .	40	
	Ta-chiu-ti Ho	30	
,, 4 . .	Pa-yen-shu-shu	45	
			175
,, 6 . .	Liu-chia Tien	20	
	Hsiao-shih Ho	10	
,, 7 . .	Wei-chia Tien	—	
	Ta-li-mo Ho	40	
	Hu-chia-wu Pu	10	
,, 8 . .	Pei Yang-mu	50	
	Nung-nung Ho	40	
,, 9 . .	Ssŭ Chan	30	
	Ting-chia Tien	30	
,, 11 . .	San Chan	30	
	Hsiang-sun Shan . . .	50	
,, 12 . .	Erh Chan	40	
	Hsiao-ku-tung Ho	30	
,, 13 . .	SANSING	30	
			410
,, 16 . .	T'ai-p'ing Chuang (first stage)	45	
	Nien-tzŭ K'ou	25	
,, 17 . .	Wei-tzŭ Ho (second stage) .	45	
,, 18 . .	Pa Yü-shu (third stage) . .	60	
,, 19 . .	Lien-hua Pao (fourth stage) .	50	
,, 20 . .	San-tao Ho-tzŭ (fourth stage from Yeh-ho)	60	
,, 21 . .	San Chan (third stage) . .	45	
,, 22 . .	Êrh Chan (second stage) . .	35	
,, 23 . .	T'ou Chan (first stage) . .	45	
,, 24 . .	Chang-shih-la-tzŭ	—	
	Hua-shu-lin-tzŭ	40	
	Tieh-ling Ho	—	
	Yeh-ho	40	
,, 26 . .	Ferry, Mu-tan Ho, or Hurka R.	40	
	NINGUTA	20	
			550

ITINERARY—Continued.

1886	Place	Distance in Chinese *li*	
Oct. 29 . .	T'ou Chan (first stage) . .	60	
„ 30 . .	Mu-la-hu-li (second stage) .	35	
„ 31 . .	Lao Sung Ling (third stage) .	60	
Nov. 1 . .	Ssŭ Chan (fourth stage) . .	60	
„ 2 . .	Ssŭ Chan (fourth stage from Hun-ch'un)	60	
	San Chan (third stage), Ha-shun	60	
„ 3 . .	Inn	34	
„ 4 . .	Ta-kan (second stage) . . .	1	
	Tê-tung	40	
„ 5 . .	Mi Chiang	60	
„ 6 . .	HUN-CH'UN	60	
			530
	Hun-ch'un to Frontier . .	30	
„ 8 . .	Frontier to Swanka	15	
„ 9 . .	Swanka to NOVO-KIEVSK	45	
			90
„ 10 . .	Novo-kievsk to Hun-ch'un .	90	
			90
	Hun-ch'un to Kirin by a mule-track	—	
„ 11 . .	Mi Chiang	60	
„ 12 . .	Liang-shui Chien-tzŭ . . .	30	
	Ka-ya Ho	60	
„ 13 . .	Hsiao Ling	10	
	Wei-tzŭ K'ou	20	
	NAN KANG-TZŬ	60	
„ 14 . .	Shui Wan-tzŭ	20	
	Chun-yang-chuan	—	
	Kuan-tou K'ou	—	
	Lao-tou K'ou	60	
„ 15 . .	Yü-shih Chuan	—	
	Wu-kou T'ing-tzŭ	40	
	Tu Mên-tzŭ	20	
	Mao-êrh K'ou	10	
„ 16 . .	Wang-pa Pao-tzŭ	10	
	Kên-yu La-tzŭ	7	
	Liang-ping Tai	10	
	Fêng-mi La-tzŭ	10	
	Chien-tsao K'ou	12	
	Ha-la-pa Ling	18	
	San-ho Shun	20	
	Pai Chia-tzŭ	5	
	Liang-shui Chien-tzŭ . . .	5	
„ 17 . .	Ta Shih-t'ou Ho	15	

ITINERARY—Continued.

1886	Place	Distance in Chinese *li*	
	Tou Yang-tzŭ	10	
	Hsing-lung Chuang . . .	10	
	Shah-k'ou Chan	8	
	Tung-o Kang-tzŭ	87	
Nov. 18 . .	Chia I-pa Ho	25	
	San-chia K'ou	25	
	O-mo-so	20	
			637
„ 19 . .	Chu-êrh-tao Ho	30	
	I-chia Sung	10	
	Wo-chia Ho	8	
	Chang-tsai Ling	—	
	Hu's Inn (East foot of pass) .	12	
„ 20 . .	Nan-tien Mên (top of pass) .	8	
	Barracks	12	
	Liao's Inn (West foot of pass)	10	
	Êrh-tao Ho-tzŭ	18	
	Wo-k'ou Shan	12	
	Pa-la-pa	8	
„ 21 . .	Ku-pu-êrh Ho	25	
	La-ma K'ou	—	
	Ta T'un	—	
	Hai-ching K'ou	45	
„ 22 . .	Hai-ching Ling	45	
	Lo-chiang K'ou ⎫ . . .	50	
	Li's Inn ⎭		
„ 23 . .	Ku Chia-tzŭ	35	
	San Chia-tzŭ	20	
„ 24 . .	Sungari (Powder Mills) . .	20	
	Kirin	5	
			373
„ 30 . .	Ta-shui Ho	45	
Dec. 1 . .	Ta Ch'iao	45	
	Shih-hui Yao-tzŭ . . .	55	
„ 2 . .	Fang-nung K'ou	35	
	K'uan Ch'êng-tzŭ, or CHANG-CHUN . . .	65	
			245
„ 4 . .	Hsiao Pa Chia-tzŭ	65	
			65
„ 6 . .	Ssŭ Chia-tzŭ	45	
	Ta Pa Chia-tzŭ, or Hua-tao Hsien	35	
	Sing-lung Pu	15	
„ 7 . .	Hsiao Ch'êng-tzŭ	55	
	Niu-chia Tien	55	

ITINERARY—Continued.

1886	Place	Distance in Chinese *li*	
Dec. 8 . .	Mai-mai Kai, or Fĕng-hsien-hsien.	35	
	Ssŭ-p'ing Kai	35	
„ 9 . .	Tzŭ-lu Shu	40	
	Yü-shih Ch'ĕng-tzŭ, or Chang-tu	60	
„ 10 . .	Ma-tien T'ai Mĕn	20	
	K'ai-yŭan	20	
	Sun-chia 'Ai	20	
	Tieh Ling	50	
„ 11 . .	Ching-shui T'ai	75	
	MOUKDEN	55	615
„ 15 . .	Pei-tu Pu	20	
	Lin-shang Pu	25	
„ 16 . .	Sha Ling	75	
„ 17 . .	Shou-shan Pu	30	
	Shah Ho	18	
	T'ang Kang-tzŭ	44	
„ 18 . .	Hai Ch'ĕng	45	
	Wang-chia Tien	60	
„ 19 . .	YINGTZŬ	50	367
„ 26 . . .	Êrh-tao Ho	20	
„ 27 . .	Kai Chou	50	
	Yang Kuan	15	
	Lung-wang Miao	30	
„ 28 . .	I-êrh Ling	5	
	Shih-chien Fĕng	45	
	Wan-fu Chuang	5	
	Hua-sha Ling-tzŭ	35	
„ 29 . .	Ta-la Ling	35	
	Cha K'ou	25	265
„ 31 . .	Li-chia Tien	30	
	Ta-chuang Ho	35	
1887. Jan. 1 . .	Shah Ho	10	
	T'ang-tzŭ Yao	20	
	Pa-la Shan	20	
	River	5	
	Liu-chia Hsiao Tien . . .	15	
	Kan-tzŭ Ti	17	
	Sung-chia Yao-tzŭ	8	
„ 2 . .	Pi-li Ho	5	
	Chin Ch'ang	20	

ITINERARY—Continued.

1887	Place	Distance in Chinese *li*	
	Wang-chia Tien	10	
	Pɪ-tzŭ Wo	35	
	Wu-chia Tien	35	
Jan. 3 . .	Li-chia Tien	45	
	Fu-chia Tien	35	
	Liu-chia Tien	5	
„ 4 . .	Kuan-chia Tien	10	
	Chin-chou T'ɪng	20	380
	Nan-kua Ling	20	
	Mu-c'hang I	40	
„ 5 . .	Ying Ch'êng-tzŭ	5	
	Shuang-t'ai K'ou	10	
	San chien Pu	20	
„ 6 . .	LÜ-SHUN K'OU (PORT ARTHUR)	25	120

SUMMARY.

	Distance in Chinese *li*
Yingtzŭ to Moukden (Hsên-yang)	348
Moukden to Shing-king	265
Shing-king to T'ung-hua Hsien	250
T'ung-hua Hsien to Mao-erh Shan	295
Mao-erh Shan to T'ang-ho K'ou	190
T'ang-ho K'ou to T'ang Shan	325
T'ang Shan to T'ang-ho K'ou	325
T'ang-ho K'ou to Kirin	611
Kirin to Lung-tan Shan and back	30
Kirin to Petuna	547
Petuna to Tsitsihar (Pu-ku'ei)	543
Tsitsihar (Pu-ku'ei) to Hu-lan	525
Hu-lan to Pei-t'uan-lin-tzŭ	175
Pei-t'uan-lin-tzŭ to Pa-yen-shu-shu	175
Pa-yen-shu-shu to Sansing	410
Sansing to Ninguta	550
Ninguta to Hun-ch'un	530
Hun-ch'un to Novo-kievak and back	180
Hun-ch'un to O-mo-so (*vid* Nan Kang-tzŭ)	637
O-mo-so to Kirin (*vid* Hai-ching Ling)	373
Kirin to K'uan Ch'êng-tzŭ	245
K'uan Ch'êng-tzŭ to Hsiao Pa Chia-tzŭ	65
Hsiao Pachia-tzŭ to Moukden	615
Moukden to Yingtzŭ	367
Yingtzŭ to Cha K'ou	265
Cha K'ou to Chin-chou T'ing	380
Chin-chou T'ing to Lü-shun K'ou (Port Arthur)	120

Total Chinese *li* . . . . 9,341[1]

[1] Equivalent to 3,113⅔ miles.

LLI

INDEX.

Hunters, deer-horn, 248
— in North-eastern Manchuria, 435
— — the Ch'ang-pai-shan, 256, 258
— sable, 258
Hurka river, 6
— — affluents of the, 337
— — at Ninguta, 341
— — — Sansing, 331
— — depth of, 337
— — scenery on the, 336
— — width of, 336
— valley, game in, 337
Huts, scanty accommodation in, 256, 275

I, GENERAL, at Hun-ch'un, 346, 357
— — dress of, 358
— — visit of, 358
Ides, Peter the Great's envoy, 109 *n*.
Idol, ancient stone, 405
— repulsive, 192
— taken from Lindan, 390
— worship, 180 *et seq.*
I-hang, rebellion at, 83
Iluam-yü, a fish, 435
Images on temple roofs, 143
Imma-keu-tzŭ, 438, 439
Immigrants, Chinese, 123, 385
Immorality among the Mongols, 302
— Chinese, 326
— discouraged by Manchus, 57
— of priests, 186
Imperial Life Guards, 116
— tombs at Moukden, 141
— — — Yungling, 231
Imports, value of, 166
— foreign, 174
Indemnity paid by Chinese, 77, 88, 94, 95
Indian opium revenue, 167, 421
Indigo, crops of, 11
Industry of the Chinese, 11, 373
Influence, geomantic, 194
— in judicial cases, 158
Inn-yard, scene in, 372
Inns, a great institution, 222, 224
— charges at, 224
— cockroaches abundant at, 225
— description of, 223, 235, 278, 306, 372
— dinners at, 224
— k'ang at, 136
— kitchen-range, primitive, at, 236

Inns, roadside, description of, 235
— signposts of, 223
Insect pests, 224, 242, 243, 296, 425
Insolence of Lin at Canton, 76
Instruments of torture, 154, 154 *n*.
Intoxicants, 165
Irish Presbyterian mission, 205, 378
Iron-foundry at Lo-chuan-kou, 239
— mine near Tieh-ling, 385
— mining, 13
Islam, decadence of, 289
Itinerary, Author's, 464
I-tung Ho river, 374

JANISSARIES or Pao-i, 116
Japan, clothing in, change of, 111
— invasion threatened by, 123
— opium prohibition in, 172
Jehol, Emperor's flight to, 87
— Lord Macartney at, 87
Jerboa rats, 208
Jesuits, survey by, 7, 32, 98, 265
Jews renouncing their religion, 289
Journey, end of Author's, 406
— itinerary of, 464
— object of, 411
Judaism, decadence of, 289
Judicial business, 149 *et seq.*, 155
Ju-i, or sceptre, *see* Ru-i
Jungo-trees at Mountain of the Sages, 400
Junk trade at Yingtzŭ, 174
Justice, administration of modern, 149 *et seq.*, 325
— amongst the Mongols, 299
— civil, in China, 155
— criminal, 150 *et seq.*
— speedy, fondness of early Manchus for, 55

KAI-CHAU, city of, 395
— — fêng-shui at, 395
— — iron pagoda at, 395
Kai-yuan, arrival at, 382
— — Ching river at, 382
— — Nurhachu's victory at, 36
— — pagoda at, 383
— — wall of, 382
Kamschatka, part of Primorsk province, 104
— supplies sent down the Amur to, 102, 103

488 — THE LONG WHITE MOUNTAIN

THE LONG WHITE MOUNTAIN

Lightning Source UK Ltd.
Milton Keynes UK
16 December 2010

164438UK00001B/49/P